Dragon Knights

Written and Illustrated by
Mineko Ohkami

Volume 5

TOKYOPOP®

Los Angeles • Tokyo

Translator - Yuki Ichimura
English Adaption - Stephanie Sheh
Retouch & Lettering - Monalisa De Asis
Cover Layout - Anna Kerbaum

Senior Editor - Luis Reyes
Production Manager - Jennifer Miller
Art Director - Matthew Alford
VP of Production & Manufacturing - Ron Klamert
President & C.O.O. - John Parker
Publisher - Stuart Levy

Email: editor@TOKYOPOP.com
Come visit us online at www.TOKYOPOP.com

A ⊙ TOKYOPOP® Manga
TOKYOPOP® is an imprint of Mixx Entertainment, Inc.
5900 Wilshire Blvd., Suite 2000, Los Angeles, CA 90036

ISBN: 1-59182-069-3

First TOKYOPOP® printing: December 2002

10 9 8 7 6 5 4 3 2 1

Printed in the USA

From the Chronicles of Dusis, the West Continent...

The Beginnings: Nadil and Lord Lykouleon

When the Yokai Nadil kidnapped the Dragon Queen Raselene, The Dragon Lord Lycouleon ventured to the Demon Realm to rescue her. He defeated Nadil by cutting off his head, thereby saving Raselene, but not before the demon leader rendered her barren, unable to give Lykouleon a child... and the Dragon Kingdom an heir. Now, the demon and Yokai forces, under the command of Shydeman and Shyrendora, plot to attack Draqueen, the Dragon Kingdom, and retrieve their leader's head in the hopes of reviving him. But they also have their sites on Cesia, a fortune teller with extraordinary hidden powers. The Alchemist Kharl and the rogue Yokai Bierrez have also entered the contest for power of all Dusis.

The Dragon Knights: A Motley Trio

Rath is the Dragon Knight of Fire and has a passion for hunting demons, though his reluctance to be entirely forthcoming about his motives may be a point of concern. Rune, in a battle with the Demon Fish Varawoo, healed the Water Dragon, thereby unlocking its seal and becoming the Dragon Knight of Water, but not without sacrificing the Elfin Princess Tintlet who remains in a sleep spell, keeping Varawoo contained. Thatz, a human thief, is the Dragon Knight of Earth and has a tempestuous history with another thief, Kitchel.

The Future: Missions Abroad

With an impending attack from the Demon Hordes looming on the horizon, and internal strife within the walls of the Dragon Castle weakening the Dragon Tribe's resolve, Lord Lykouleon has dispatched the Dragon Knights to three different corners of the world: Rath has been sent to accompany Cesia on a quest to Mt. Mfartha to resurrect the Dragon Dog Crewger. Rune has journeyed to the Faerie Forest to learn the fate of the elves and, perhaps, rescue Tintlet. And Thatz has joined Kitchel on her quest to find the Three Treasures for the Dragon Lord, a quest for which they must first find fragments of a map that have been scattered throughout the world. They've nearly found all of the map fragments already and seek the last piece in the land of Luwa...

CONTENTS

Treasure Hunt **5**
Bertha's Curse **153**

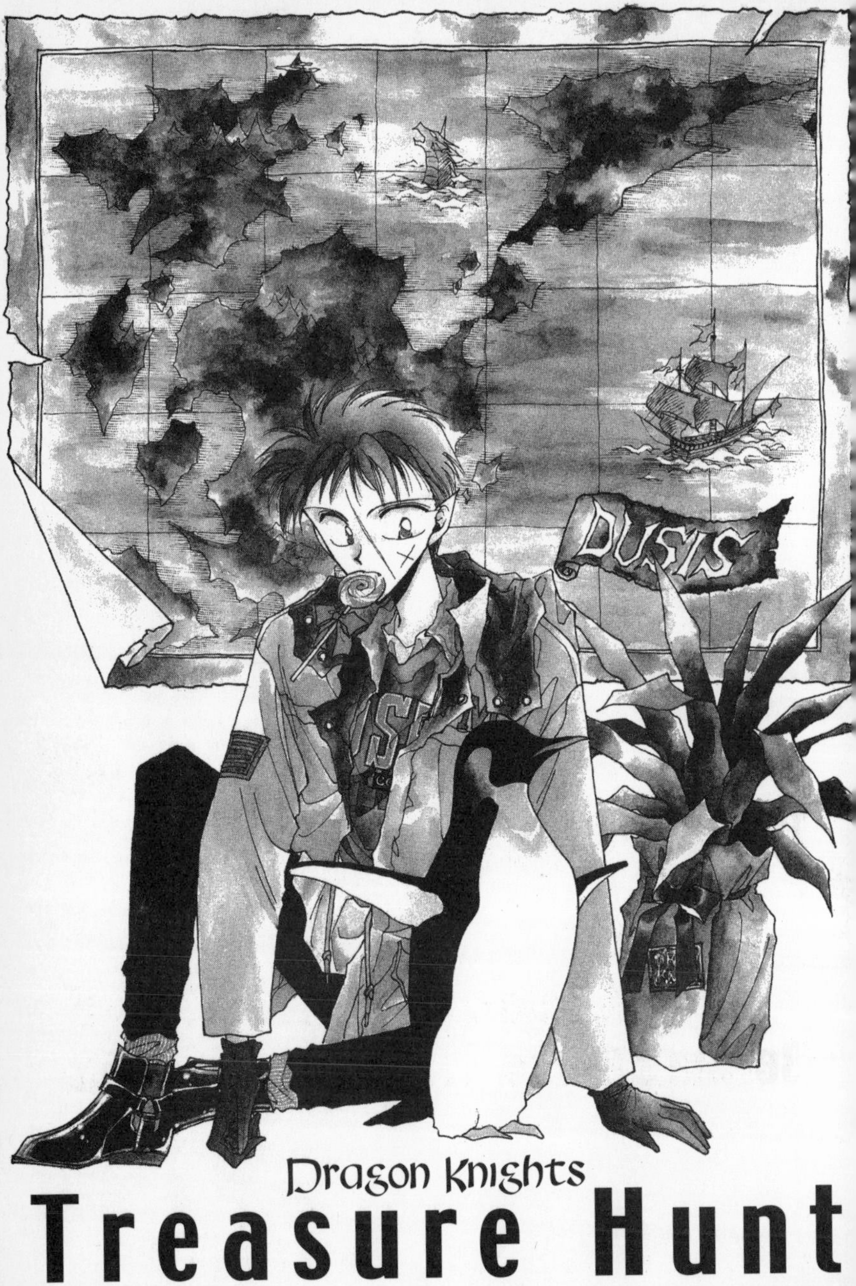
DUSIS

Dragon Knights

Treasure Hunt

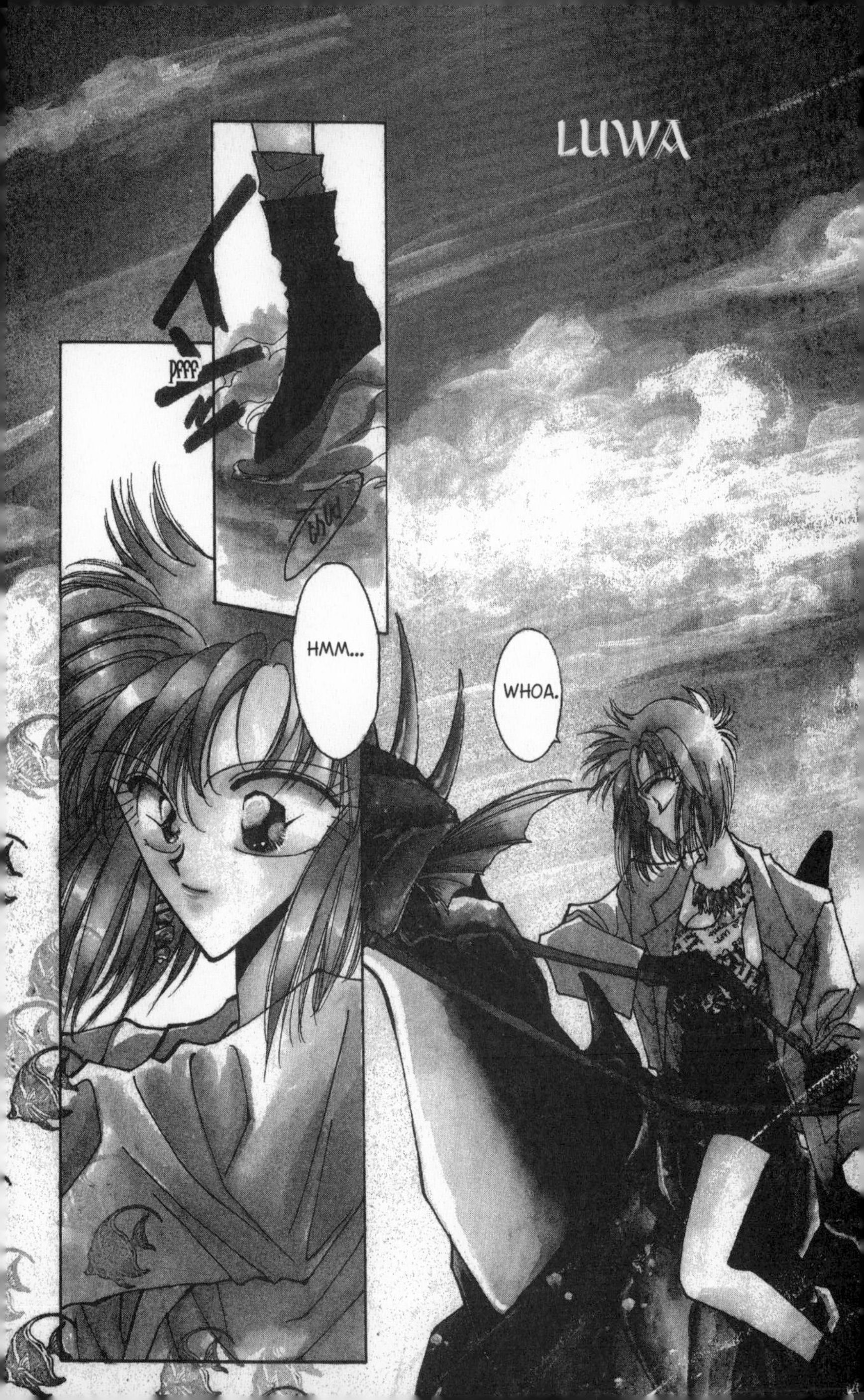
LUWA
pfff
WHOA.
HMM...

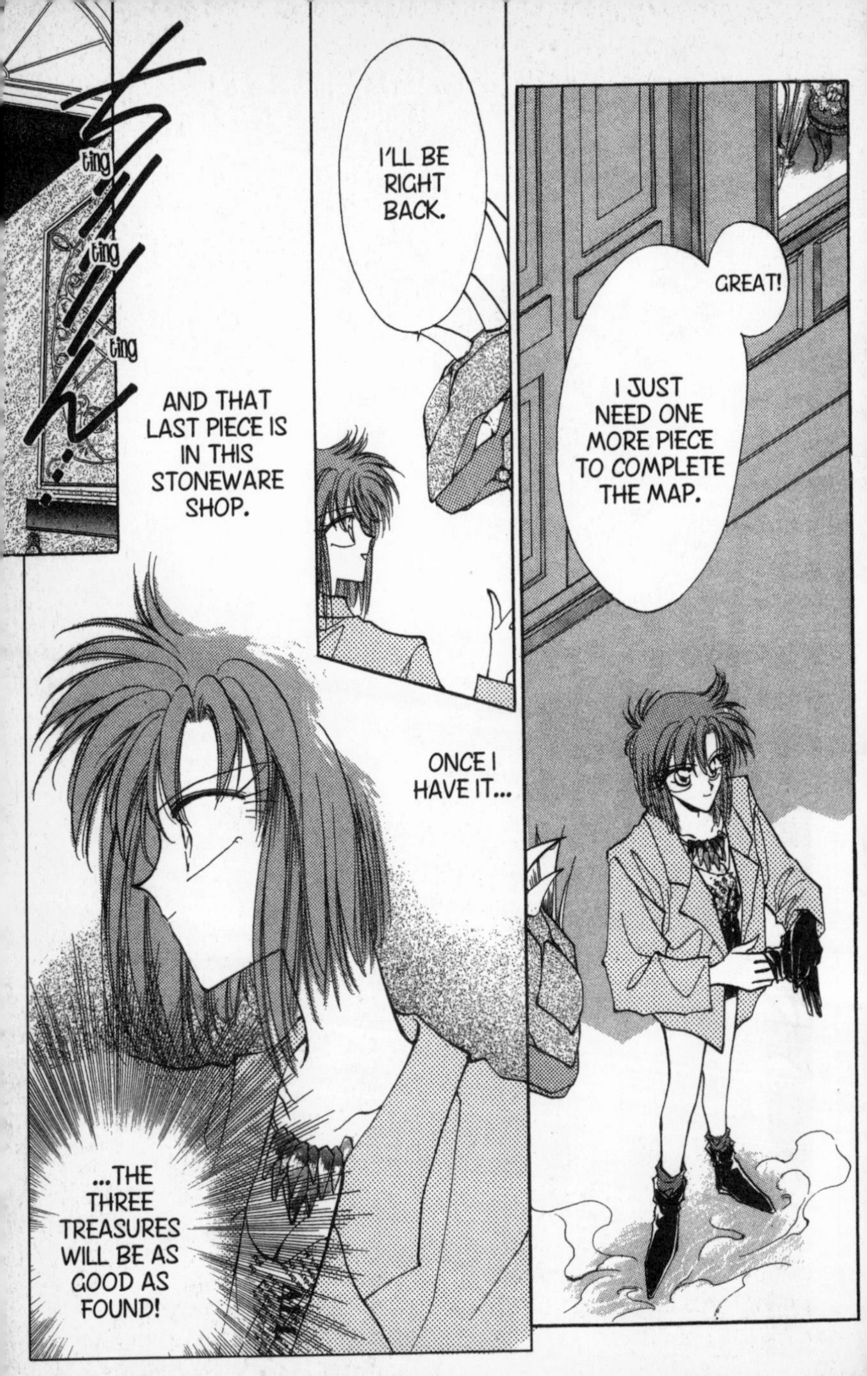
GREAT!
I JUST NEED ONE MORE PIECE TO COMPLETE THE MAP.
I'LL BE RIGHT BACK.
ting
ting
ting
AND THAT LAST PIECE IS IN THIS STONEWARE SHOP.
ONCE I HAVE IT...
...THE THREE TREASURES WILL BE AS GOOD AS FOUND!

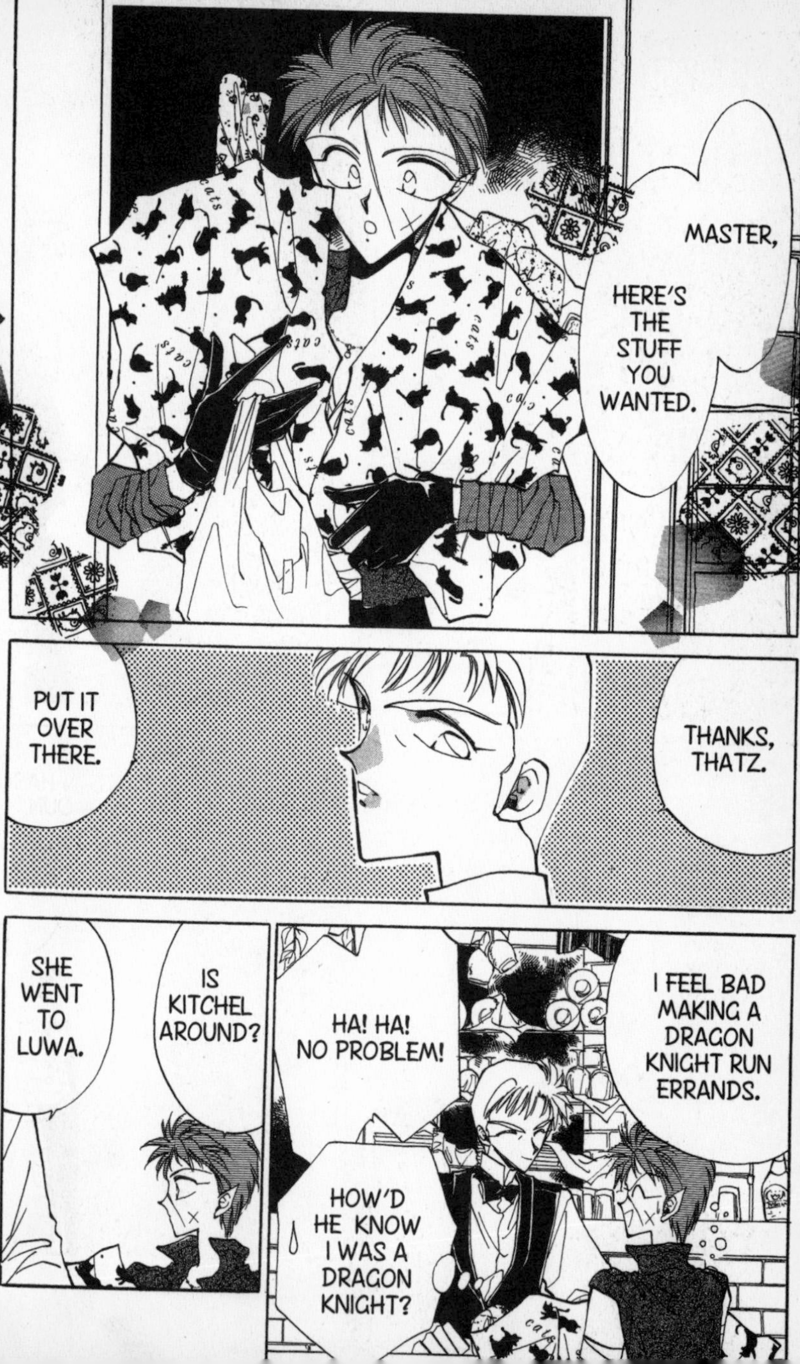
MASTER,
HERE'S THE STUFF YOU WANTED.
THANKS, THATZ.
PUT IT OVER THERE.
I FEEL BAD MAKING A DRAGON KNIGHT RUN ERRANDS.
HA! HA! NO PROBLEM!
HOW'D HE KNOW I WAS A DRAGON KNIGHT?
IS KITCHEL AROUND?
SHE WENT TO LUWA.

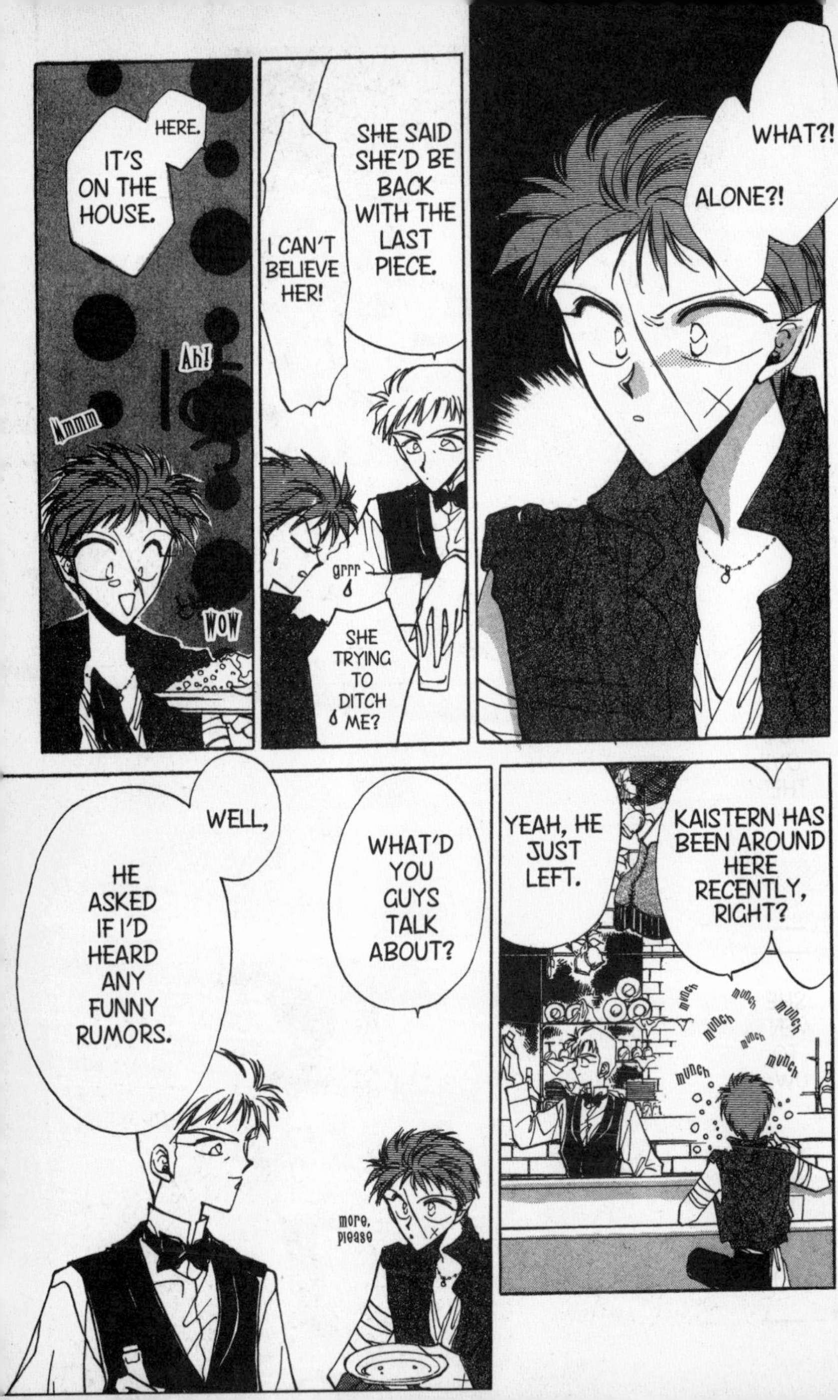
WHAT?!
ALONE?!
SHE SAID SHE'D BE BACK WITH THE LAST PIECE.
I CAN'T BELIEVE HER!
grrr
SHE TRYING TO DITCH ME?
HERE.
IT'S ON THE HOUSE.
Ah!
Mmmm
WOW
KAISTERN HAS BEEN AROUND HERE RECENTLY, RIGHT?
YEAH, HE JUST LEFT.
munch munch munch munch munch munch munch
WHAT'D YOU GUYS TALK ABOUT?
WELL,
HE ASKED IF I'D HEARD ANY FUNNY RUMORS.
more, please

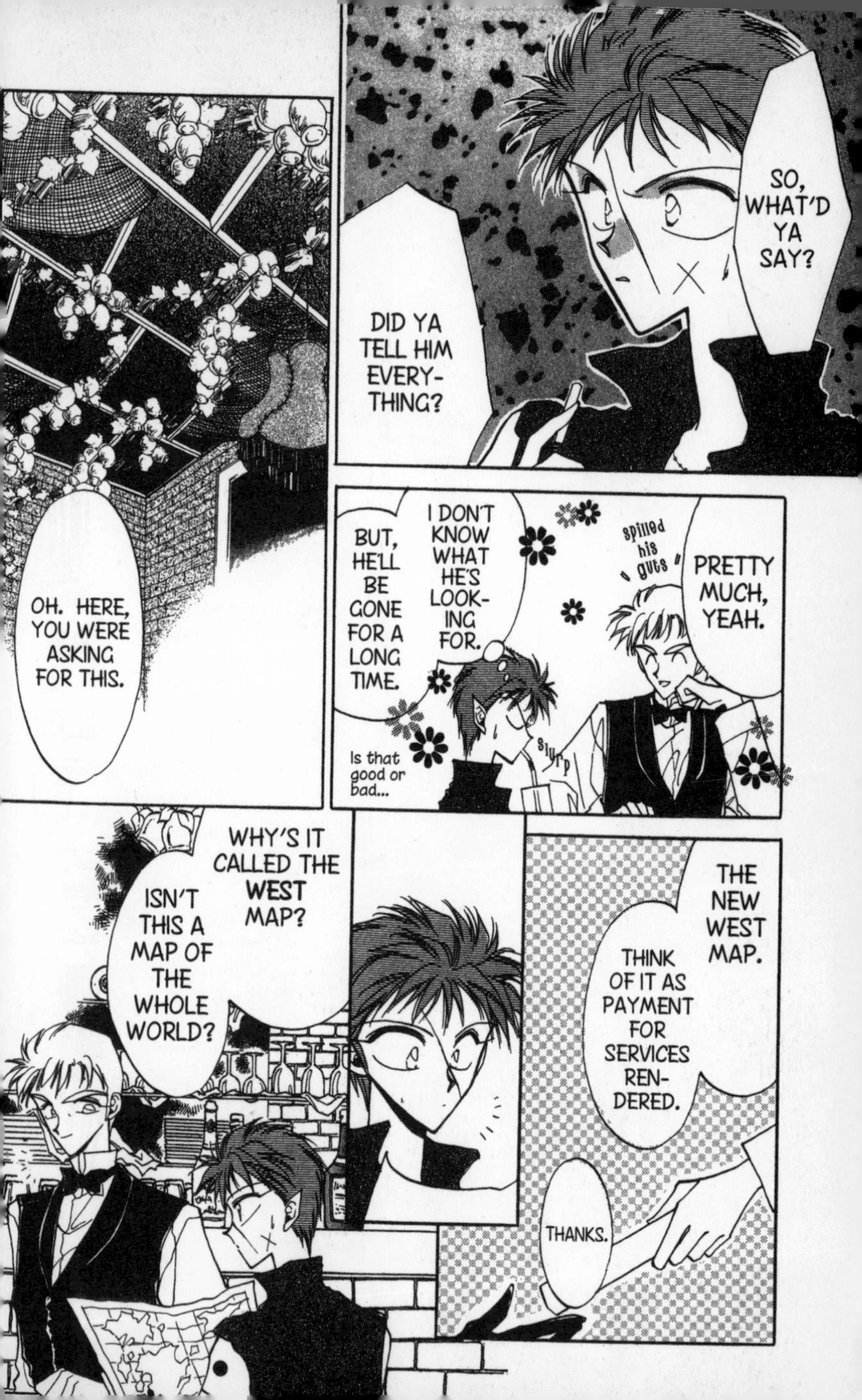
SO, WHAT'D YA SAY?
DID YA TELL HIM EVERY-THING?
PRETTY MUCH, YEAH.
spilled his guts
I DON'T KNOW WHAT HE'S LOOK-ING FOR.
BUT, HE'LL BE GONE FOR A LONG TIME.
slurp
Is that good or bad...
OH. HERE, YOU WERE ASKING FOR THIS.
THE NEW WEST MAP.
THINK OF IT AS PAYMENT FOR SERVICES REN-DERED.
THANKS.
WHY'S IT CALLED THE WEST MAP?
ISN'T THIS A MAP OF THE WHOLE WORLD?

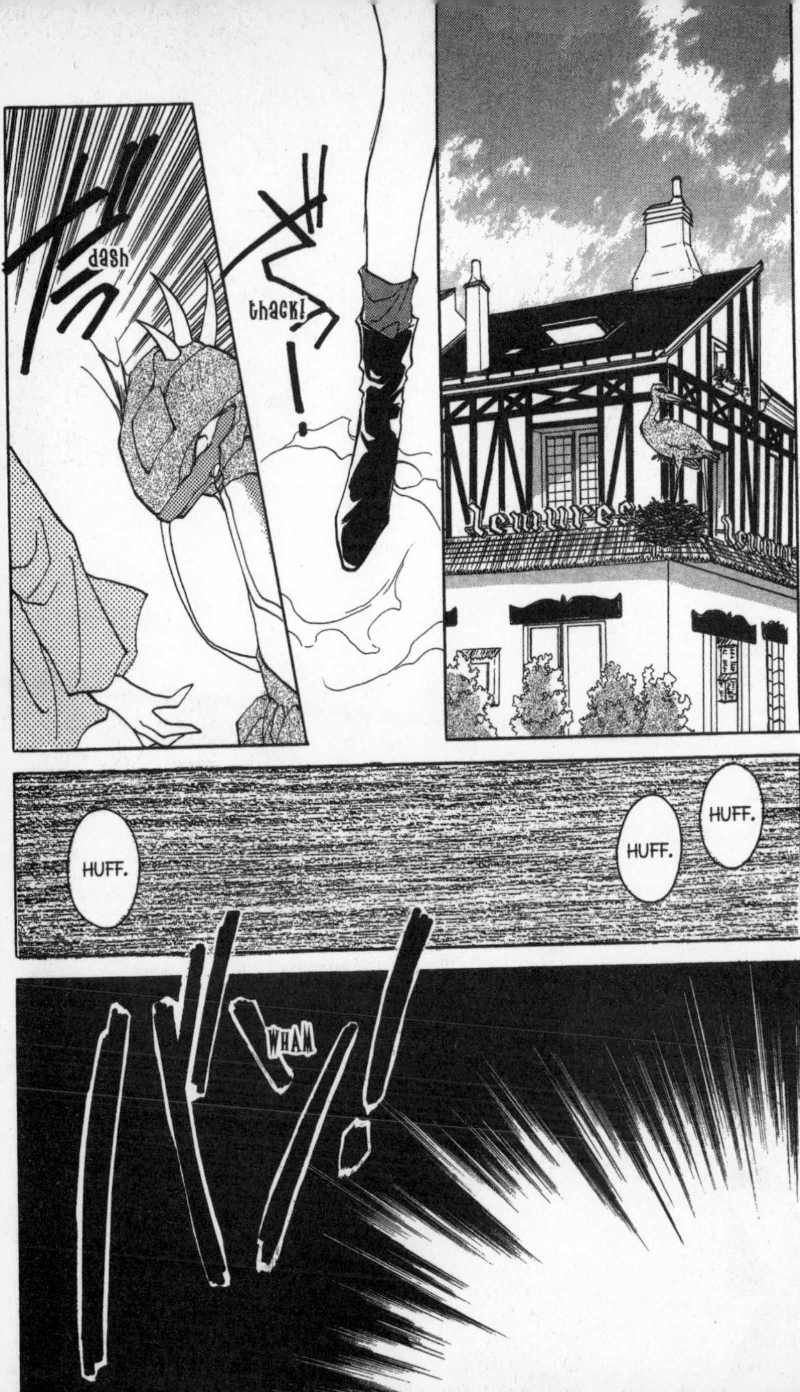

Lemures
thack!
dash
HUFF.
HUFF.
HUFF.
WHAM

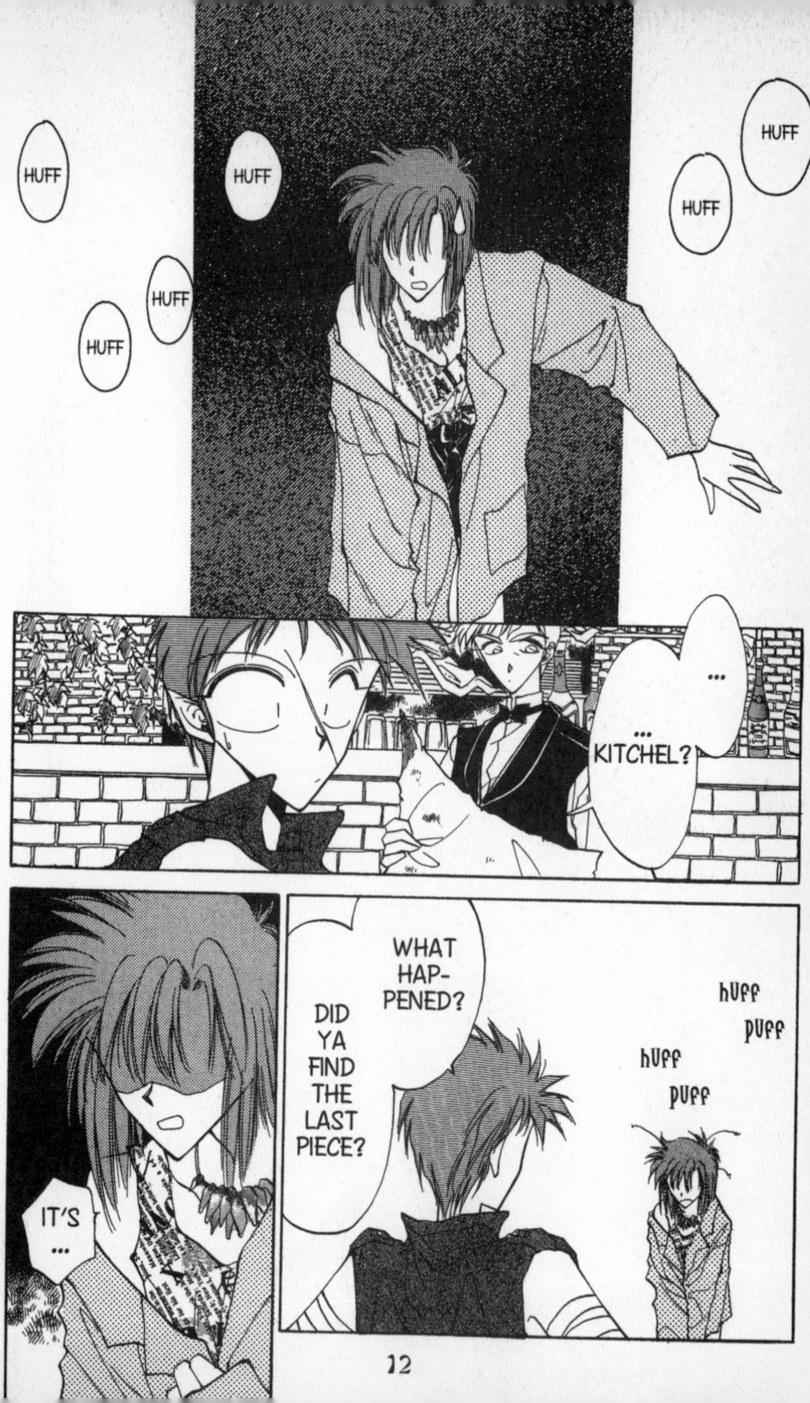
HUFF
HUFF
HUFF
HUFF
HUFF
HUFF
...
... KITCHEL?
hUFF
pUFF
hUFF
pUFF
WHAT HAP-PENED?
DID YA FIND THE LAST PIECE?
IT'S ...

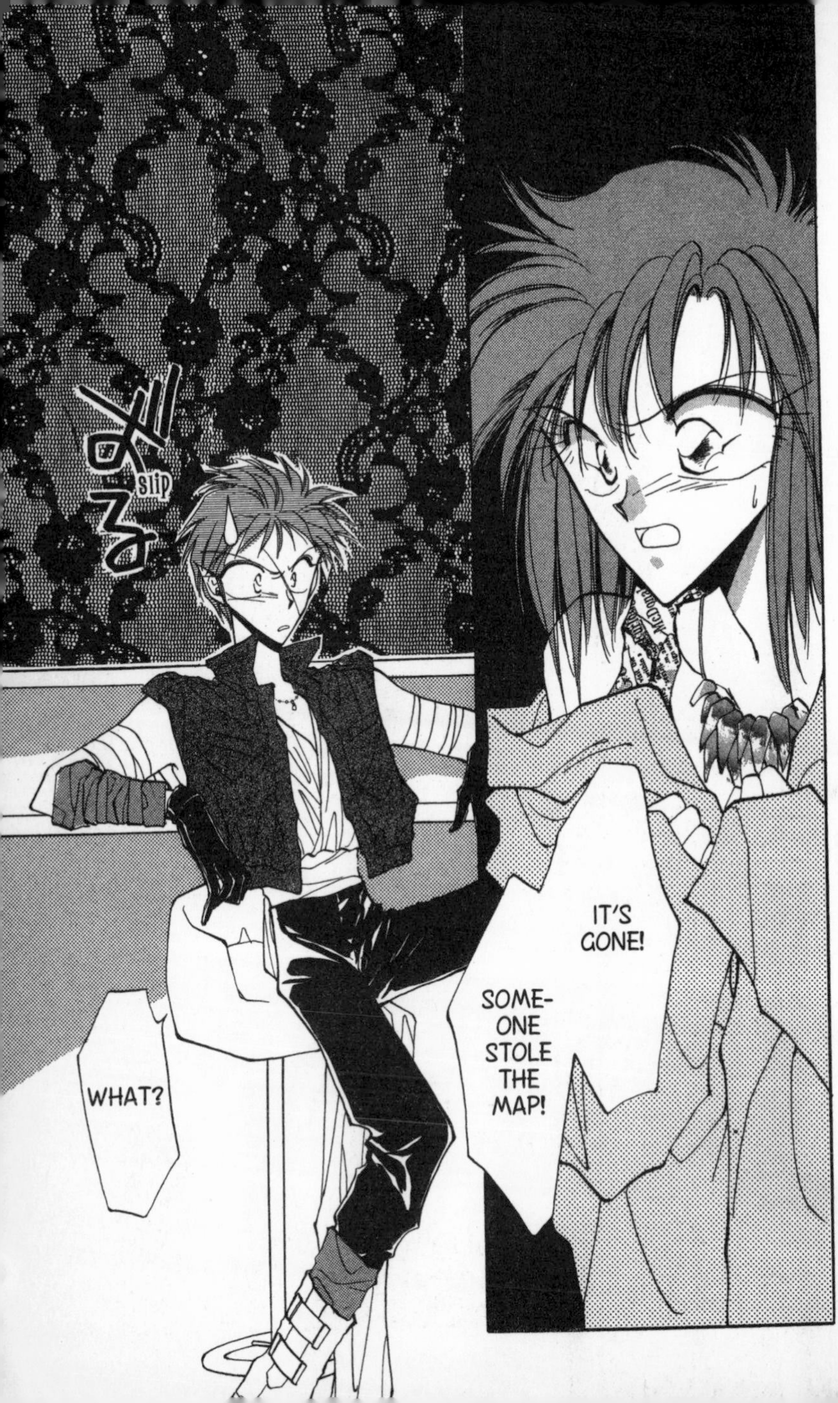
IT'S GONE!
SOME-ONE STOLE THE MAP!
slip
WHAT?

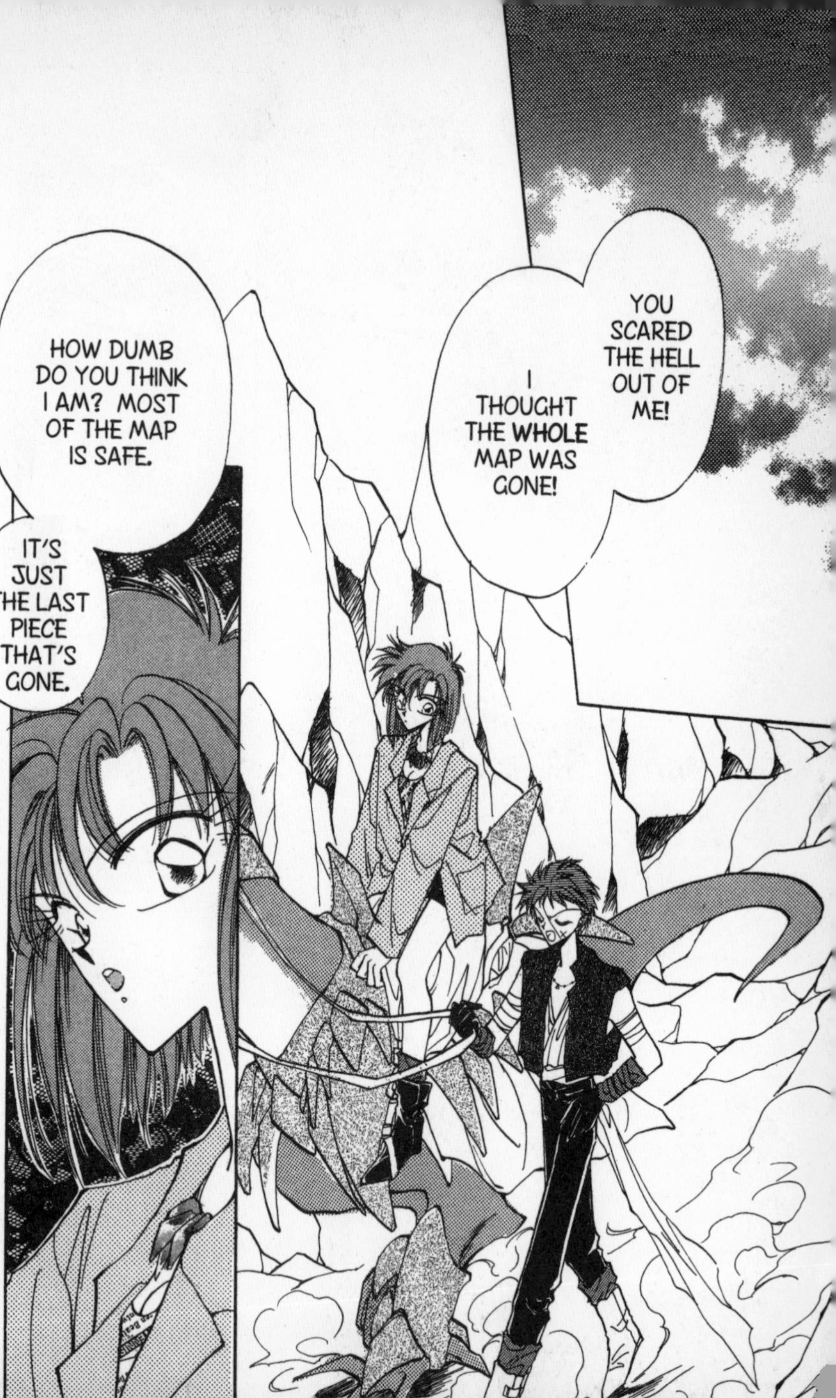
YOU SCARED THE HELL OUT OF ME!
I THOUGHT THE WHOLE MAP WAS GONE!
HOW DUMB DO YOU THINK I AM? MOST OF THE MAP IS SAFE.
IT'S JUST THE LAST PIECE THAT'S GONE.

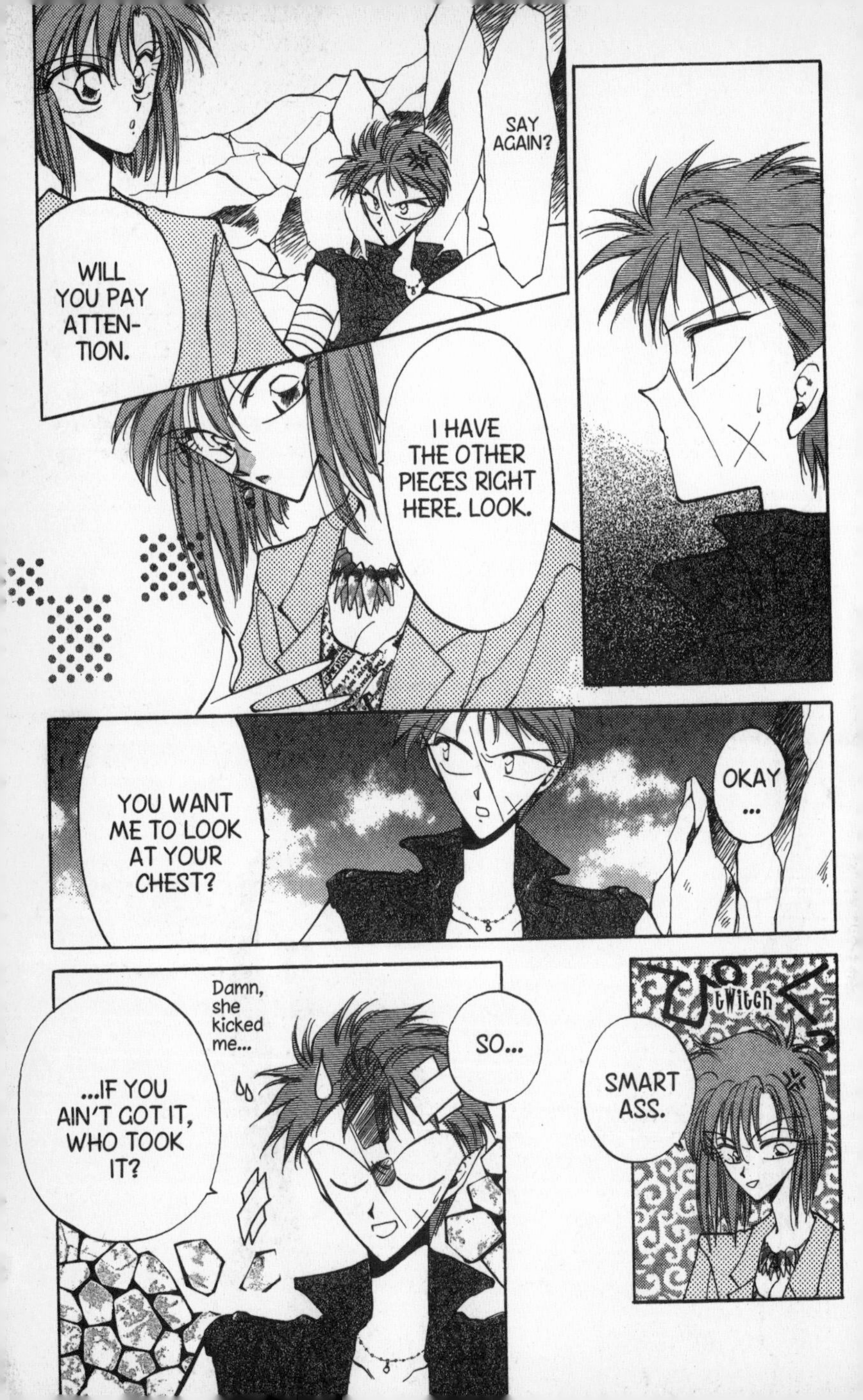
SAY AGAIN?
WILL YOU PAY ATTENTION.
I HAVE THE OTHER PIECES RIGHT HERE. LOOK.
OKAY ...
YOU WANT ME TO LOOK AT YOUR CHEST?
TWITCH
SMART ASS.
SO...
Damn, she kicked me...
...IF YOU AIN'T GOT IT, WHO TOOK IT?

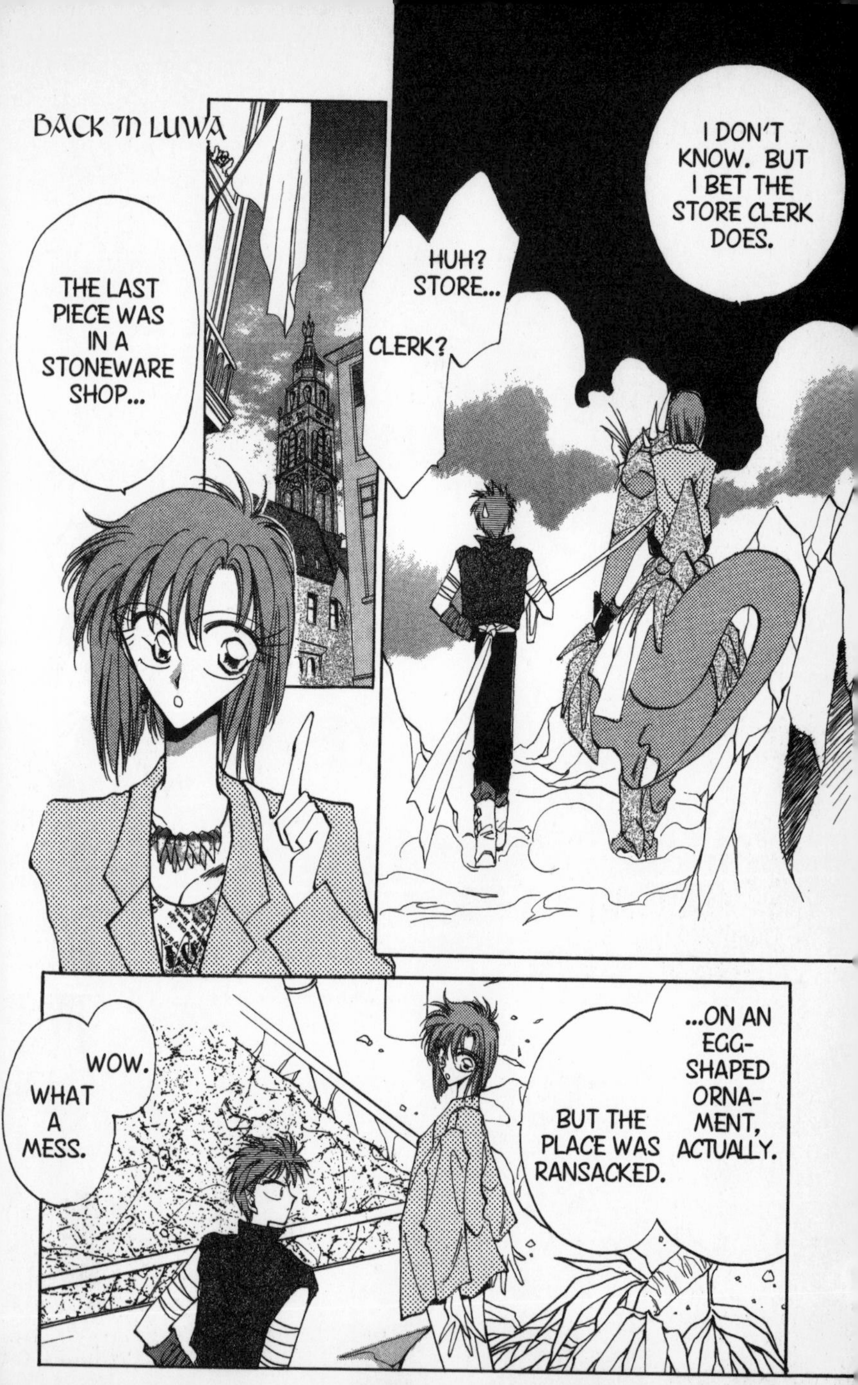
I DON'T KNOW. BUT I BET THE STORE CLERK DOES.
HUH? STORE...
CLERK?
BACK IN LUWA
THE LAST PIECE WAS IN A STONEWARE SHOP...
...ON AN EGG-SHAPED ORNAMENT, ACTUALLY.
BUT THE PLACE WAS RANSACKED.
WOW. WHAT A MESS.

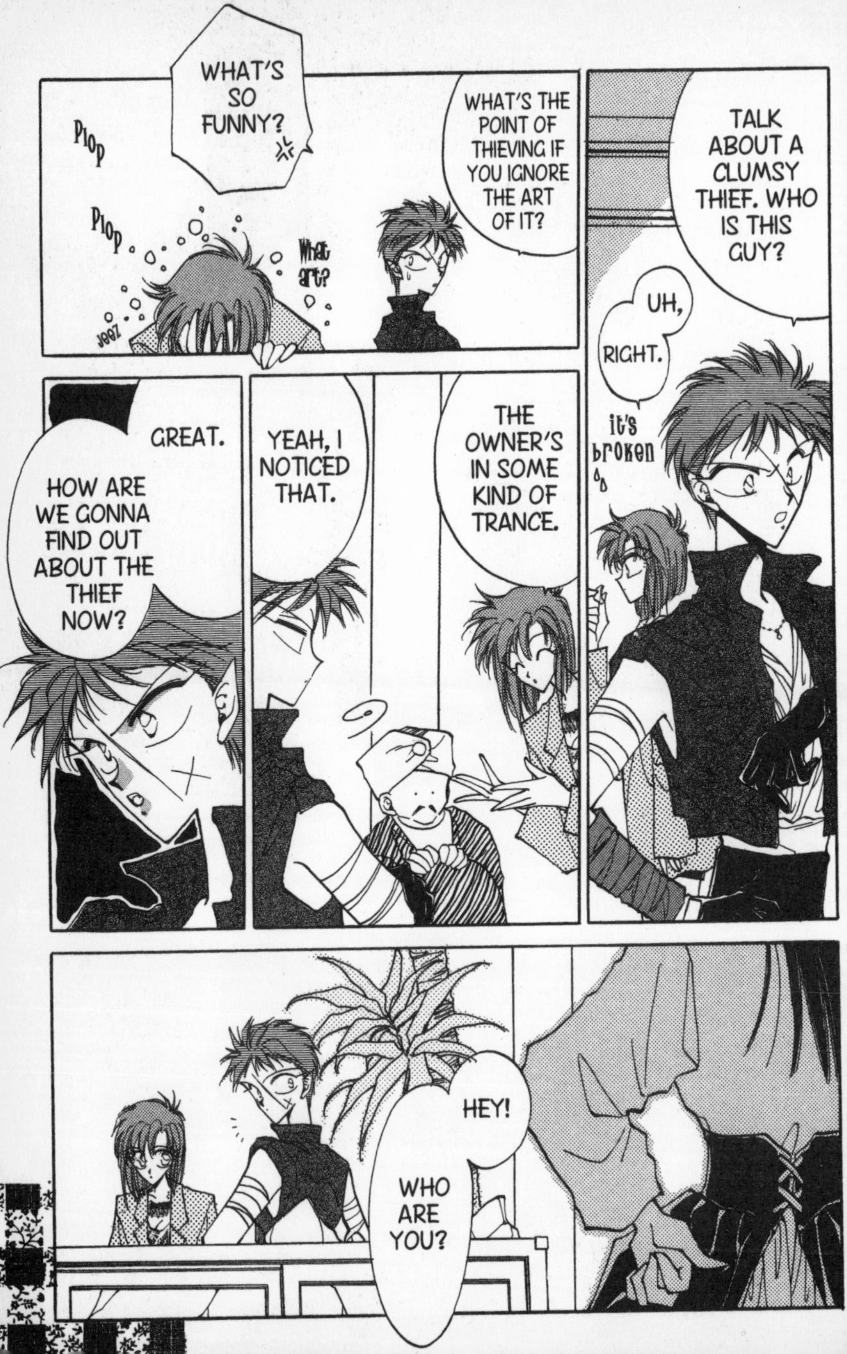

TALK ABOUT A CLUMSY THIEF. WHO IS THIS GUY?
UH,
RIGHT.
it's broken
WHAT'S THE POINT OF THIEVING IF YOU IGNORE THE ART OF IT?
What art?
WHAT'S SO FUNNY?
Plop
Plop
Jeez
THE OWNER'S IN SOME KIND OF TRANCE.
YEAH, I NOTICED THAT.
GREAT.
HOW ARE WE GONNA FIND OUT ABOUT THE THIEF NOW?
HEY!
WHO ARE YOU?

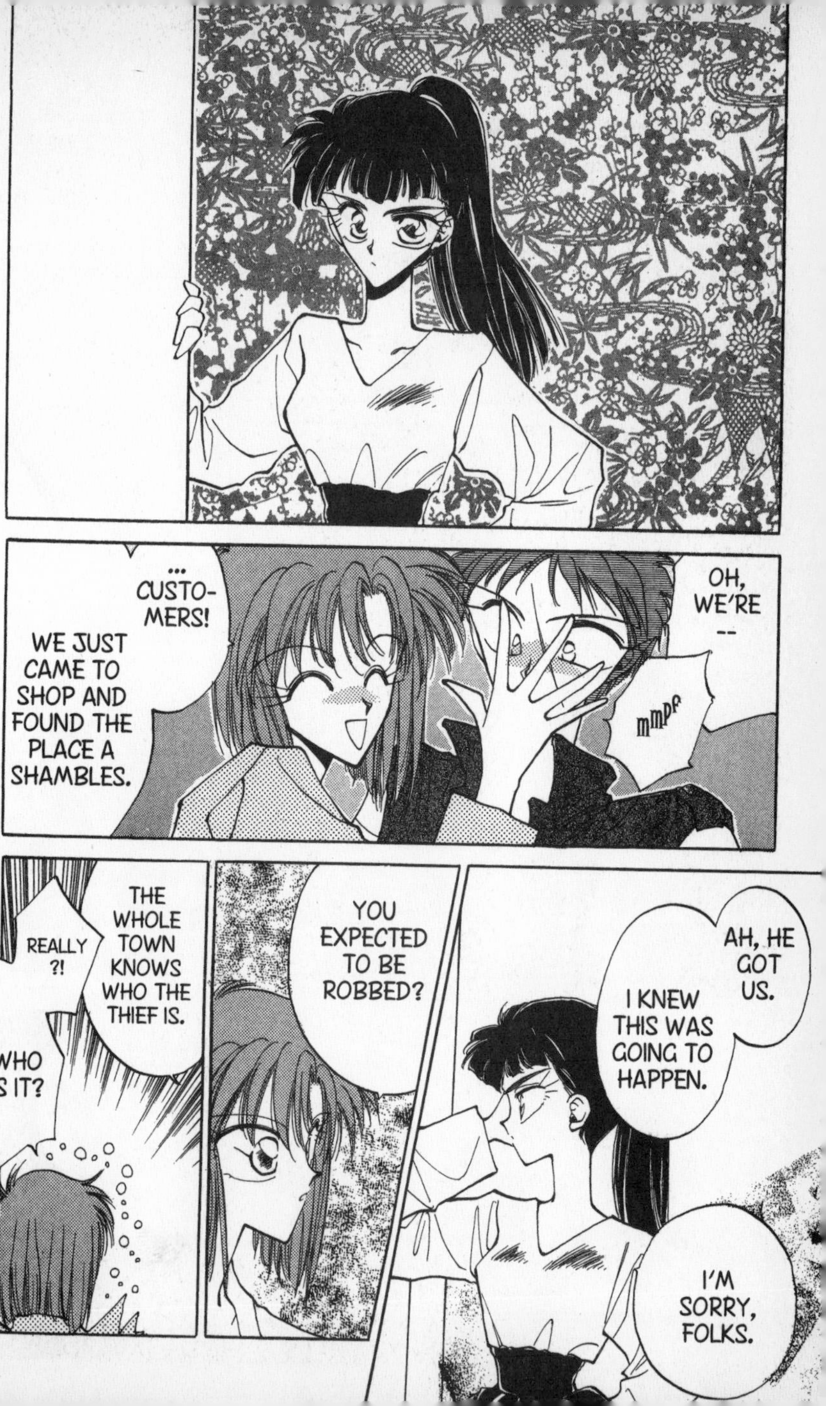
OH, WE'RE --
mmpf
... CUSTO-MERS!
WE JUST CAME TO SHOP AND FOUND THE PLACE A SHAMBLES.
AH, HE GOT US.
I KNEW THIS WAS GOING TO HAPPEN.
I'M SORRY, FOLKS.
YOU EXPECTED TO BE ROBBED?
THE WHOLE TOWN KNOWS WHO THE THIEF IS.
REALLY ?!
WHO IS IT?

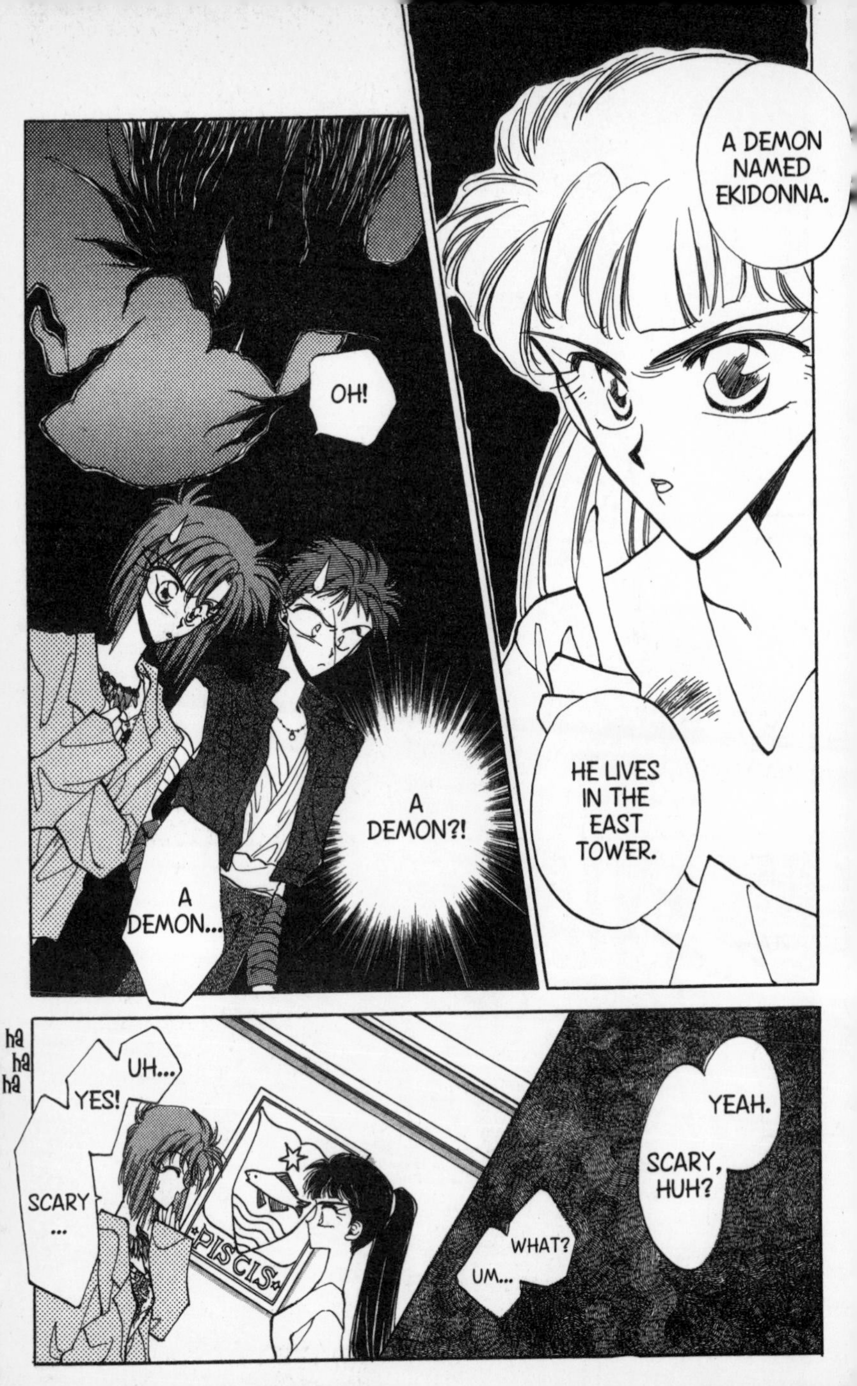
A DEMON NAMED EKIDONNA.
HE LIVES IN THE EAST TOWER.
OH!
A DEMON?!
A DEMON...
YEAH.
SCARY, HUH?
WHAT?
UM...
UH...
YES!
ha ha ha
SCARY ...

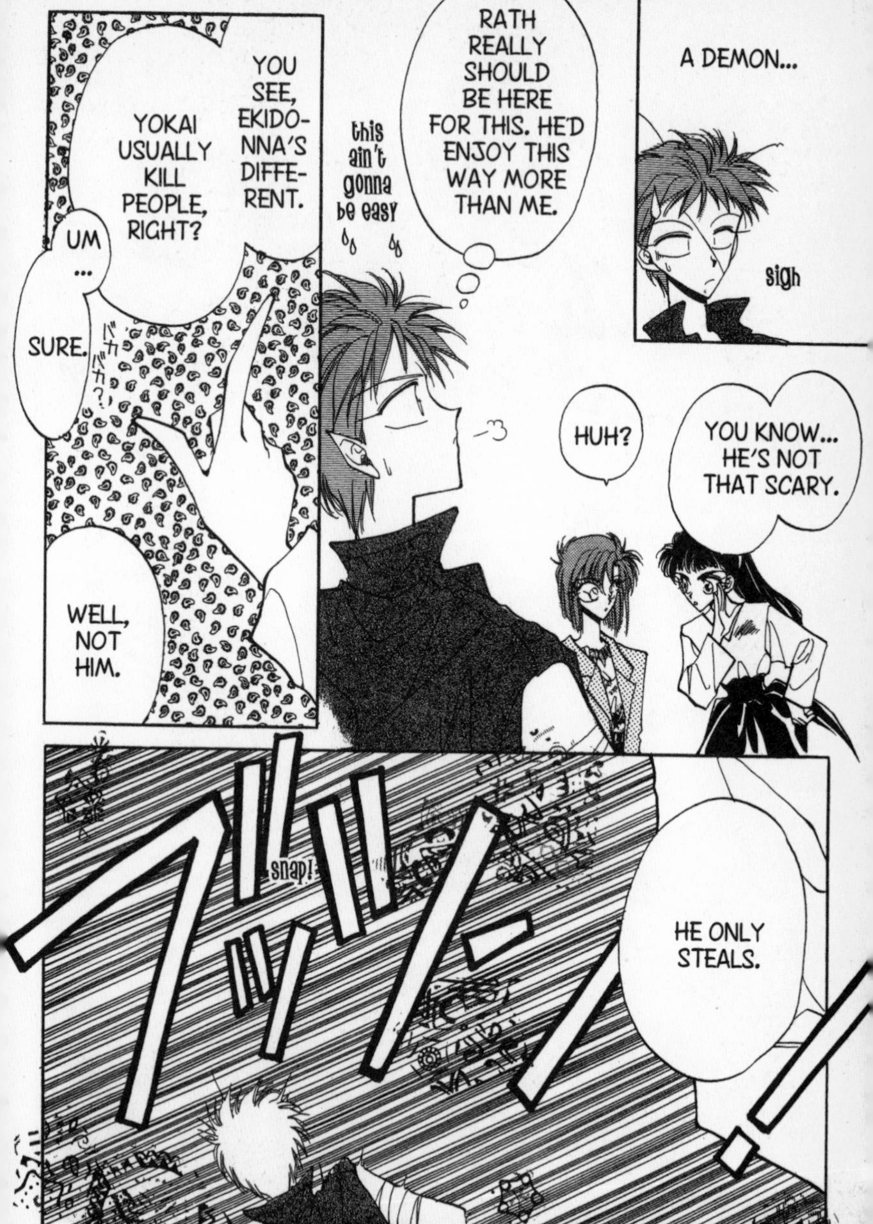
A DEMON...
sigh
YOU KNOW... HE'S NOT THAT SCARY.
HUH?
RATH REALLY SHOULD BE HERE FOR THIS. HE'D ENJOY THIS WAY MORE THAN ME.
this ain't gonna be easy
YOU SEE, EKIDONNA'S DIFFERENT.
YOKAI USUALLY KILL PEOPLE, RIGHT?
UM... SURE.
WELL, NOT HIM.
HE ONLY STEALS.
snap!

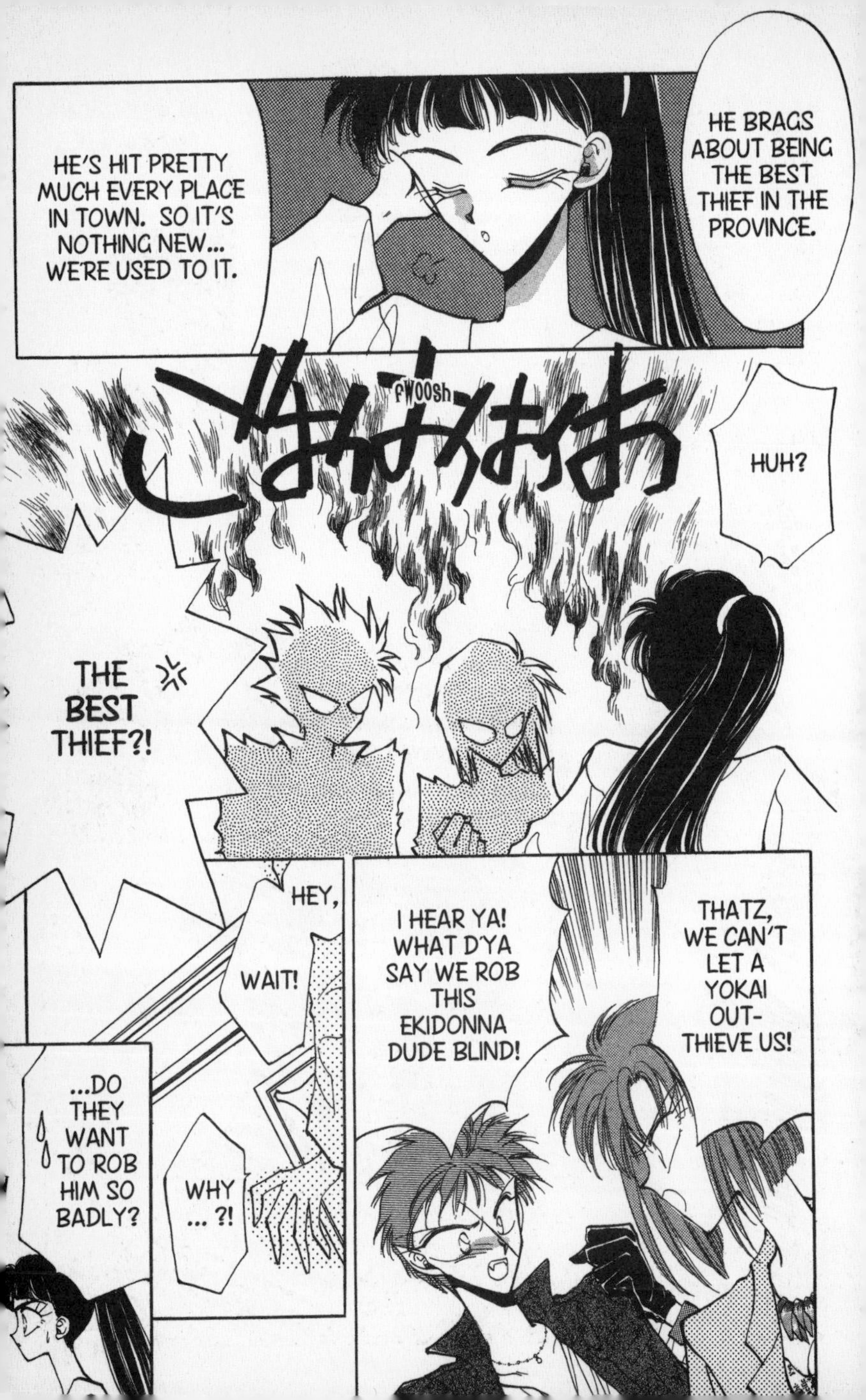
HE BRAGS ABOUT BEING THE BEST THIEF IN THE PROVINCE.
HE'S HIT PRETTY MUCH EVERY PLACE IN TOWN. SO IT'S NOTHING NEW... WE'RE USED TO IT.
HUH?
fWOOsh
THE BEST THIEF?!
THATZ, WE CAN'T LET A YOKAI OUT-THIEVE US!
I HEAR YA! WHAT D'YA SAY WE ROB THIS EKIDONNA DUDE BLIND!
HEY,
WAIT!
WHY ... ?!
...DO THEY WANT TO ROB HIM SO BADLY?

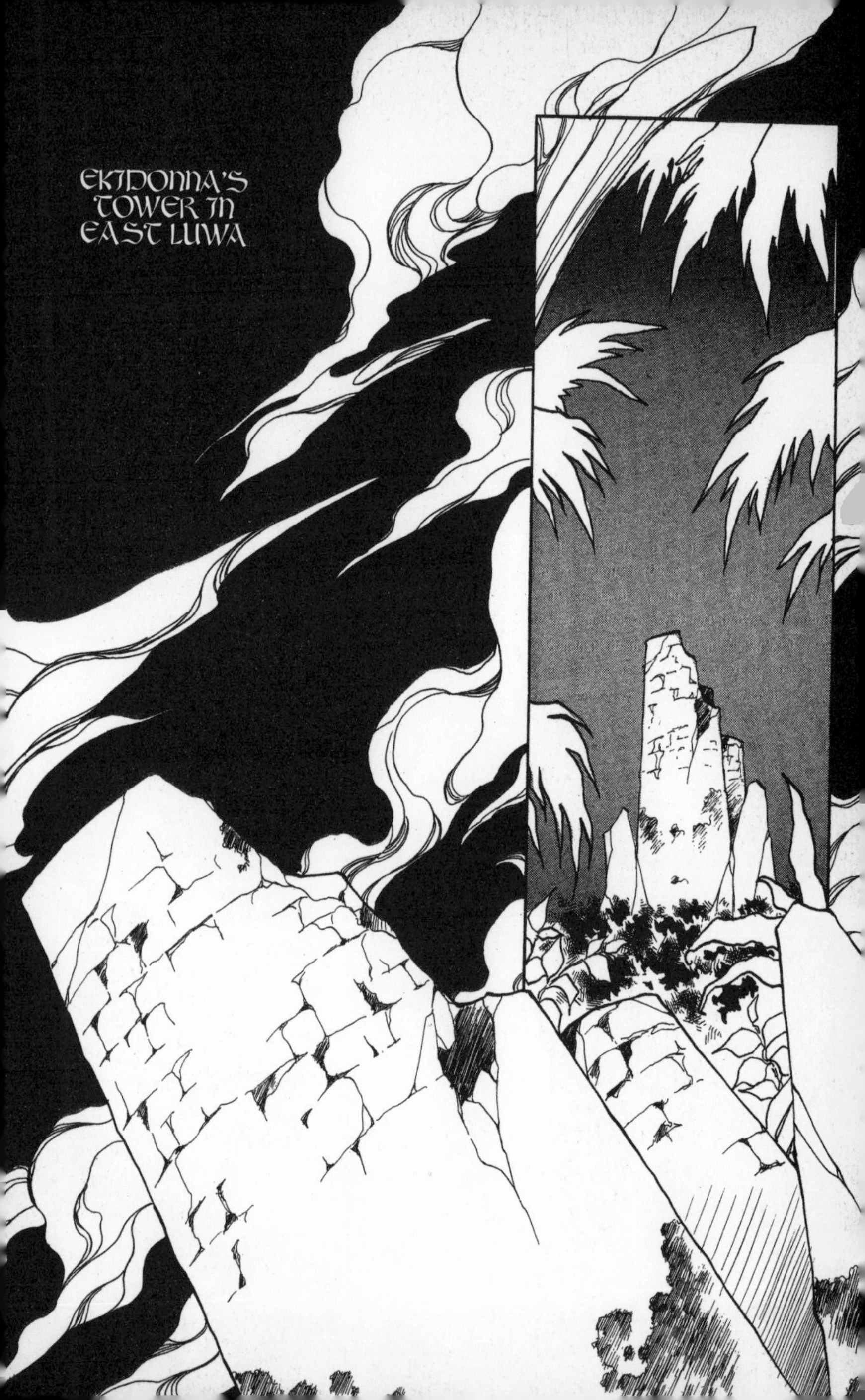
EKIDONNA'S TOWER IN EAST LUWA

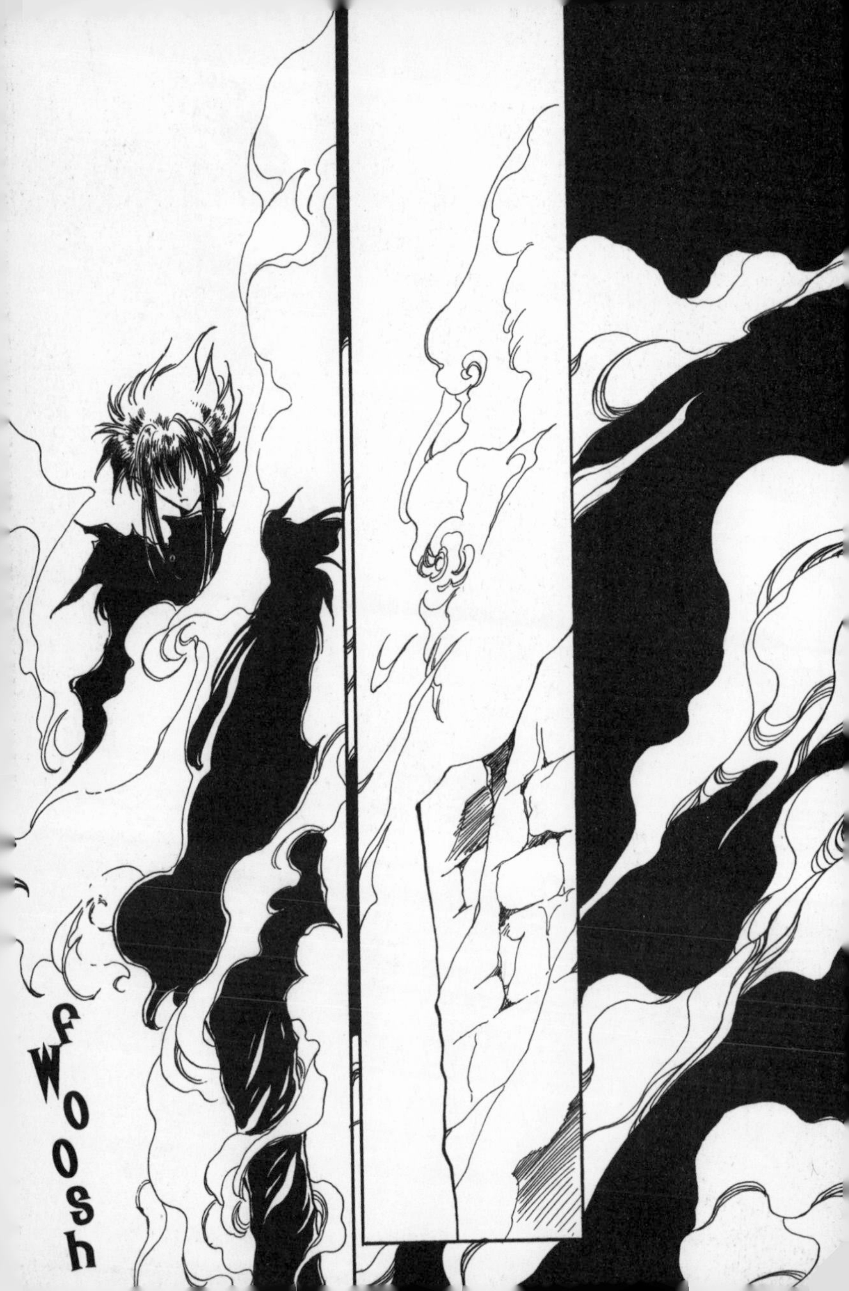
fwoosh

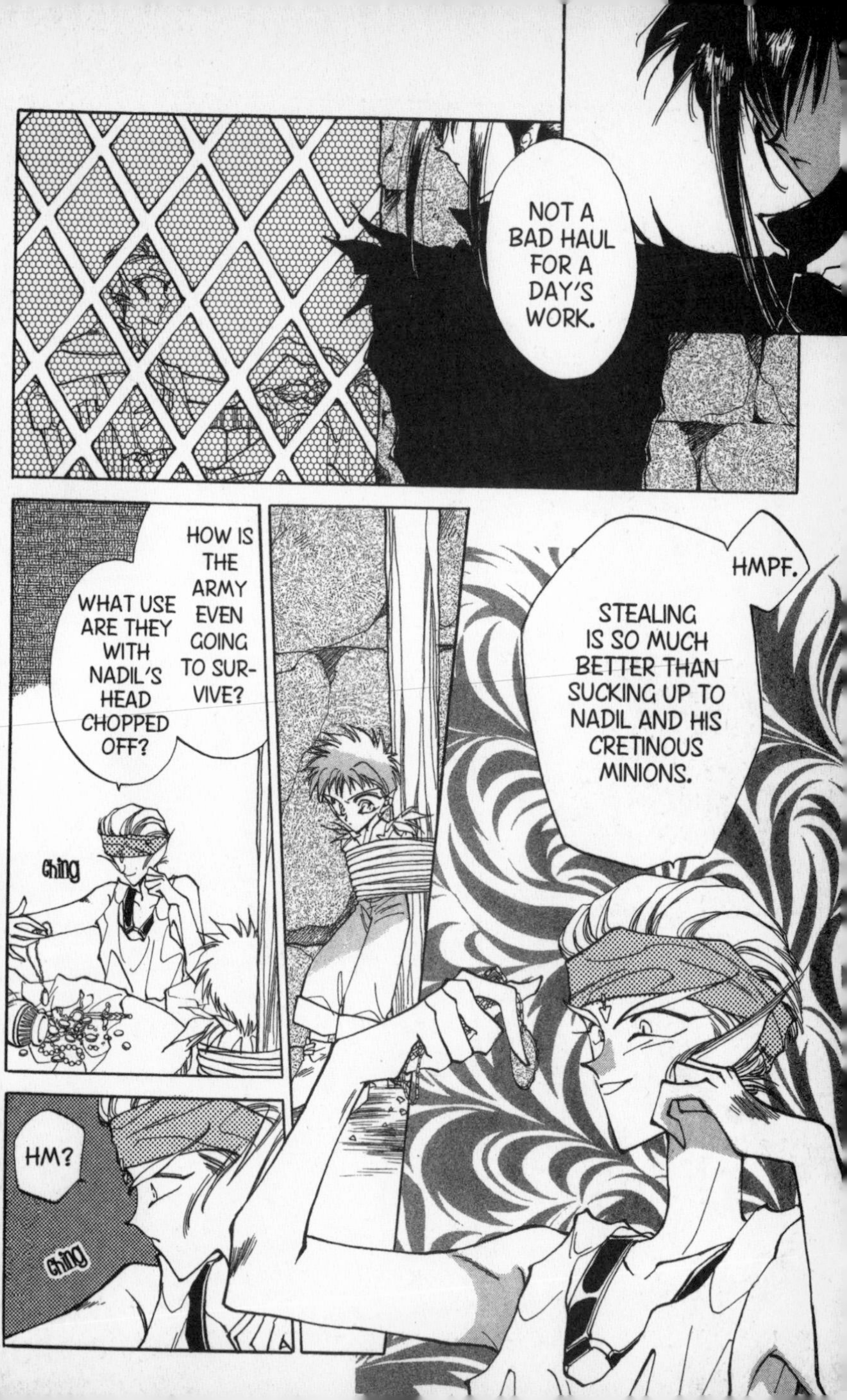
NOT A BAD HAUL FOR A DAY'S WORK.
HMPF.
STEALING IS SO MUCH BETTER THAN SUCKING UP TO NADIL AND HIS CRETINOUS MINIONS.
HOW IS THE ARMY EVEN GOING TO SURVIVE?
WHAT USE ARE THEY WITH NADIL'S HEAD CHOPPED OFF?
Ching
Ching
HM?

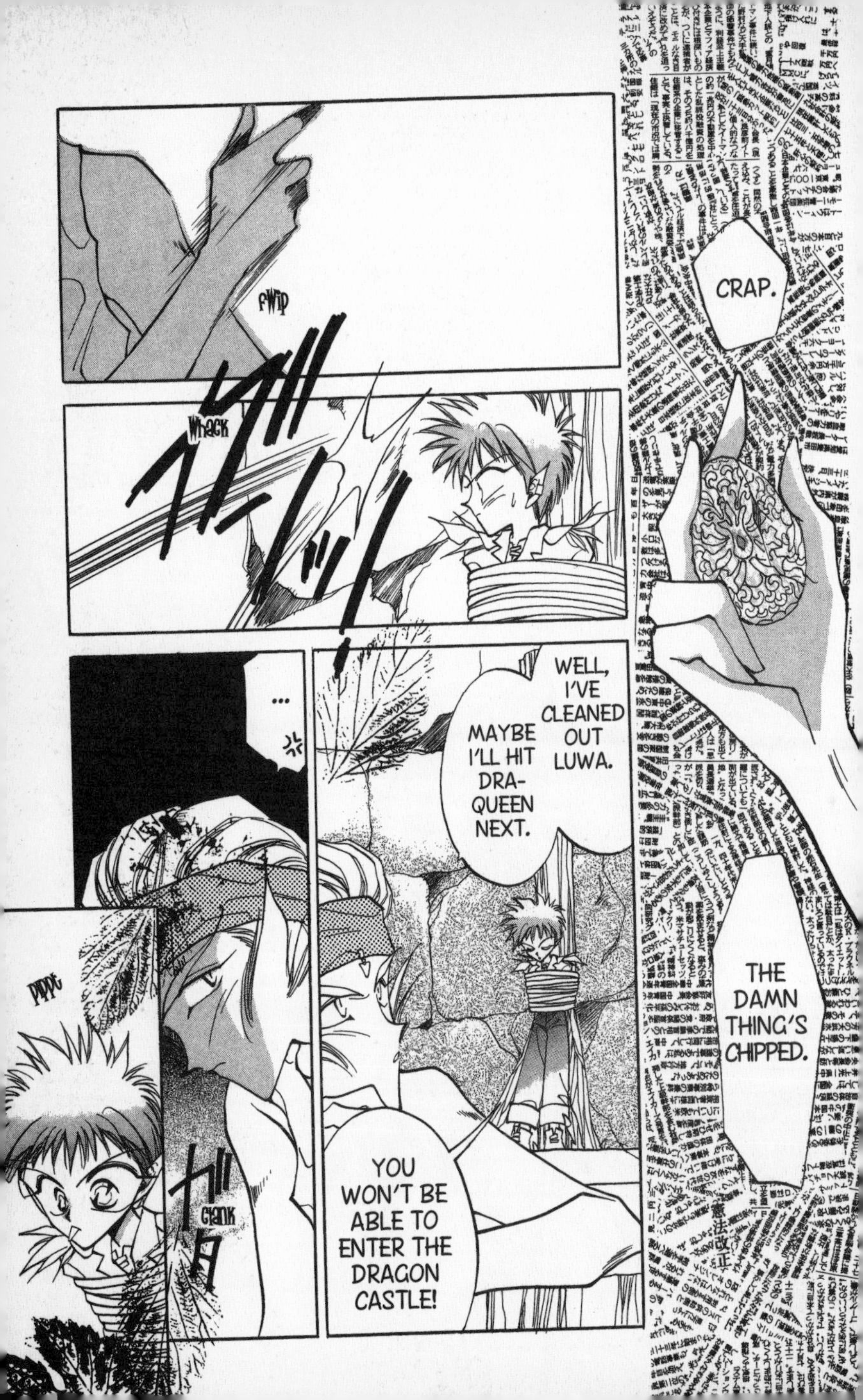
CRAP.
THE DAMN THING'S CHIPPED.
FWIP
WHACK
WELL, I'VE CLEANED OUT LUWA.
MAYBE I'LL HIT DRA-QUEEN NEXT.
...
YOU WON'T BE ABLE TO ENTER THE DRAGON CASTLE!
CLANK
PIPPT

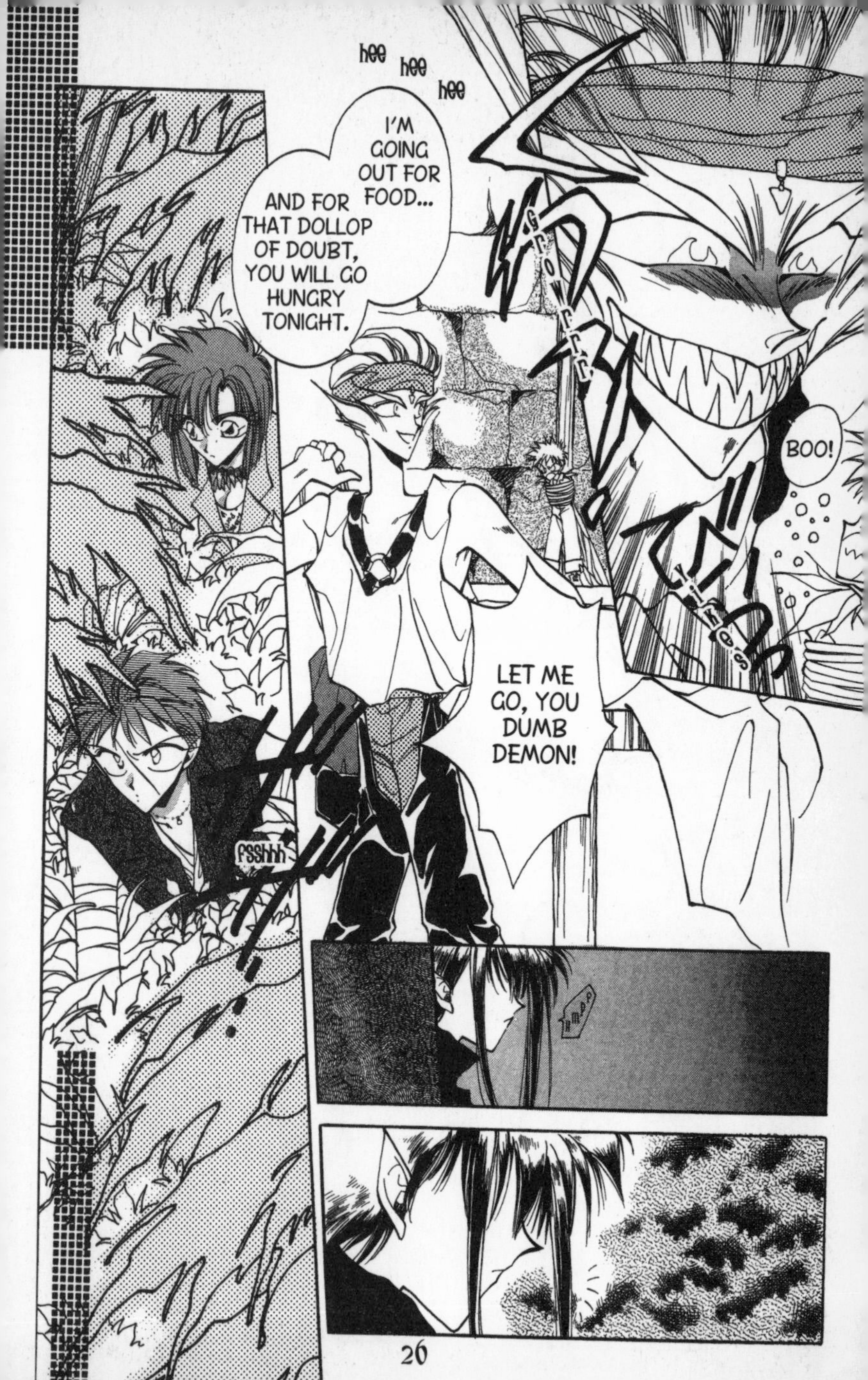
BOO!
GROWRRR
YIKES
hee hee hee
I'M GOING OUT FOR FOOD...
AND FOR THAT DOLLOP OF DOUBT, YOU WILL GO HUNGRY TONIGHT.
LET ME GO, YOU DUMB DEMON!
fsshhh
HMPP

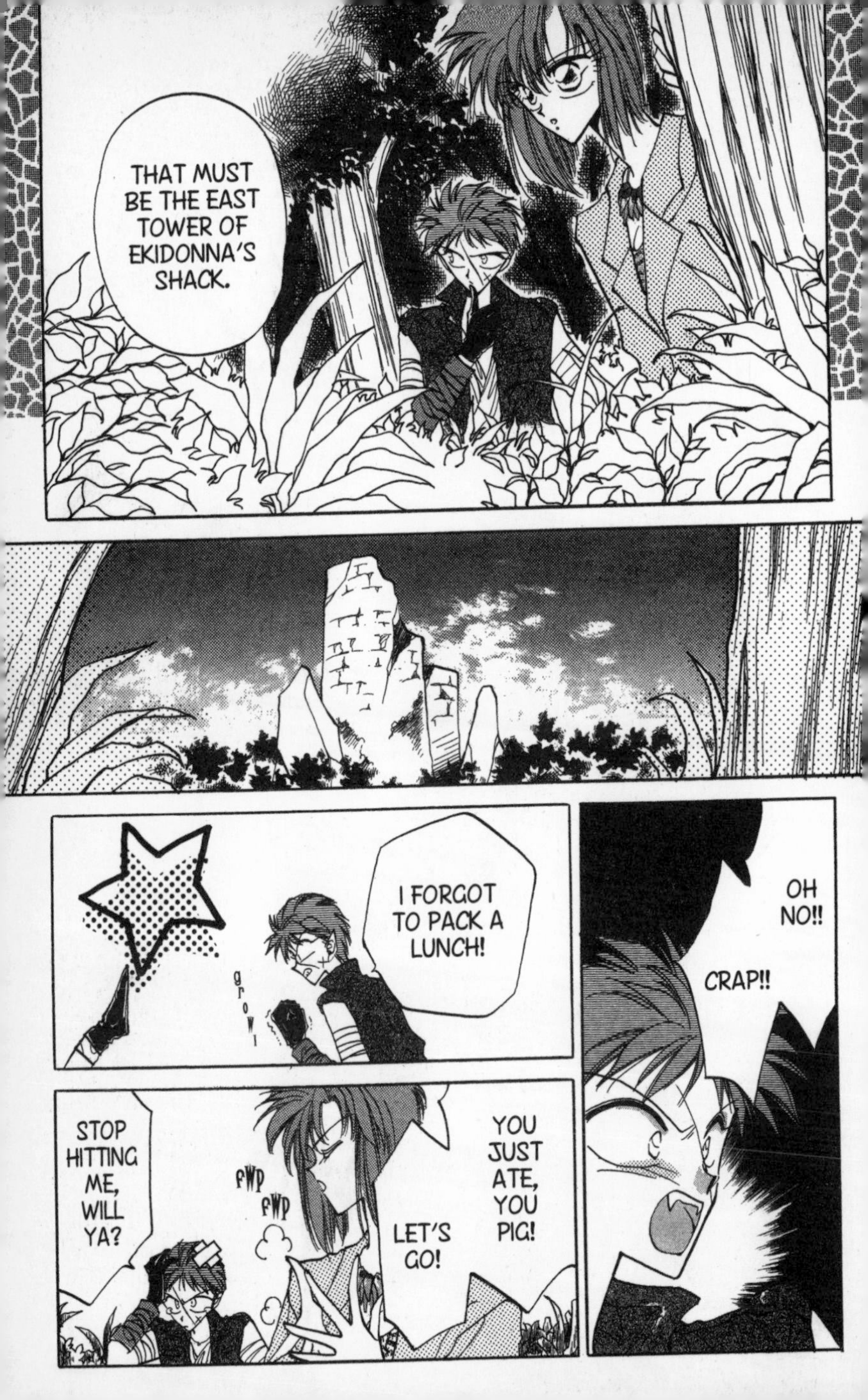
THAT MUST BE THE EAST TOWER OF EKIDONNA'S SHACK.
OH NO!!
CRAP!!
I FORGOT TO PACK A LUNCH!
growl
YOU JUST ATE, YOU PIG!
LET'S GO!
fwp
fwp
STOP HITTING ME, WILL YA?

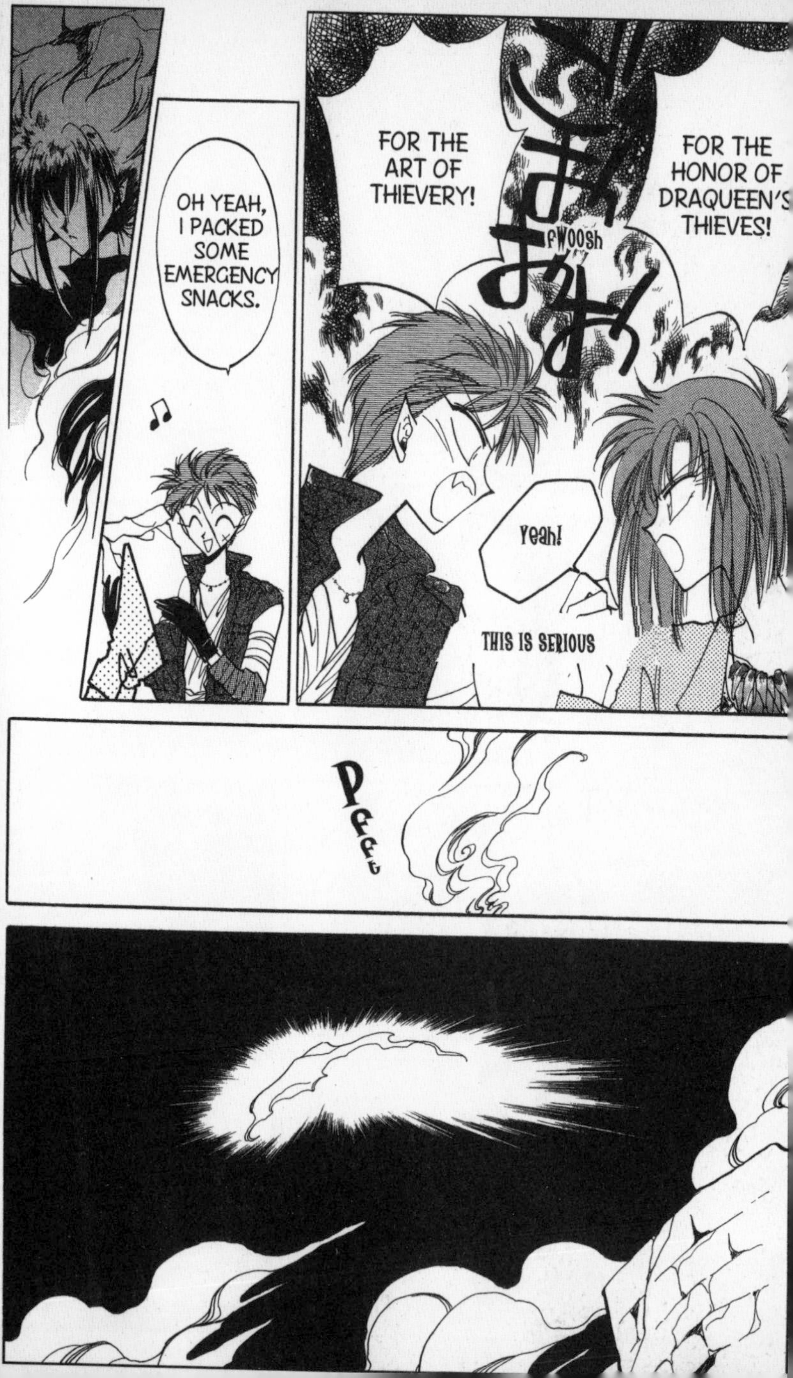

FOR THE HONOR OF DRAQUEEN'S THIEVES!
FOR THE ART OF THIEVERY!
fWOOSh
Yeah!
THIS IS SERIOUS
OH YEAH, I PACKED SOME EMERGENCY SNACKS.
♪
Pfff

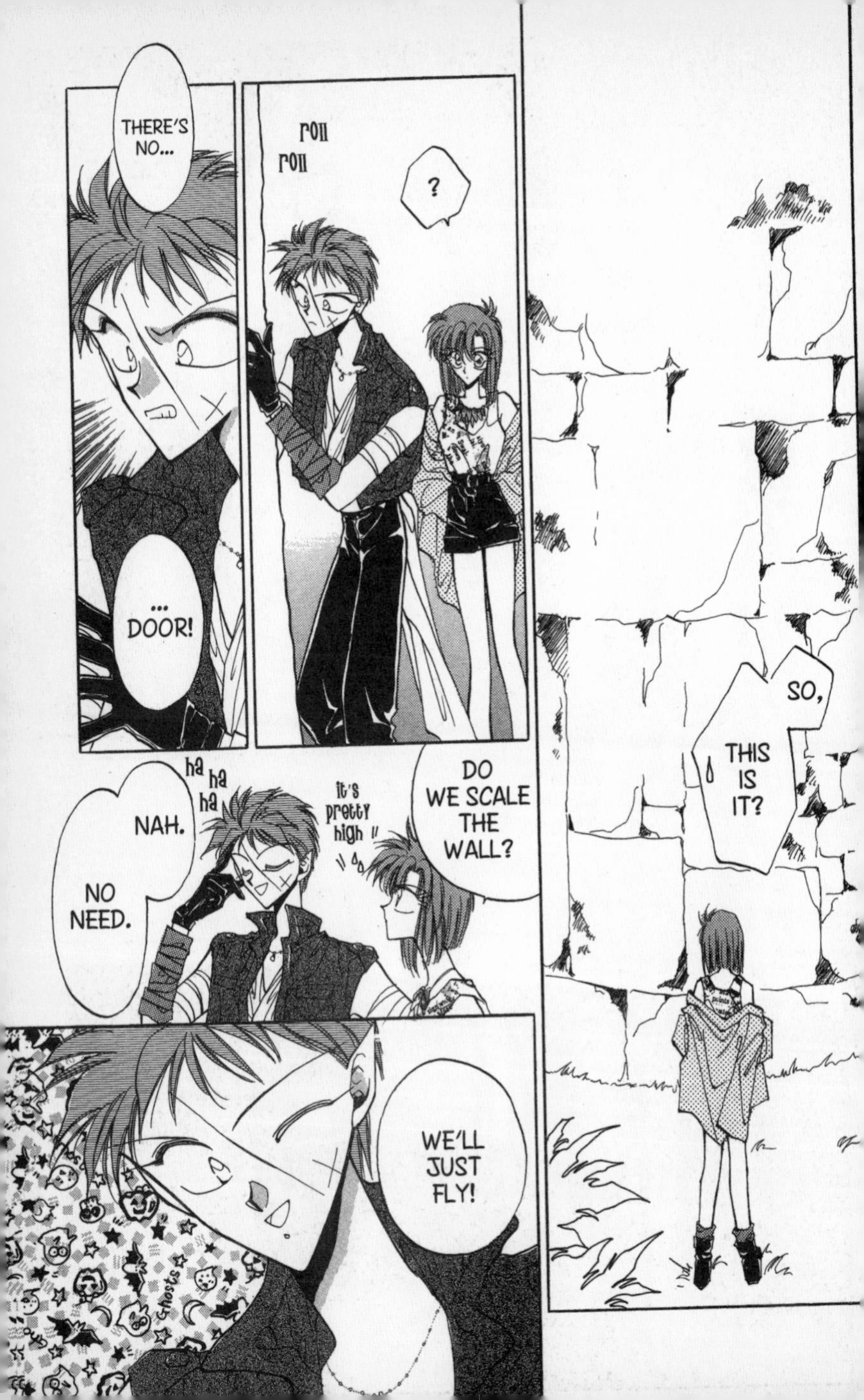
SO,
THIS IS IT?
roll
roll
?
THERE'S NO...
...DOOR!
DO WE SCALE THE WALL?
it's pretty high
ha ha ha
NAH.
NO NEED.
WE'LL JUST FLY!

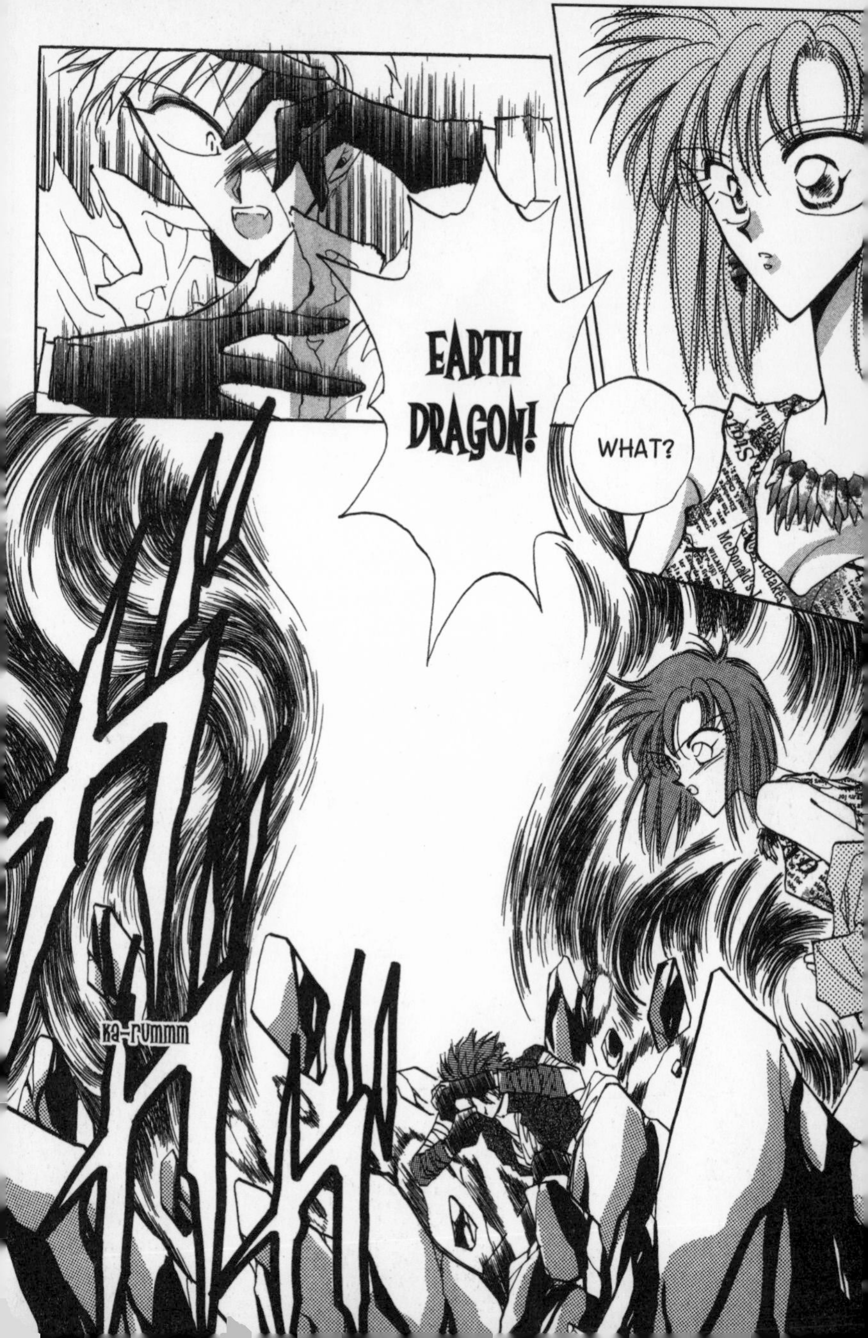
WHAT?
EARTH DRAGON!
KA-RUMMM

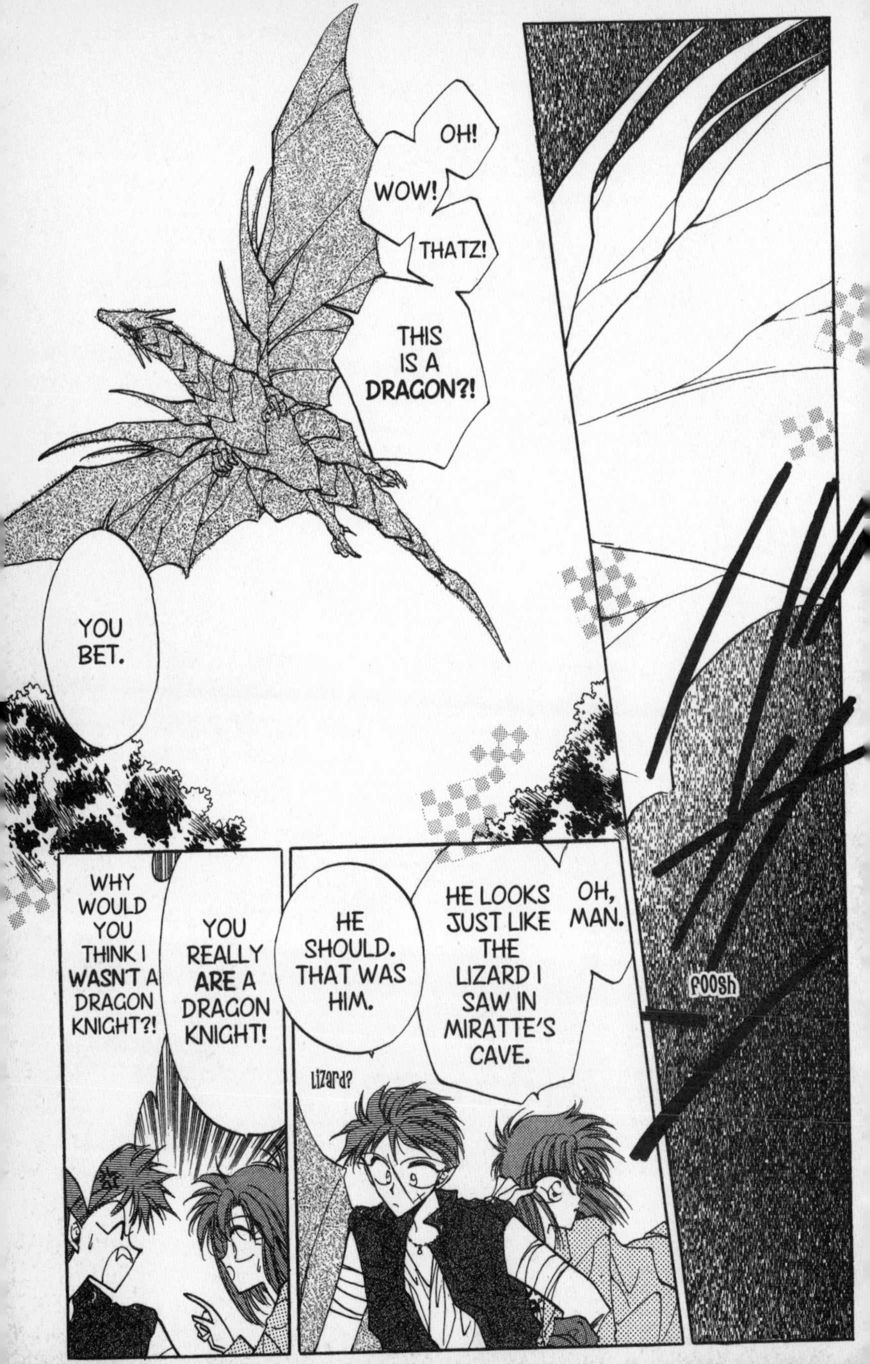
foosh
OH!
WOW!
THATZ!
THIS IS A DRAGON?!
YOU BET.
OH, MAN.
HE LOOKS JUST LIKE THE LIZARD I SAW IN MIRATTE'S CAVE.
Lizard?
HE SHOULD. THAT WAS HIM.
YOU REALLY ARE A DRAGON KNIGHT!
WHY WOULD YOU THINK I WASN'T A DRAGON KNIGHT?!

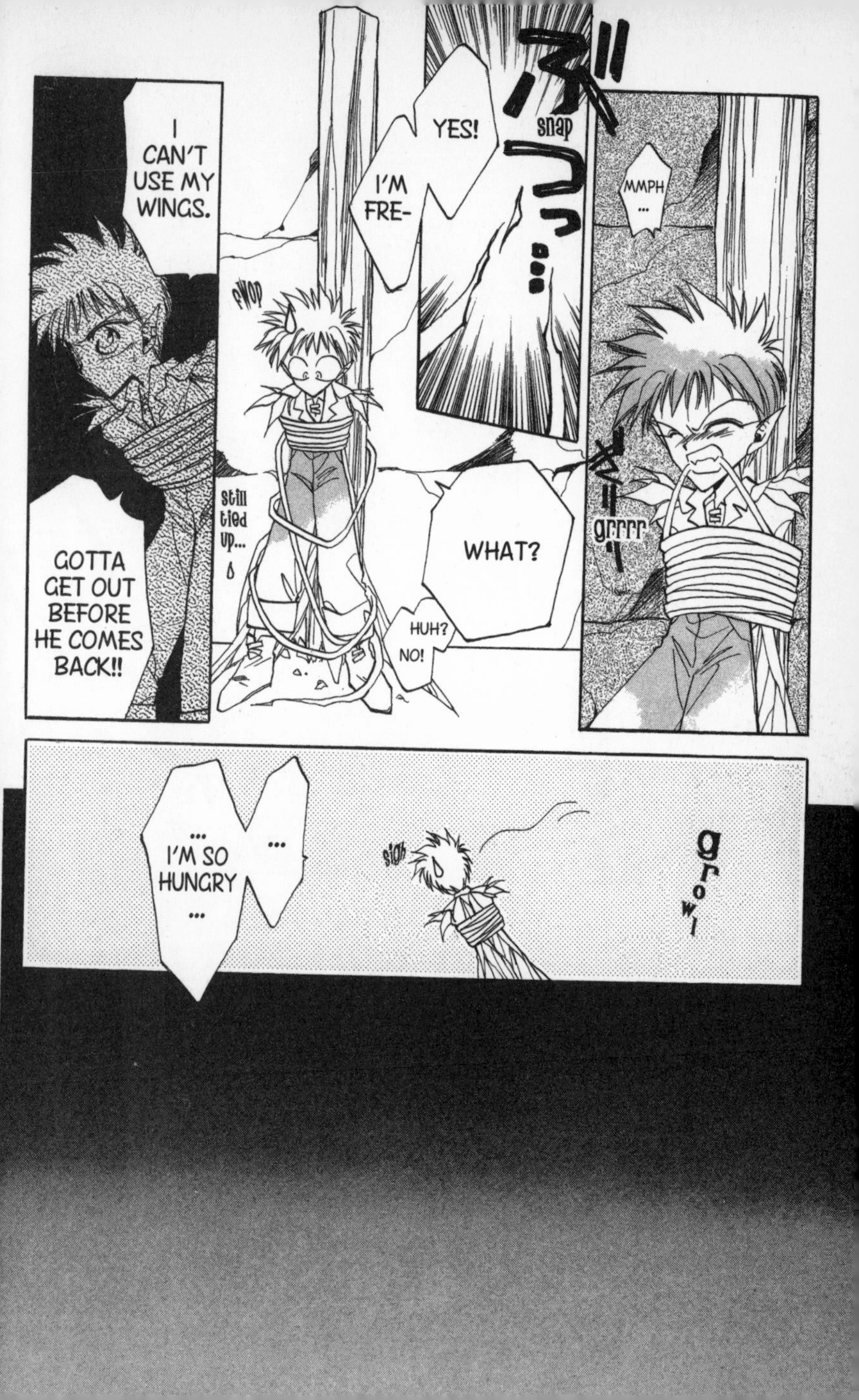

MMPH ...
grrrr
ぶつっ…
snap
YES!
I'M FRE-
fwop
WHAT?
HUH?
NO!
still tied up...
I CAN'T USE MY WINGS.
GOTTA GET OUT BEFORE HE COMES BACK!!
growl
sigh
...
... I'M SO HUNGRY ...

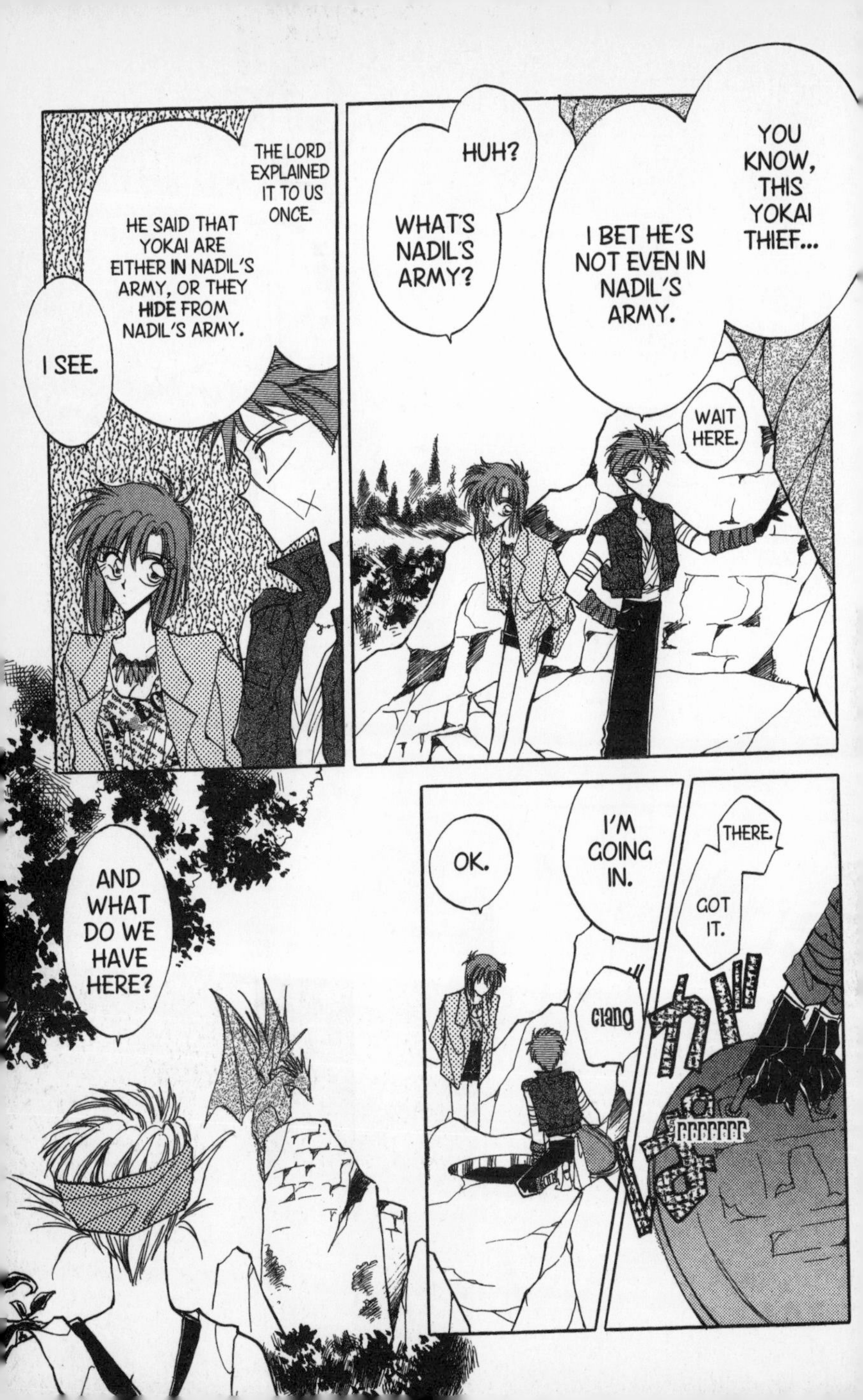
YOU KNOW, THIS YOKAI THIEF...
I BET HE'S NOT EVEN IN NADIL'S ARMY.
HUH?
WHAT'S NADIL'S ARMY?
WAIT HERE.
THE LORD EXPLAINED IT TO US ONCE.
HE SAID THAT YOKAI ARE EITHER IN NADIL'S ARMY, OR THEY HIDE FROM NADIL'S ARMY.
I SEE.
THERE.
GOT IT.
rrrrrrr
I'M GOING IN.
OK.
clang
AND WHAT DO WE HAVE HERE?

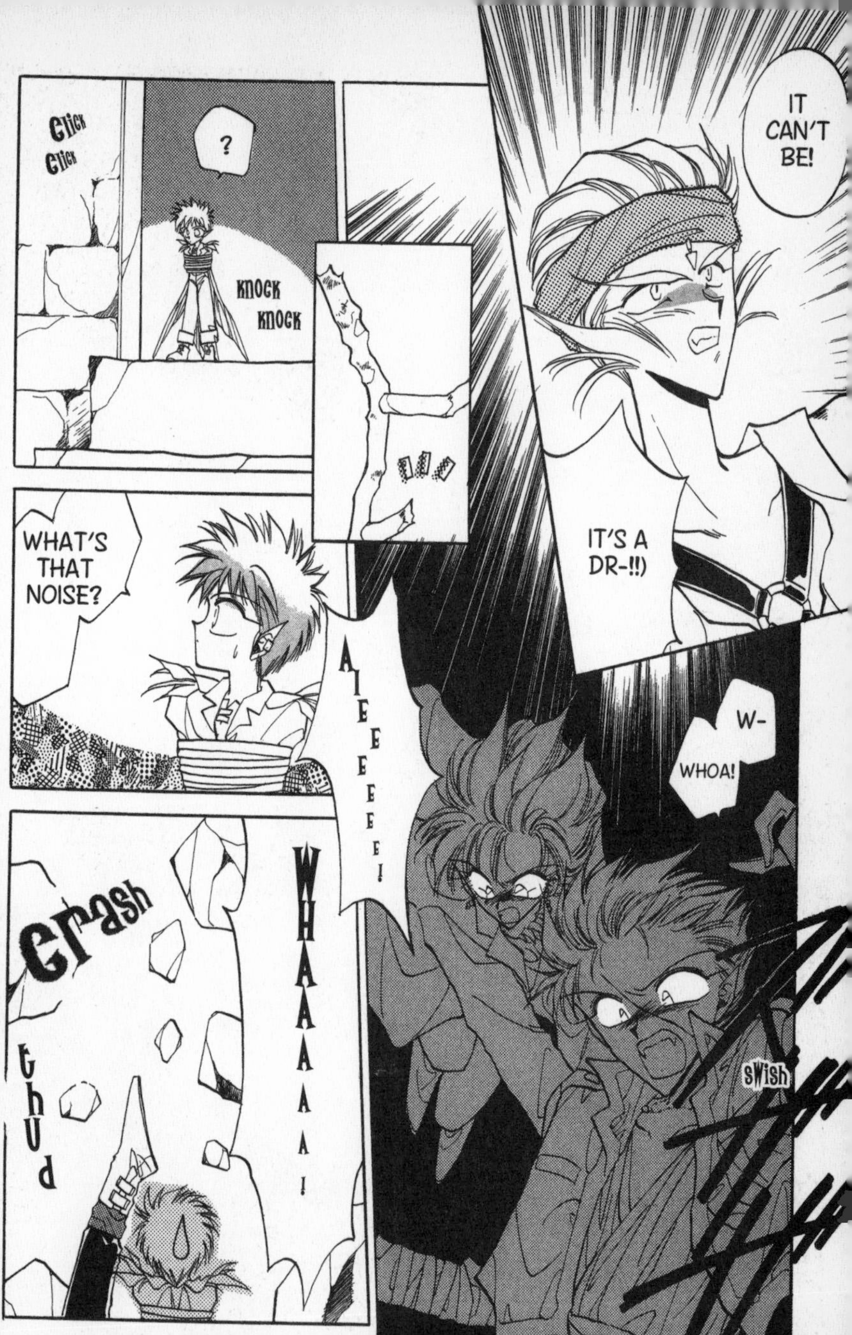
IT CAN'T BE!
IT'S A DR-!!)
CLICK
CLICK
?
KNOCK
KNOCK
WHAT'S THAT NOISE?
AIEEEEEEE!
W- WHOA!
SWISH
WHAAAAAAAA!
CRASH
THUD

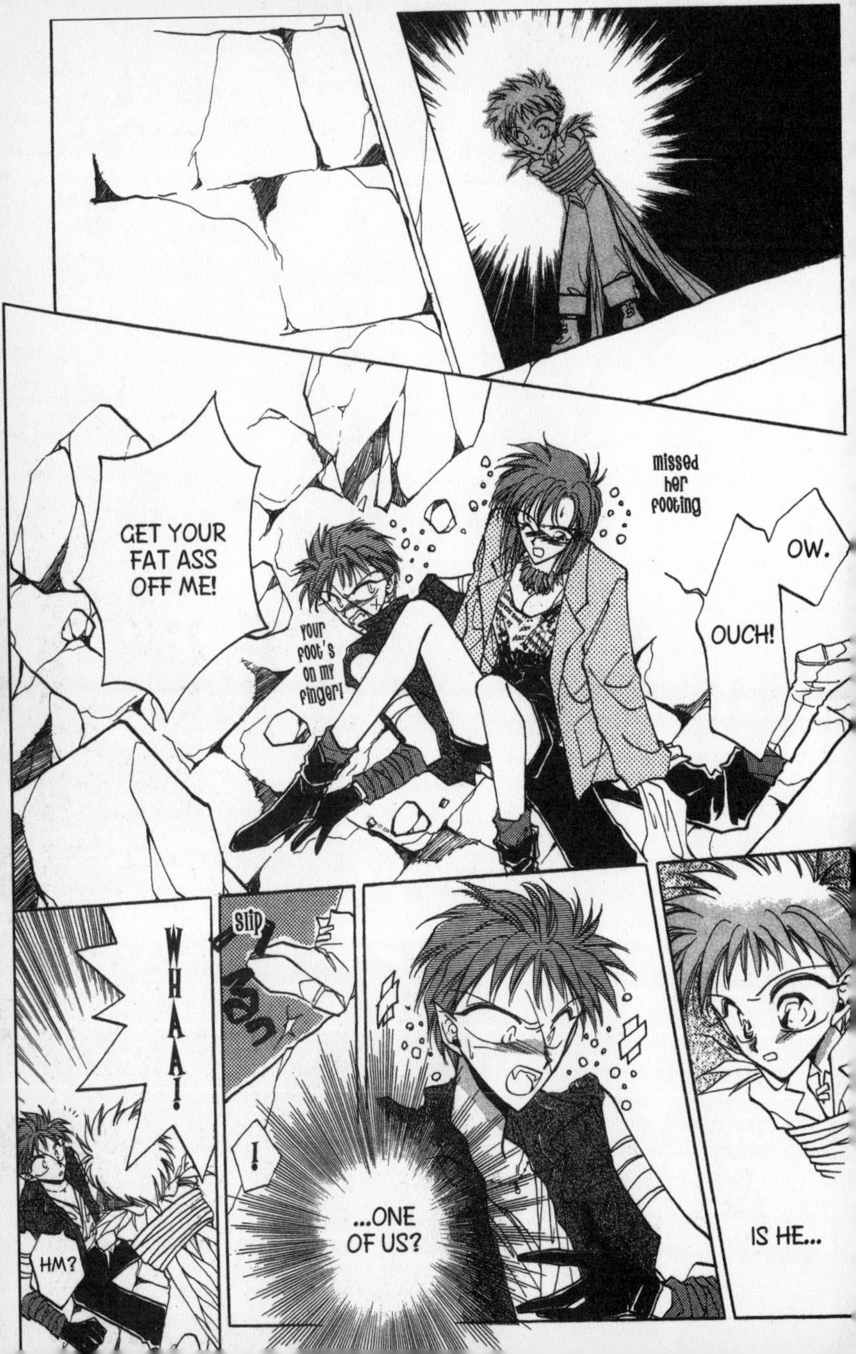
missed her footing
OW.
OUCH!
GET YOUR FAT ASS OFF ME!
your foot's on my finger!
IS HE...
!
...ONE OF US?
slip
WHAAA!
HM?

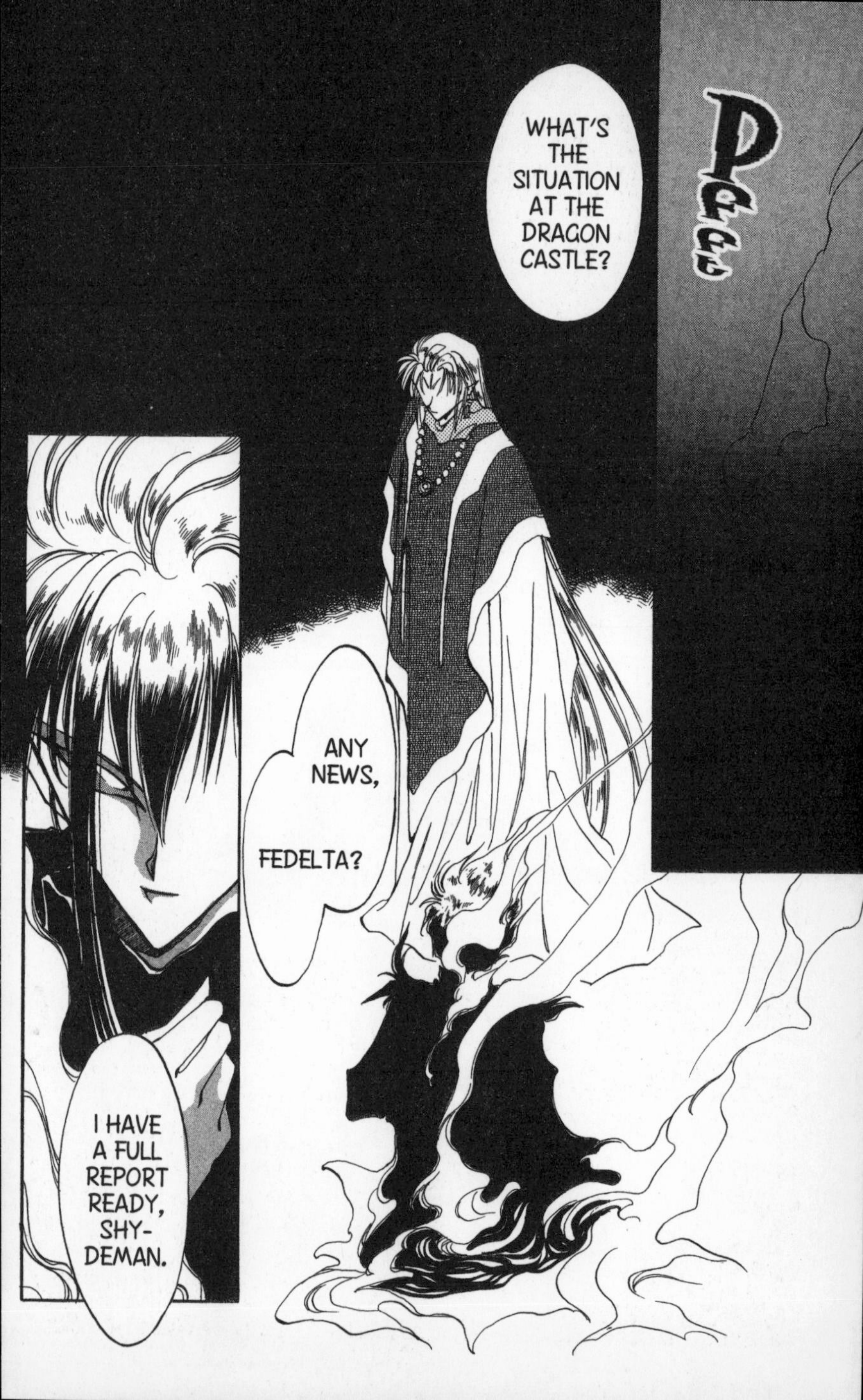
WHAT'S THE SITUATION AT THE DRAGON CASTLE?
ANY NEWS, FEDELTA?
I HAVE A FULL REPORT READY, SHY-DEMAN.

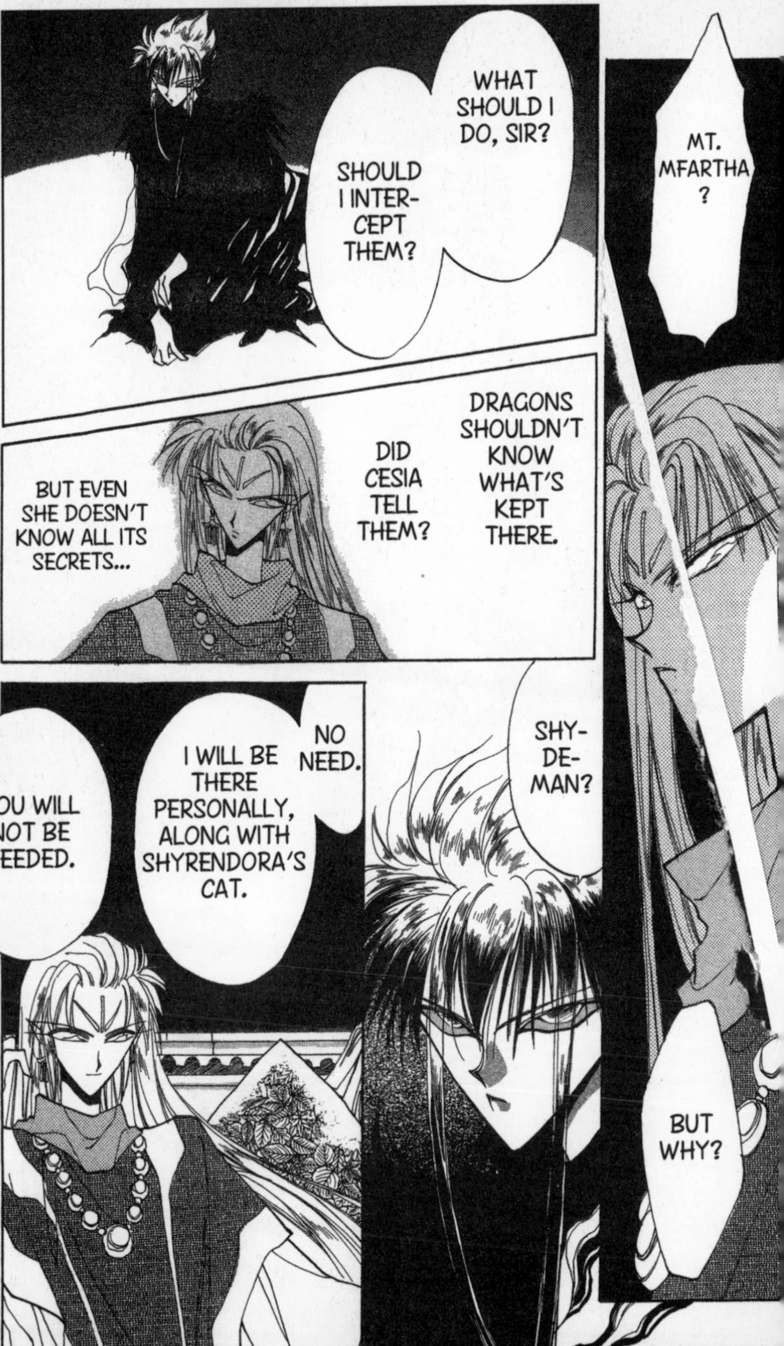
MT. MFARTHA?
BUT WHY?
WHAT SHOULD I DO, SIR?
SHOULD I INTERCEPT THEM?
DRAGONS SHOULDN'T KNOW WHAT'S KEPT THERE.
DID CESIA TELL THEM?
BUT EVEN SHE DOESN'T KNOW ALL ITS SECRETS...
SHY-DE-MAN?
NO NEED.
I WILL BE THERE PERSONALLY, ALONG WITH SHYRENDORA'S CAT.
YOU WILL NOT BE NEEDED.

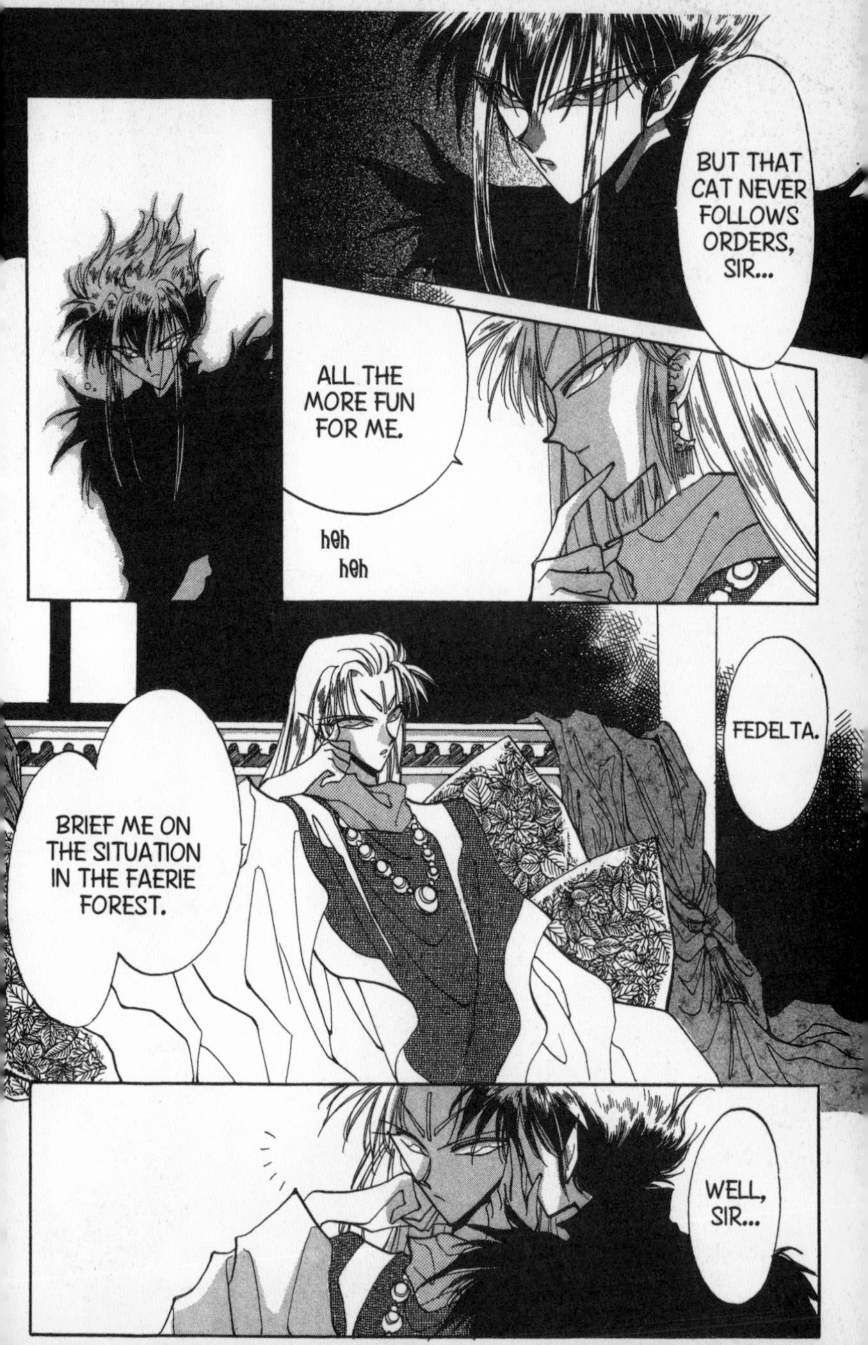
BUT THAT CAT NEVER FOLLOWS ORDERS, SIR...
ALL THE MORE FUN FOR ME.
heh heh
FEDELTA.
BRIEF ME ON THE SITUATION IN THE FAERIE FOREST.
WELL, SIR...

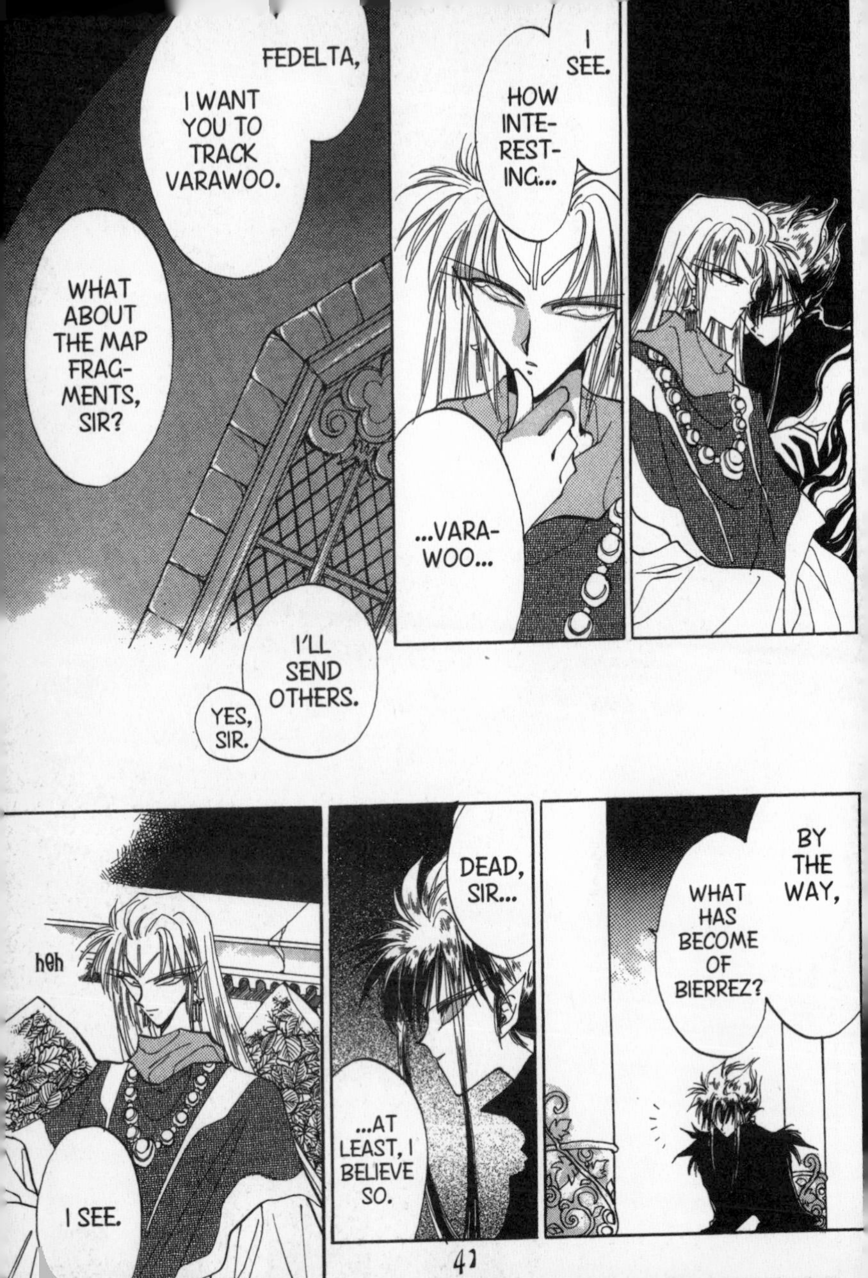
I SEE.
HOW INTE-REST-ING...
...VARA-WOO...
FEDELTA,
I WANT YOU TO TRACK VARAWOO.
WHAT ABOUT THE MAP FRAG-MENTS, SIR?
I'LL SEND OTHERS.
YES, SIR.
BY THE WAY,
WHAT HAS BECOME OF BIERREZ?
DEAD, SIR...
...AT LEAST, I BELIEVE SO.
heh
I SEE.

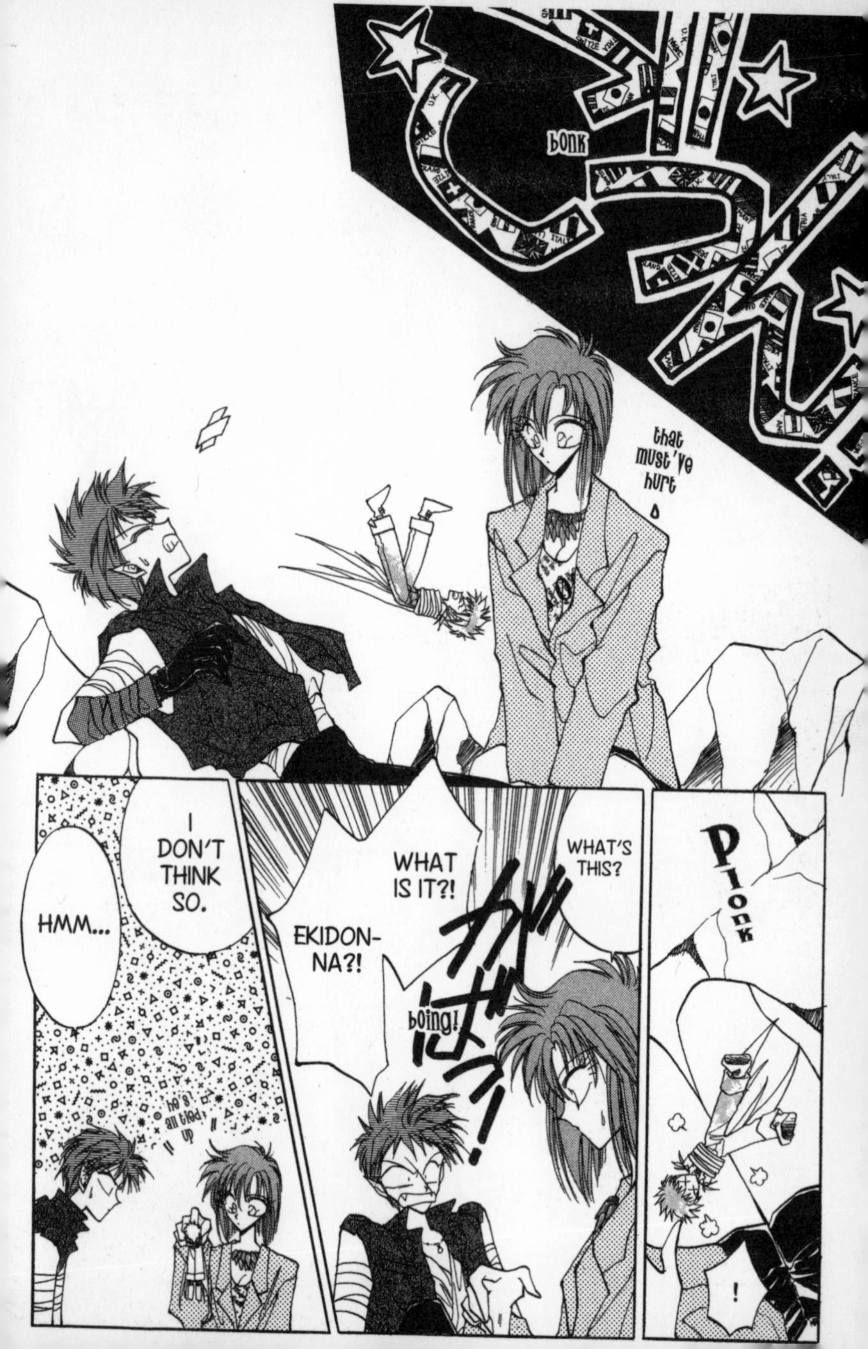
bonk
that must've hurt
Plonk
!
WHAT'S THIS?
WHAT IS IT?!
EKIDON-NA?!
boing!
I DON'T THINK SO.
HMM...
he's all tied up

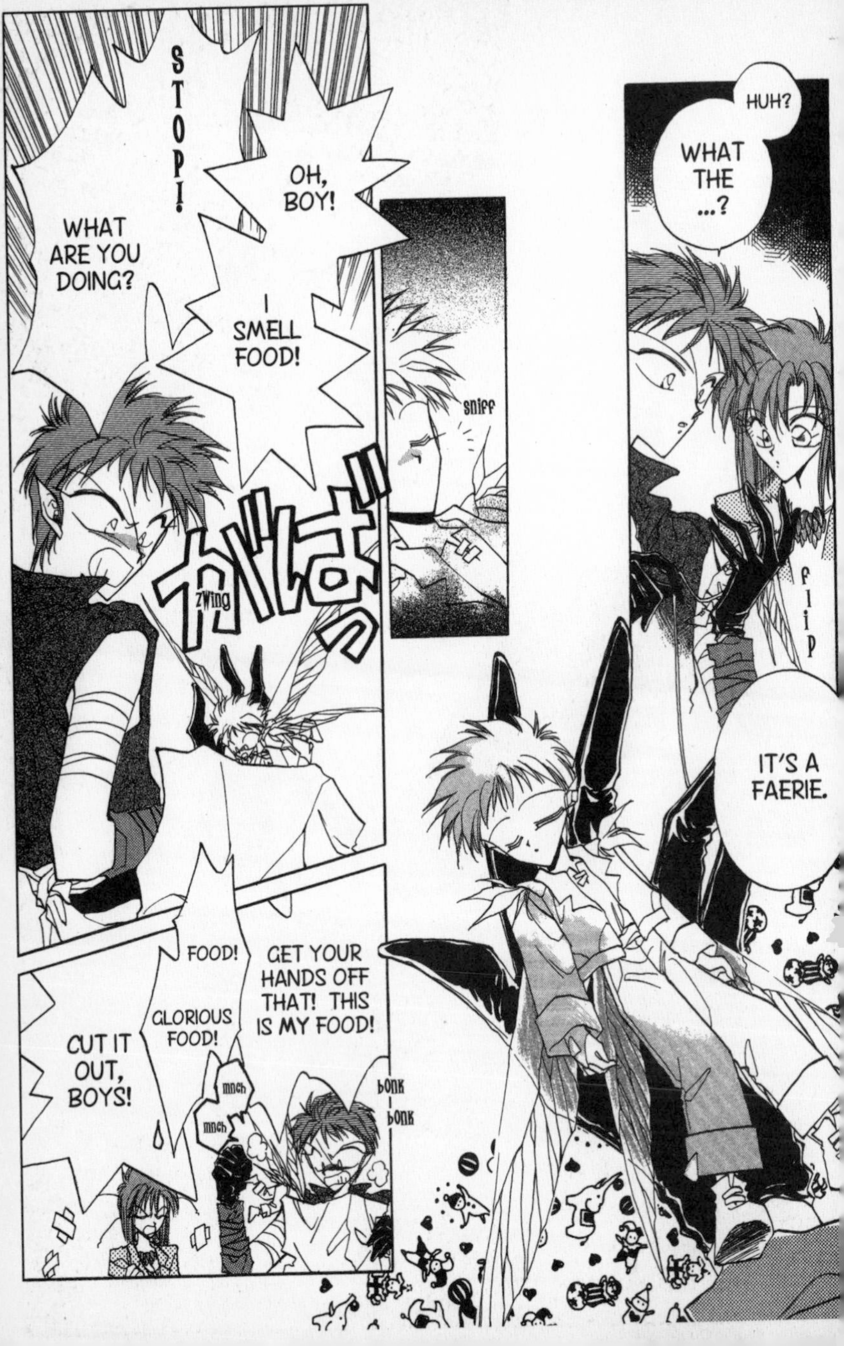
HUH?
WHAT THE ...?
flip
IT'S A FAERIE.
sniff
STOP!
WHAT ARE YOU DOING?
OH, BOY!
I SMELL FOOD!
zwing
GET YOUR HANDS OFF THAT! THIS IS MY FOOD!
FOOD!
GLORIOUS FOOD!
CUT IT OUT, BOYS!
mnch
mnch
bonk
bonk

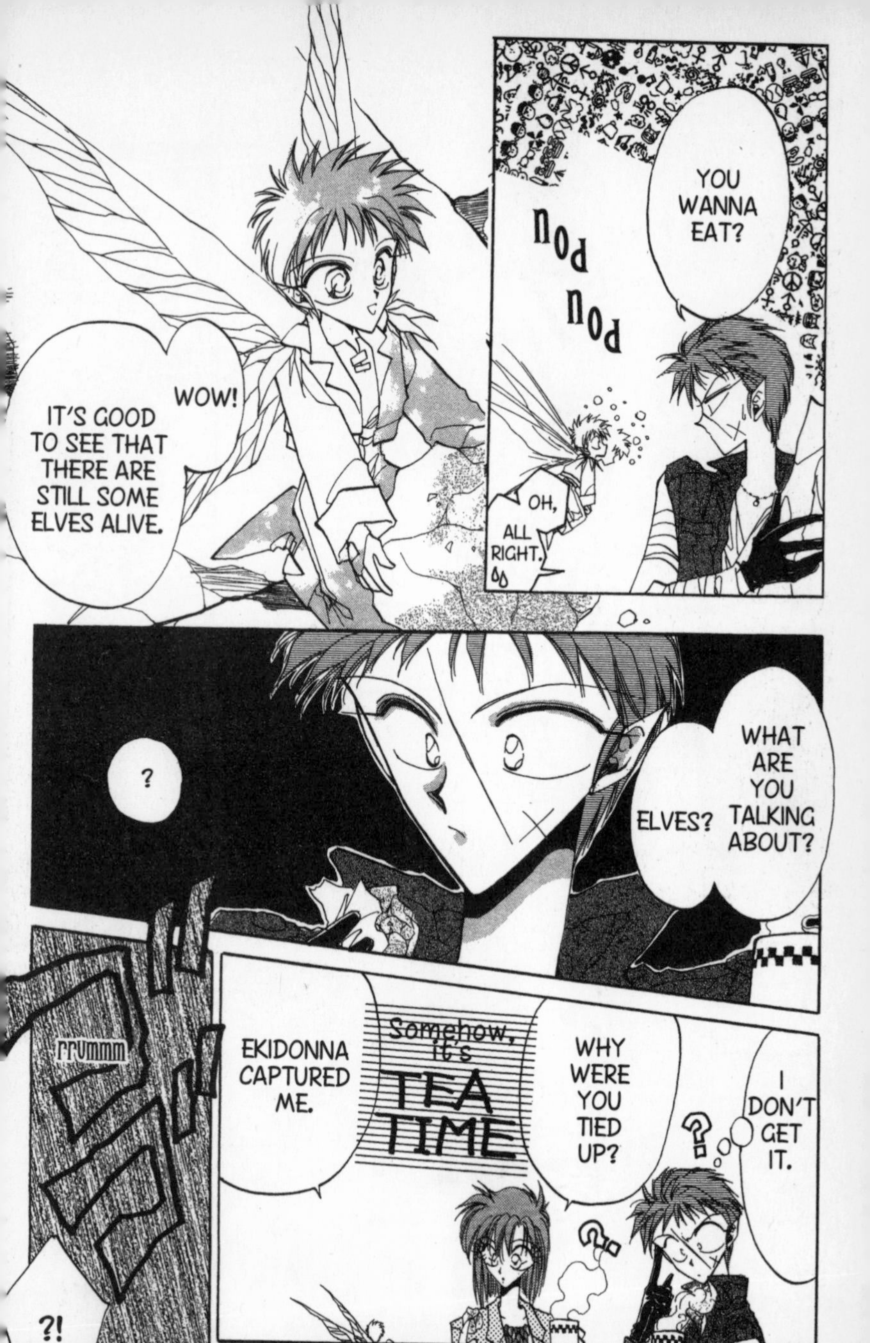
YOU WANNA EAT?
nod nod
OH, ALL RIGHT.
WOW!
IT'S GOOD TO SEE THAT THERE ARE STILL SOME ELVES ALIVE.
WHAT ARE YOU TALKING ABOUT?
ELVES?
?
I DON'T GET IT.
WHY WERE YOU TIED UP?
Somehow, it's TEA TIME
EKIDONNA CAPTURED ME.
rrummm
?!

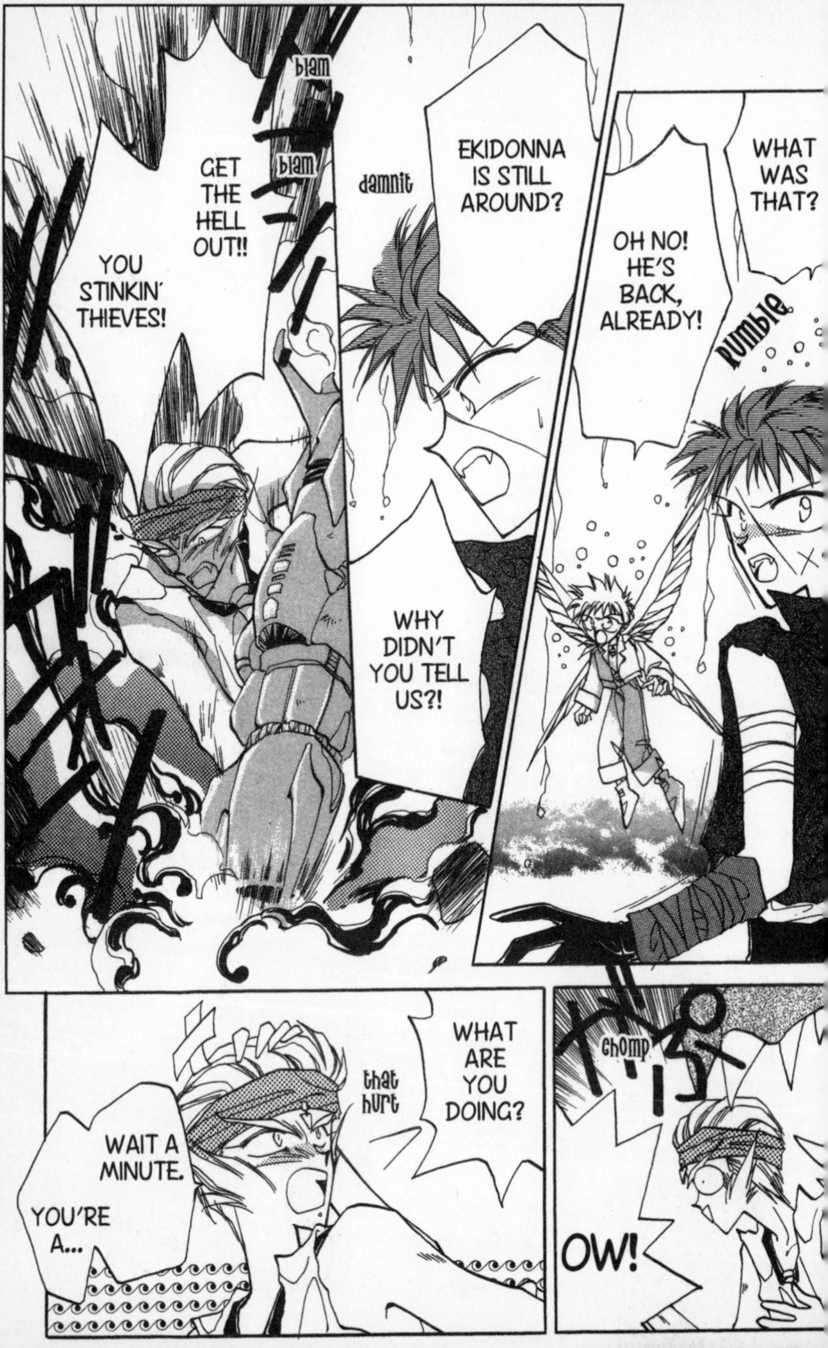
WHAT WAS THAT?
RUMBLE
OH NO! HE'S BACK, ALREADY!
EKIDONNA IS STILL AROUND?
damnit
WHY DIDN'T YOU TELL US?!
blam
blam
GET THE HELL OUT!!
YOU STINKIN' THIEVES!
chomp
OW!
WHAT ARE YOU DOING?
that hurt
WAIT A MINUTE.
YOU'RE A...

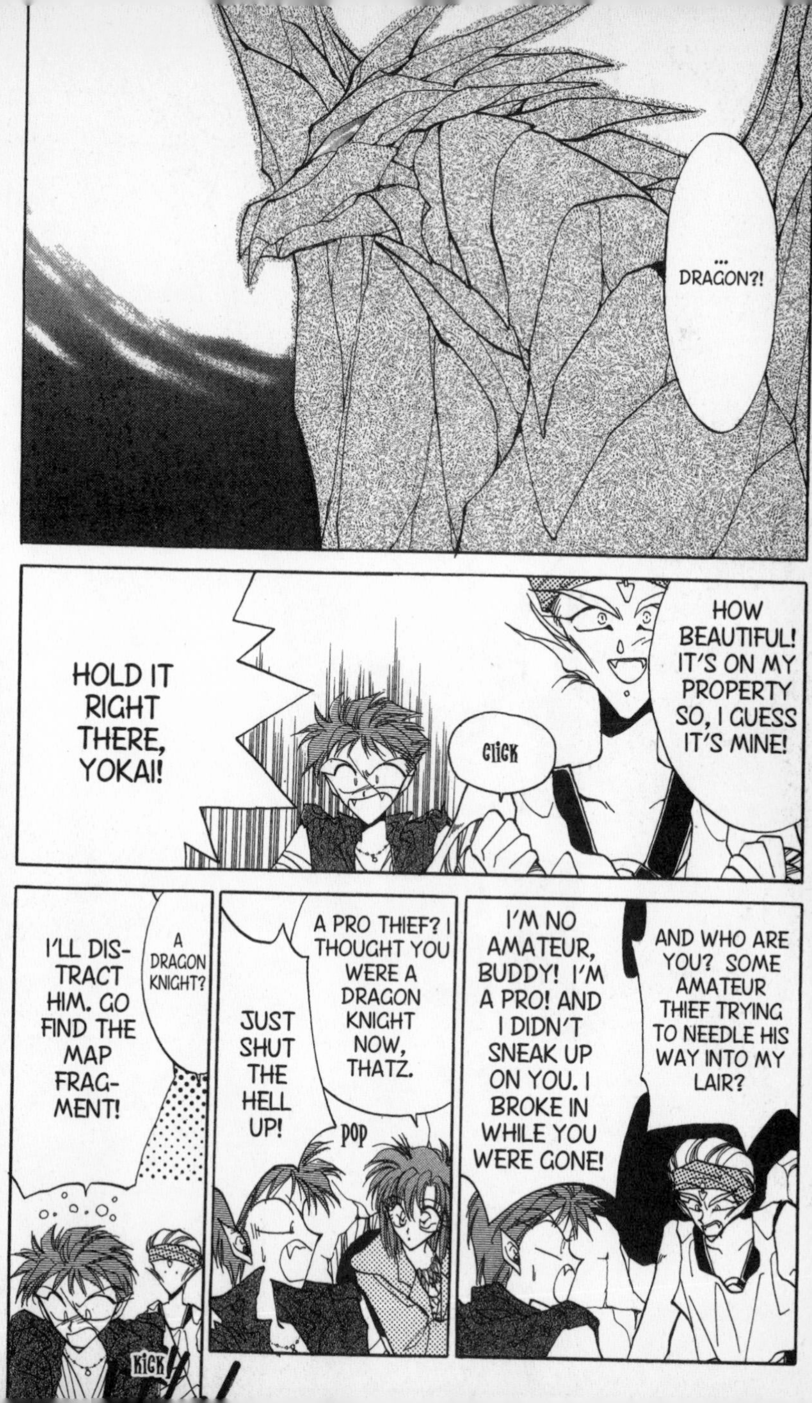

... DRAGON?!
HOW BEAUTIFUL! IT'S ON MY PROPERTY SO, I GUESS IT'S MINE!
CLICK
HOLD IT RIGHT THERE, YOKAI!
AND WHO ARE YOU? SOME AMATEUR THIEF TRYING TO NEEDLE HIS WAY INTO MY LAIR?
I'M NO AMATEUR, BUDDY! I'M A PRO! AND I DIDN'T SNEAK UP ON YOU. I BROKE IN WHILE YOU WERE GONE!
A PRO THIEF? I THOUGHT YOU WERE A DRAGON KNIGHT NOW, THATZ.
JUST SHUT THE HELL UP!
POP
A DRAGON KNIGHT?
I'LL DIS-TRACT HIM. GO FIND THE MAP FRAG-MENT!
KICK

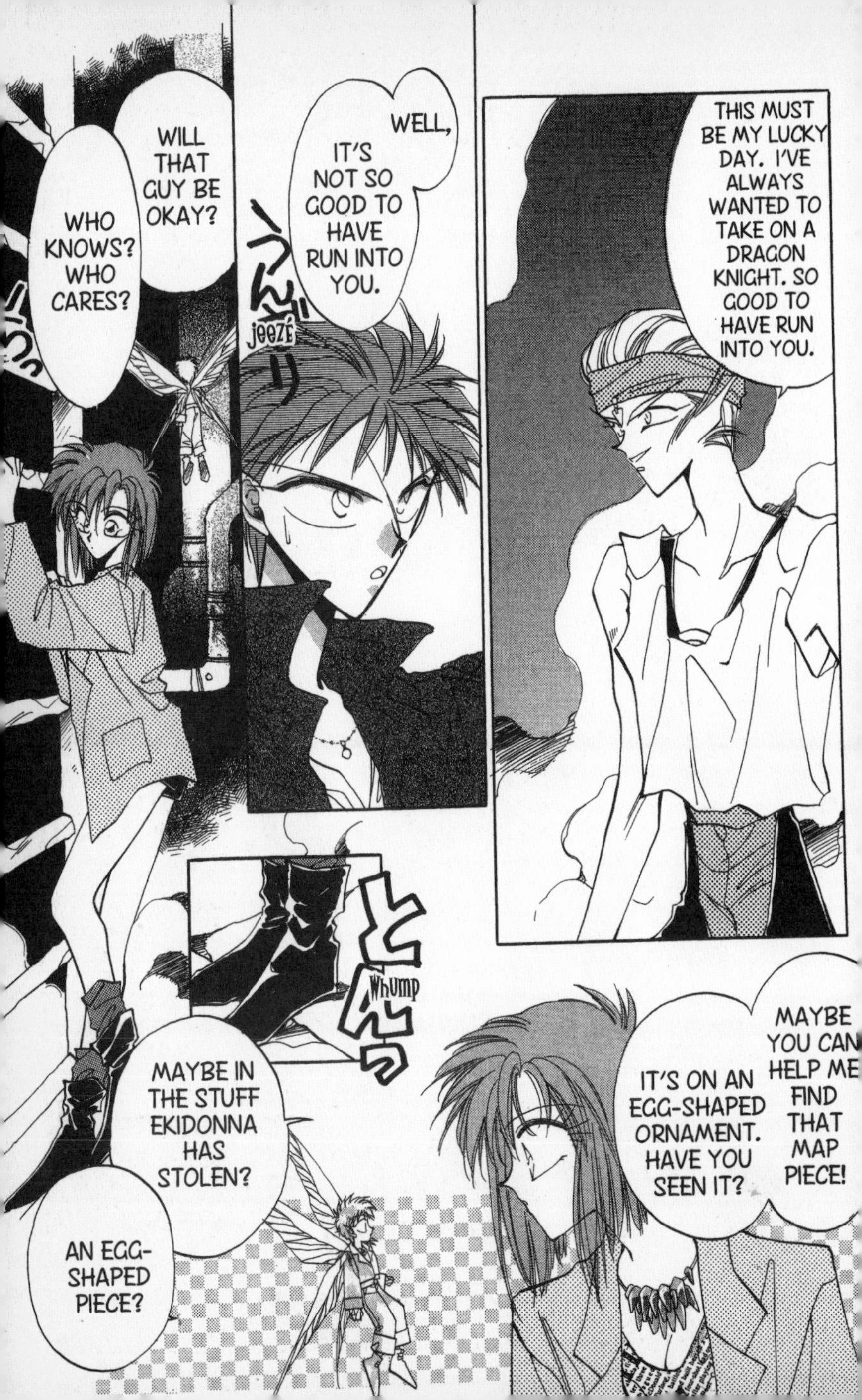
THIS MUST BE MY LUCKY DAY. I'VE ALWAYS WANTED TO TAKE ON A DRAGON KNIGHT. SO GOOD TO HAVE RUN INTO YOU.
WELL, IT'S NOT SO GOOD TO HAVE RUN INTO YOU.
うんざり
jeeze
WILL THAT GUY BE OKAY?
WHO KNOWS? WHO CARES?
MAYBE YOU CAN HELP ME FIND THAT MAP PIECE!
IT'S ON AN EGG-SHAPED ORNAMENT. HAVE YOU SEEN IT?
とんっ
Whump
MAYBE IN THE STUFF EKIDONNA HAS STOLEN?
AN EGG-SHAPED PIECE?

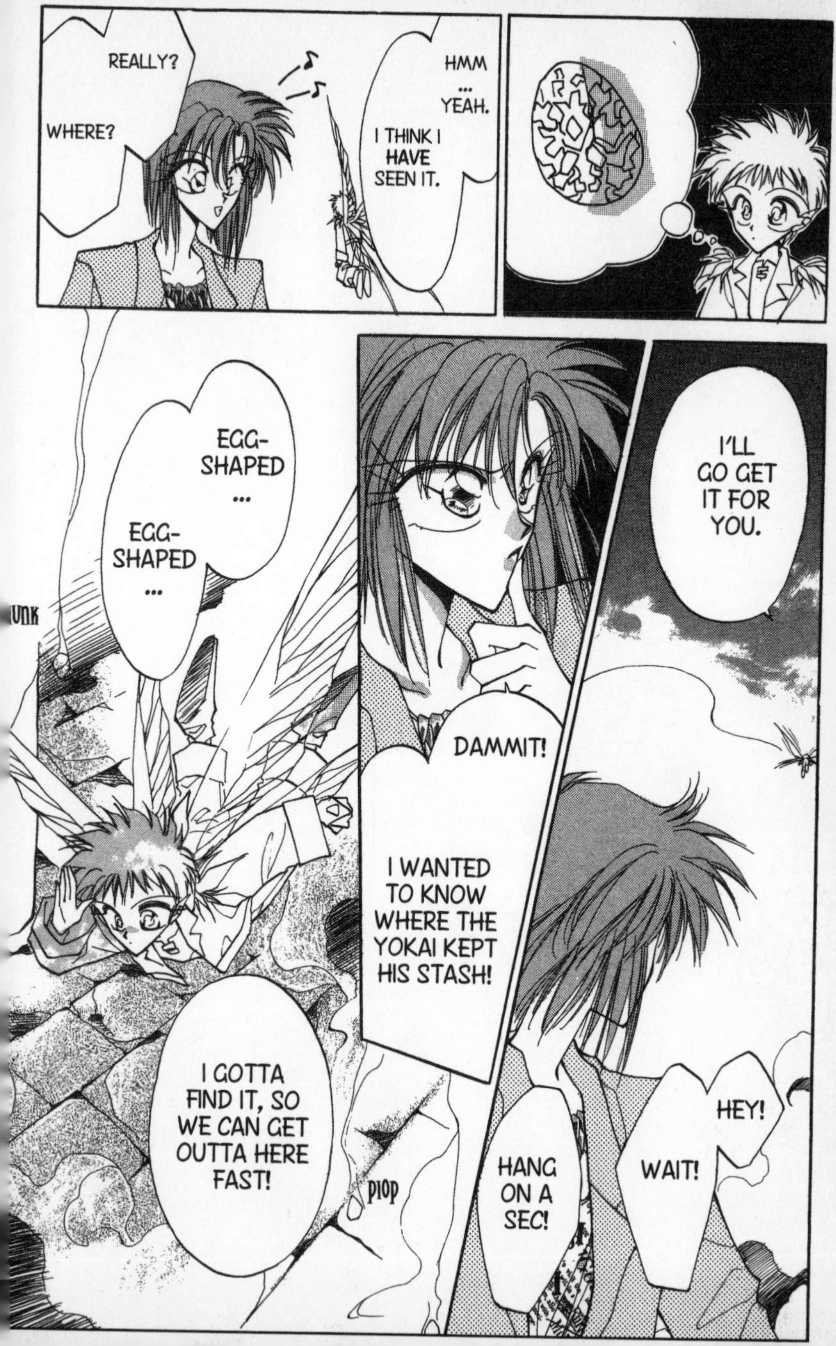

HMM ... YEAH.
I THINK I HAVE SEEN IT.
REALLY?
WHERE?
I'LL GO GET IT FOR YOU.
DAMMIT!
I WANTED TO KNOW WHERE THE YOKAI KEPT HIS STASH!
HEY!
WAIT!
HANG ON A SEC!
plop
EGG-SHAPED ...
EGG-SHAPED ...
I GOTTA FIND IT, SO WE CAN GET OUTTA HERE FAST!

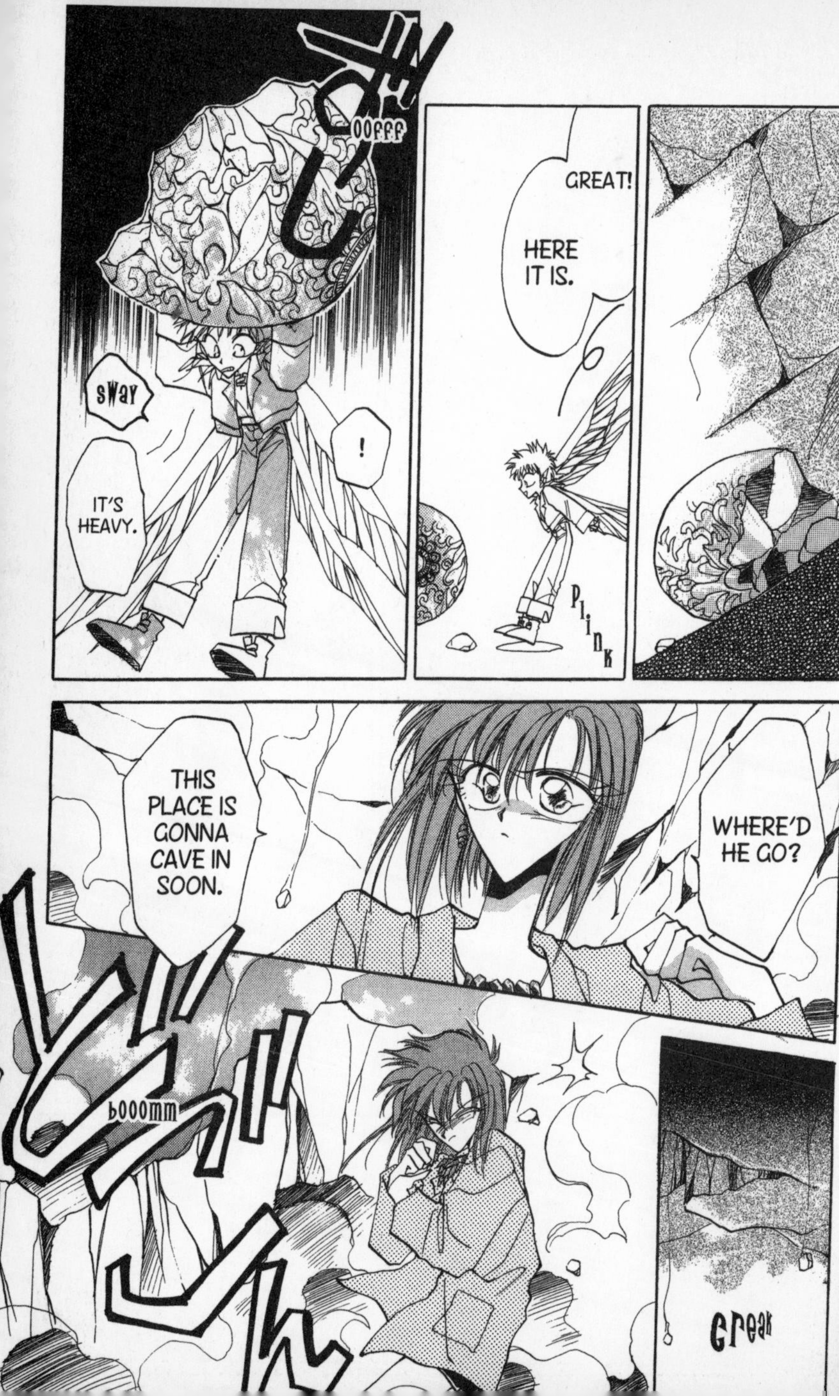
GREAT!
HERE IT IS.
PLINK
OOFFF
SWAY
!
IT'S HEAVY.
WHERE'D HE GO?
THIS PLACE IS GONNA CAVE IN SOON.
CREAK
BOOOMM

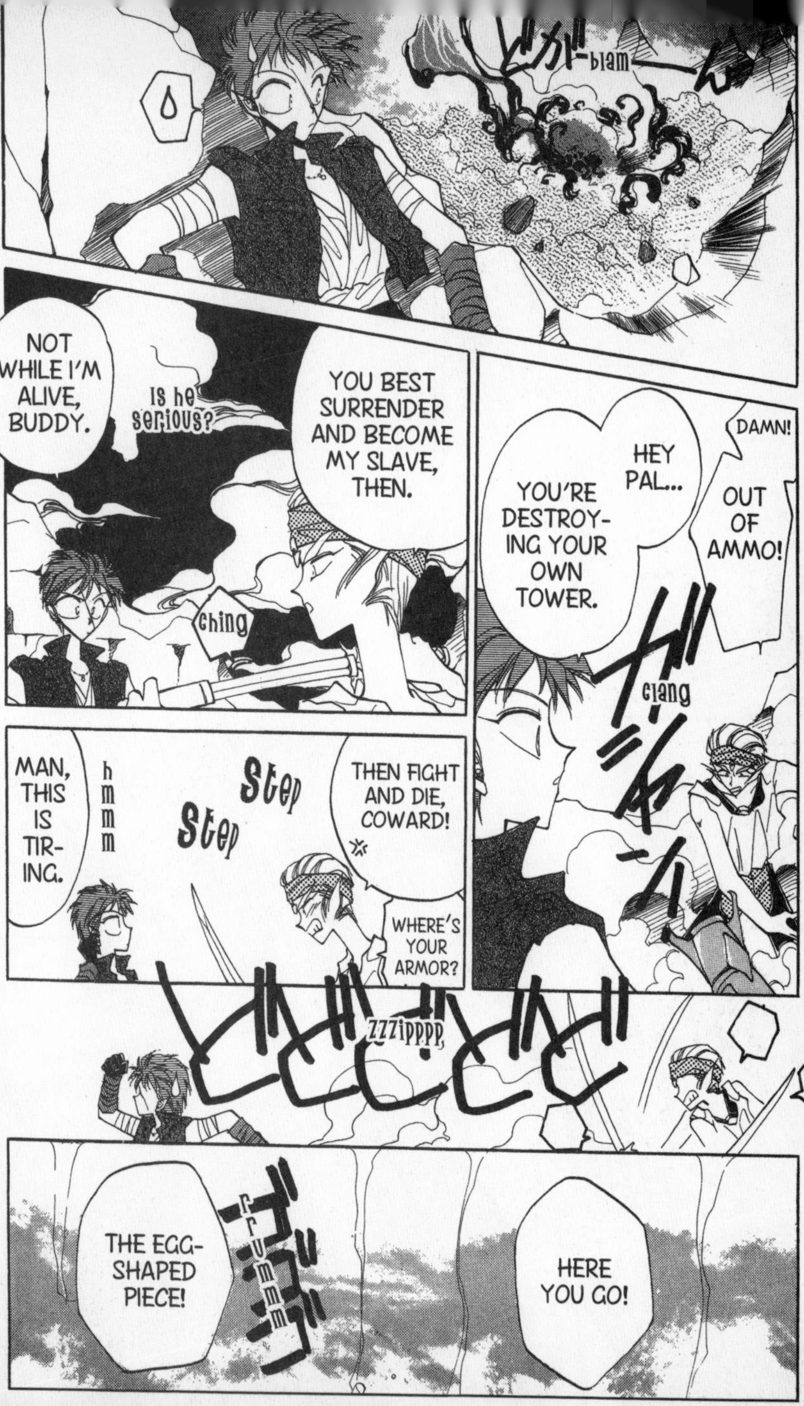
blam
DAMN!
OUT OF AMMO!
HEY PAL...
YOU'RE DESTROYING YOUR OWN TOWER.
clang
YOU BEST SURRENDER AND BECOME MY SLAVE, THEN.
ching
is he serious?
NOT WHILE I'M ALIVE, BUDDY.
THEN FIGHT AND DIE, COWARD!
WHERE'S YOUR ARMOR?
step
step
hmmm
MAN, THIS IS TIRING.
zzzipppp
HERE YOU GO!
rrummm
THE EGG-SHAPED PIECE!

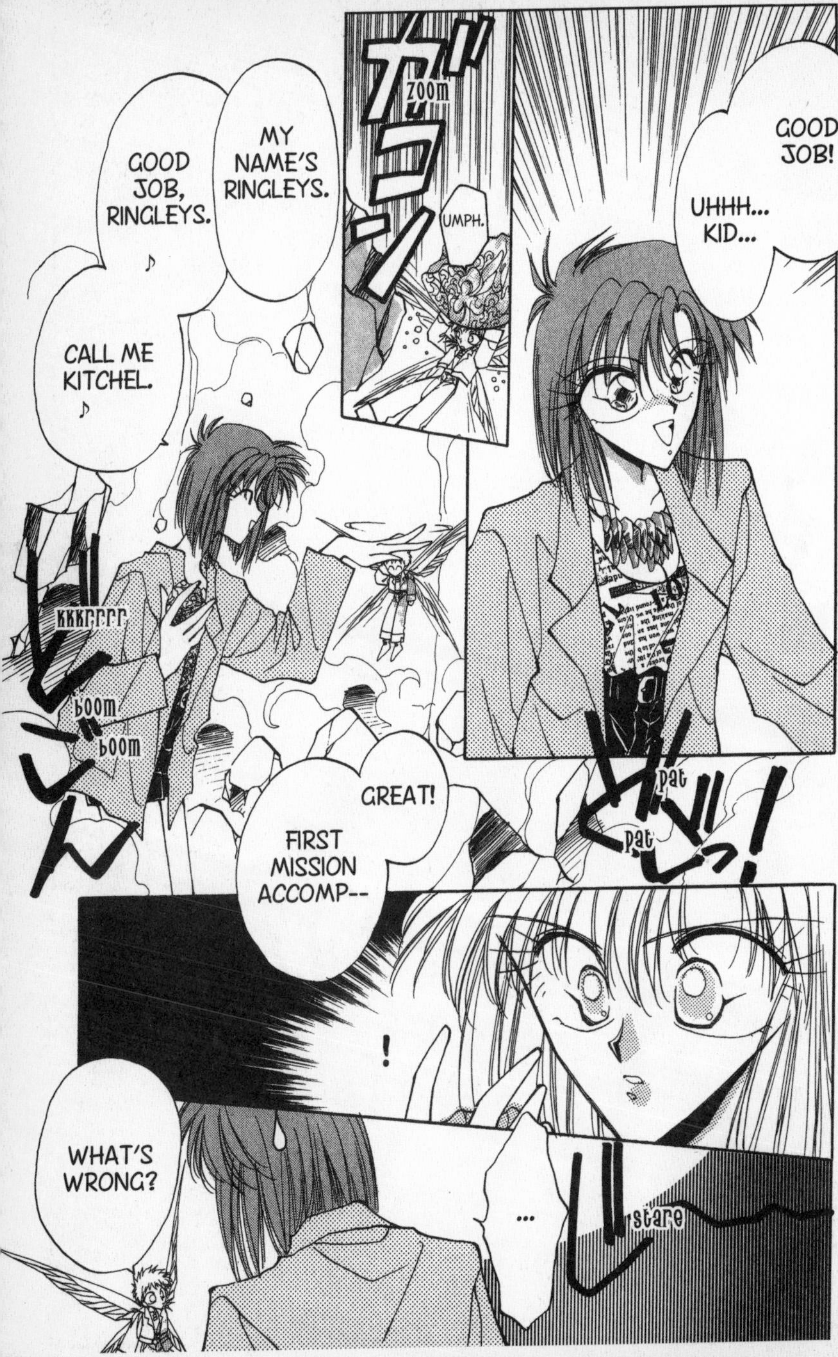
GOOD JOB!
UHHH... KID...
zoom
UMPH.
MY NAME'S RINGLEYS.
GOOD JOB, RINGLEYS. ♪
CALL ME KITCHEL. ♪
kkkrrrr
boom
boom
pat
pat
GREAT!
FIRST MISSION ACCOMP--
!
WHAT'S WRONG?
...
stare

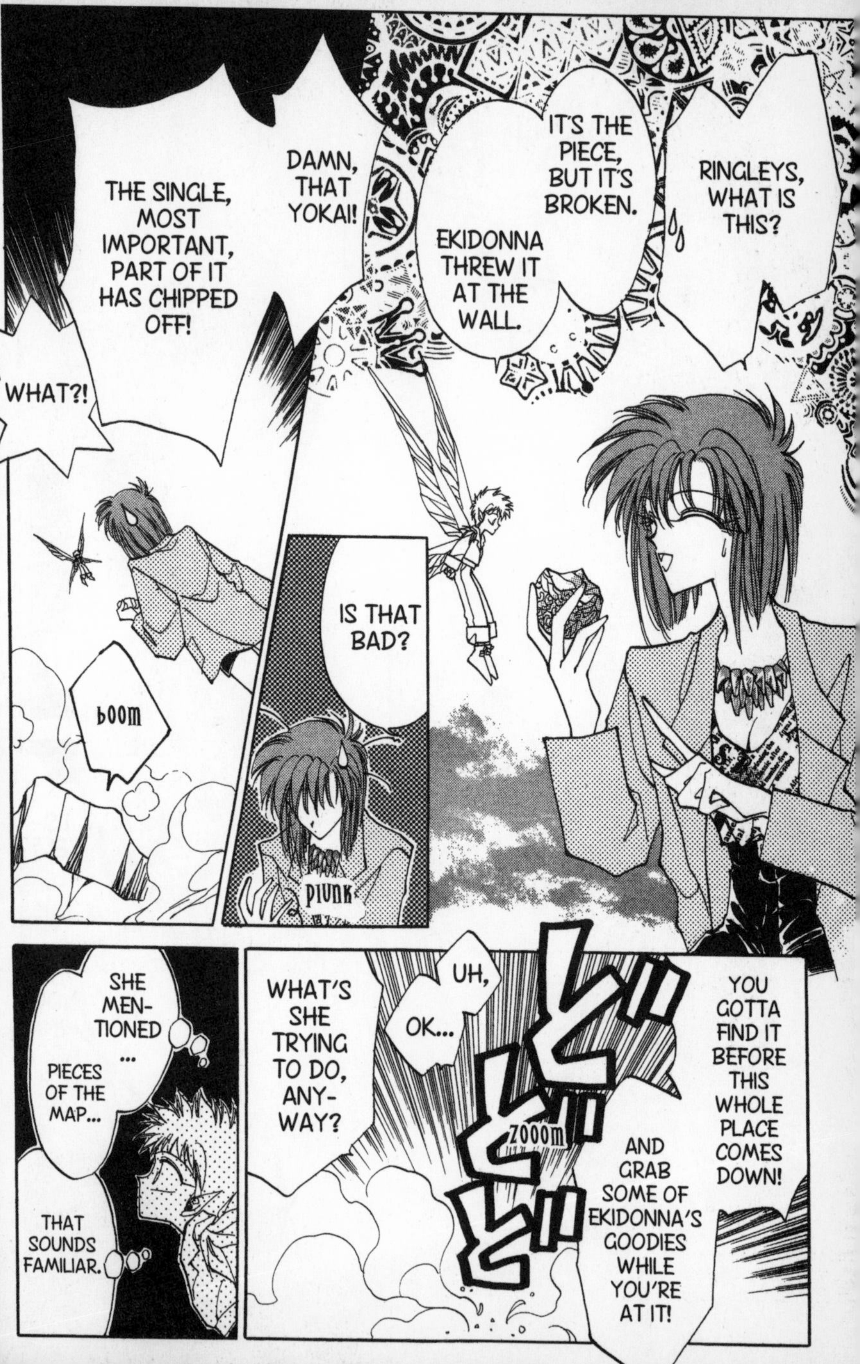
RINGLEYS, WHAT IS THIS?
IT'S THE PIECE, BUT IT'S BROKEN.
EKIDONNA THREW IT AT THE WALL.
DAMN, THAT YOKAI!
THE SINGLE, MOST IMPORTANT, PART OF IT HAS CHIPPED OFF!
WHAT?!
IS THAT BAD?
PLUNK
boom
YOU GOTTA FIND IT BEFORE THIS WHOLE PLACE COMES DOWN!
AND GRAB SOME OF EKIDONNA'S GOODIES WHILE YOU'RE AT IT!
UH, OK...
zooom
WHAT'S SHE TRYING TO DO, ANY-WAY?
SHE MEN-TIONED ...
PIECES OF THE MAP...
THAT SOUNDS FAMILIAR.

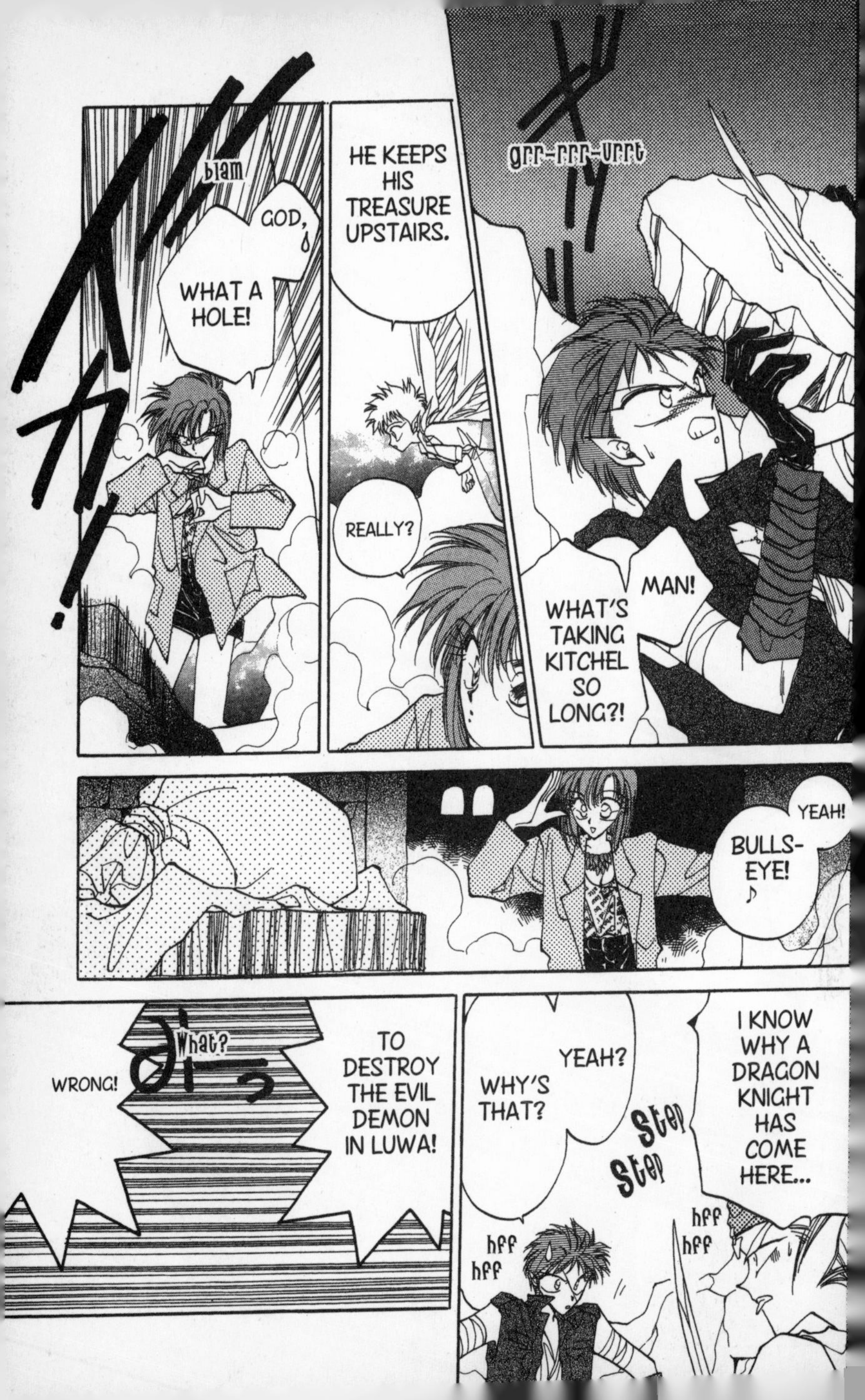
grr-rrr-urrt
MAN!
WHAT'S TAKING KITCHEL SO LONG?!
HE KEEPS HIS TREASURE UPSTAIRS.
REALLY?
blam
GOD, WHAT A HOLE!
YEAH!
BULLS-EYE! ♪
I KNOW WHY A DRAGON KNIGHT HAS COME HERE...
Step
Step
hff
hff
YEAH?
WHY'S THAT?
hff
hff
TO DESTROY THE EVIL DEMON IN LUWA!
What?
WRONG!

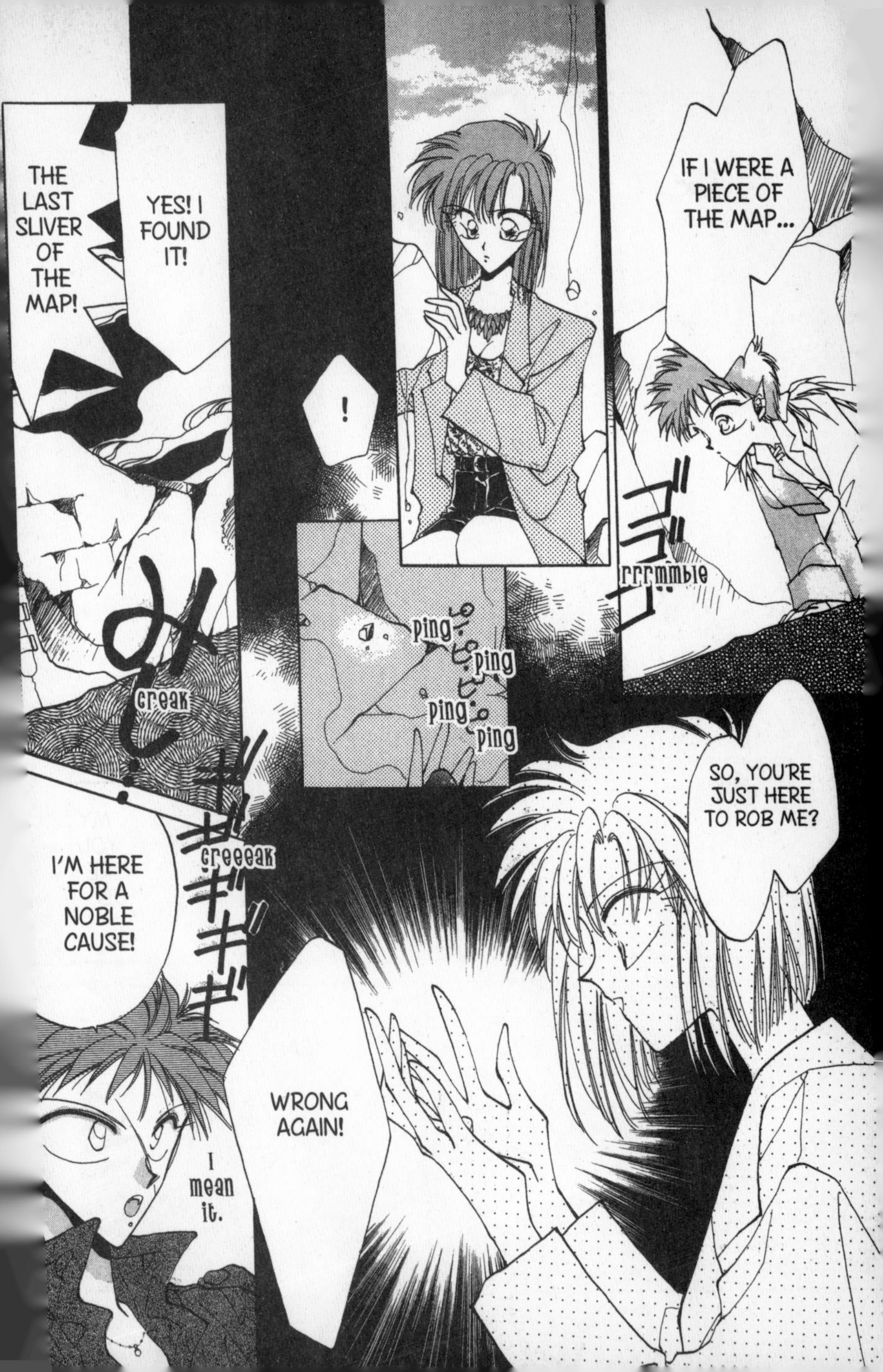
IF I WERE A PIECE OF THE MAP...
rrrmmble
!
ping
ping
ping
ping
YES! I FOUND IT!
THE LAST SLIVER OF THE MAP!
creak
creeeak
SO, YOU'RE JUST HERE TO ROB ME?
WRONG AGAIN!
I'M HERE FOR A NOBLE CAUSE!
I mean it.

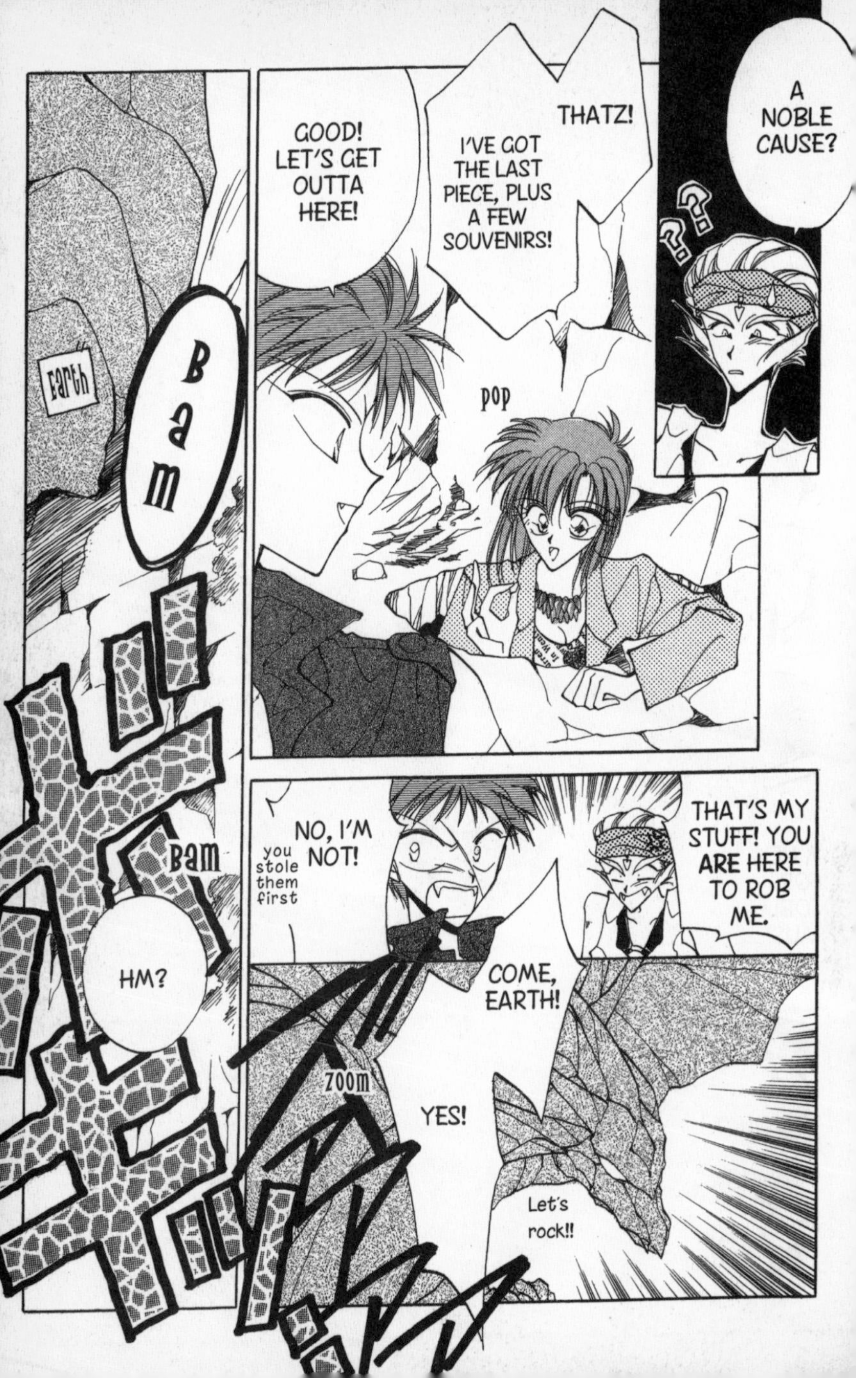
A NOBLE CAUSE?
THATZ!
I'VE GOT THE LAST PIECE, PLUS A FEW SOUVENIRS!
GOOD! LET'S GET OUTTA HERE!
pop
THAT'S MY STUFF! YOU **ARE** HERE TO ROB ME.
NO, I'M NOT!
you stole them first
COME, EARTH!
Let's rock!!
YES!
zoom
Earth
Bam
Bam
HM?

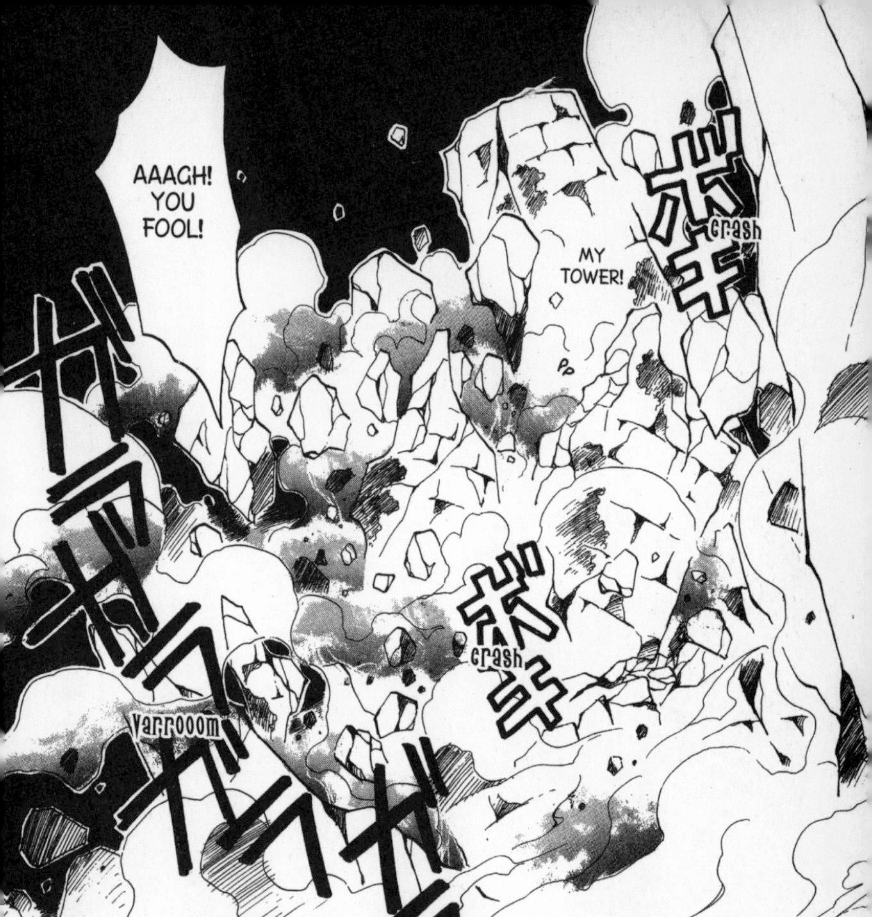
crash
MY TOWER!
AAAGH! YOU FOOL!
crash
varrooom
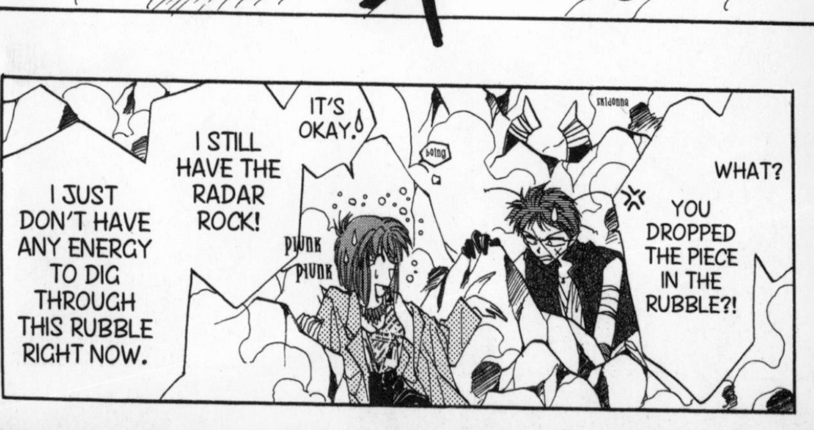
WHAT?
YOU DROPPED THE PIECE IN THE RUBBLE?!
IT'S OKAY.
I STILL HAVE THE RADAR ROCK!
plunk
plunk
I JUST DON'T HAVE ANY ENERGY TO DIG THROUGH THIS RUBBLE RIGHT NOW.

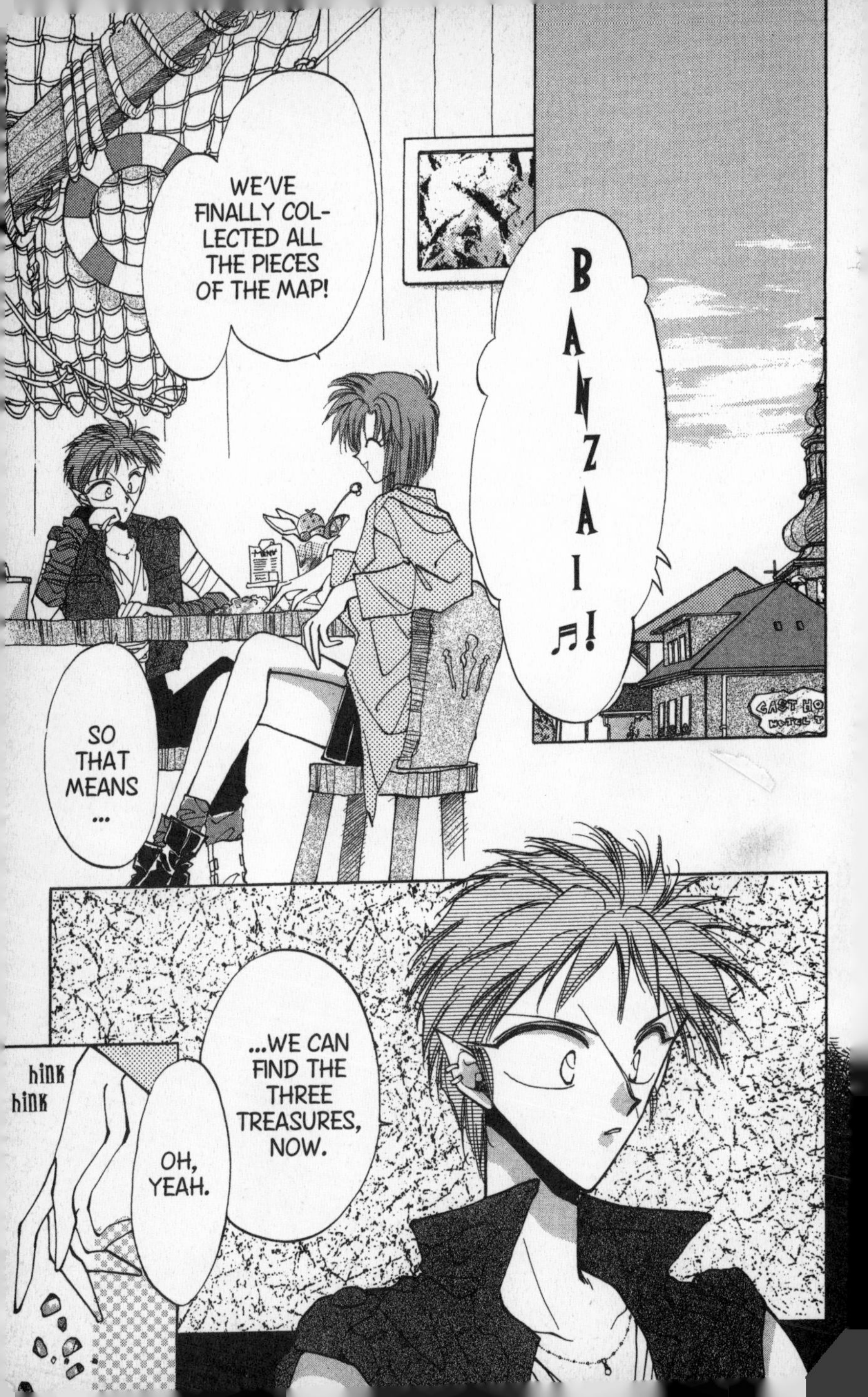
WE'VE FINALLY COL-LECTED ALL THE PIECES OF THE MAP!
BANZAI♬!
SO THAT MEANS...
...WE CAN FIND THE THREE TREASURES, NOW.
OH, YEAH.
hink hink

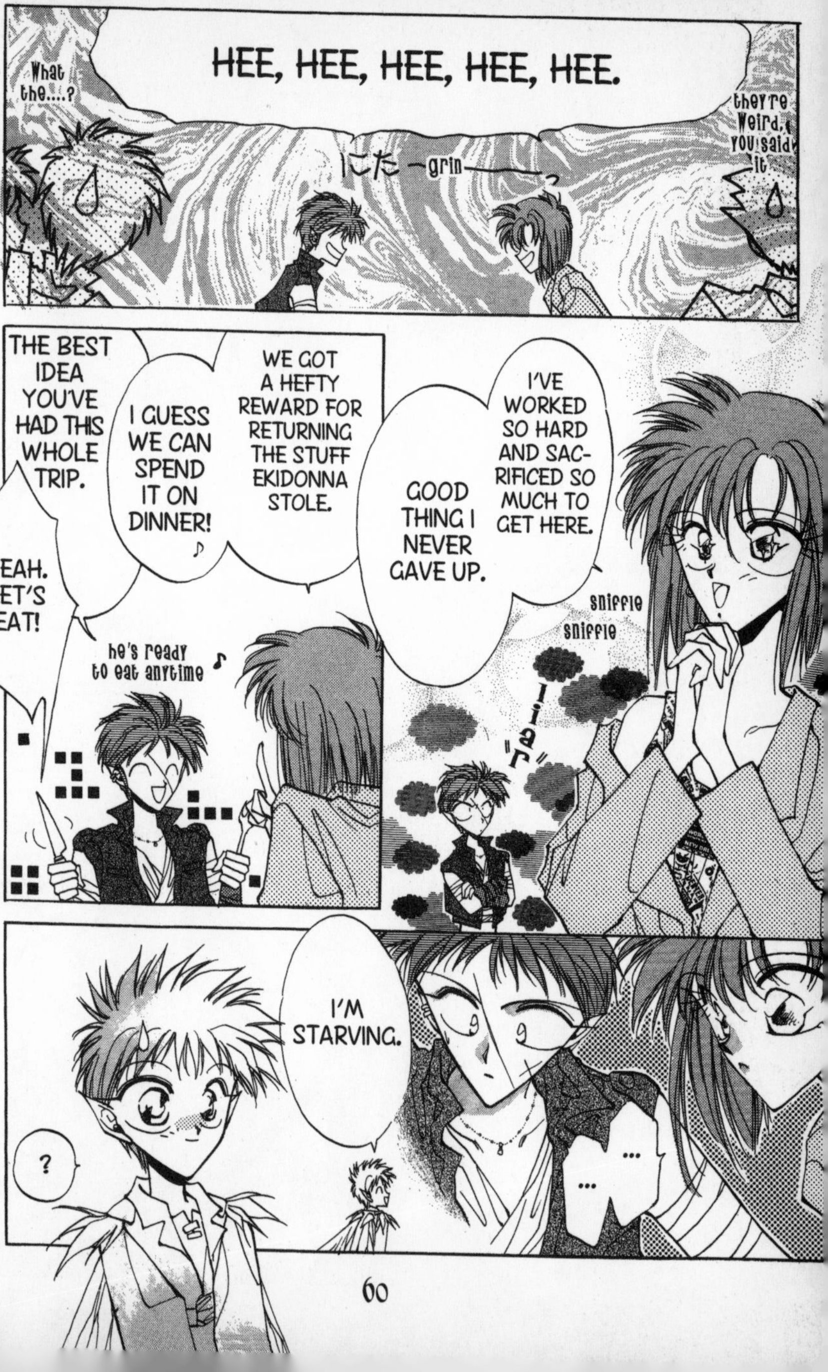
they're Weird, you said it
HEE, HEE, HEE, HEE, HEE.
にた—grin——
What the....?
I'VE WORKED SO HARD AND SACRIFICED SO MUCH TO GET HERE.
GOOD THING I NEVER GAVE UP.
sniffle sniffle
"liar"
WE GOT A HEFTY REWARD FOR RETURNING THE STUFF EKIDONNA STOLE.
I GUESS WE CAN SPEND IT ON DINNER! ♪
THE BEST IDEA YOU'VE HAD THIS WHOLE TRIP.
YEAH. LET'S EAT!
he's ready to eat anytime ♪
...
...
I'M STARVING.
?

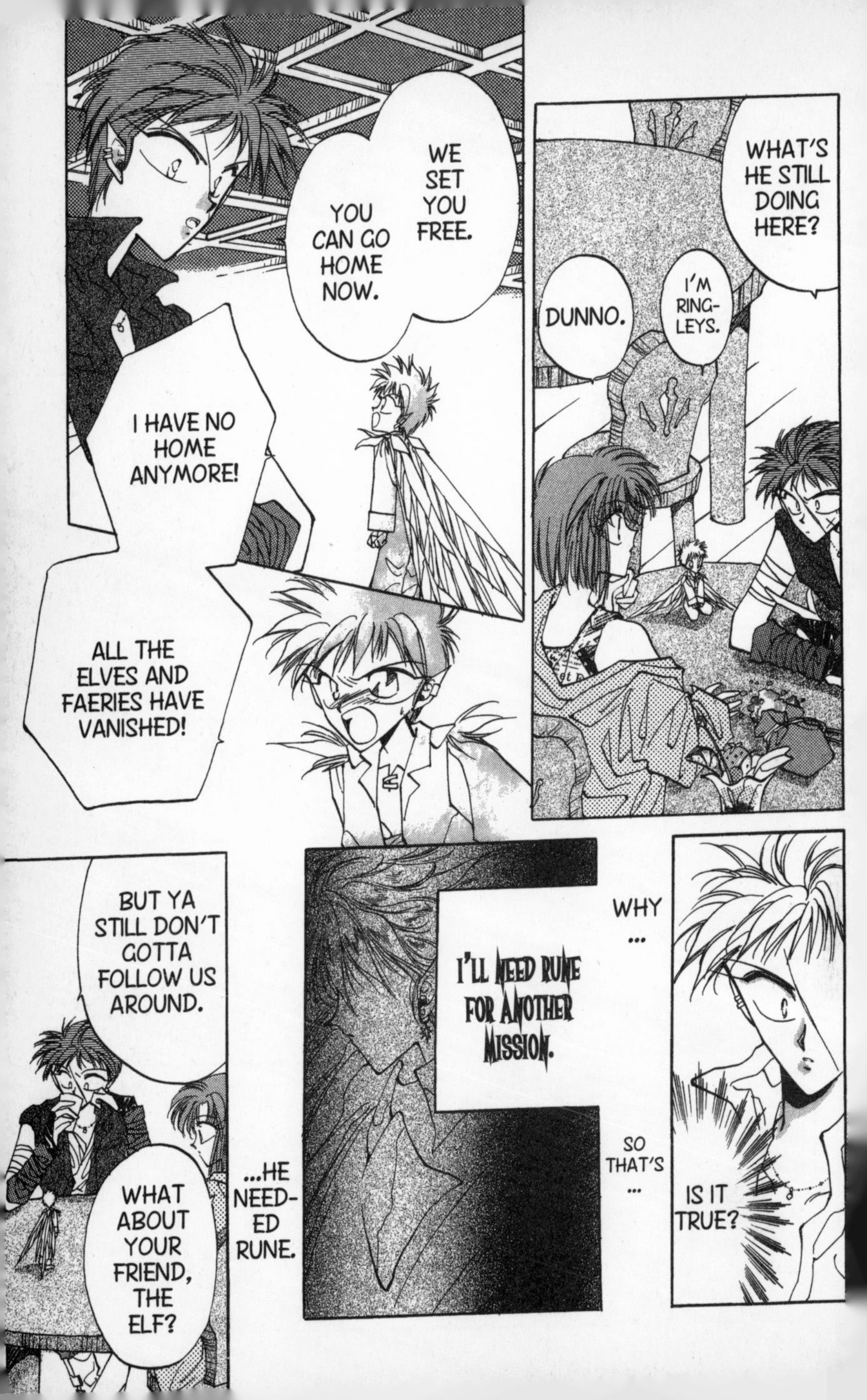
WHAT'S HE STILL DOING HERE?
I'M RINGLEYS.
DUNNO.
WE SET YOU FREE.
YOU CAN GO HOME NOW.
I HAVE NO HOME ANYMORE!
ALL THE ELVES AND FAERIES HAVE VANISHED!
WHY ...
SO THAT'S ...
IS IT TRUE?
I'LL NEED RUNE FOR ANOTHER MISSION.
...HE NEEDED RUNE.
BUT YA STILL DON'T GOTTA FOLLOW US AROUND.
WHAT ABOUT YOUR FRIEND, THE ELF?

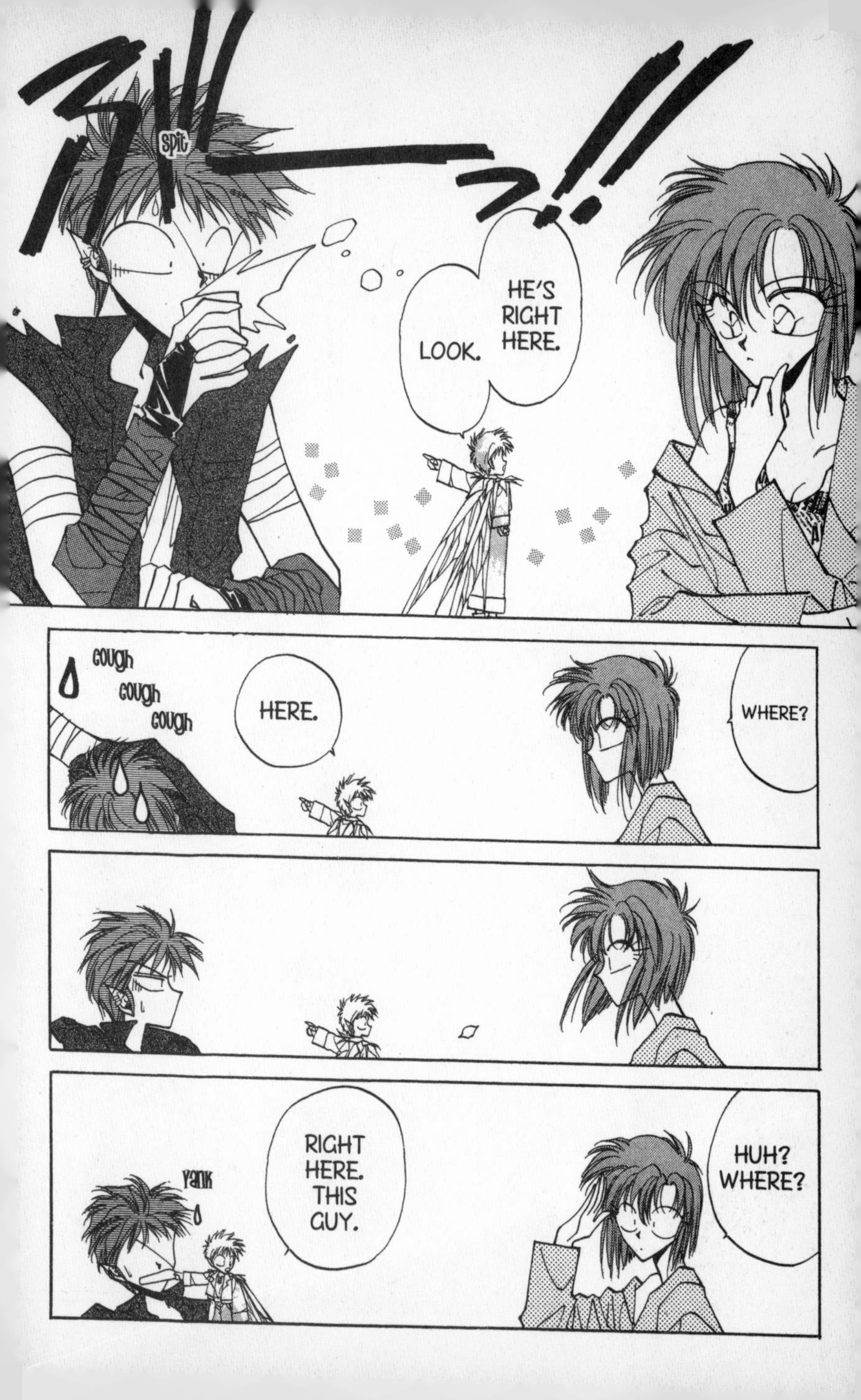
spit
HE'S RIGHT HERE.
LOOK.
WHERE?
HERE.
COUGH
COUGH
COUGH
HUH? WHERE?
RIGHT HERE. THIS GUY.
YANK

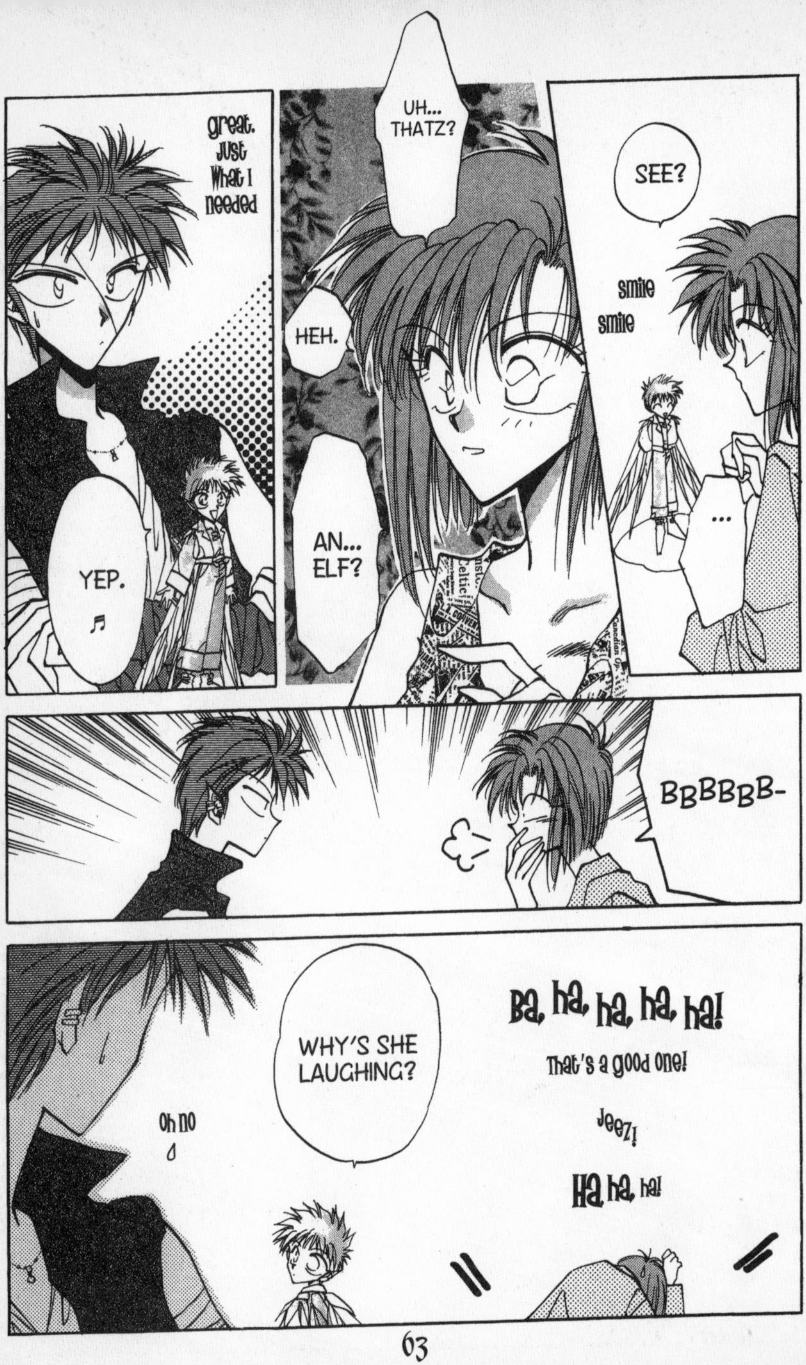
SEE?
smile
smile
...
UH... THATZ?
HEH.
AN... ELF?
great. Just What I needed
YEP. ♪
BBBBBB-
Ba, ha, ha, ha, ha!
That's a good one!
Jeez!
Ha, ha, ha!
WHY'S SHE LAUGHING?
Oh no

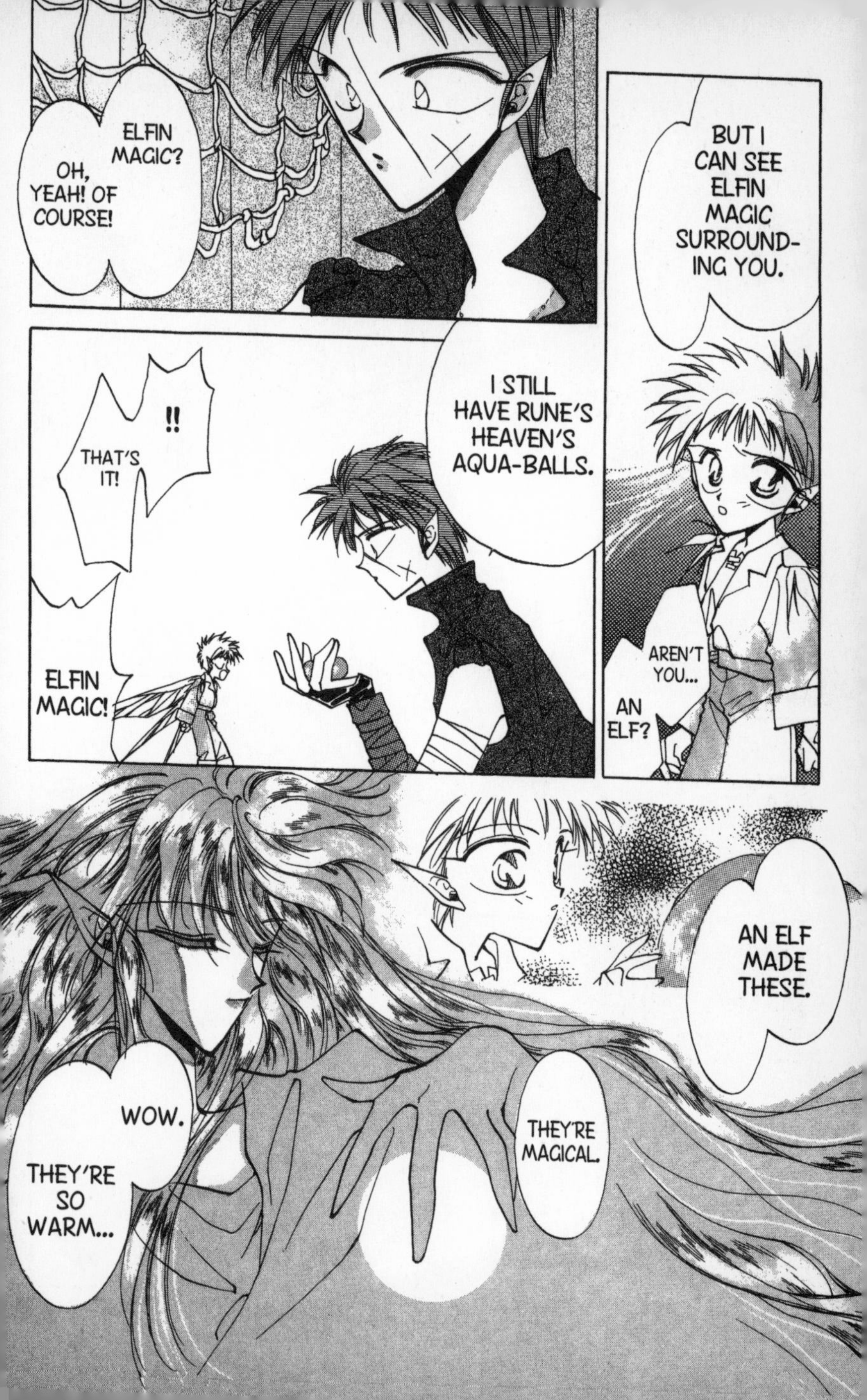

BUT I CAN SEE ELFIN MAGIC SURROUNDING-ING YOU.
AREN'T YOU...
AN ELF?
ELFIN MAGIC?
OH, YEAH! OF COURSE!
I STILL HAVE RUNE'S HEAVEN'S AQUA-BALLS.
!!
THAT'S IT!
ELFIN MAGIC!
AN ELF MADE THESE.
THEY'RE MAGICAL.
WOW.
THEY'RE SO WARM...

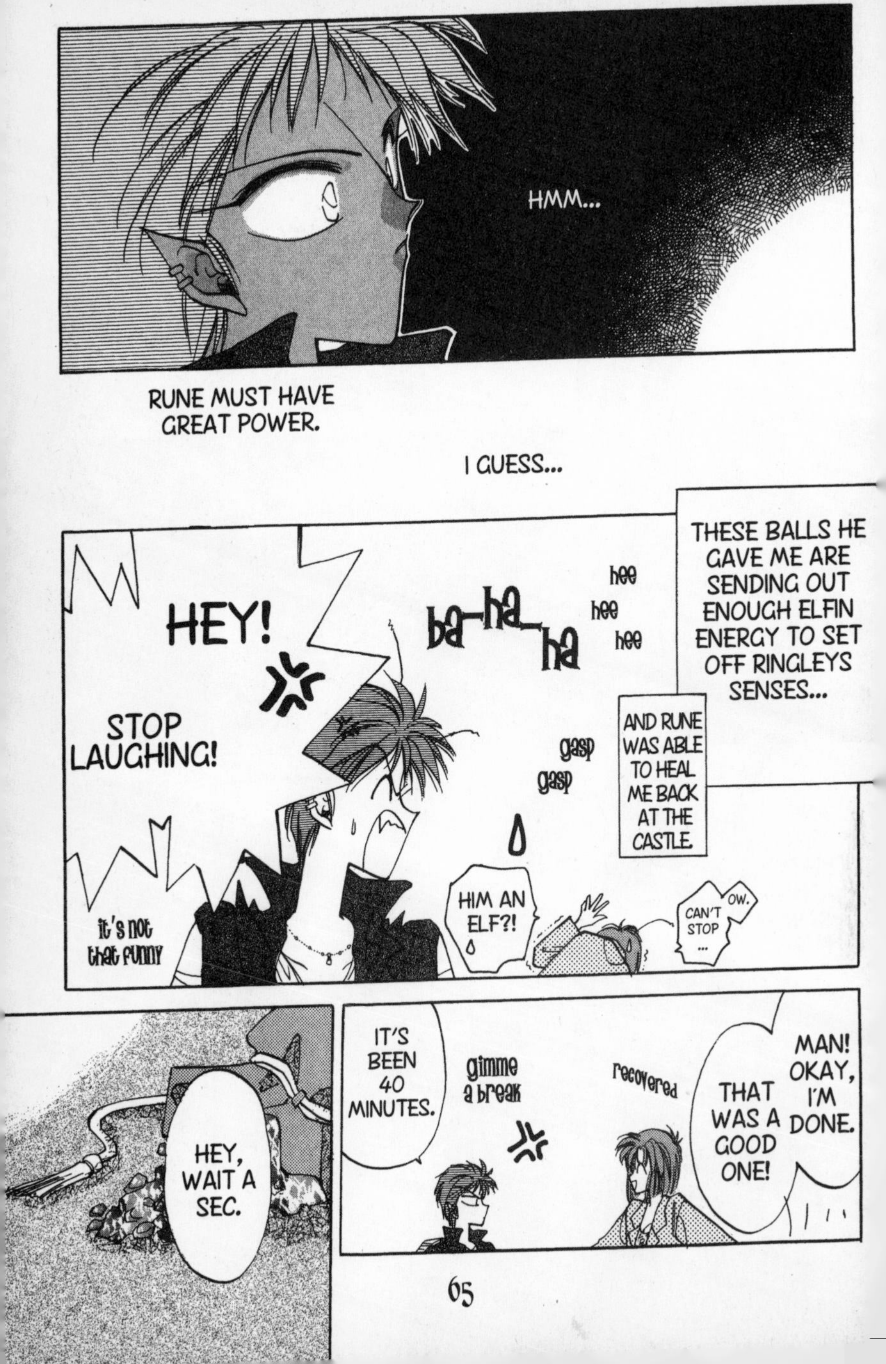
HMM...
RUNE MUST HAVE GREAT POWER.
I GUESS...
THESE BALLS HE GAVE ME ARE SENDING OUT ENOUGH ELFIN ENERGY TO SET OFF RINGLEYS SENSES...
AND RUNE WAS ABLE TO HEAL ME BACK AT THE CASTLE.
hee hee hee
ba-ha-ha
HEY!
STOP LAUGHING!
gasp gasp
OW.
CAN'T STOP ...
HIM AN ELF?!
it's not that funny
MAN! OKAY, I'M DONE.
THAT WAS A GOOD ONE!
recovered
gimme a break
IT'S BEEN 40 MINUTES.
HEY, WAIT A SEC.

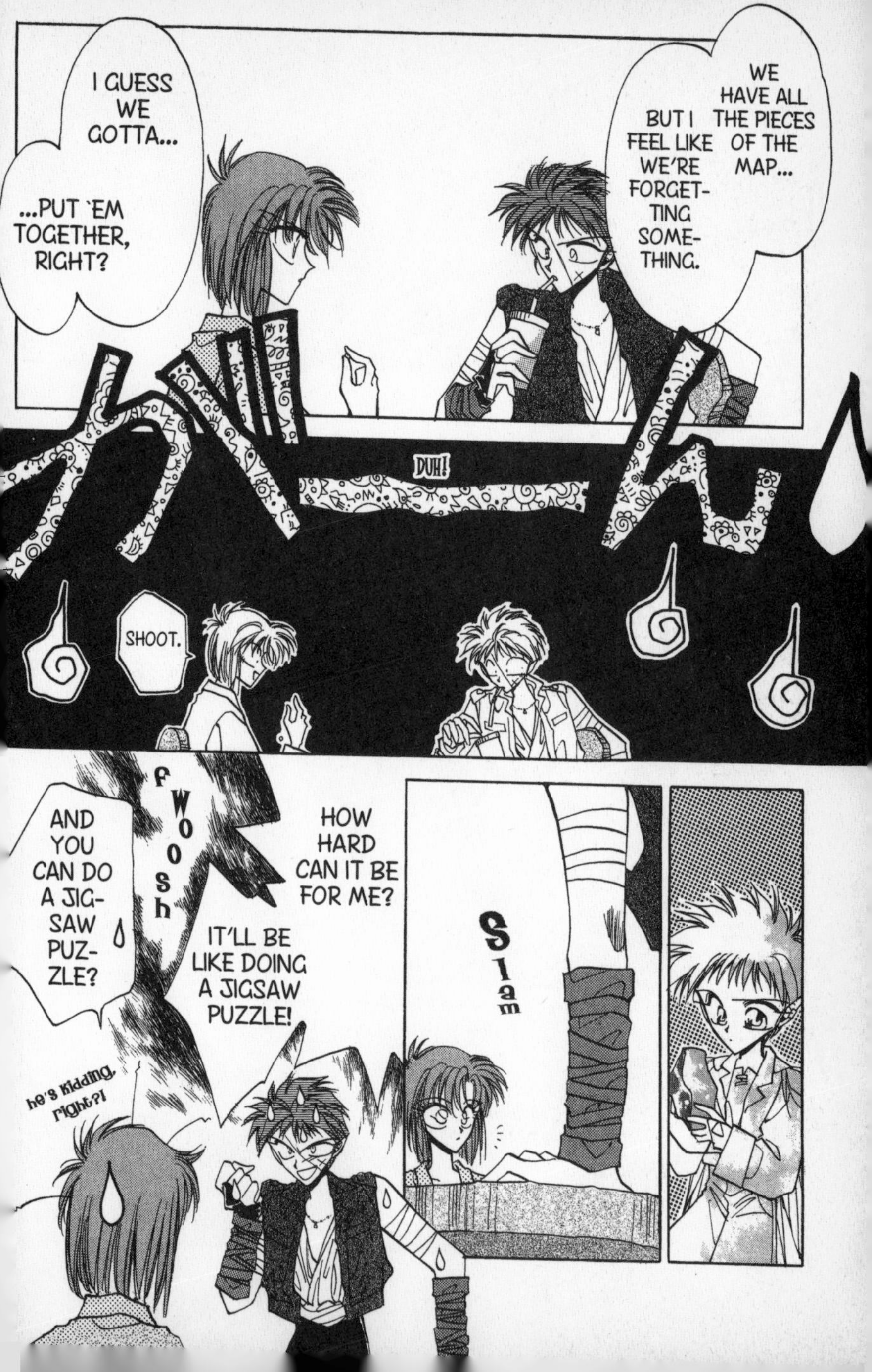
WE HAVE ALL THE PIECES OF THE MAP...
BUT I FEEL LIKE WE'RE FORGET-TING SOME-THING.
I GUESS WE GOTTA...
...PUT `EM TOGETHER, RIGHT?
DUH!
SHOOT.
Slam
HOW HARD CAN IT BE FOR ME?
IT'LL BE LIKE DOING A JIGSAW PUZZLE!
fwoosh
AND YOU CAN DO A JIG-SAW PUZ-ZLE?
he's kidding, right?!

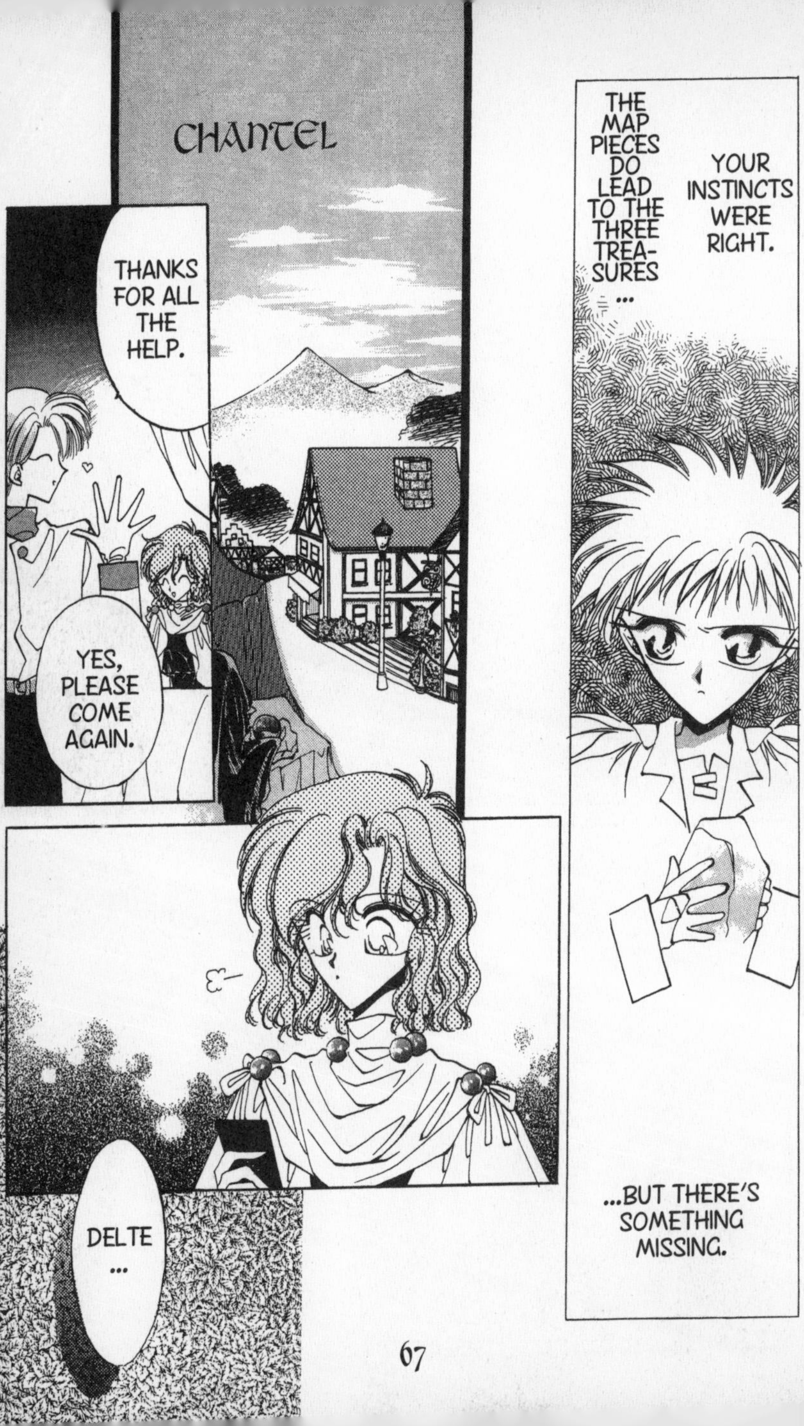
YOUR INSTINCTS WERE RIGHT.
THE MAP PIECES DO LEAD TO THE THREE TREA-SURES...
...BUT THERE'S SOMETHING MISSING.
CHANTEL
THANKS FOR ALL THE HELP.
YES, PLEASE COME AGAIN.
DELTE...

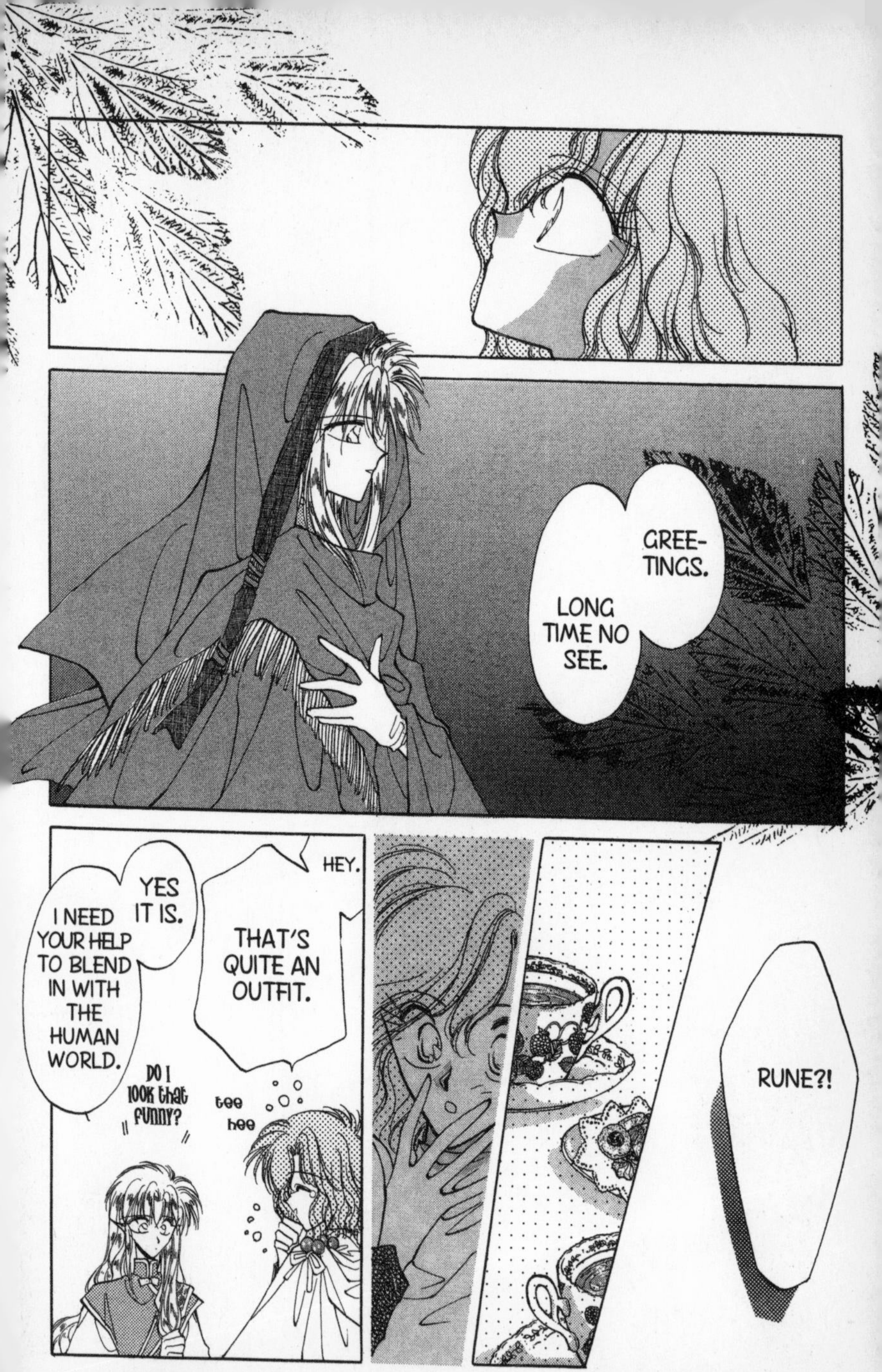
GREE-TINGS.
LONG TIME NO SEE.
RUNE?!
HEY.
THAT'S QUITE AN OUTFIT.
YES IT IS.
I NEED YOUR HELP TO BLEND IN WITH THE HUMAN WORLD.
tee hee
DO I LOOK THAT FUNNY?

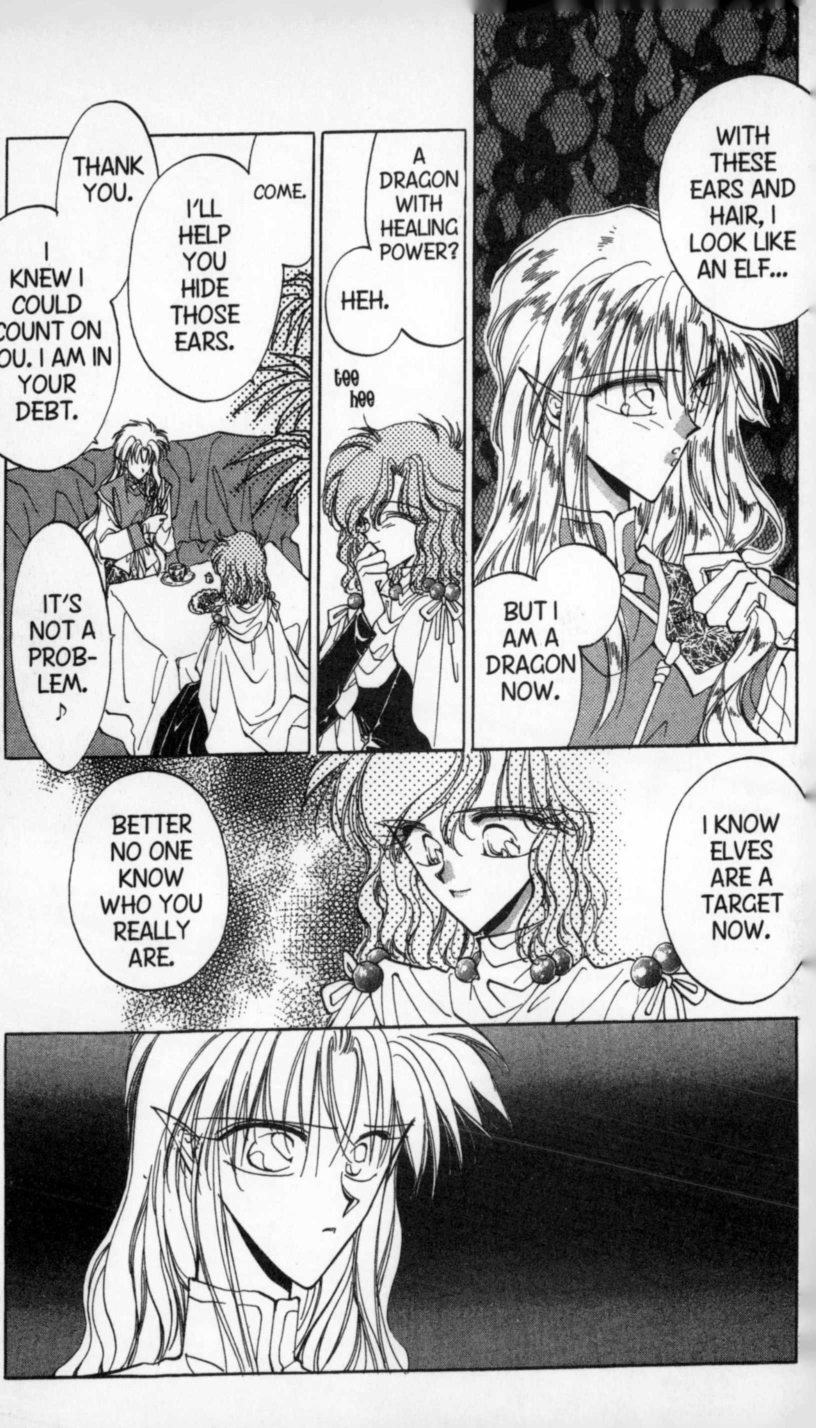
WITH THESE EARS AND HAIR, I LOOK LIKE AN ELF...
BUT I AM A DRAGON NOW.
A DRAGON WITH HEALING POWER?
HEH.
tee hee
COME.
I'LL HELP YOU HIDE THOSE EARS.
THANK YOU.
I KNEW I COULD COUNT ON YOU. I AM IN YOUR DEBT.
IT'S NOT A PROBLEM. ♪
I KNOW ELVES ARE A TARGET NOW.
BETTER NO ONE KNOW WHO YOU REALLY ARE.

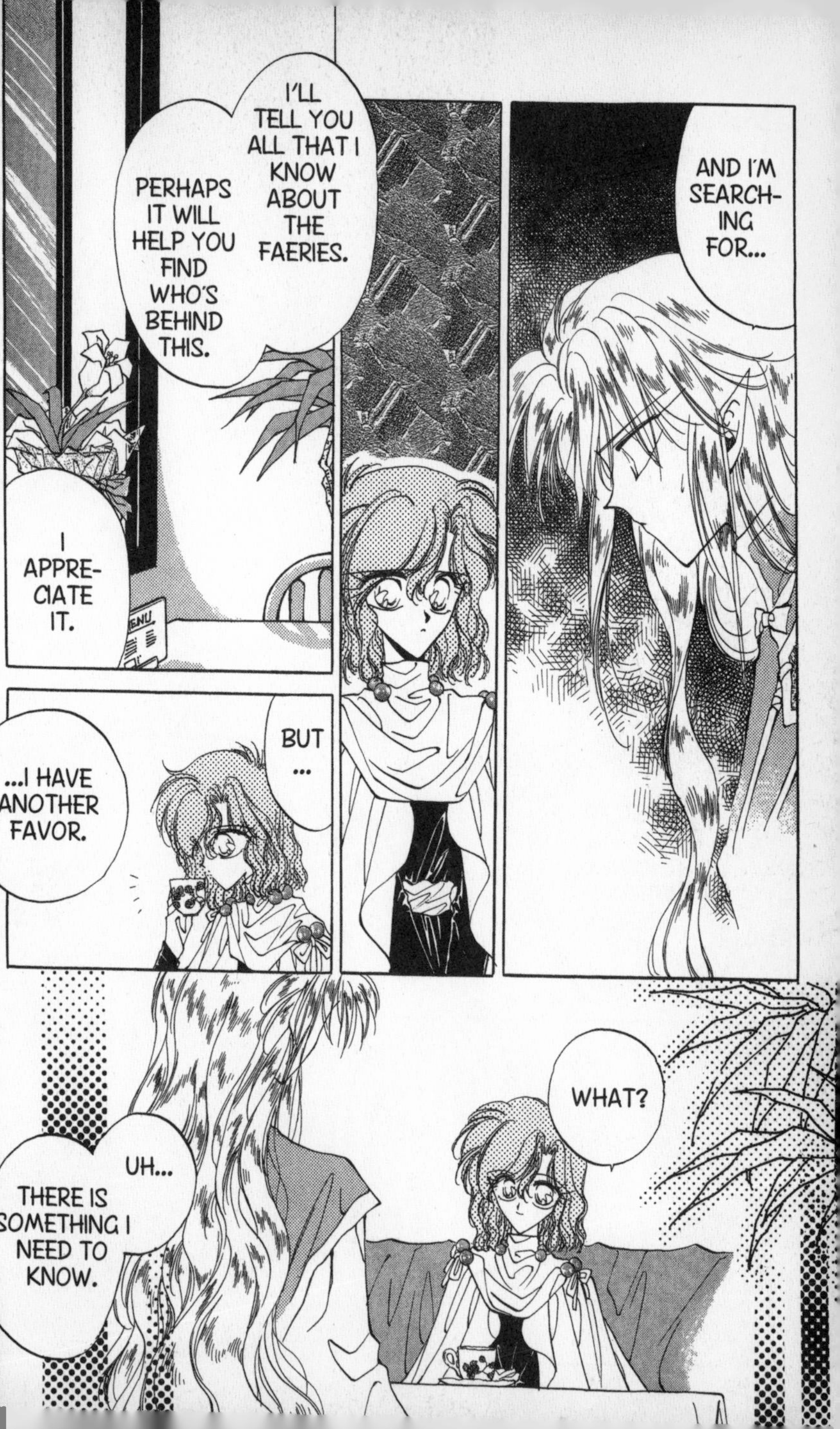
AND I'M SEARCH-ING FOR...
I'LL TELL YOU ALL THAT I KNOW ABOUT THE FAERIES.
PERHAPS IT WILL HELP YOU FIND WHO'S BEHIND THIS.
I APPRE-CIATE IT.
MENU
BUT ...
...I HAVE ANOTHER FAVOR.
WHAT?
UH...
THERE IS SOMETHING I NEED TO KNOW.

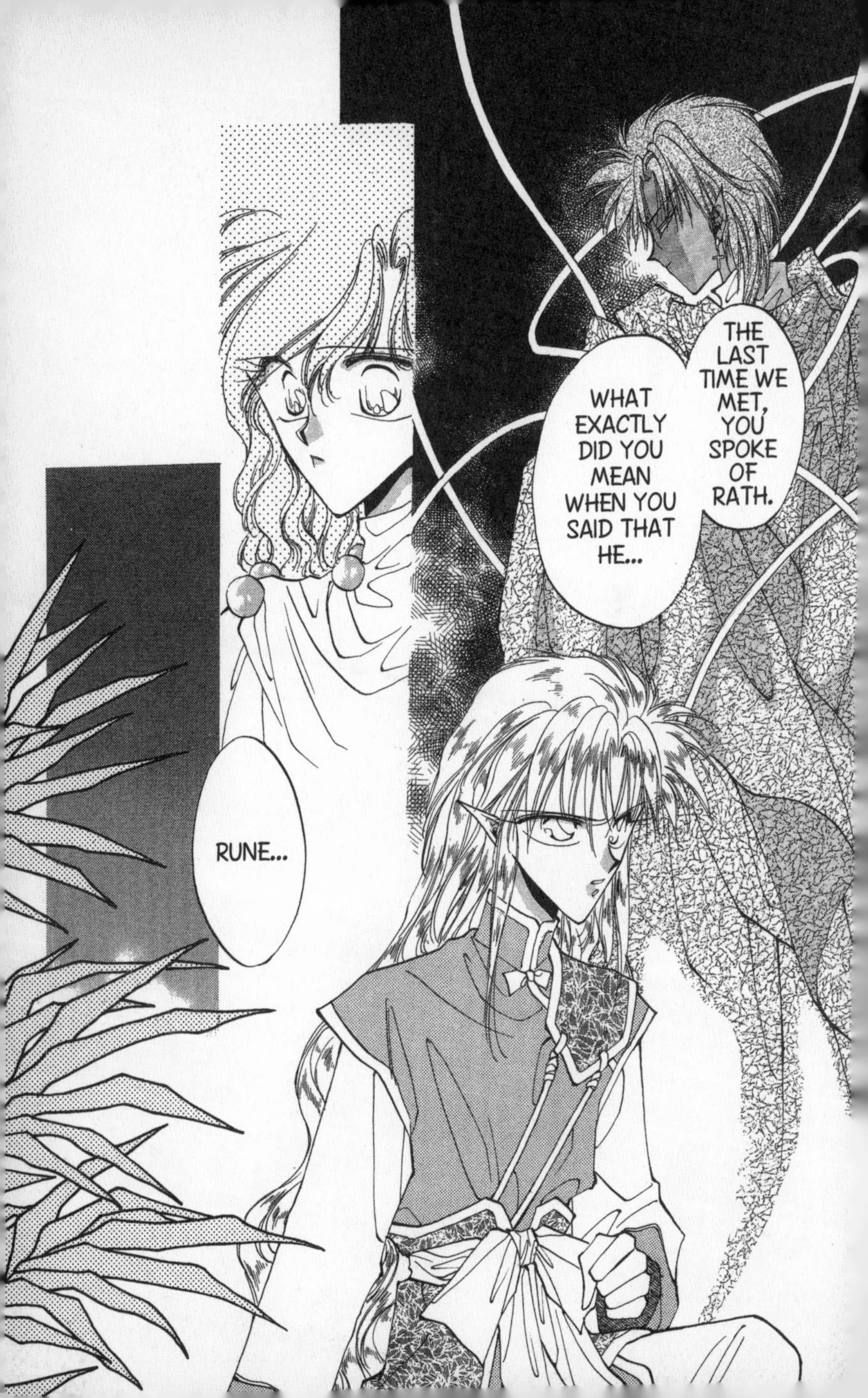
THE LAST TIME WE MET, YOU SPOKE OF RATH.
WHAT EXACTLY DID YOU MEAN WHEN YOU SAID THAT HE...
RUNE...

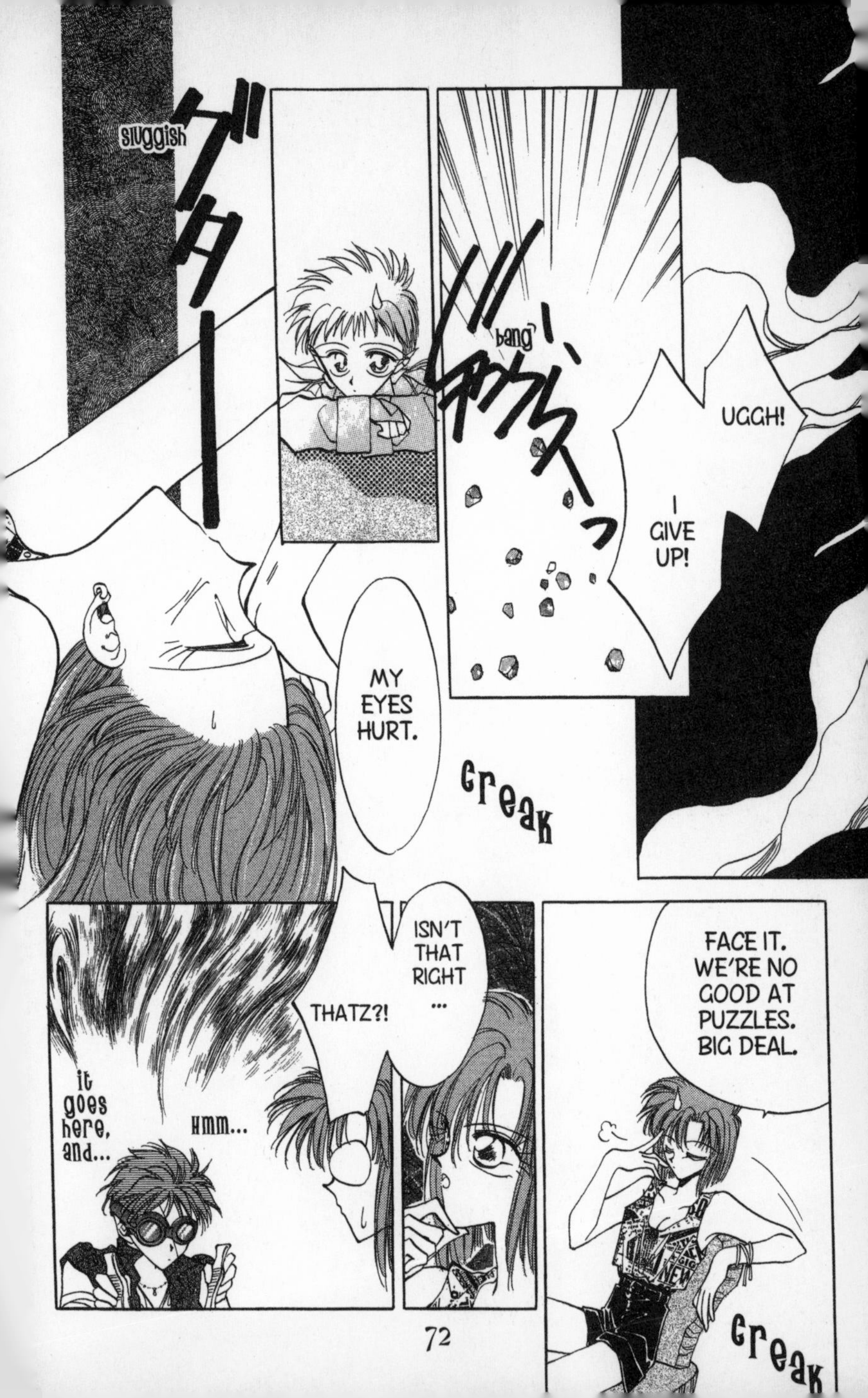
UGGH!
I GIVE UP!
bang
sluggish
MY EYES HURT.
creak
FACE IT. WE'RE NO GOOD AT PUZZLES. BIG DEAL.
creak
ISN'T THAT RIGHT ...
THATZ?!
it goes here, and...
HMM...

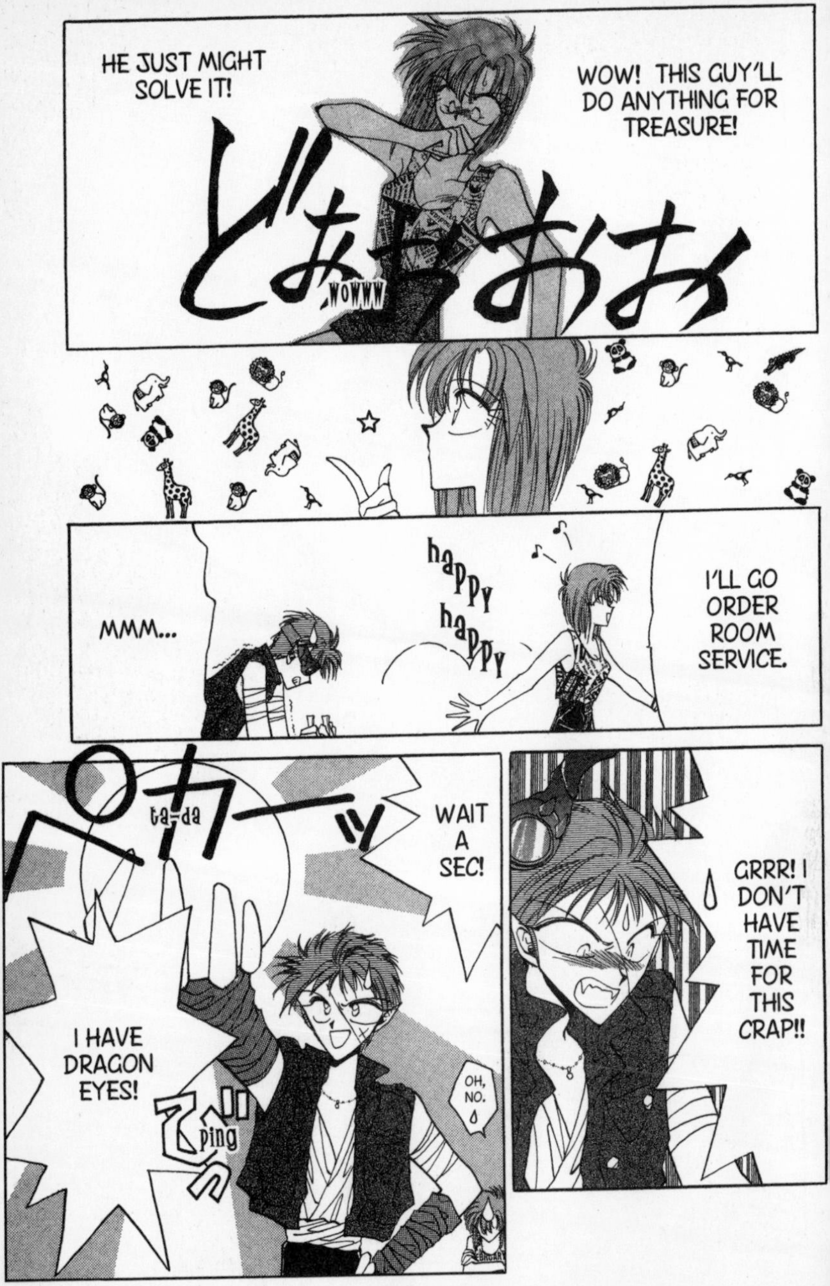
WOW! THIS GUY'LL DO ANYTHING FOR TREASURE!
HE JUST MIGHT SOLVE IT!
WOWWW
I'LL GO ORDER ROOM SERVICE.
happy happy
MMM...
GRRR! I DON'T HAVE TIME FOR THIS CRAP!!
WAIT A SEC!
ta-da
I HAVE DRAGON EYES!
ping
OH, NO.

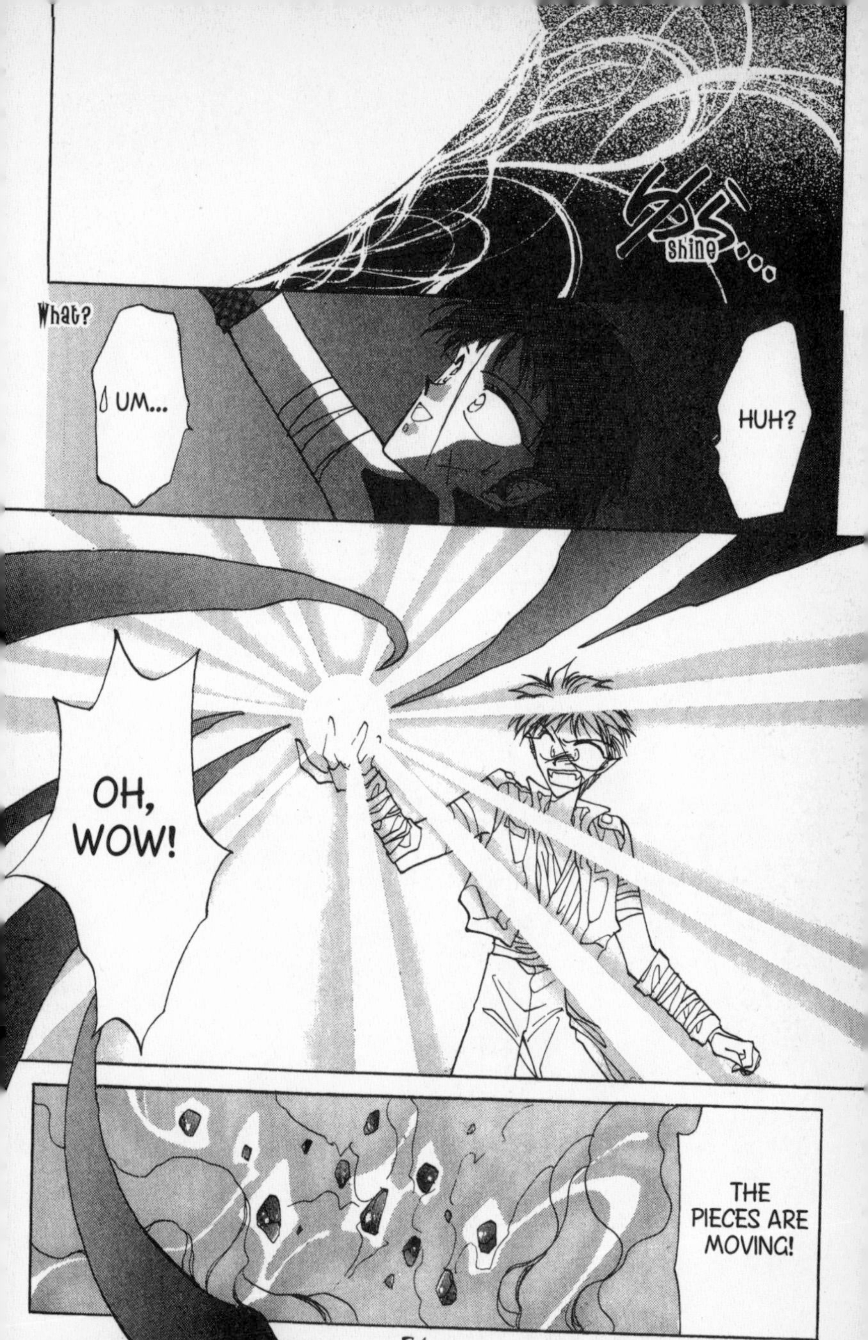
shine...
HUH?
What?
UM...
OH, WOW!
THE PIECES ARE MOVING!

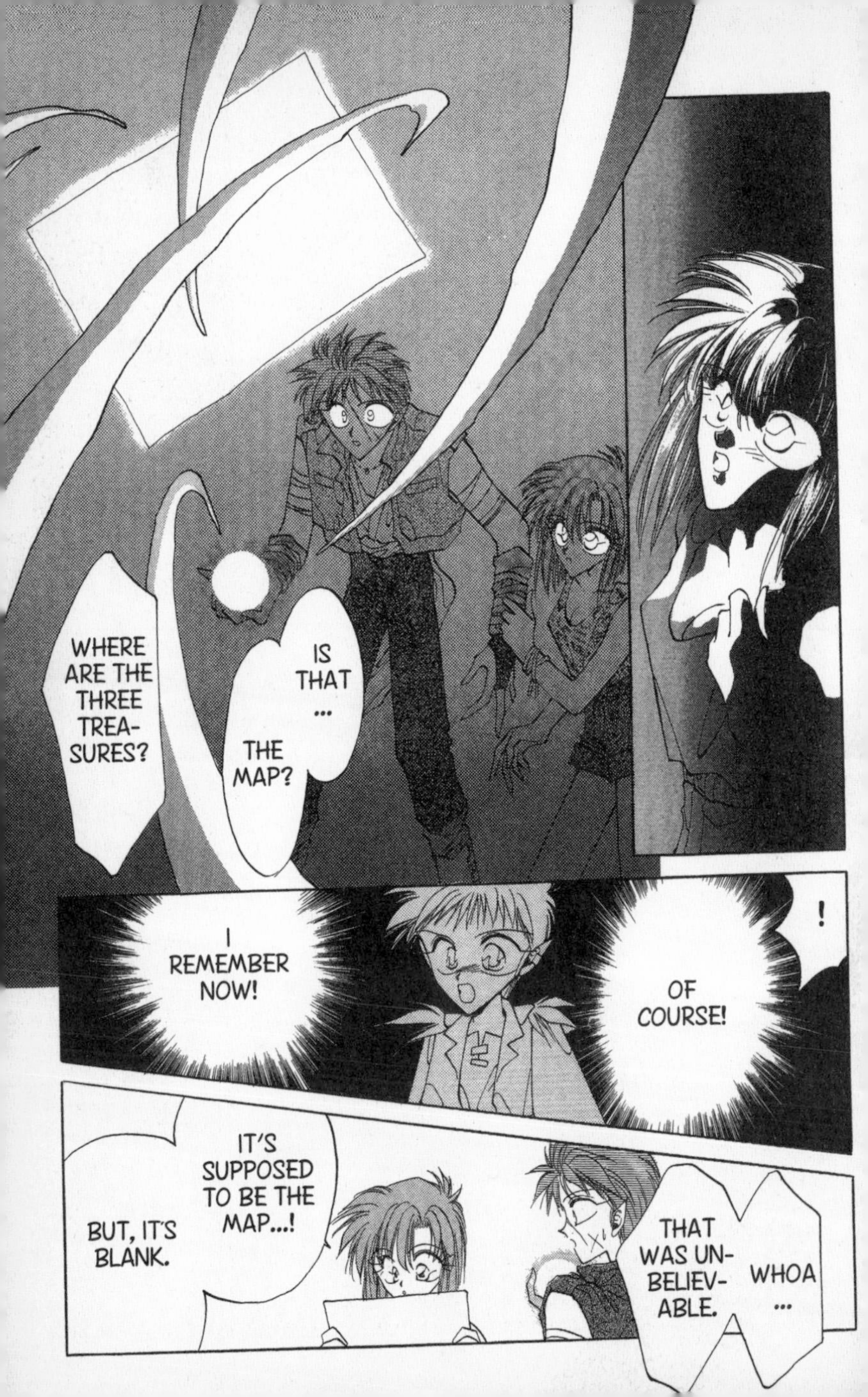
IS THAT ... THE MAP?
WHERE ARE THE THREE TREA-SURES?
!
OF COURSE!
I REMEMBER NOW!
WHOA ...
THAT WAS UN-BELIEV-ABLE.
IT'S SUPPOSED TO BE THE MAP...!
BUT, IT'S BLANK.

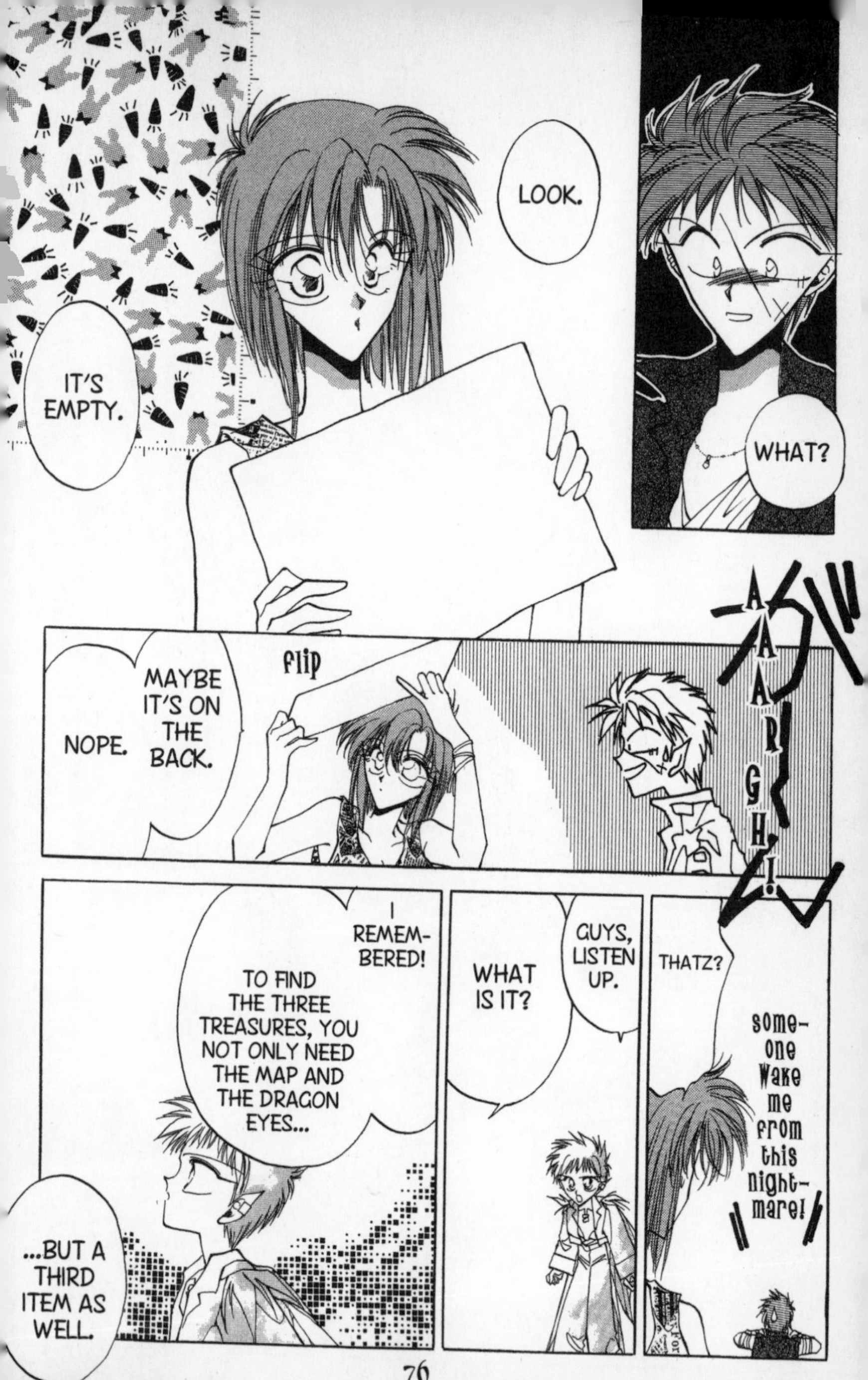
WHAT?
LOOK.
IT'S EMPTY.
AAARGH!
flip
MAYBE IT'S ON THE BACK.
NOPE.
THATZ?
someone Wake me from this nightmare!
GUYS, LISTEN UP.
WHAT IS IT?
I REMEMBERED!
TO FIND THE THREE TREASURES, YOU NOT ONLY NEED THE MAP AND THE DRAGON EYES...
...BUT A THIRD ITEM AS WELL.

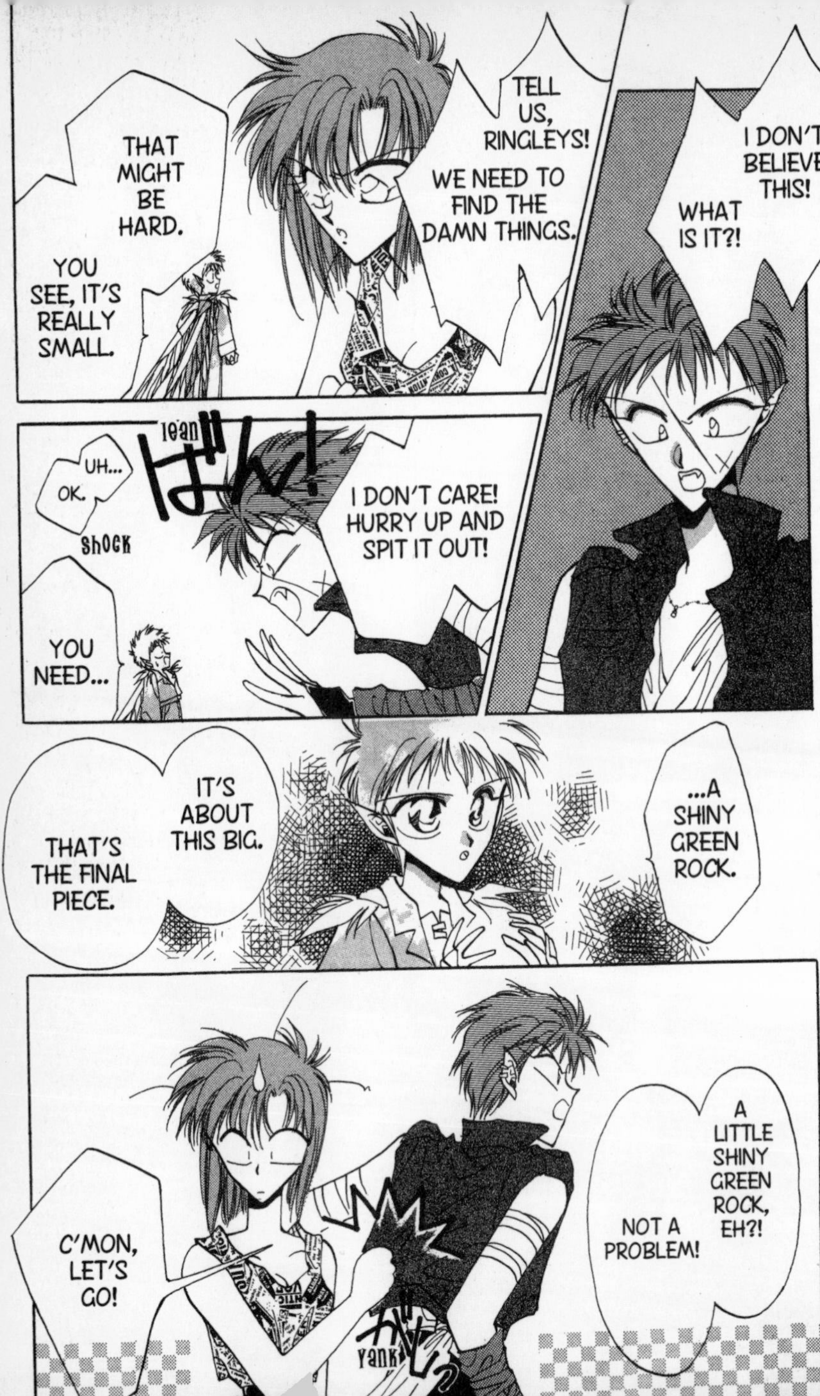
I DON'T BELIEVE THIS!
WHAT IS IT?!
TELL US, RINGLEYS!
WE NEED TO FIND THE DAMN THINGS.
THAT MIGHT BE HARD.
YOU SEE, IT'S REALLY SMALL.
ばん!
lean
I DON'T CARE! HURRY UP AND SPIT IT OUT!
UH... OK.
SHOCK
YOU NEED...
...A SHINY GREEN ROCK.
IT'S ABOUT THIS BIG.
THAT'S THE FINAL PIECE.
A LITTLE SHINY GREEN ROCK, EH?!
NOT A PROBLEM!
C'MON, LET'S GO!
YANK

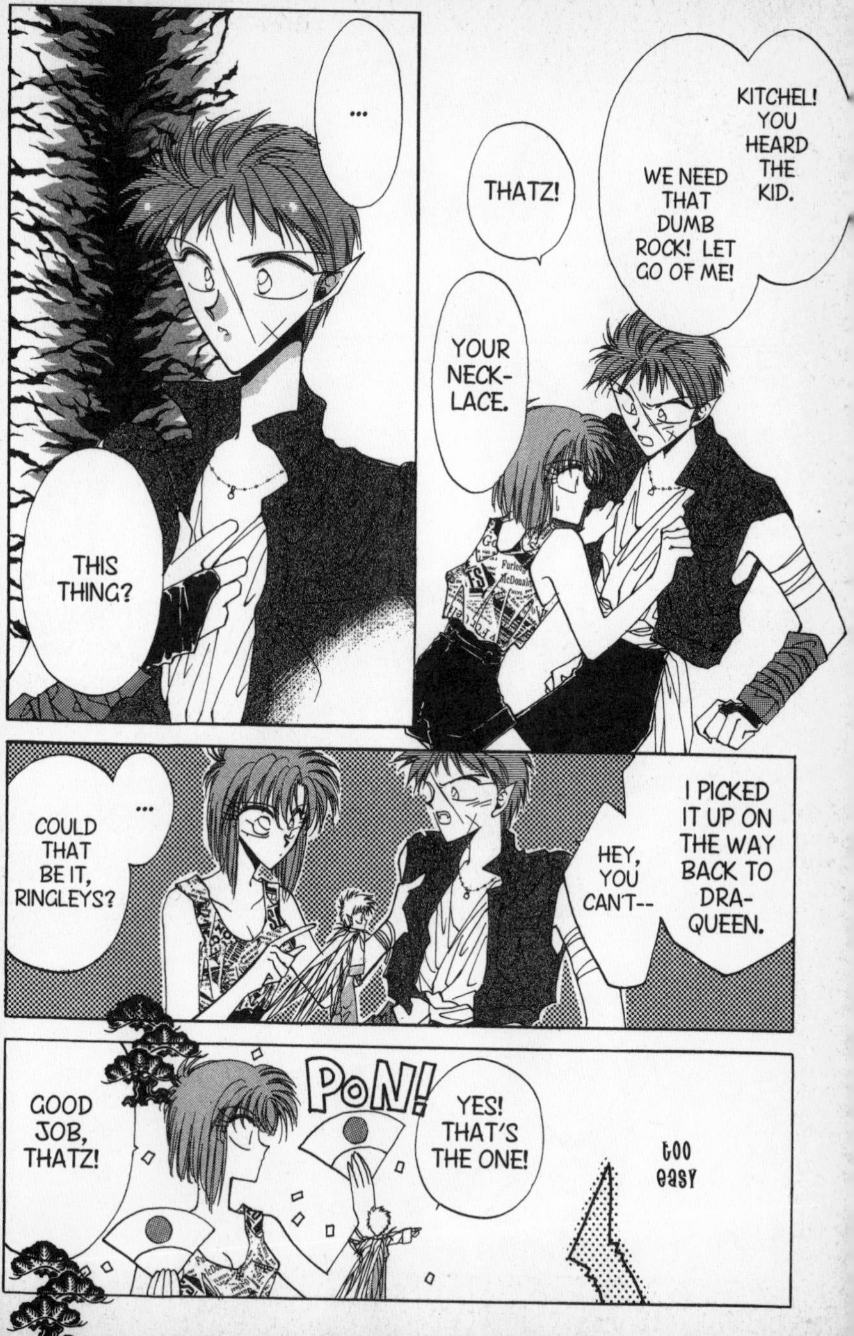
KITCHEL! YOU HEARD THE KID.
WE NEED THAT DUMB ROCK! LET GO OF ME!
THATZ!
YOUR NECKLACE.
...
THIS THING?
I PICKED IT UP ON THE WAY BACK TO DRA-QUEEN.
HEY, YOU CAN'T--
...
COULD THAT BE IT, RINGLEYS?
too easy
PoN!
YES! THAT'S THE ONE!
GOOD JOB, THATZ!

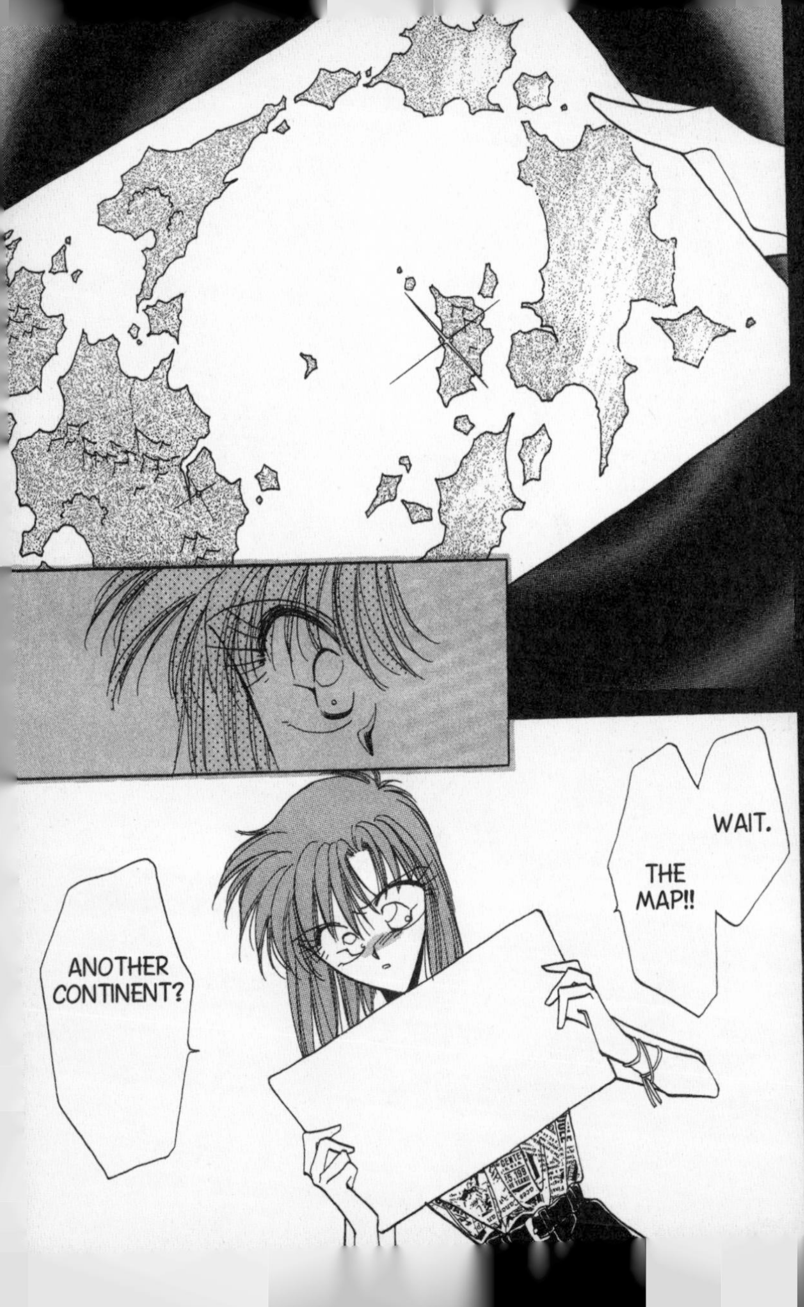
WAIT.
THE MAP!!
ANOTHER CONTINENT?

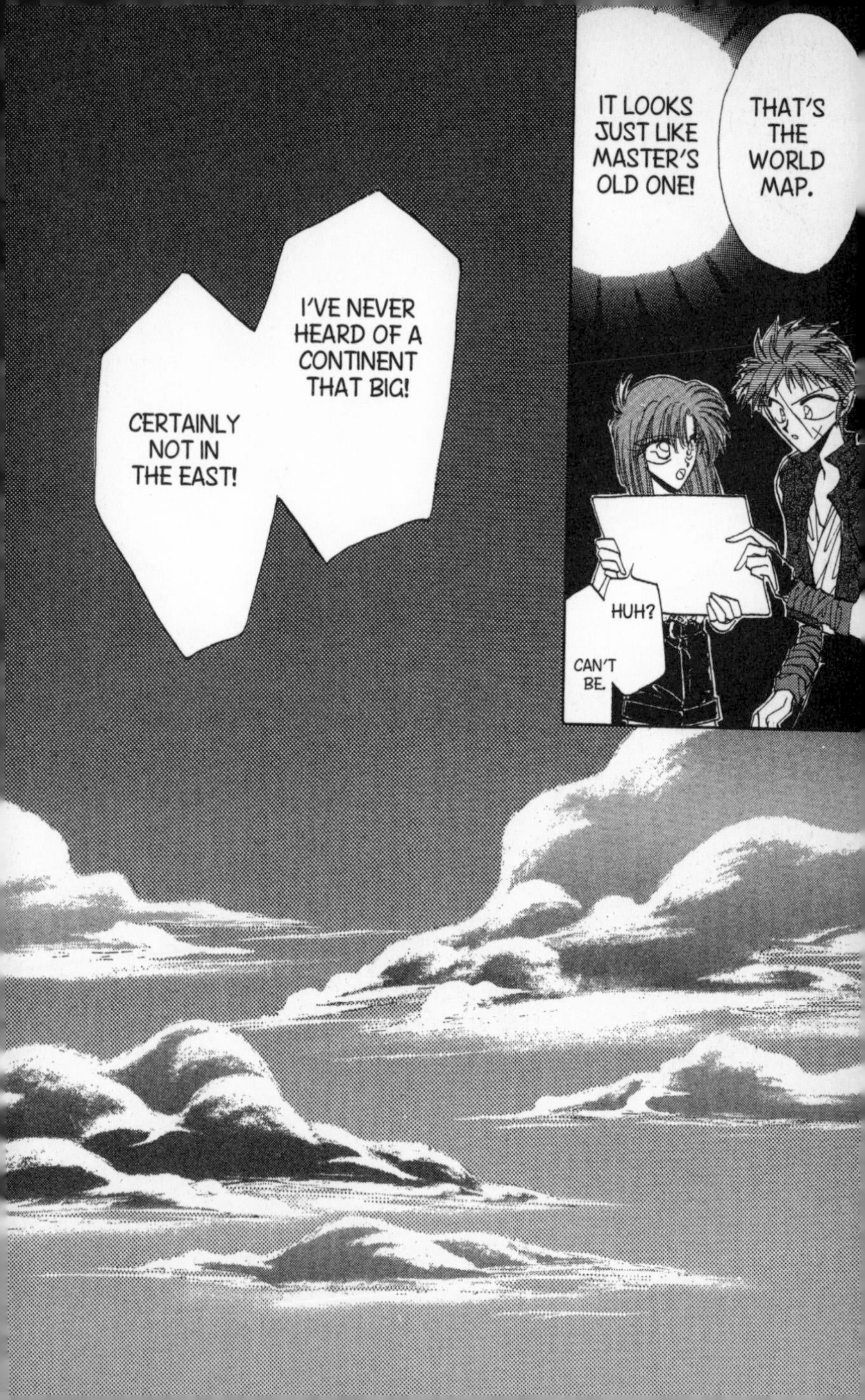
THAT'S THE WORLD MAP.
IT LOOKS JUST LIKE MASTER'S OLD ONE!
HUH?
CAN'T BE.
I'VE NEVER HEARD OF A CONTINENT THAT BIG!
CERTAINLY NOT IN THE EAST!

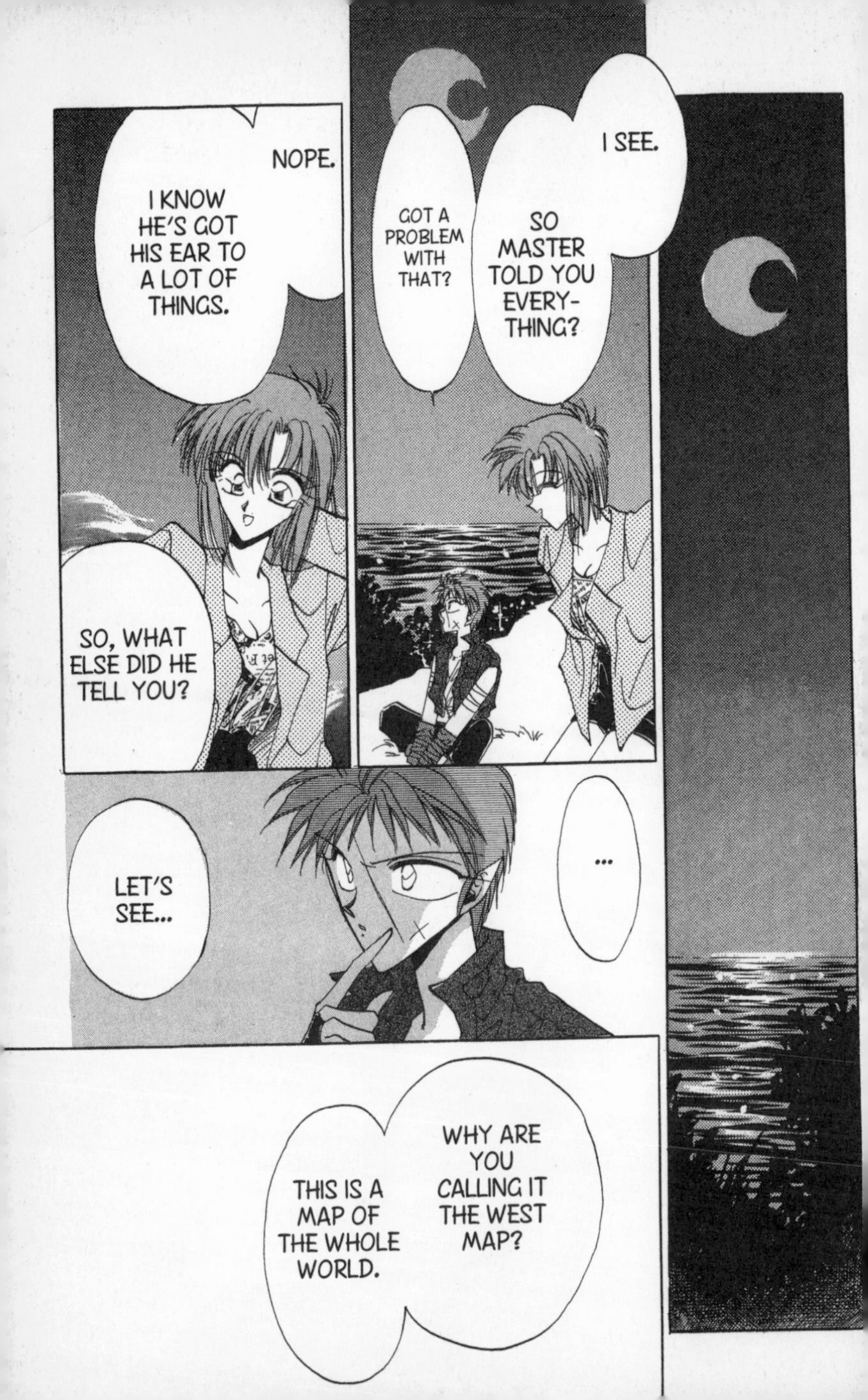
I SEE.
SO MASTER TOLD YOU EVERYTHING?
GOT A PROBLEM WITH THAT?
NOPE.
I KNOW HE'S GOT HIS EAR TO A LOT OF THINGS.
SO, WHAT ELSE DID HE TELL YOU?
...
LET'S SEE...
WHY ARE YOU CALLING IT THE WEST MAP?
THIS IS A MAP OF THE WHOLE WORLD.

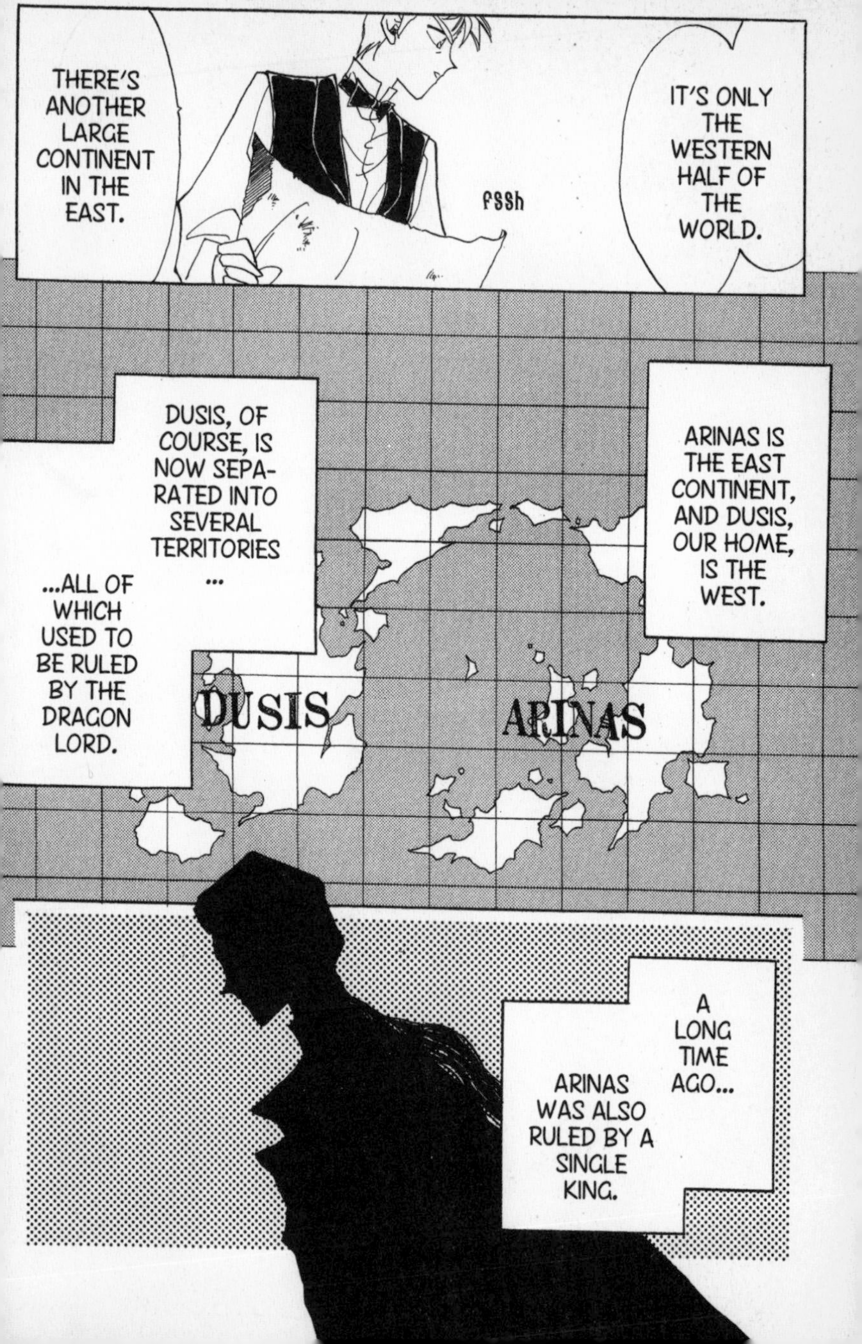
IT'S ONLY THE WESTERN HALF OF THE WORLD.
fssh
THERE'S ANOTHER LARGE CONTINENT IN THE EAST.
ARINAS IS THE EAST CONTINENT, AND DUSIS, OUR HOME, IS THE WEST.
DUSIS, OF COURSE, IS NOW SEPA-RATED INTO SEVERAL TERRITORIES ...
...ALL OF WHICH USED TO BE RULED BY THE DRAGON LORD.
ARINAS
DUSIS
A LONG TIME AGO...
ARINAS WAS ALSO RULED BY A SINGLE KING.

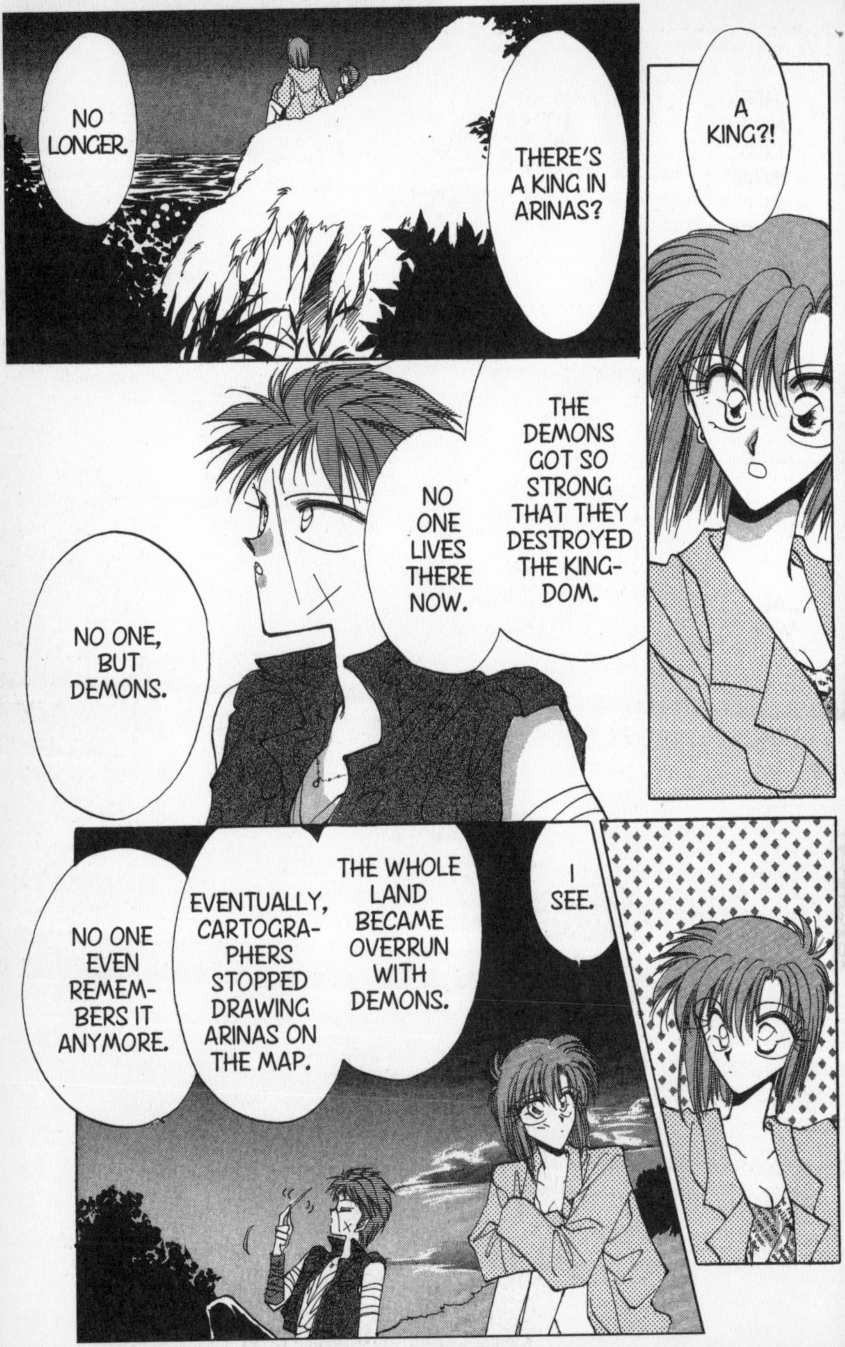
THERE'S A KING IN ARINAS?
NO LONGER.
A KING?!
THE DEMONS GOT SO STRONG THAT THEY DESTROYED THE KING-DOM.
NO ONE LIVES THERE NOW.
NO ONE, BUT DEMONS.
I SEE.
THE WHOLE LAND BECAME OVERRUN WITH DEMONS.
EVENTUALLY, CARTOGRA-PHERS STOPPED DRAWING ARINAS ON THE MAP.
NO ONE EVEN REMEM-BERS IT ANYMORE.

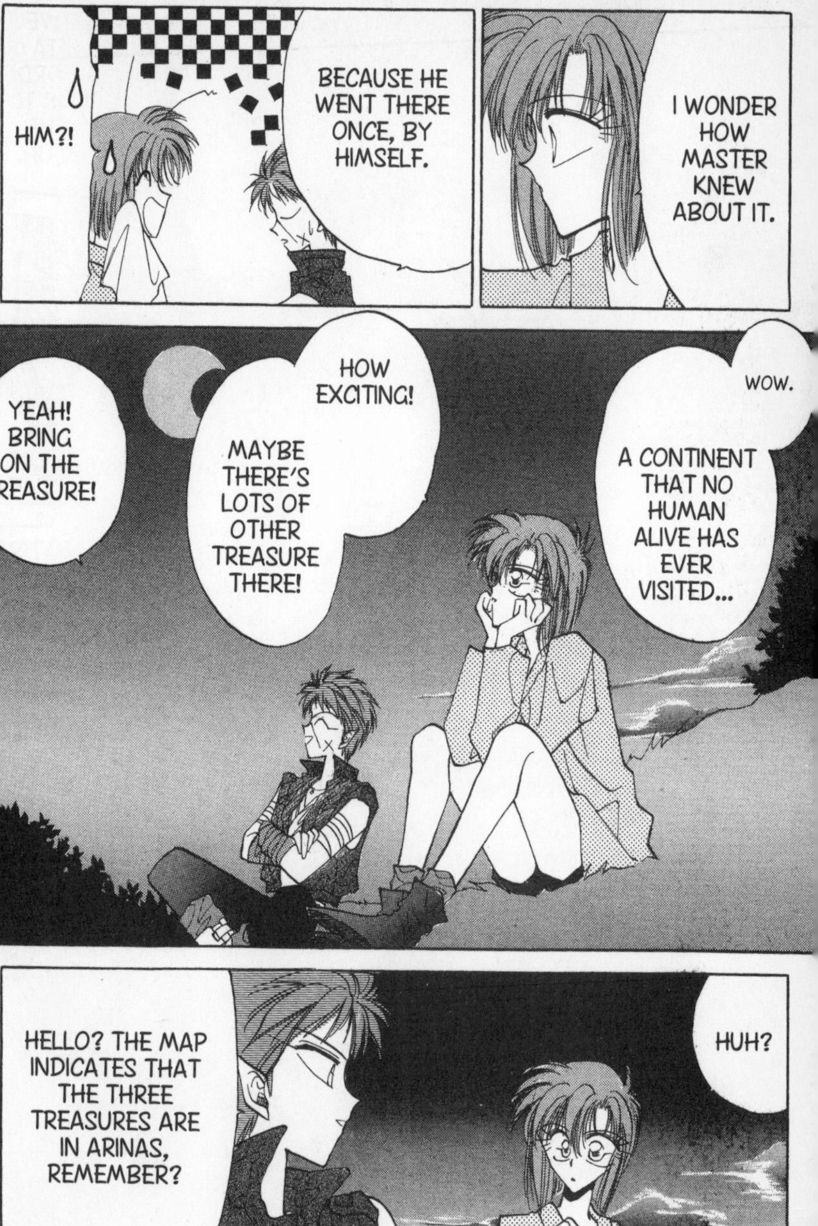
I WONDER HOW MASTER KNEW ABOUT IT.
BECAUSE HE WENT THERE ONCE, BY HIMSELF.
HIM?!
WOW.
A CONTINENT THAT NO HUMAN ALIVE HAS EVER VISITED...
HOW EXCITING!
MAYBE THERE'S LOTS OF OTHER TREASURE THERE!
YEAH! BRING ON THE TREASURE!
HUH?
HELLO? THE MAP INDICATES THAT THE THREE TREASURES ARE IN ARINAS, REMEMBER?

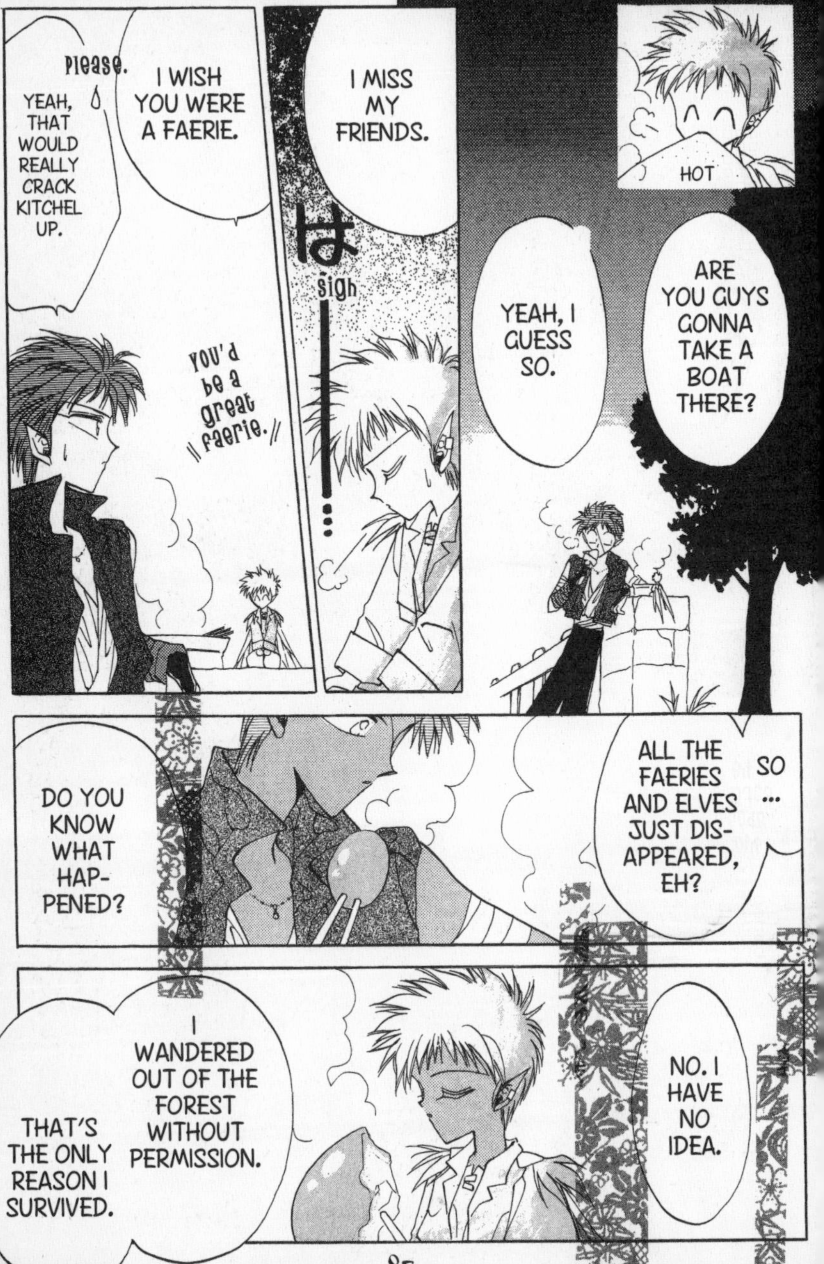
HOT
ARE YOU GUYS GONNA TAKE A BOAT THERE?
YEAH, I GUESS SO.
I MISS MY FRIENDS.
は
sigh
I WISH YOU WERE A FAERIE.
Please.
YEAH, THAT WOULD REALLY CRACK KITCHEL UP.
You'd be a great faerie.
SO...
ALL THE FAERIES AND ELVES JUST DIS-APPEARED, EH?
DO YOU KNOW WHAT HAP-PENED?
NO. I HAVE NO IDEA.
I WANDERED OUT OF THE FOREST WITHOUT PERMISSION.
THAT'S THE ONLY REASON I SURVIVED.

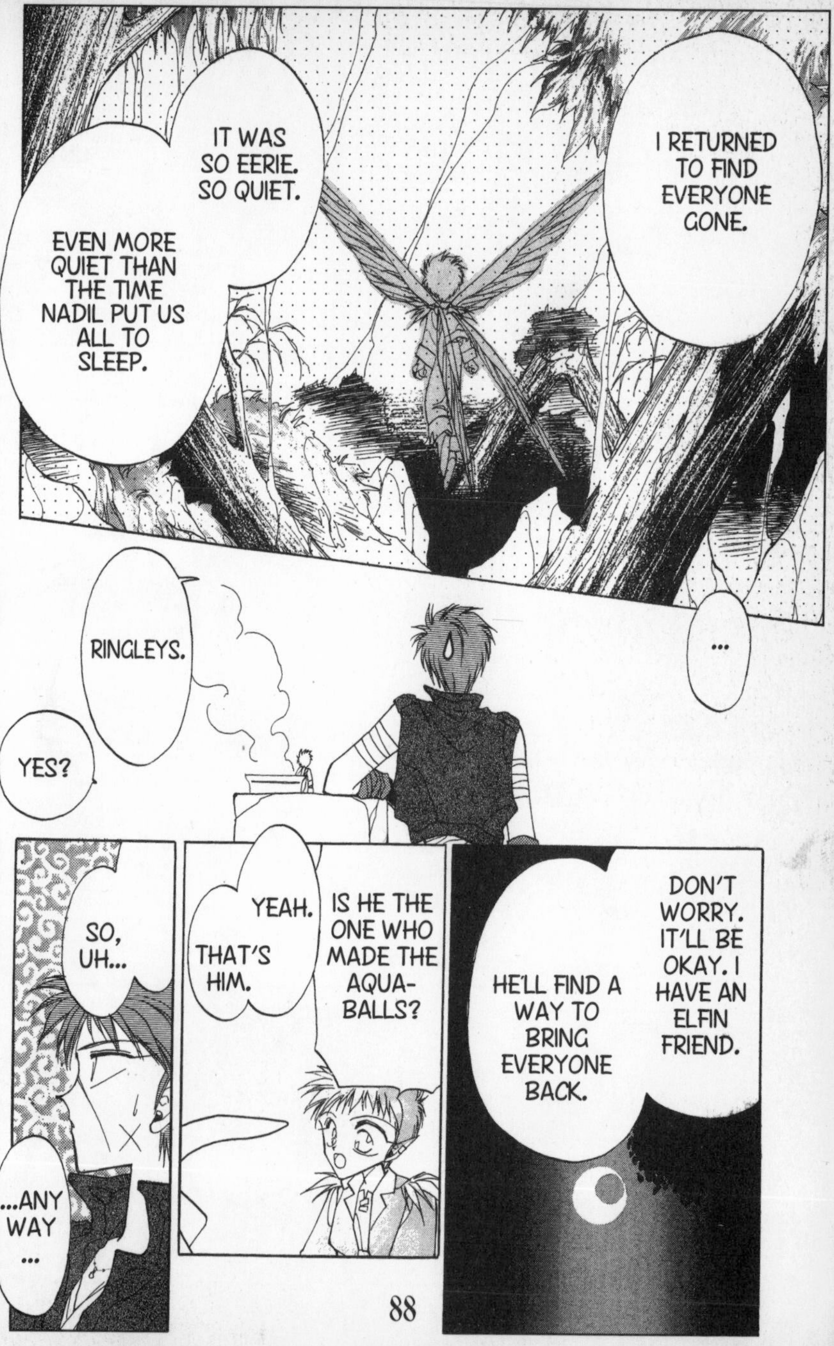
I RETURNED TO FIND EVERYONE GONE.
IT WAS SO EERIE. SO QUIET.
EVEN MORE QUIET THAN THE TIME NADIL PUT US ALL TO SLEEP.
...
RINGLEYS.
YES?
DON'T WORRY. IT'LL BE OKAY. I HAVE AN ELFIN FRIEND.
HE'LL FIND A WAY TO BRING EVERYONE BACK.
IS HE THE ONE WHO MADE THE AQUA-BALLS?
YEAH.
THAT'S HIM.
SO, UH...
...ANY WAY ...

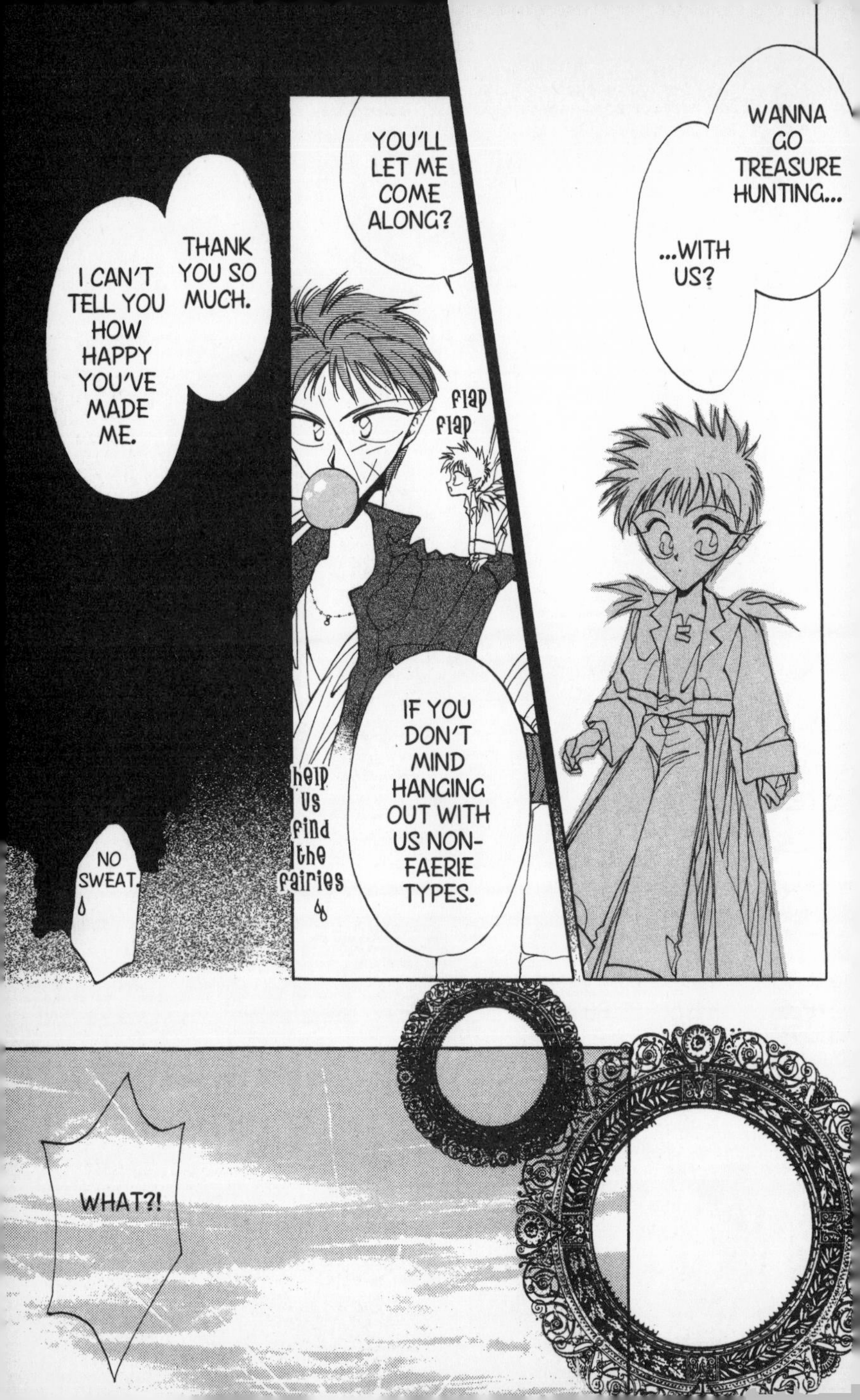
WANNA GO TREASURE HUNTING...
...WITH US?
YOU'LL LET ME COME ALONG?
flap flap
IF YOU DON'T MIND HANGING OUT WITH US NON-FAERIE TYPES.
help us find the fairies
THANK YOU SO MUCH.
I CAN'T TELL YOU HOW HAPPY YOU'VE MADE ME.
NO SWEAT.
WHAT?!

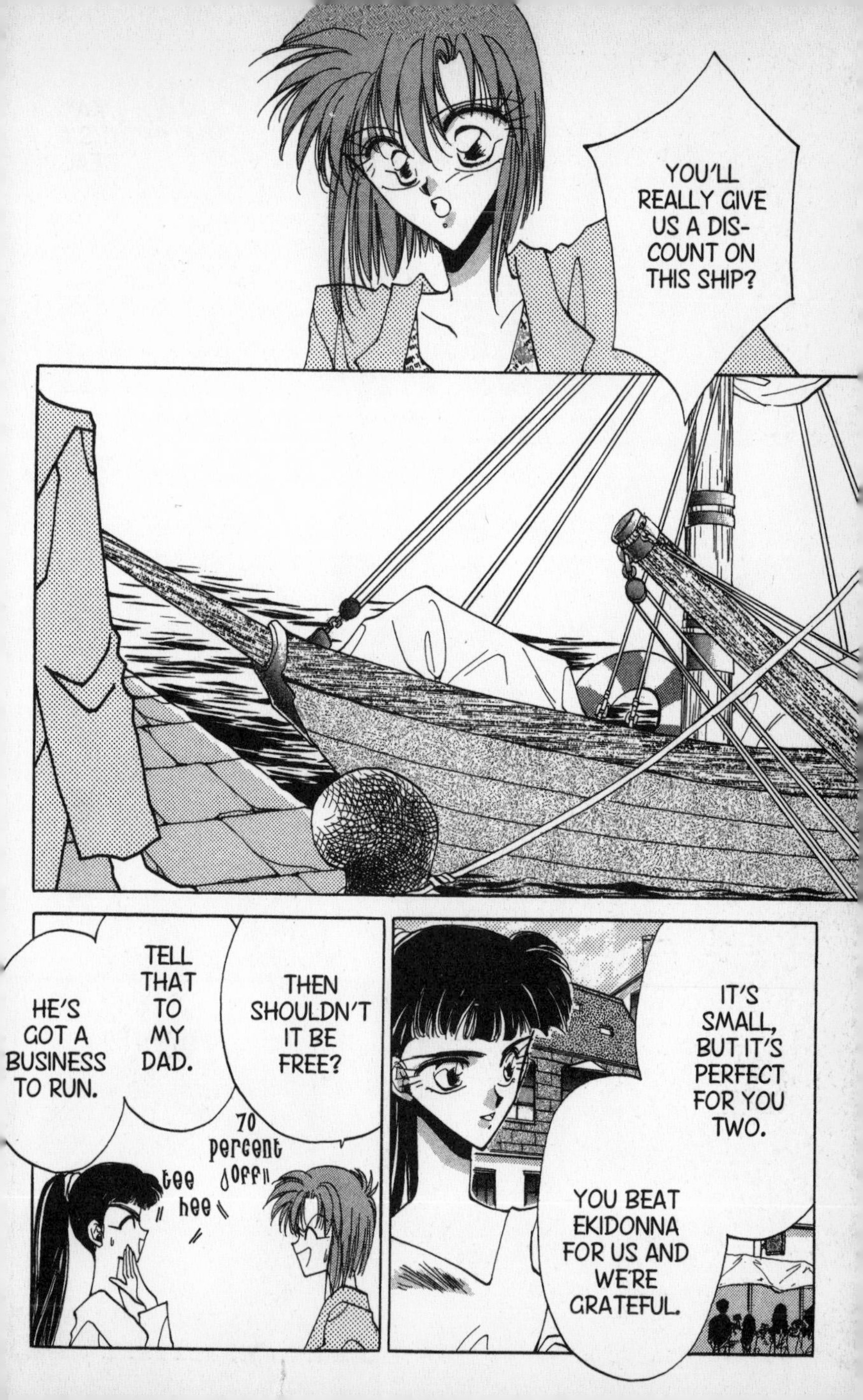
YOU'LL REALLY GIVE US A DIS-COUNT ON THIS SHIP?
IT'S SMALL, BUT IT'S PERFECT FOR YOU TWO.
YOU BEAT EKIDONNA FOR US AND WE'RE GRATEFUL.
THEN SHOULDN'T IT BE FREE?
TELL THAT TO MY DAD.
HE'S GOT A BUSINESS TO RUN.
70 percent off
tee hee

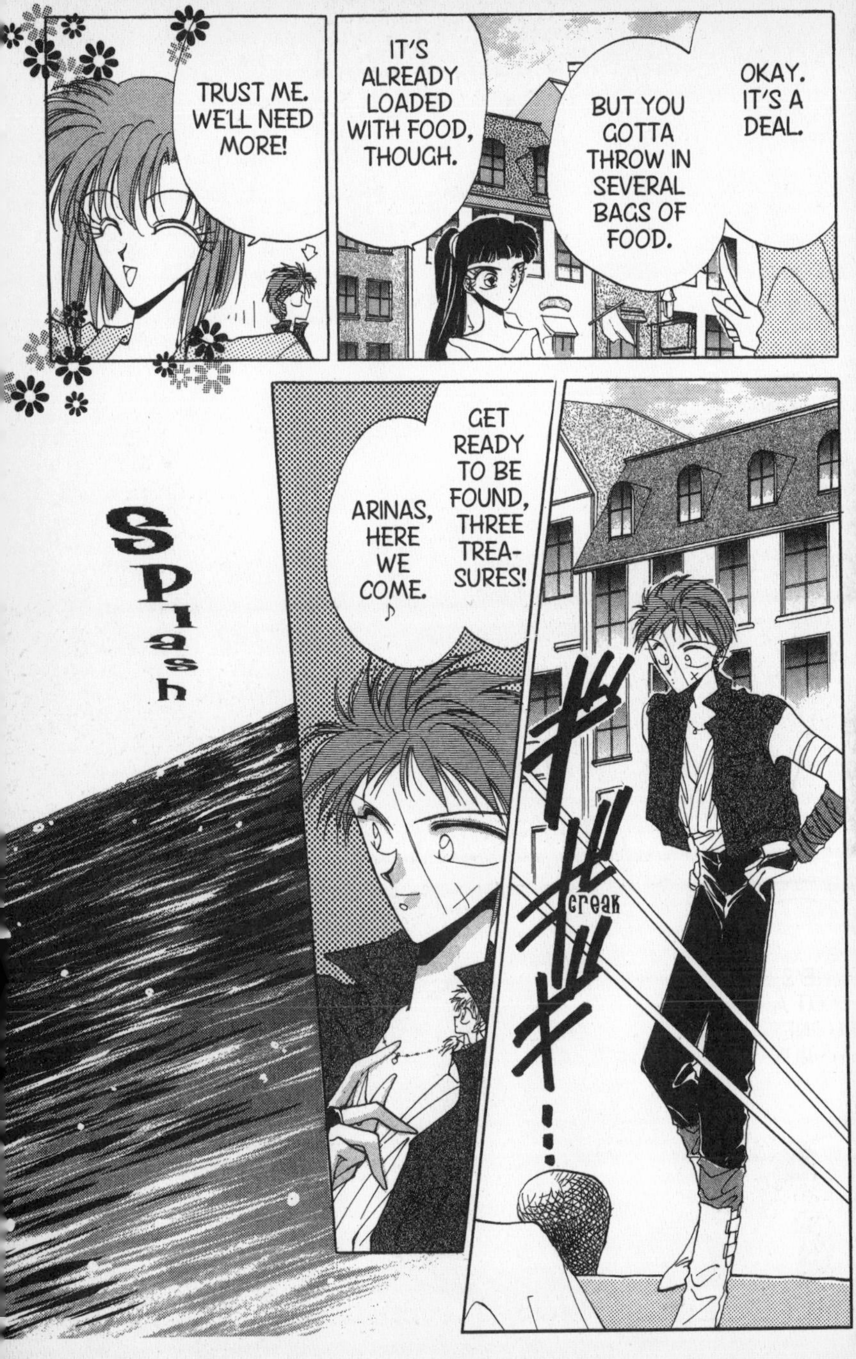
OKAY. IT'S A DEAL.
BUT YOU GOTTA THROW IN SEVERAL BAGS OF FOOD.
IT'S ALREADY LOADED WITH FOOD, THOUGH.
TRUST ME. WE'LL NEED MORE!
creak
GET READY TO BE FOUND, THREE TREASURES!
ARINAS, HERE WE COME. ♪
Splash

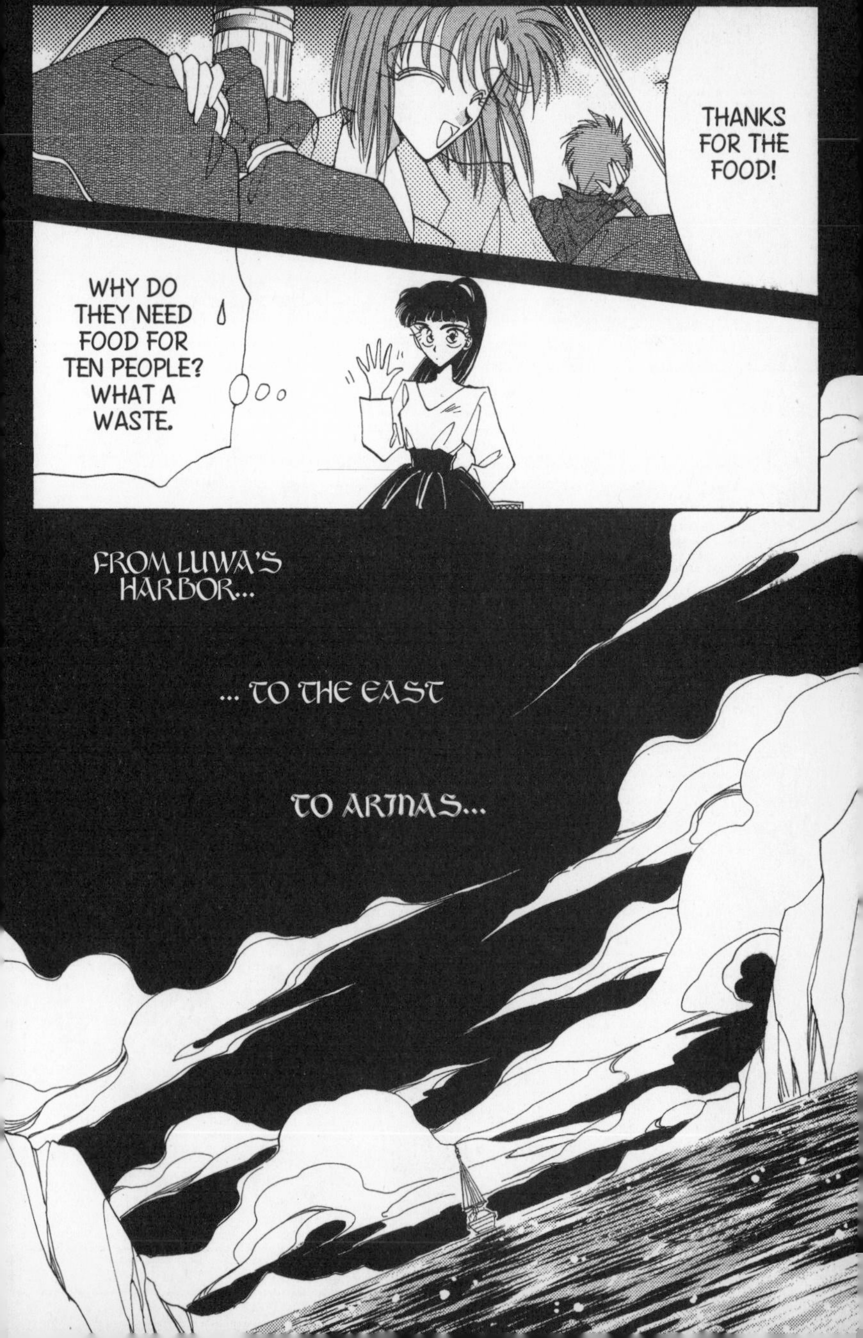
THANKS FOR THE FOOD!
WHY DO THEY NEED FOOD FOR TEN PEOPLE? WHAT A WASTE.
FROM LUWA'S HARBOR...
... TO THE EAST
TO ARINAS...

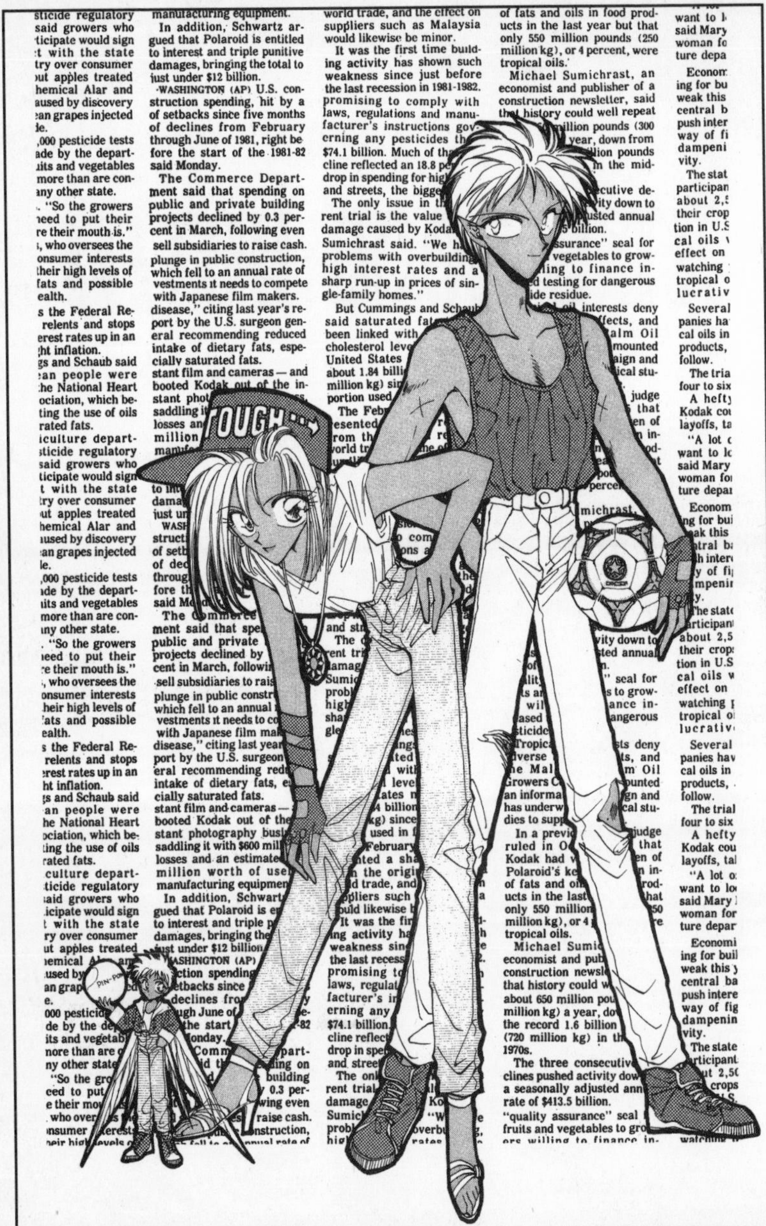
TOUGH
PIN-PON

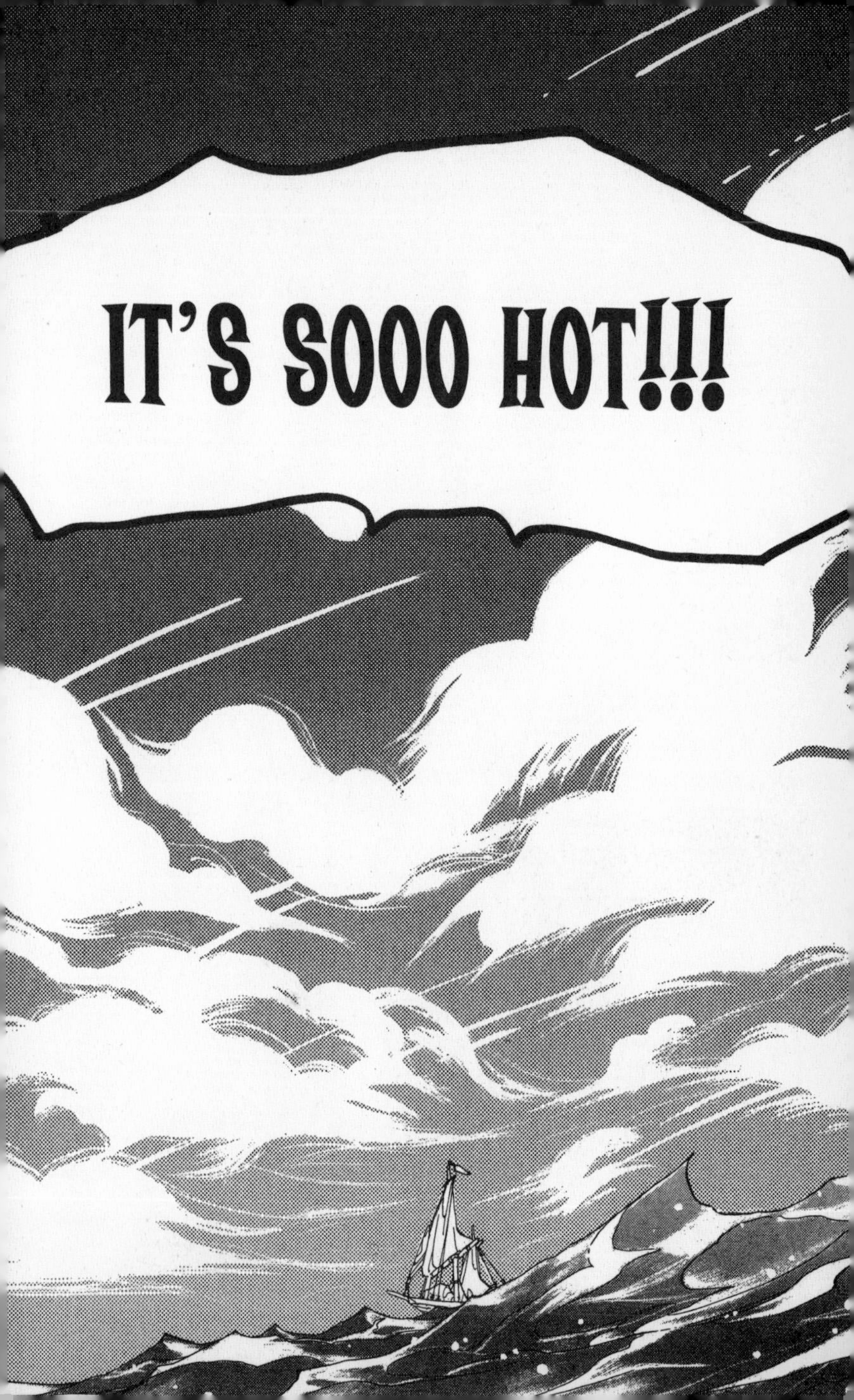
IT'S SOOO HOT!!!

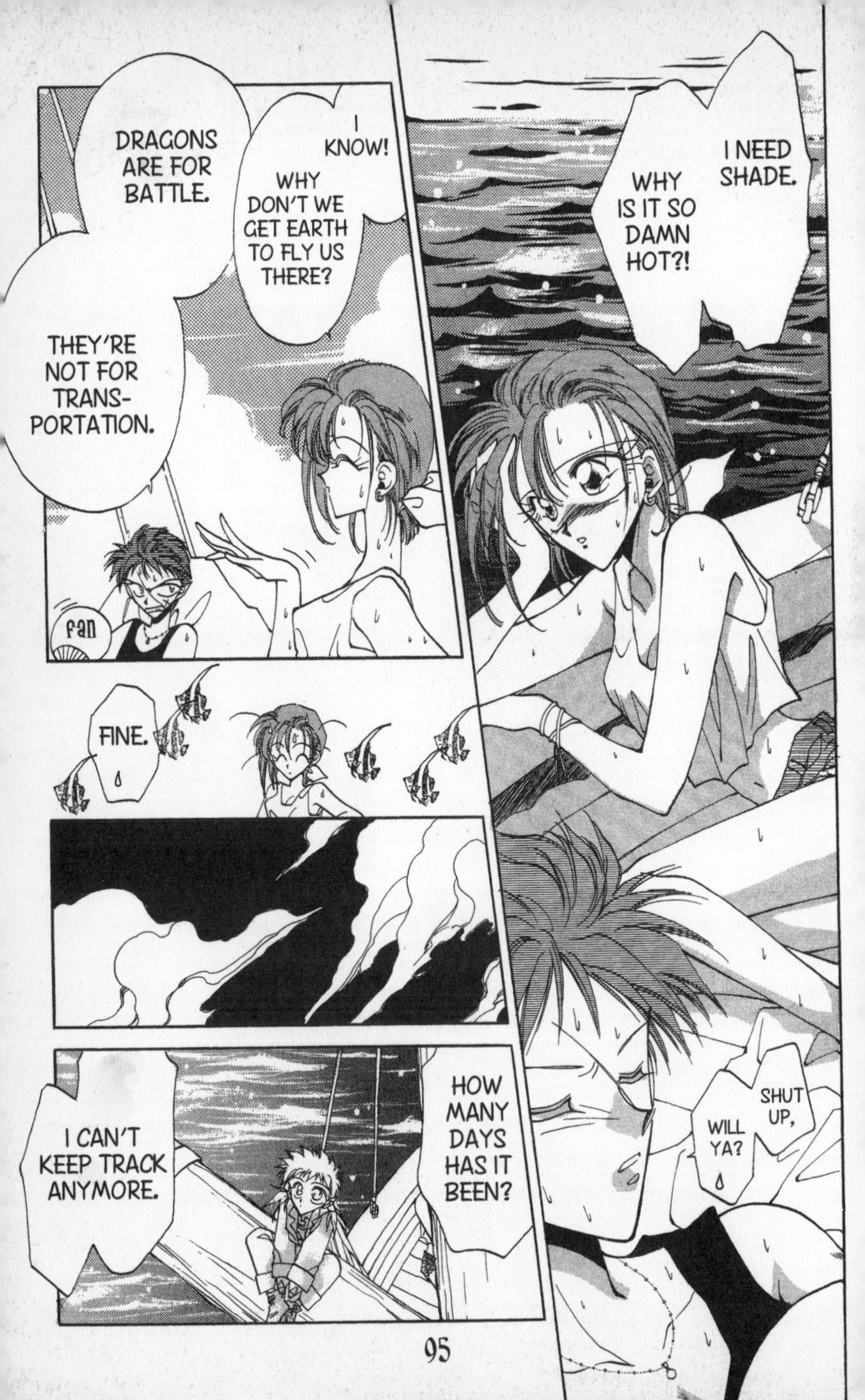
I NEED SHADE.
WHY IS IT SO DAMN HOT?!
SHUT UP, WILL YA?
I KNOW!
WHY DON'T WE GET EARTH TO FLY US THERE?
DRAGONS ARE FOR BATTLE.
THEY'RE NOT FOR TRANS-PORTATION.
fan
FINE.
HOW MANY DAYS HAS IT BEEN?
I CAN'T KEEP TRACK ANYMORE.

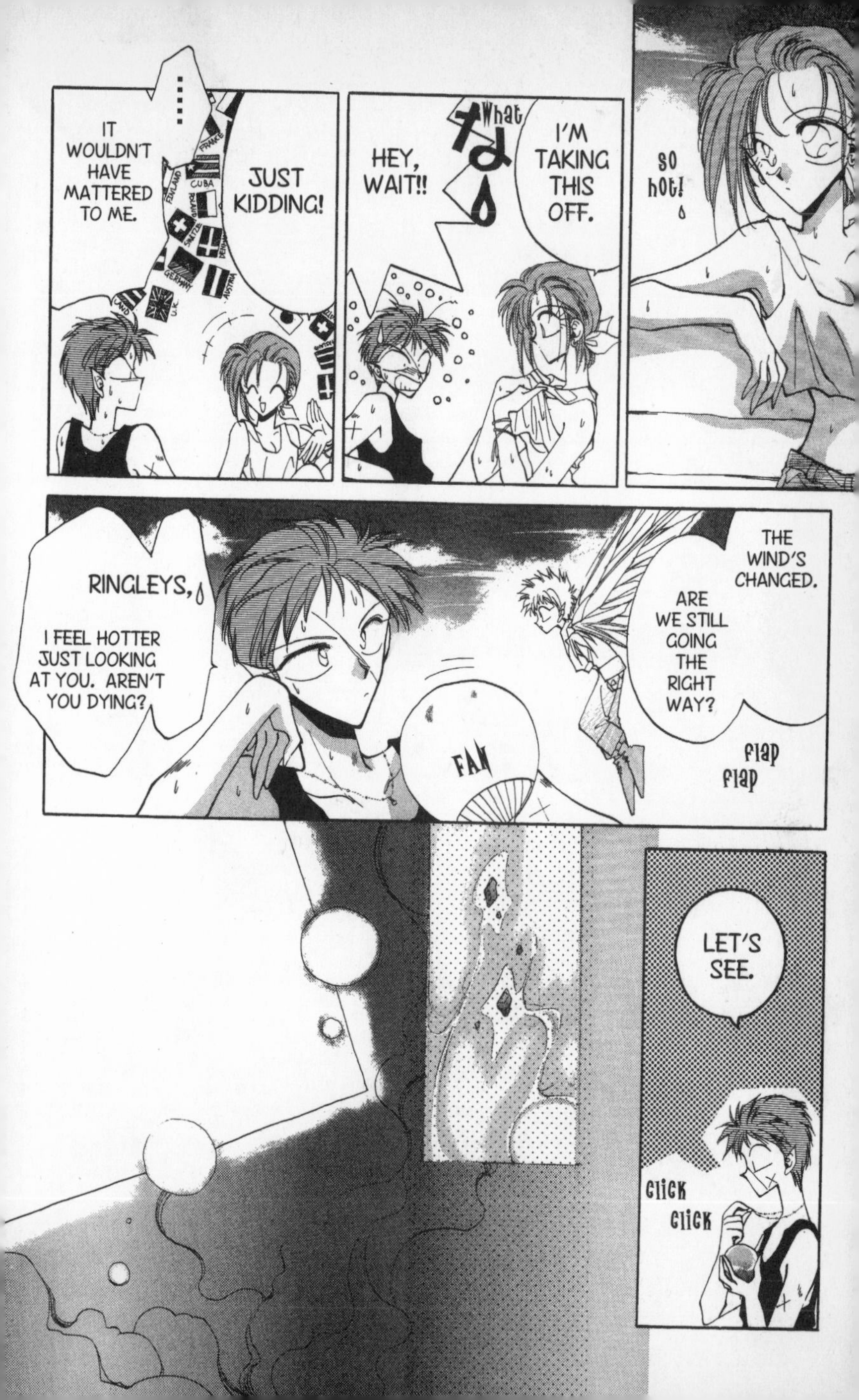
so hot!
I'M TAKING THIS OFF.
What
HEY, WAIT!!
JUST KIDDING!
.....
IT WOULDN'T HAVE MATTERED TO ME.
THE WIND'S CHANGED.
ARE WE STILL GOING THE RIGHT WAY?
flap flap
FAN
RINGLEYS,
I FEEL HOTTER JUST LOOKING AT YOU. AREN'T YOU DYING?
LET'S SEE.
click click

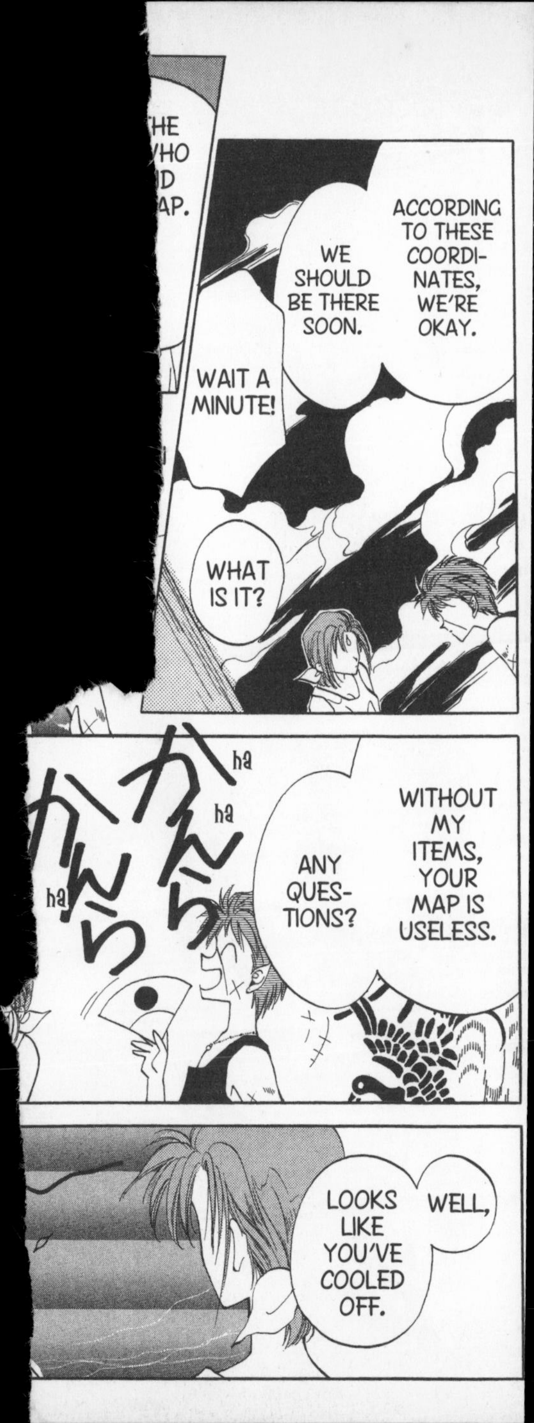
ACCORDING TO THESE COORDI-NATES, WE'RE OKAY.
WE SHOULD BE THERE SOON.
WAIT A MINUTE!
WHAT IS IT?
WITHOUT MY ITEMS, YOUR MAP IS USELESS.
ANY QUES-TIONS?
かんら
ha
ha
かんら
ha
WELL,
LOOKS LIKE YOU'VE COOLED OFF.

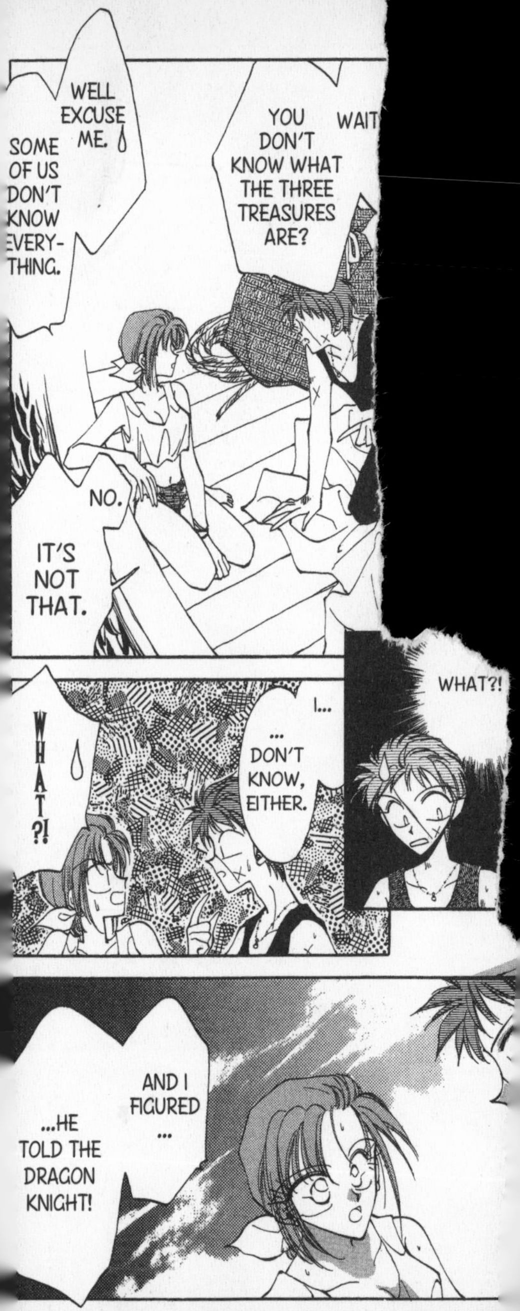
WAIT
YOU DON'T KNOW WHAT THE THREE TREASURES ARE?
WELL EXCUSE ME.
SOME OF US DON'T KNOW EVERY-THING.
NO.
IT'S NOT THAT.
WHAT?!
I...
...DON'T KNOW, EITHER.
WHAT?!
AND I FIGURED...
...HE TOLD THE DRAGON KNIGHT!

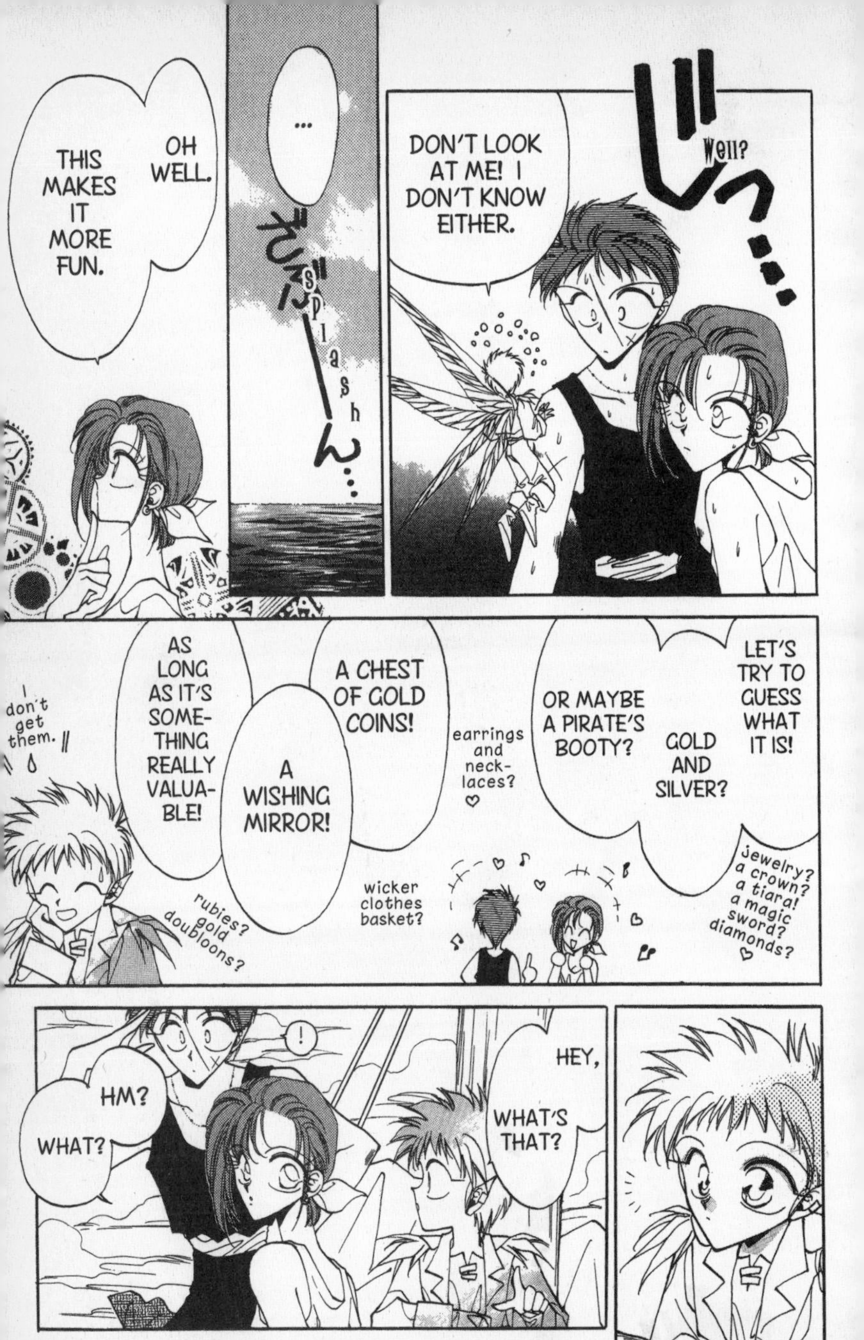
じっ
Well?
DON'T LOOK AT ME! I DON'T KNOW EITHER.
...
splash
OH WELL.
THIS MAKES IT MORE FUN.
LET'S TRY TO GUESS WHAT IT IS!
GOLD AND SILVER?
jewelry? a crown? a tiara! a magic sword? diamonds?
OR MAYBE A PIRATE'S BOOTY?
earrings and necklaces?
A CHEST OF GOLD COINS!
wicker clothes basket?
A WISHING MIRROR!
AS LONG AS IT'S SOMETHING REALLY VALUABLE!
rubies? gold doubloons?
I don't get them.
HEY, WHAT'S THAT?
!
HM?
WHAT?

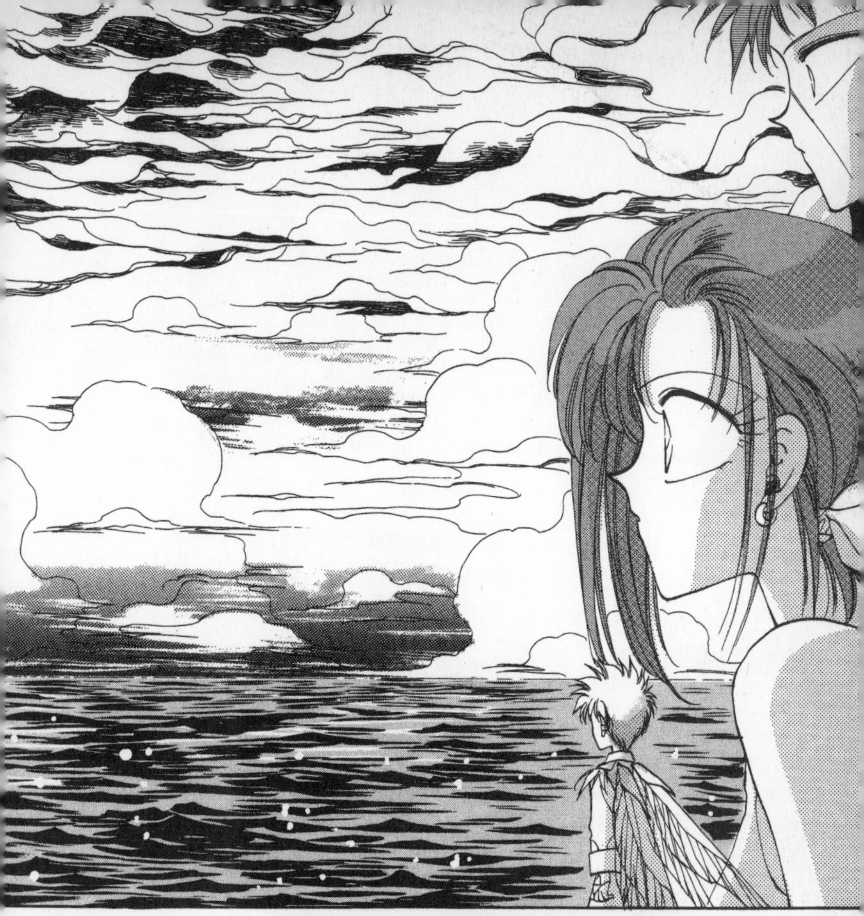

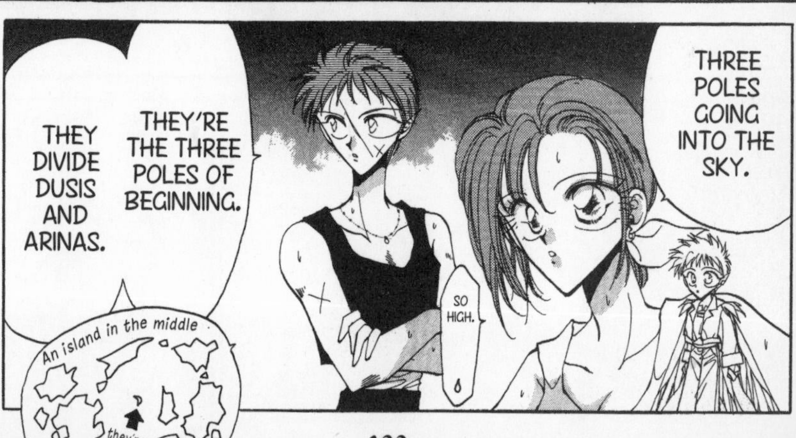
THREE POLES GOING INTO THE SKY.
SO HIGH.
THEY'RE THE THREE POLES OF BEGINNING.
THEY DIVIDE DUSIS AND ARINAS.
An island in the middle
they're here

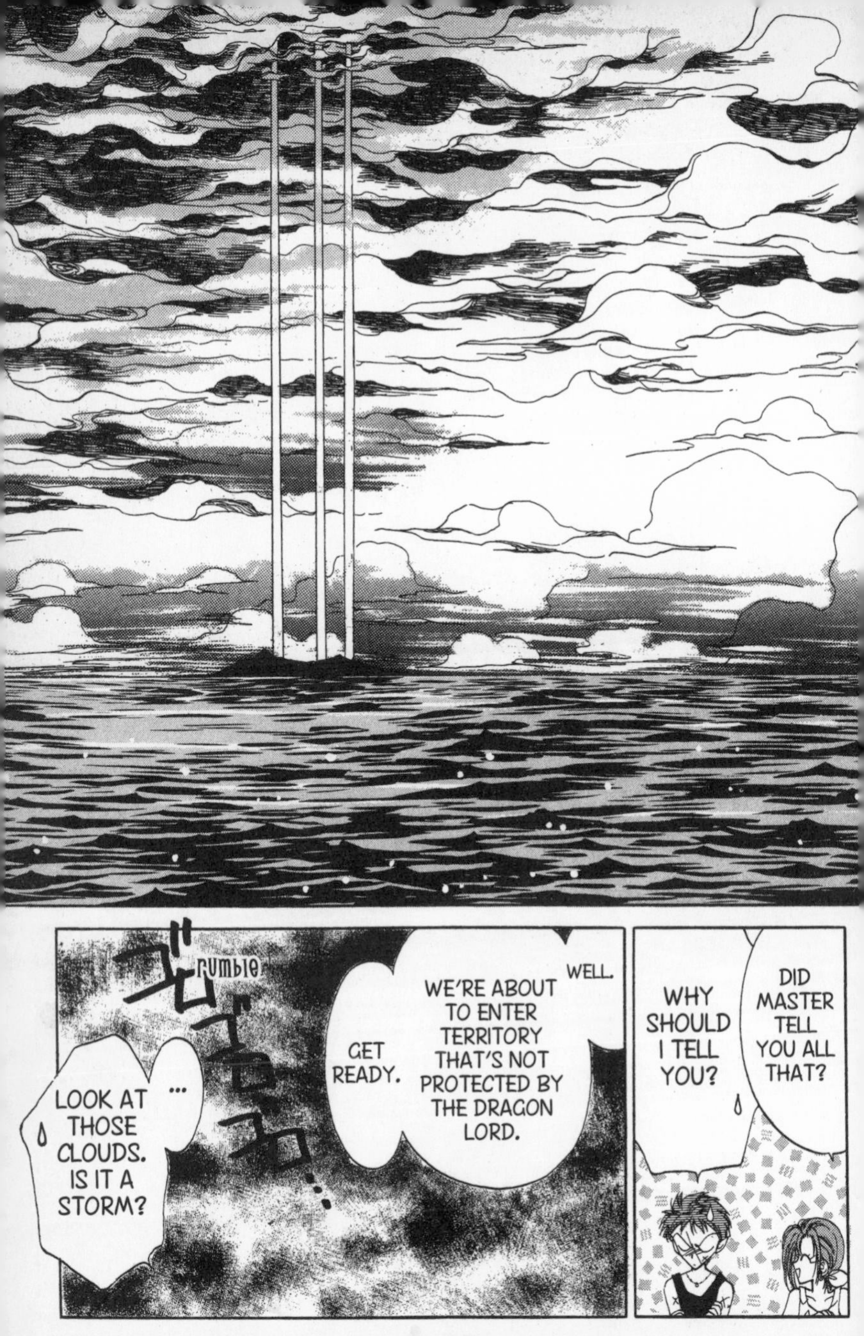
DID MASTER TELL YOU ALL THAT?
WHY SHOULD I TELL YOU?
WELL.
WE'RE ABOUT TO ENTER TERRITORY THAT'S NOT PROTECTED BY THE DRAGON LORD.
GET READY.
rumble
...
LOOK AT THOSE CLOUDS. IS IT A STORM?

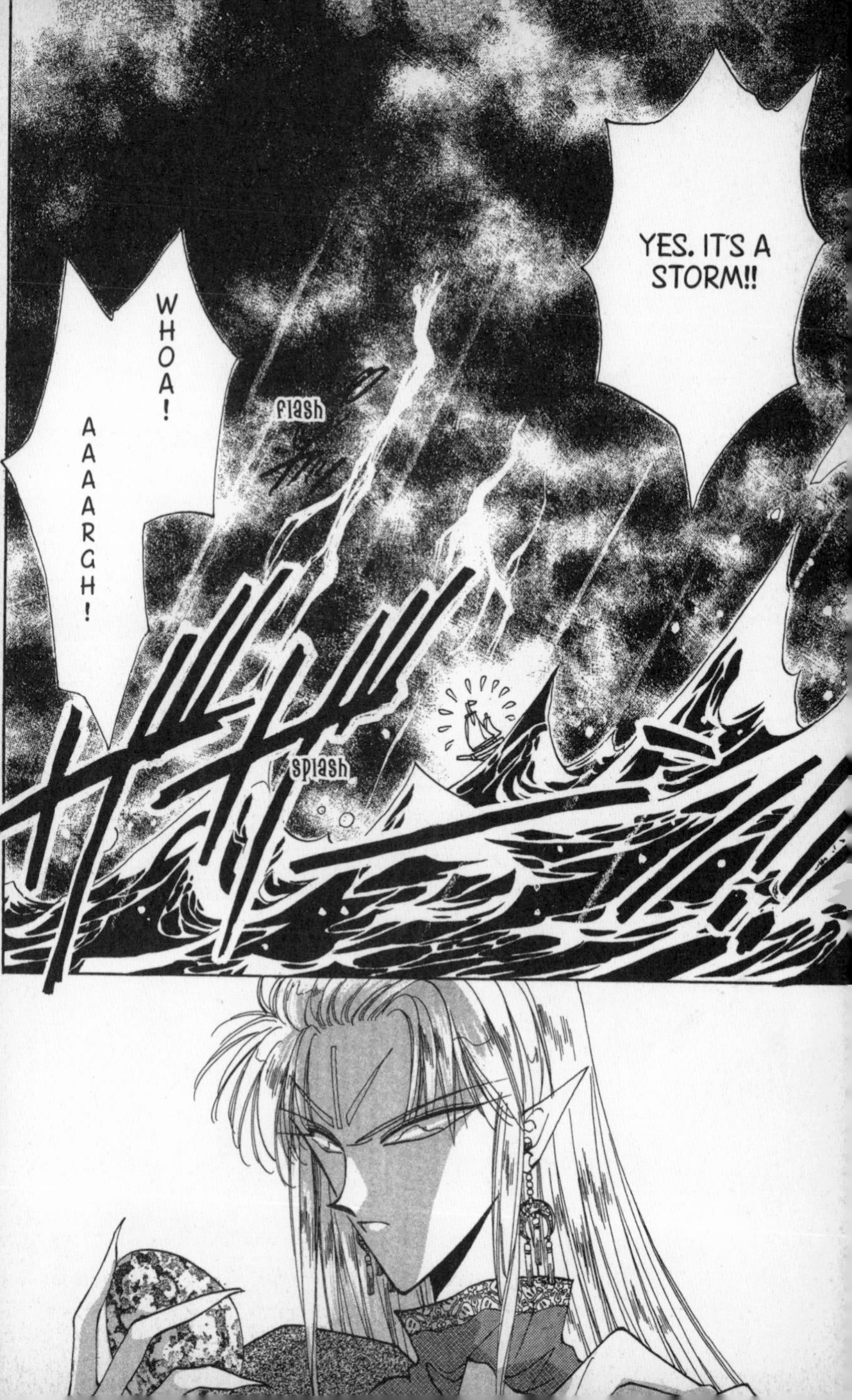
YES. IT'S A STORM!!
WHOA!
AAAAARGH!
flash
splash

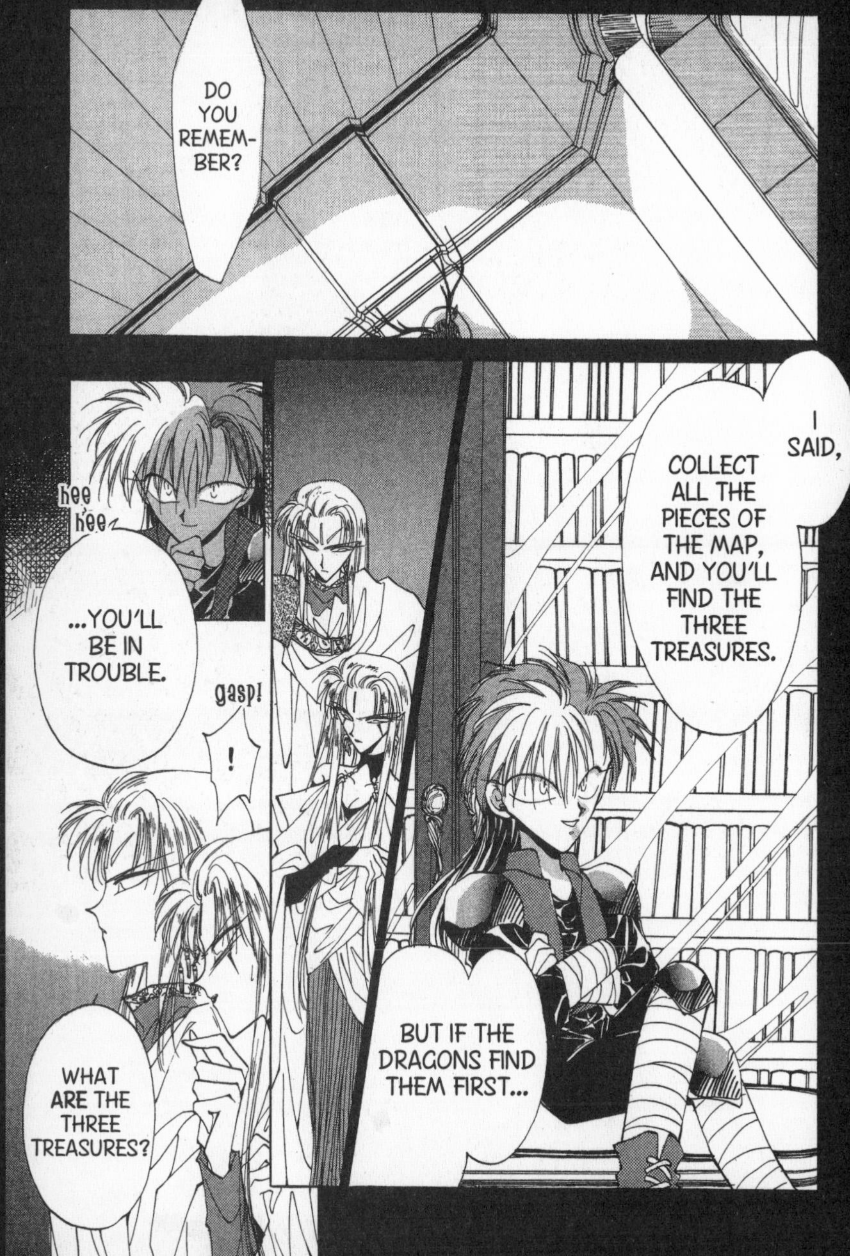
DO YOU REMEMBER?
I SAID, COLLECT ALL THE PIECES OF THE MAP, AND YOU'LL FIND THE THREE TREASURES.
BUT IF THE DRAGONS FIND THEM FIRST...
hee hee
...YOU'LL BE IN TROUBLE.
gasp!
!
WHAT ARE THE THREE TREASURES?

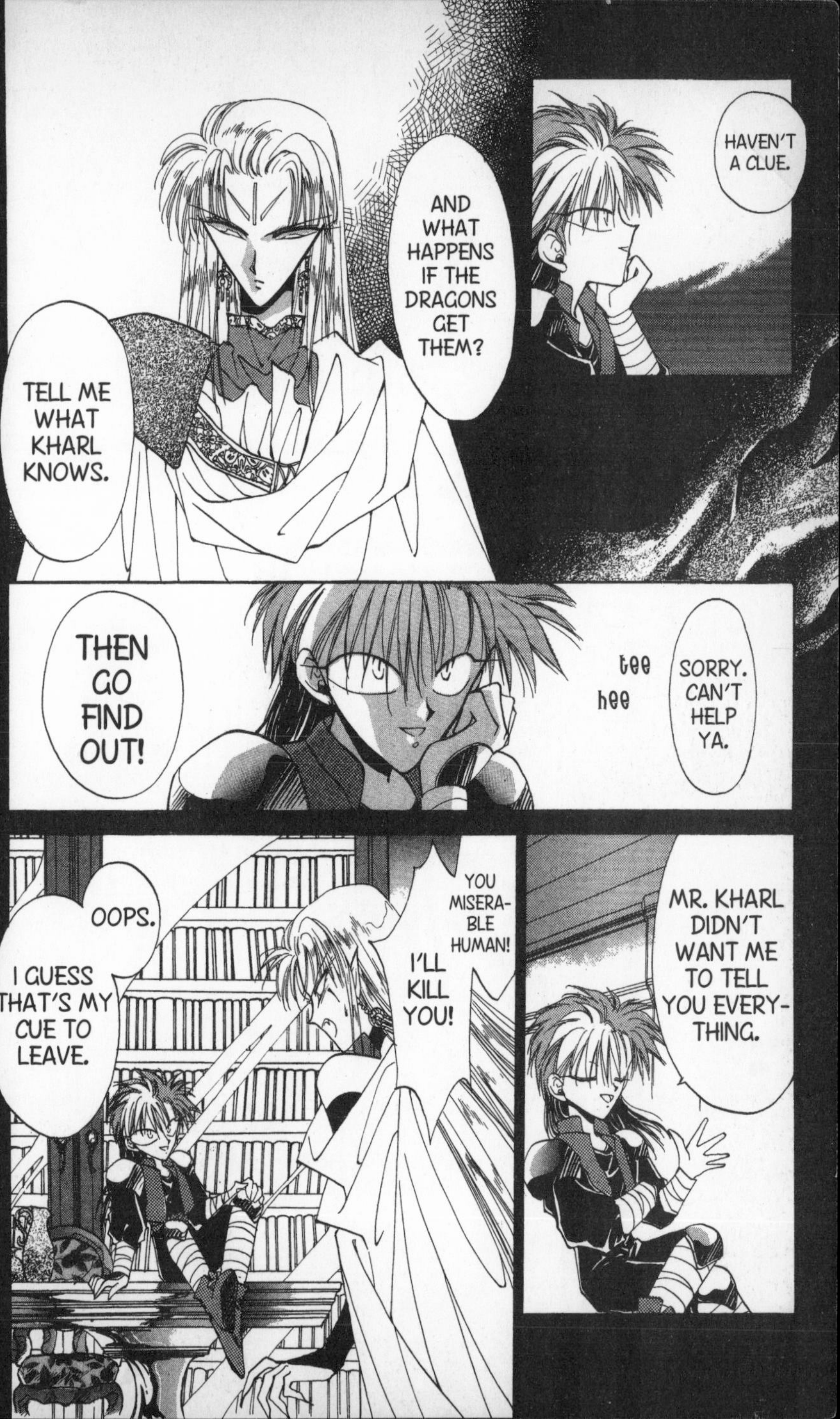
AND WHAT HAPPENS IF THE DRAGONS GET THEM?
HAVEN'T A CLUE.
TELL ME WHAT KHARL KNOWS.
SORRY. CAN'T HELP YA.
tee hee
THEN GO FIND OUT!
MR. KHARL DIDN'T WANT ME TO TELL YOU EVERY-THING.
YOU MISERA-BLE HUMAN!
I'LL KILL YOU!
OOPS.
I GUESS THAT'S MY CUE TO LEAVE.

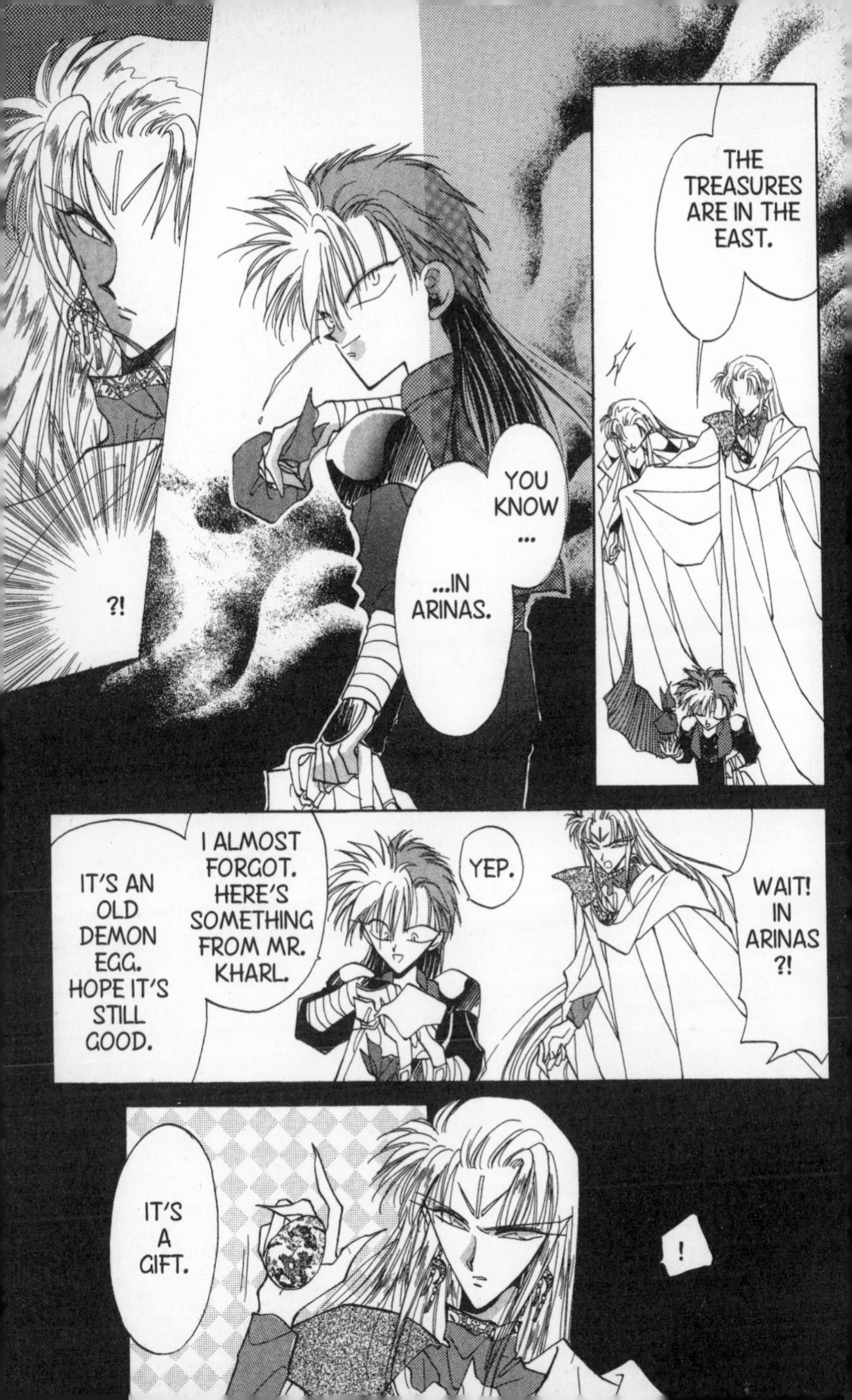
THE TREASURES ARE IN THE EAST.
YOU KNOW ...
...IN ARINAS.
?!
WAIT! IN ARINAS ?!
YEP.
I ALMOST FORGOT. HERE'S SOMETHING FROM MR. KHARL.
IT'S AN OLD DEMON EGG. HOPE IT'S STILL GOOD.
!
IT'S A GIFT.

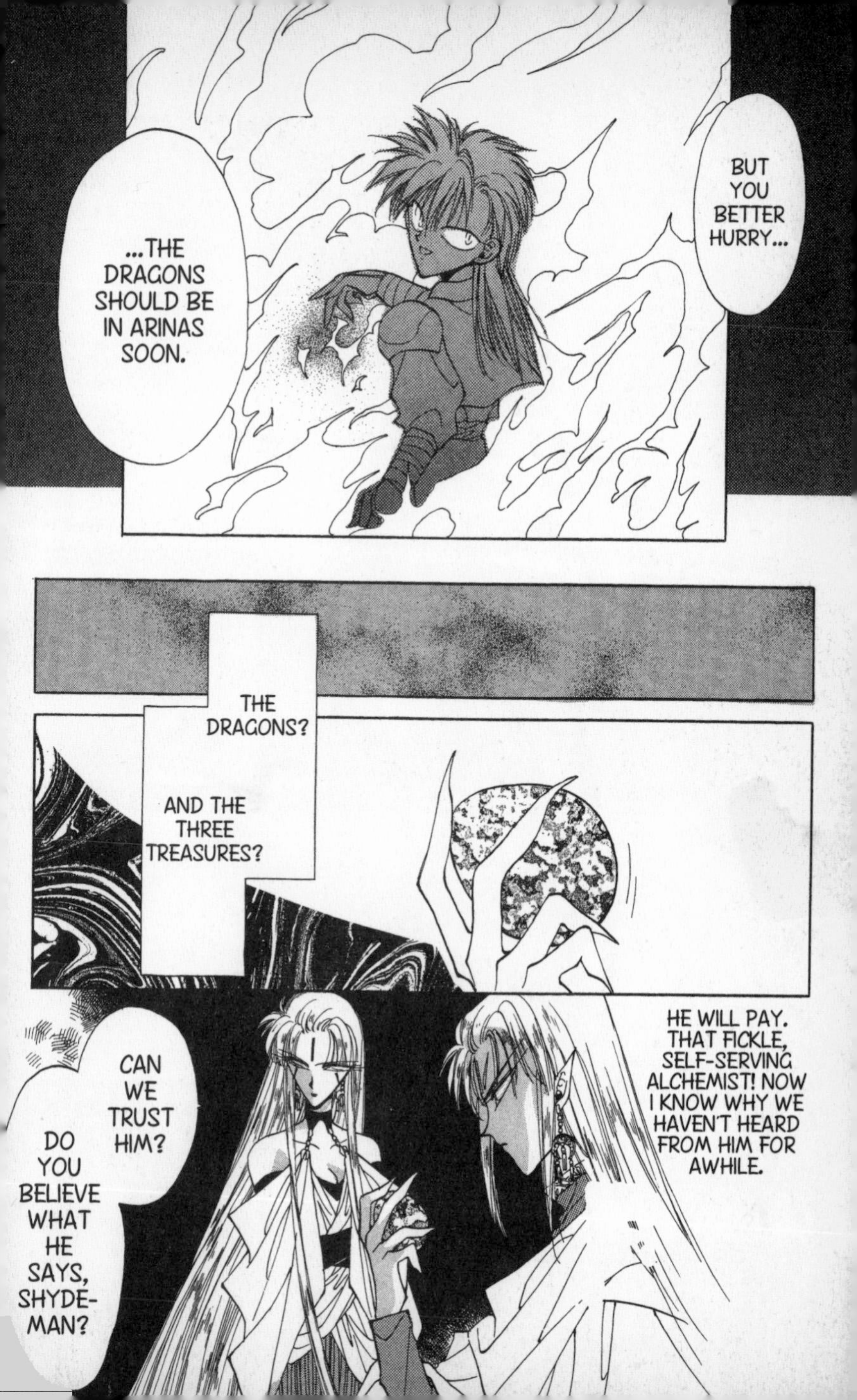
BUT YOU BETTER HURRY...
...THE DRAGONS SHOULD BE IN ARINAS SOON.
THE DRAGONS?
AND THE THREE TREASURES?
HE WILL PAY. THAT FICKLE, SELF-SERVING ALCHEMIST! NOW I KNOW WHY WE HAVEN'T HEARD FROM HIM FOR AWHILE.
CAN WE TRUST HIM?
DO YOU BELIEVE WHAT HE SAYS, SHYDE-MAN?

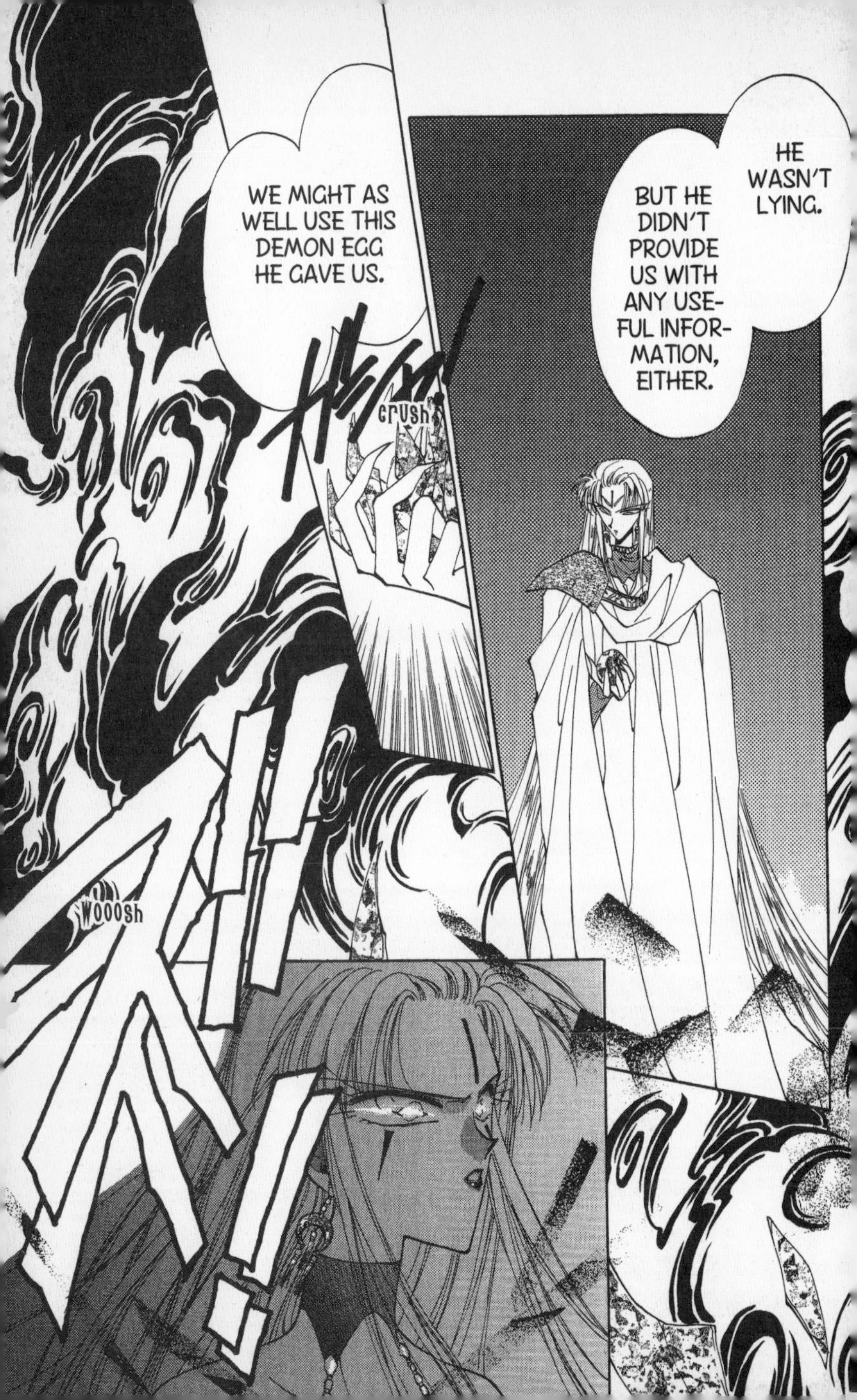
HE WASN'T LYING.
BUT HE DIDN'T PROVIDE US WITH ANY USE-FUL INFOR-MATION, EITHER.
WE MIGHT AS WELL USE THIS DEMON EGG HE GAVE US.
crush
Wooosh

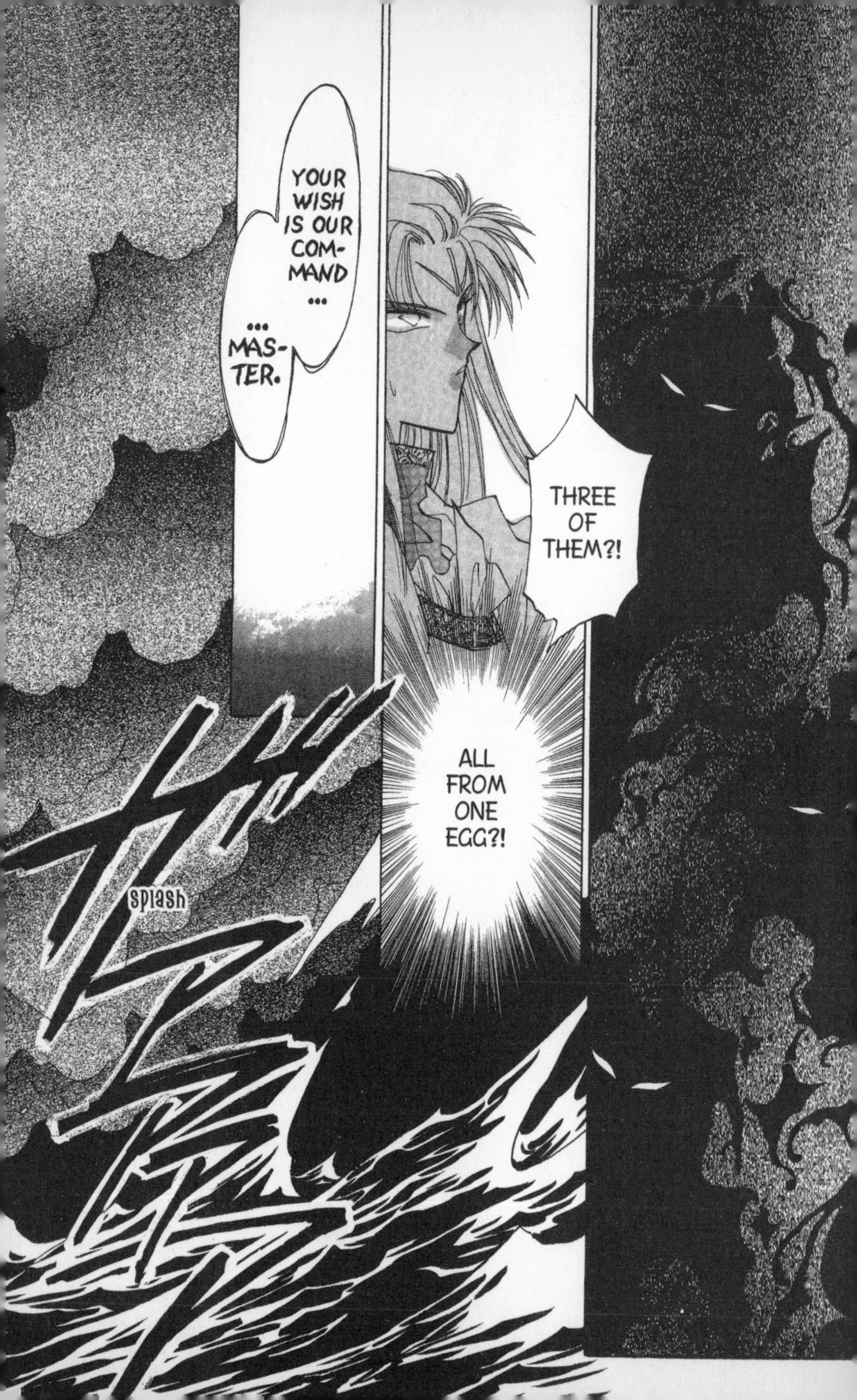
THREE OF THEM?!
ALL FROM ONE EGG?!
YOUR WISH IS OUR COMMAND ...
... MASTER.
splash

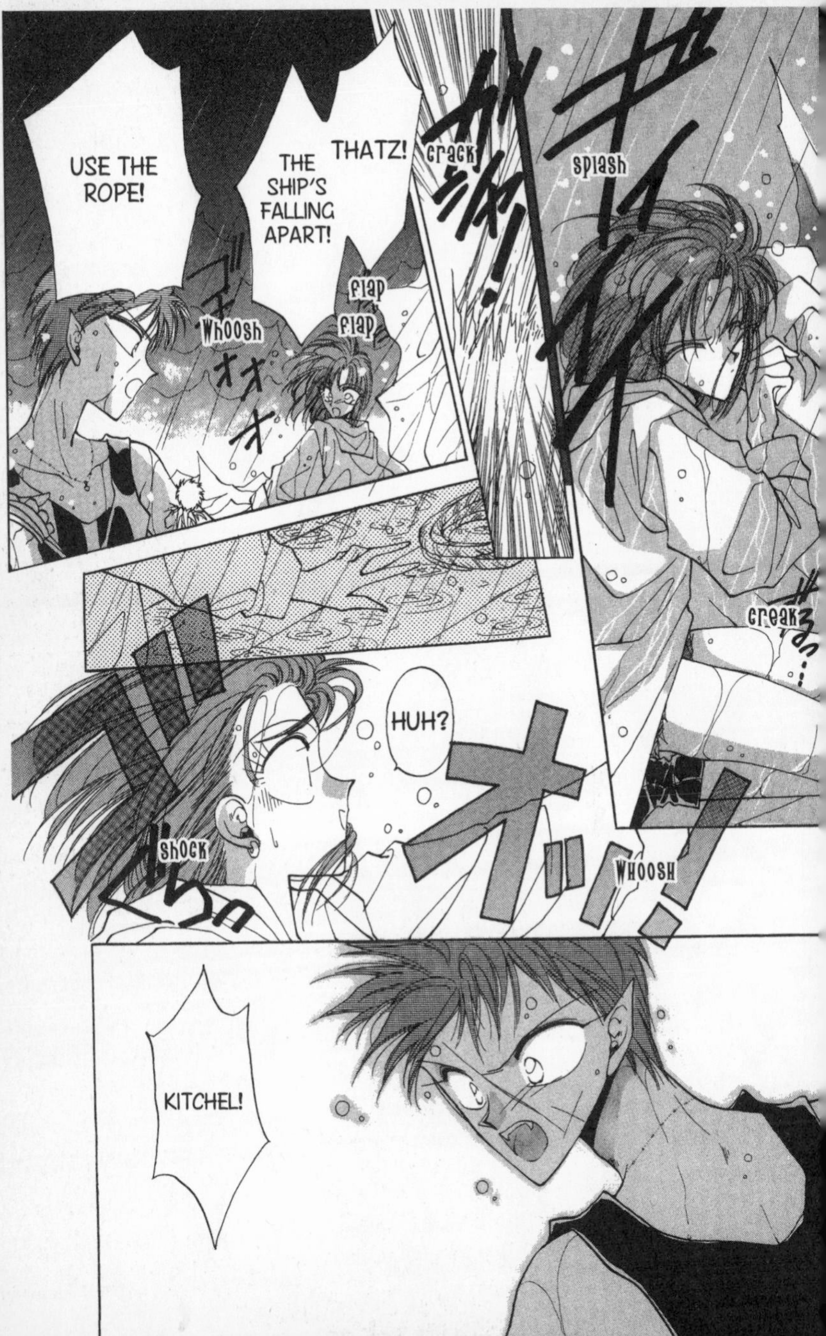
crack
splash
creak
THATZ!
THE SHIP'S FALLING APART!
USE THE ROPE!
flap flap
Whoosh
HUH?
WHOOSH
shock
KITCHEL!

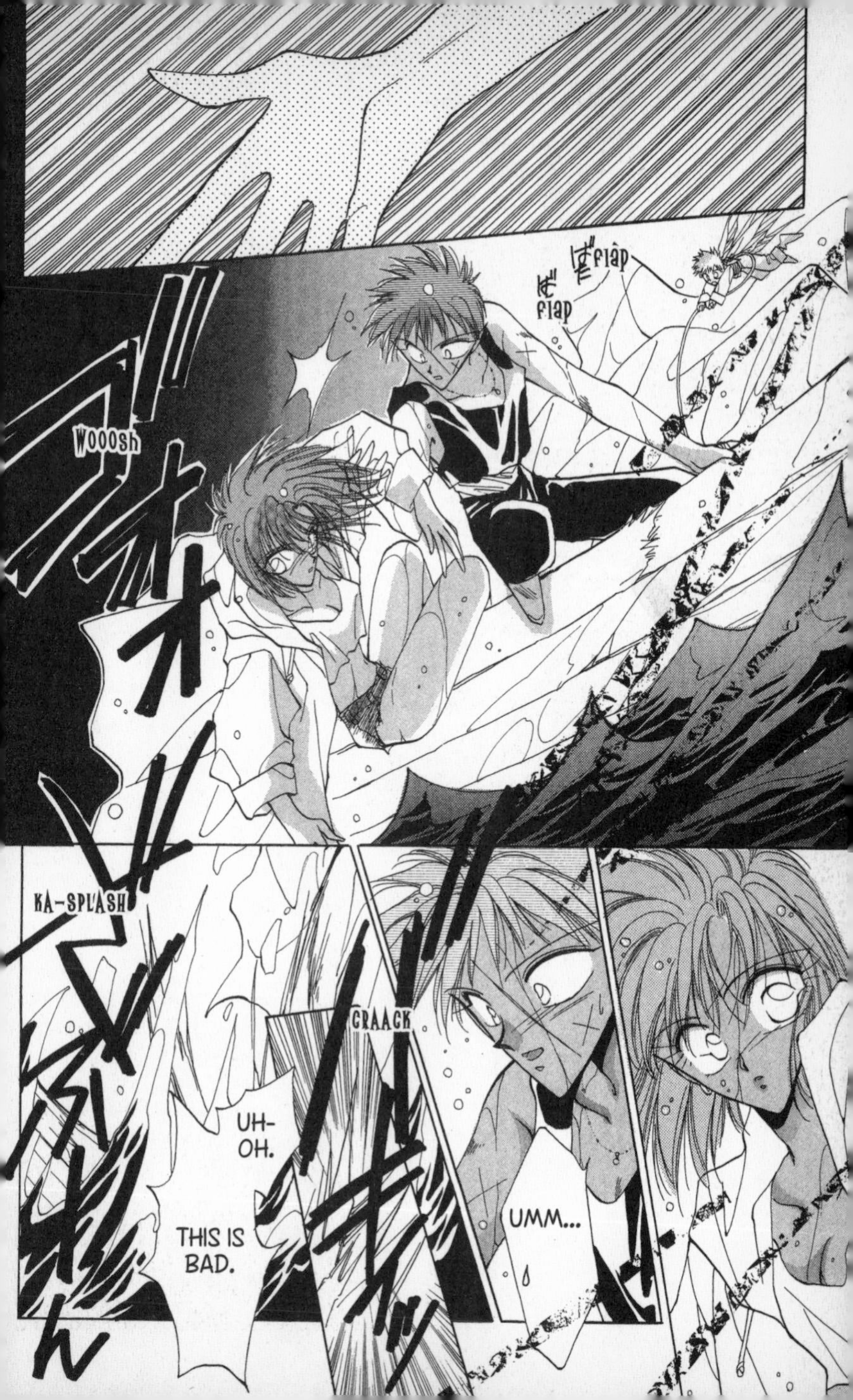
flap
flap
WOOOSH
UMM...
CRAACK
UH-OH.
THIS IS BAD.
KA-SPLASH

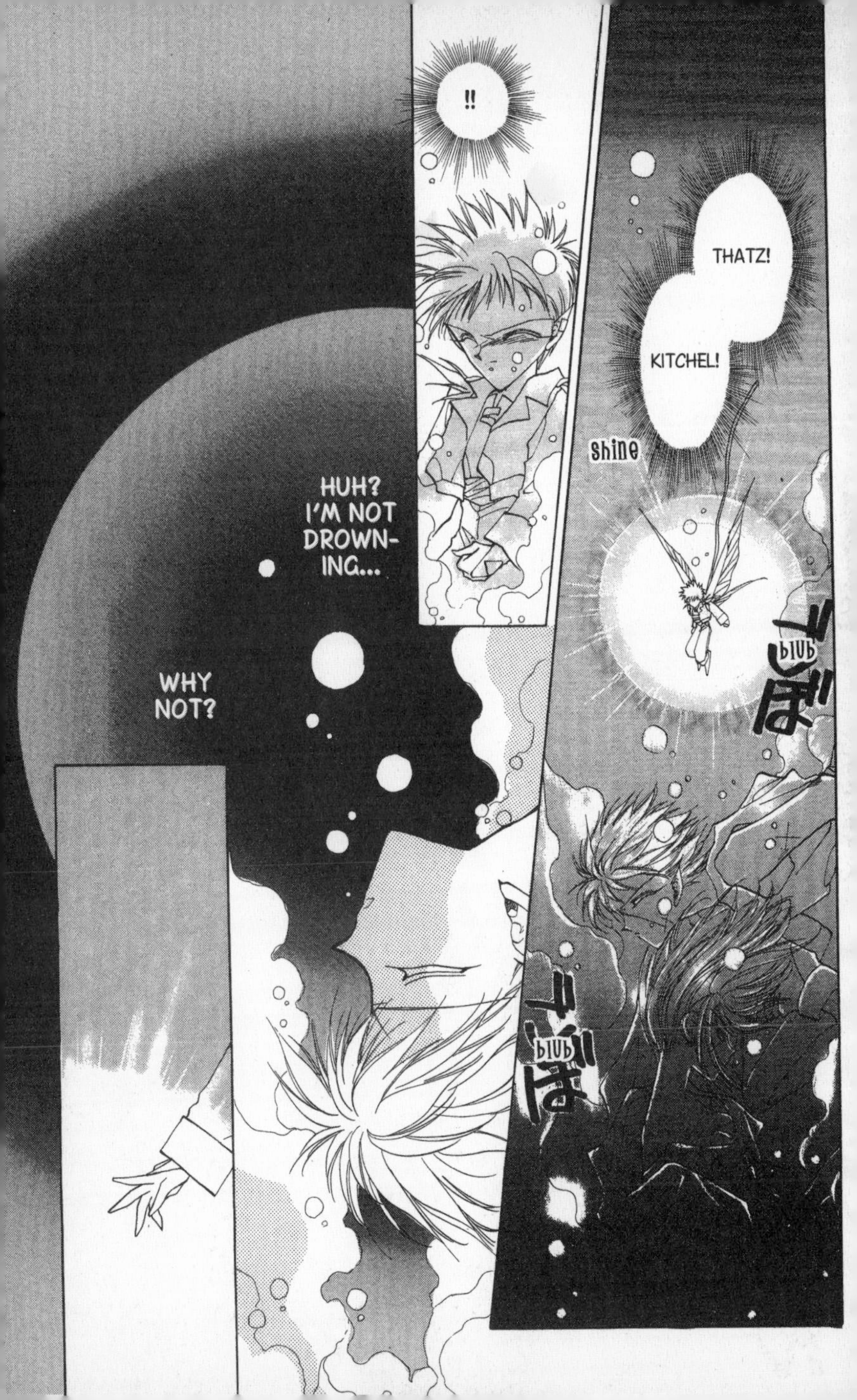
THATZ!
KITCHEL!
shine
blub
blub
!!
HUH? I'M NOT DROWNING...
WHY NOT?

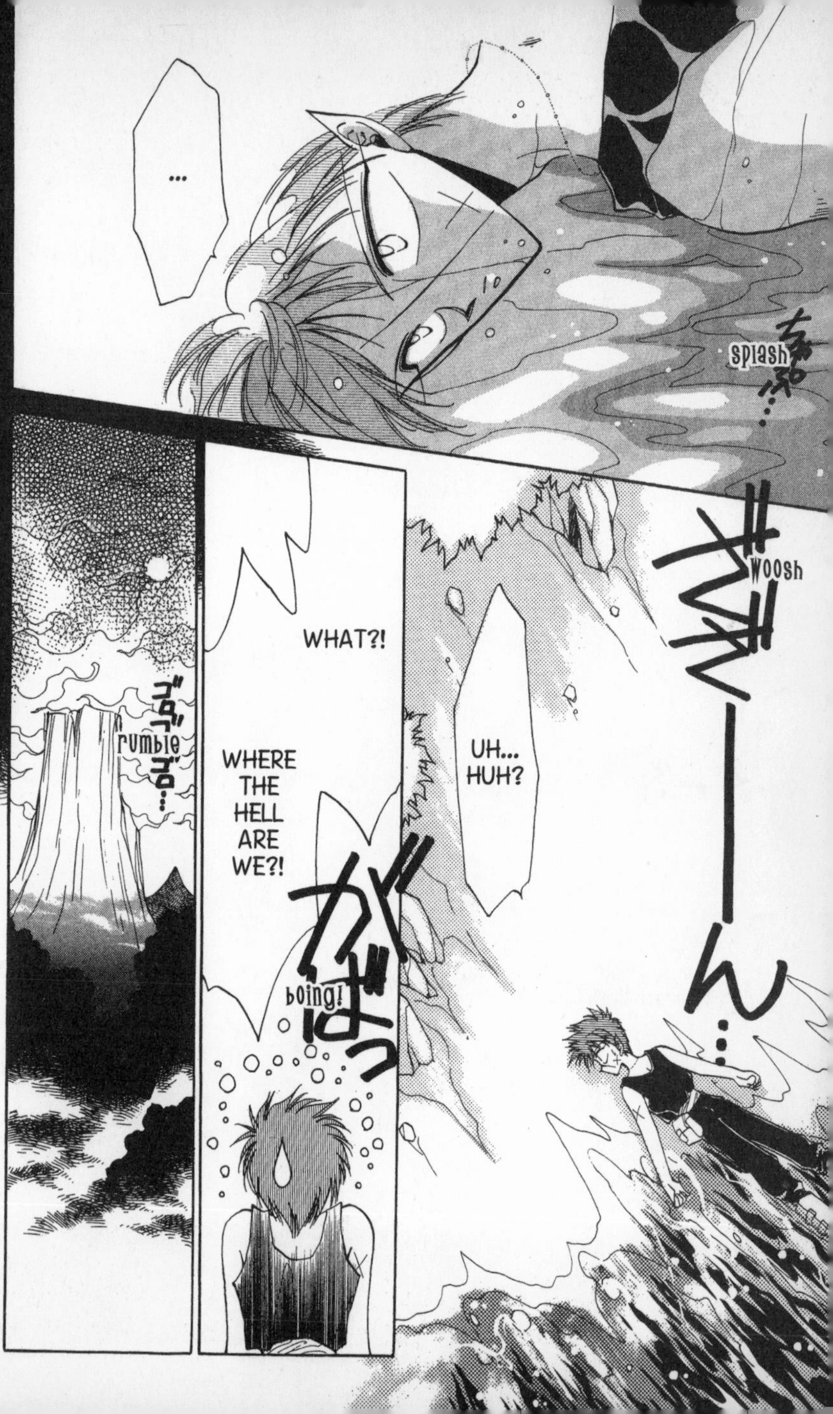
...
splash
woosh
UH... HUH?
WHAT?!
WHERE THE HELL ARE WE?!
boing!
rumble

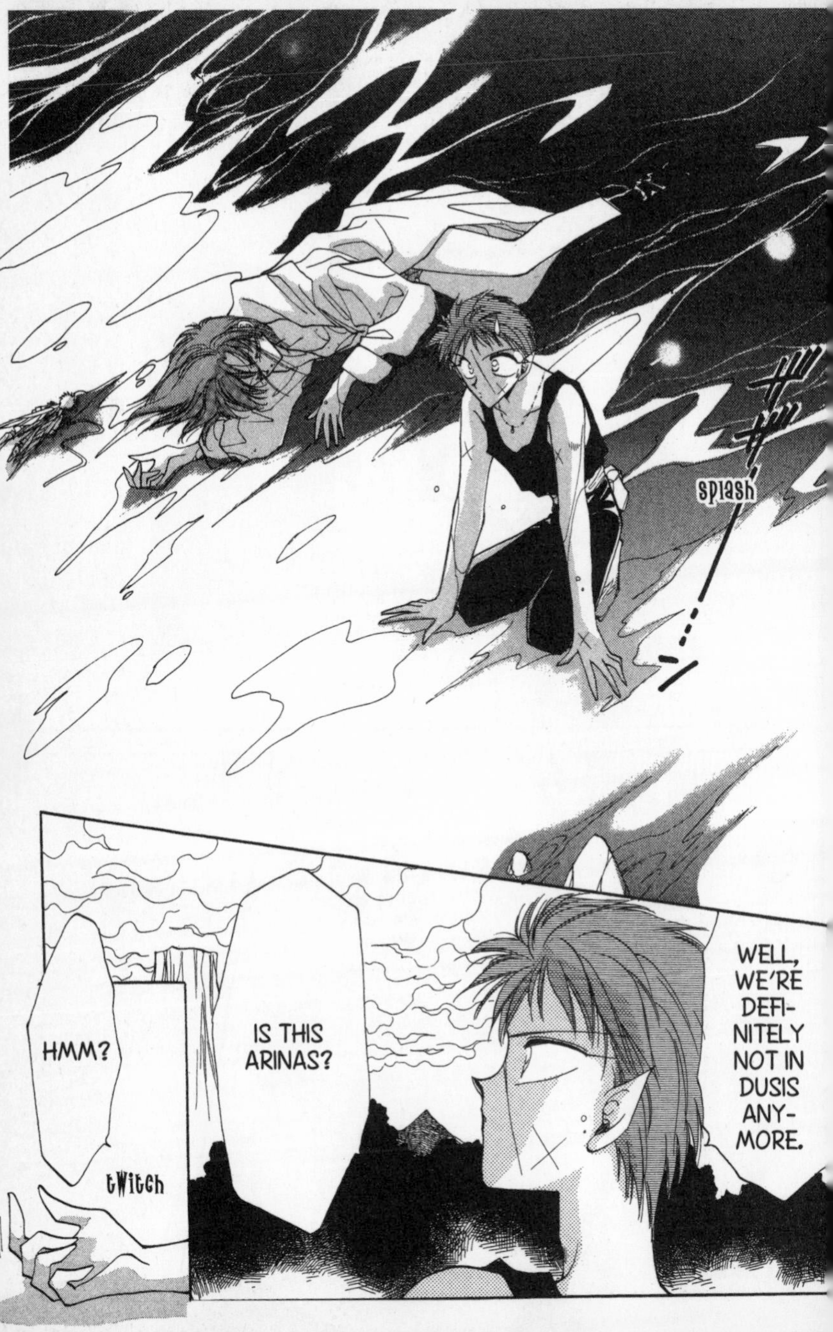
splash
WELL, WE'RE DEFINITELY NOT IN DUSIS ANYMORE.
IS THIS ARINAS?
HMM?
twitch

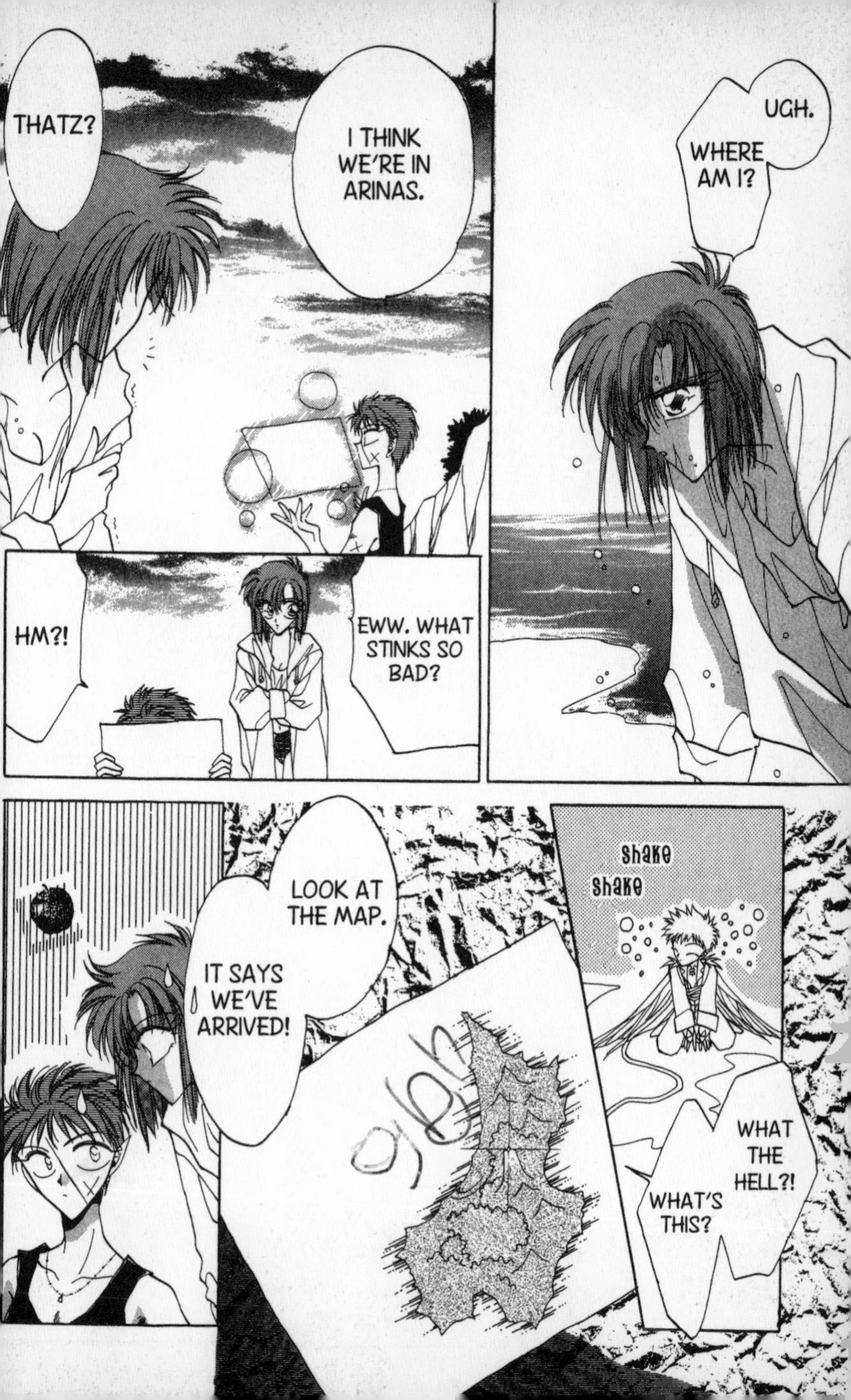
UGH.
WHERE AM I?
I THINK WE'RE IN ARINAS.
THATZ?
EWW. WHAT STINKS SO BAD?
HM?!
Shake
Shake
WHAT THE HELL?!
WHAT'S THIS?
LOOK AT THE MAP.
IT SAYS WE'VE ARRIVED!

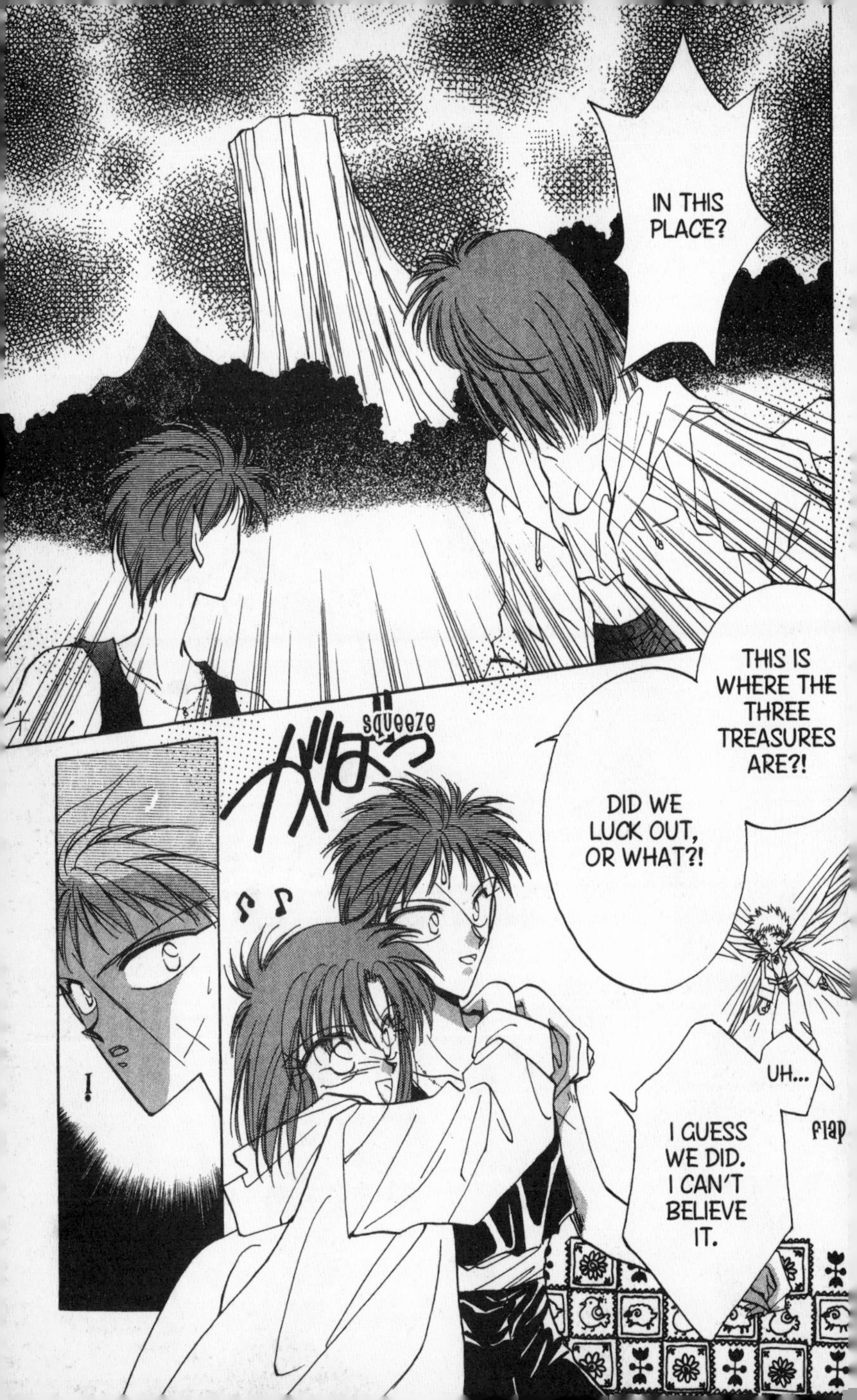
IN THIS PLACE?
THIS IS WHERE THE THREE TREASURES ARE?!
がばっ
squeeze
DID WE LUCK OUT, OR WHAT?!
UH...
I GUESS WE DID. I CAN'T BELIEVE IT.
flap
!

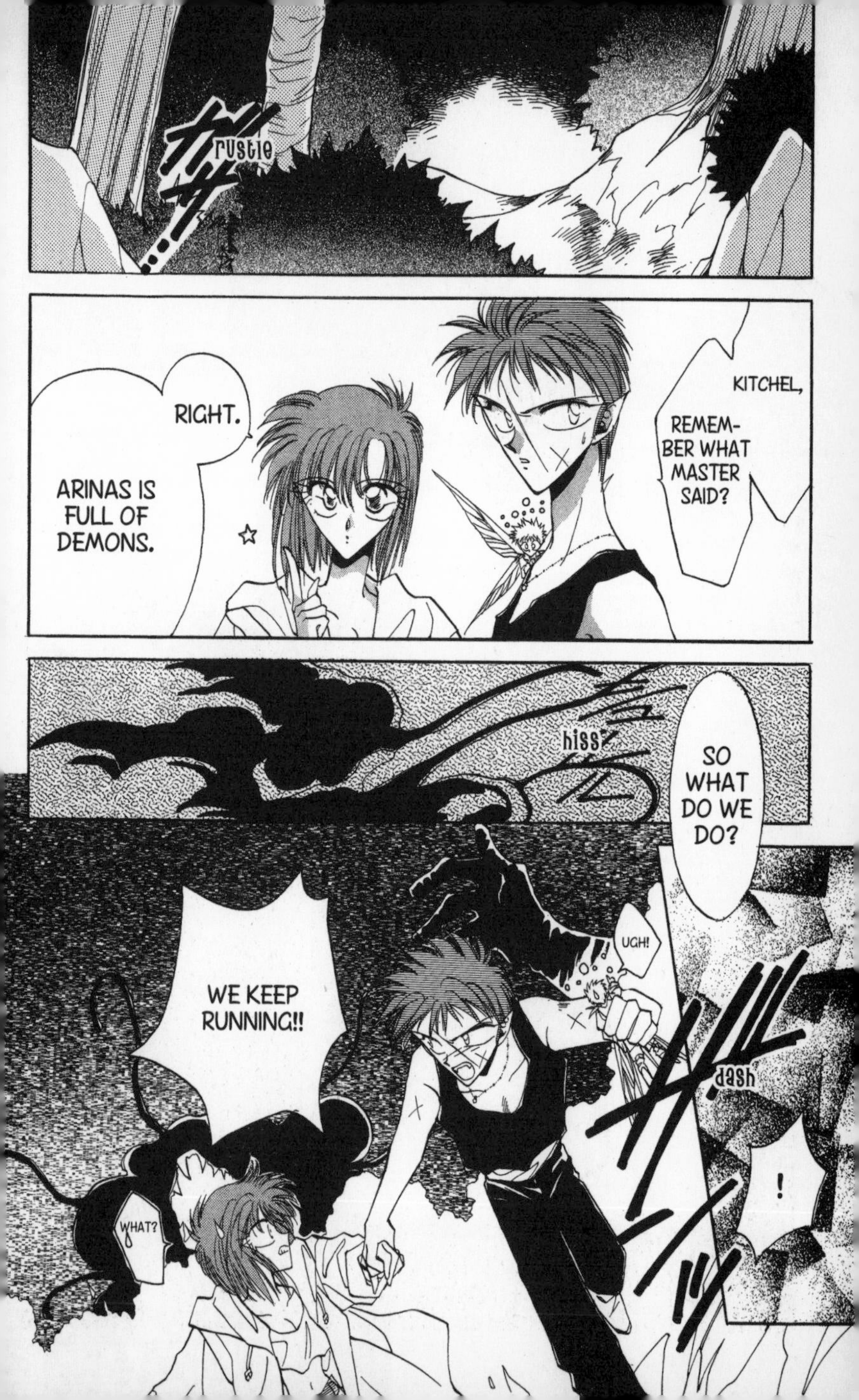
rustle
KITCHEL,
REMEM-BER WHAT MASTER SAID?
RIGHT.
ARINAS IS FULL OF DEMONS.
hiss
SO WHAT DO WE DO?
!
dash
UGH!
WE KEEP RUNNING!!
WHAT?

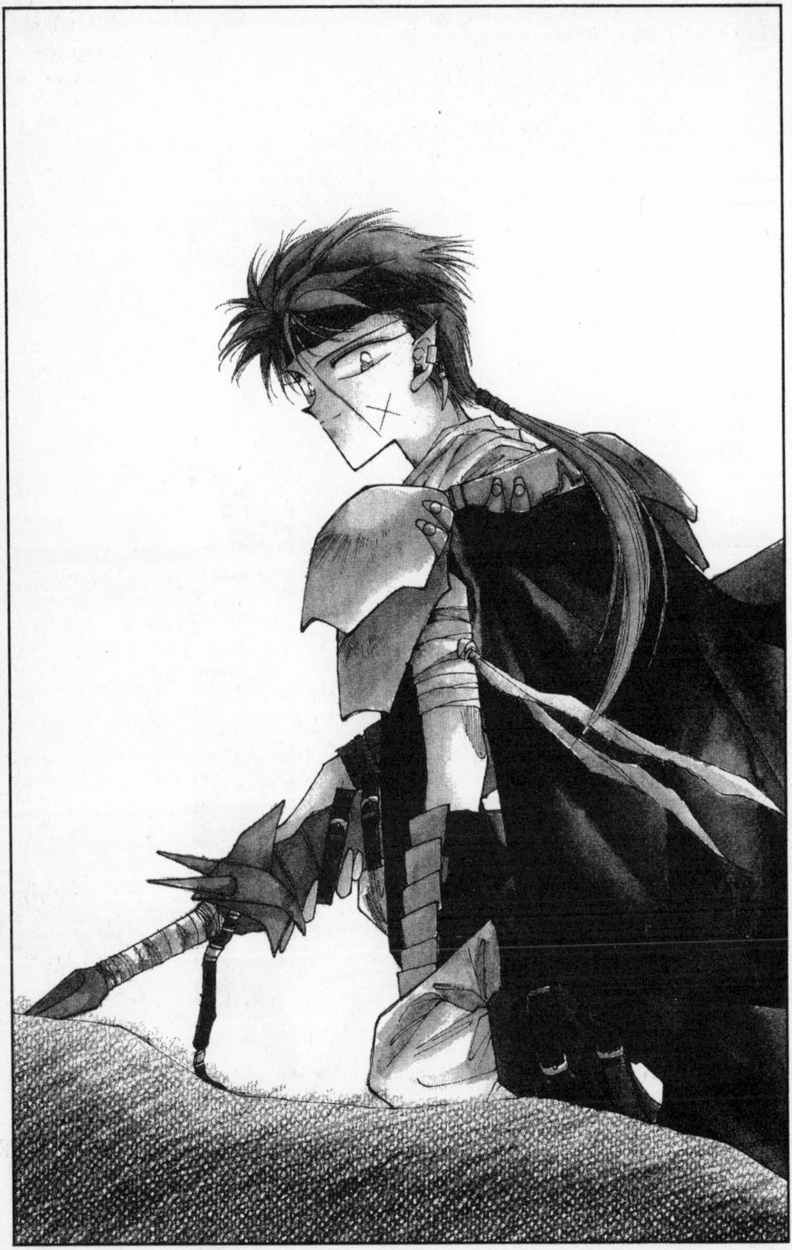

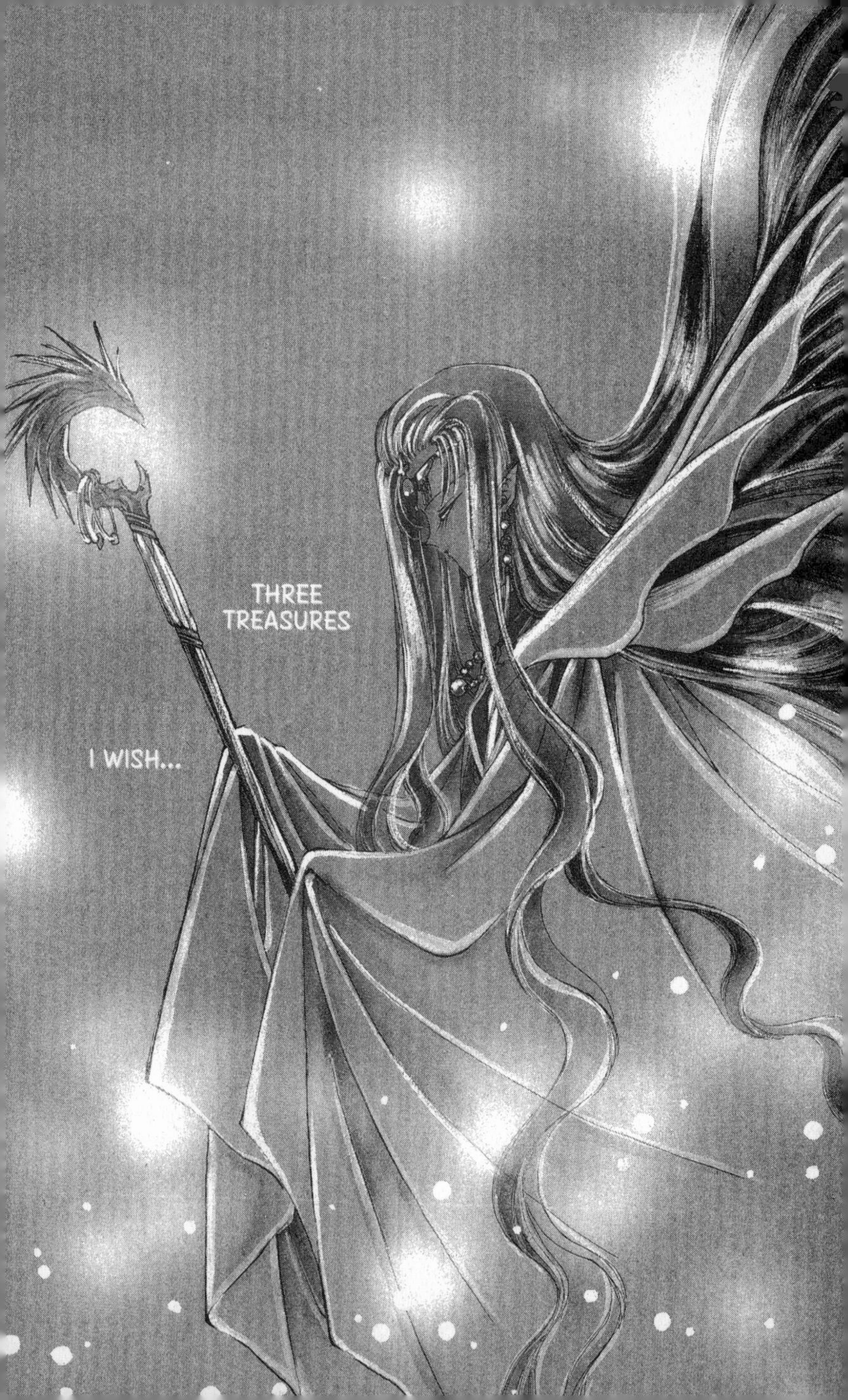
THREE TREASURES
I WISH...

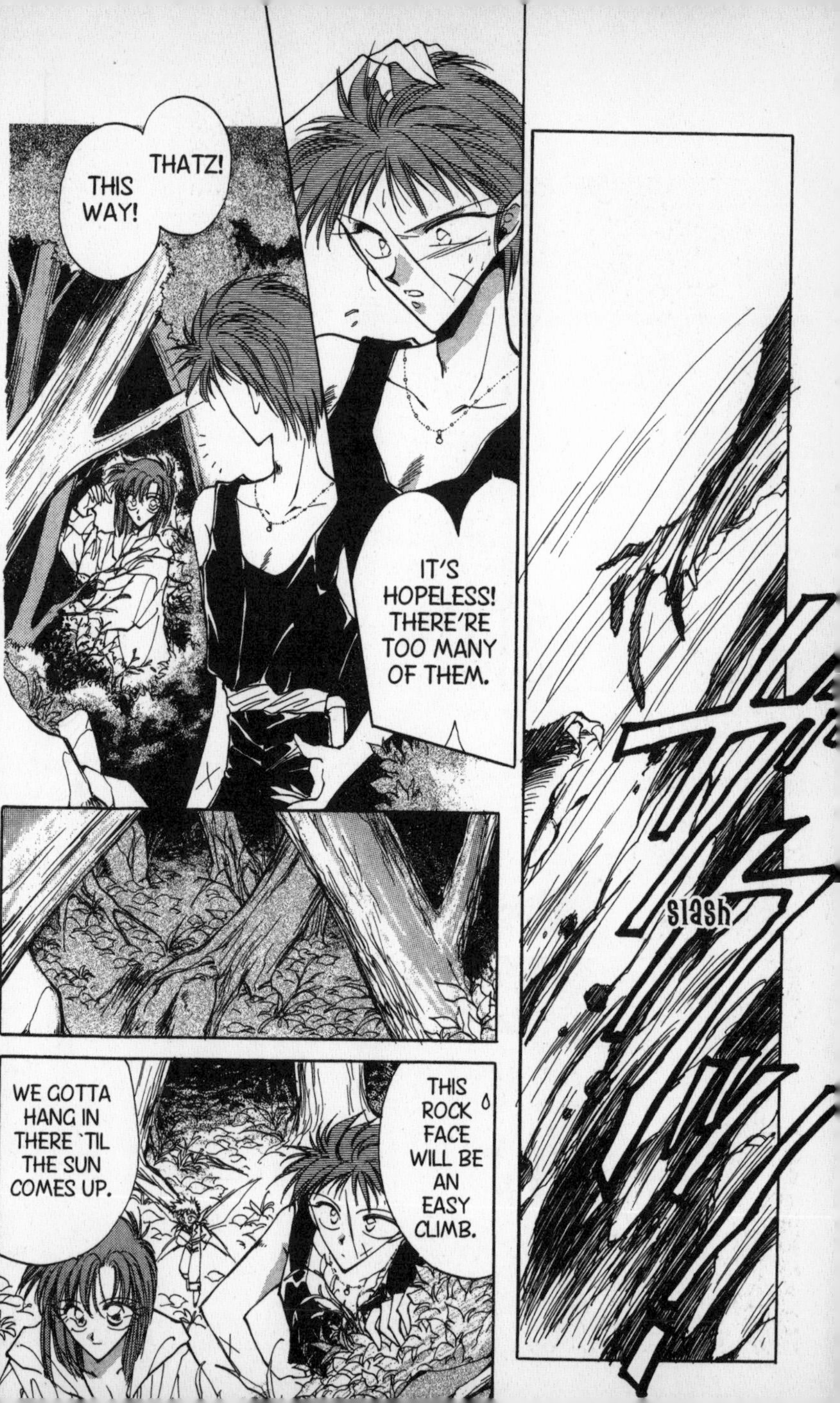
slash
THATZ! THIS WAY!
IT'S HOPELESS! THERE'RE TOO MANY OF THEM.
THIS ROCK FACE WILL BE AN EASY CLIMB.
WE GOTTA HANG IN THERE `TIL THE SUN COMES UP.

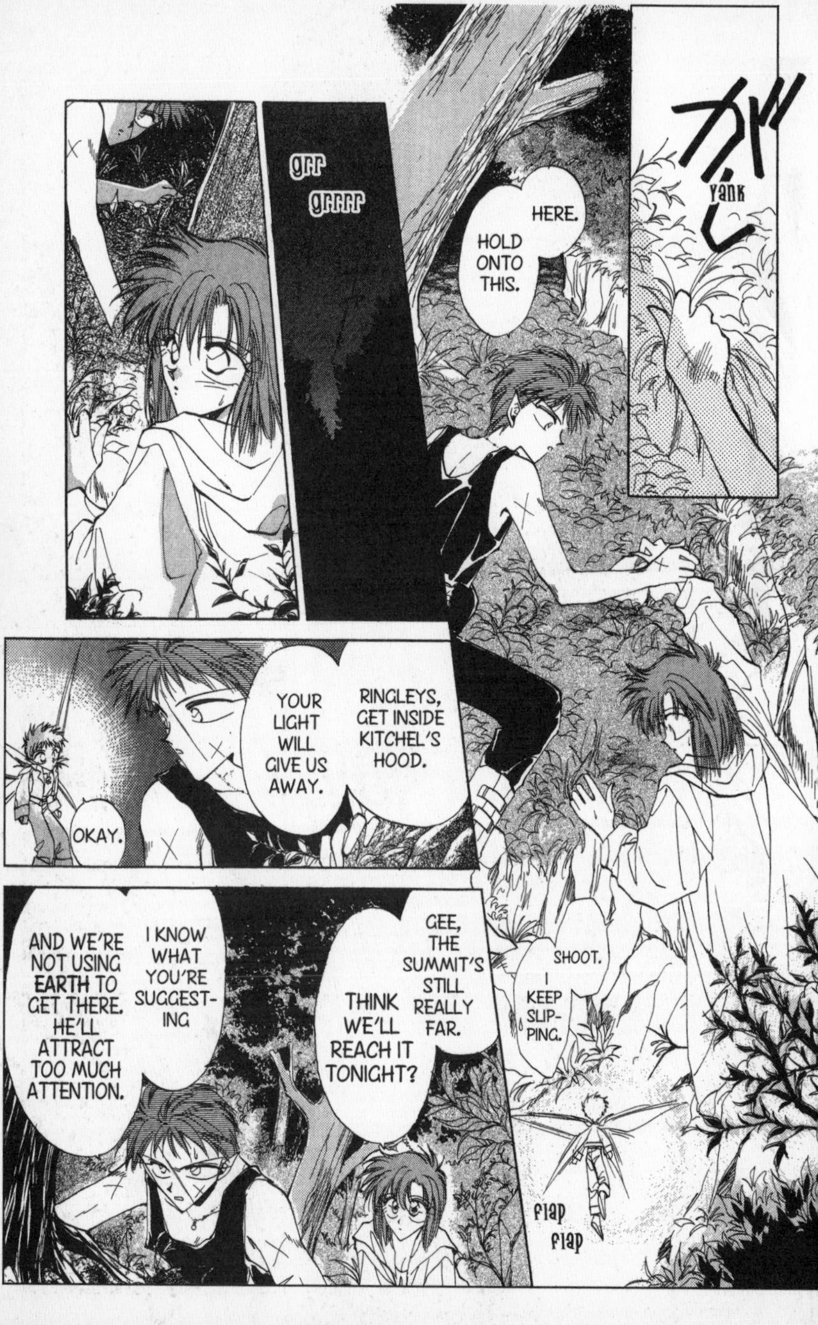
yank
HERE.
HOLD ONTO THIS.
SHOOT.
I KEEP SLIPPING.
flap
flap
grr
grrrr
RINGLEYS, GET INSIDE KITCHEL'S HOOD.
YOUR LIGHT WILL GIVE US AWAY.
OKAY.
GEE, THE SUMMIT'S STILL REALLY FAR.
THINK WE'LL REACH IT TONIGHT?
I KNOW WHAT YOU'RE SUGGESTING
AND WE'RE NOT USING EARTH TO GET THERE. HE'LL ATTRACT TOO MUCH ATTENTION.

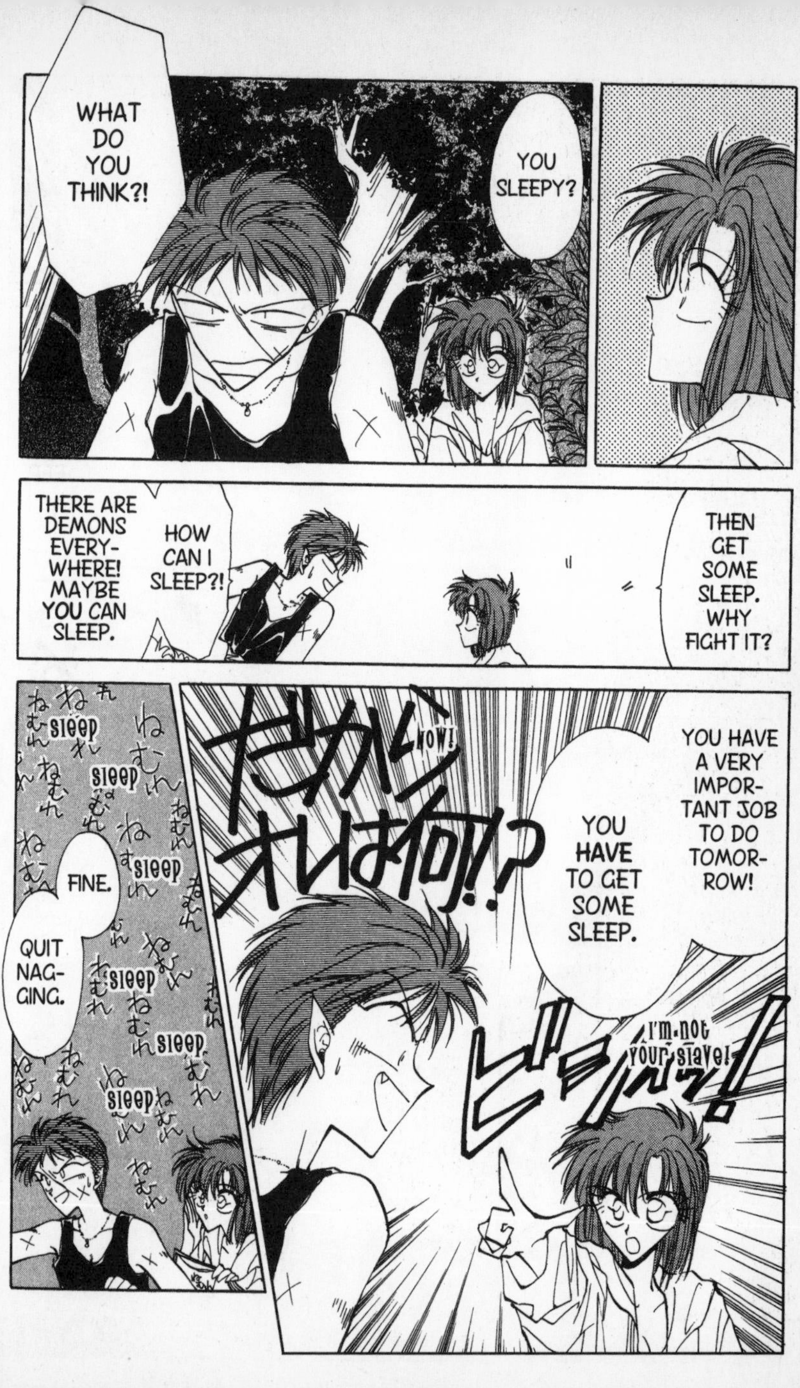
YOU SLEEPY?
WHAT DO YOU THINK?!
THEN GET SOME SLEEP. WHY FIGHT IT?
HOW CAN I SLEEP?!
THERE ARE DEMONS EVERY-WHERE! MAYBE YOU CAN SLEEP.
YOU HAVE A VERY IMPOR-TANT JOB TO DO TOMOR-ROW!
YOU HAVE TO GET SOME SLEEP.
だから
NOW!
オレは何!!?
I'm not your slave!
FINE.
QUIT NAG-GING.
sleep
sleep
sleep
sleep
sleep
sleep

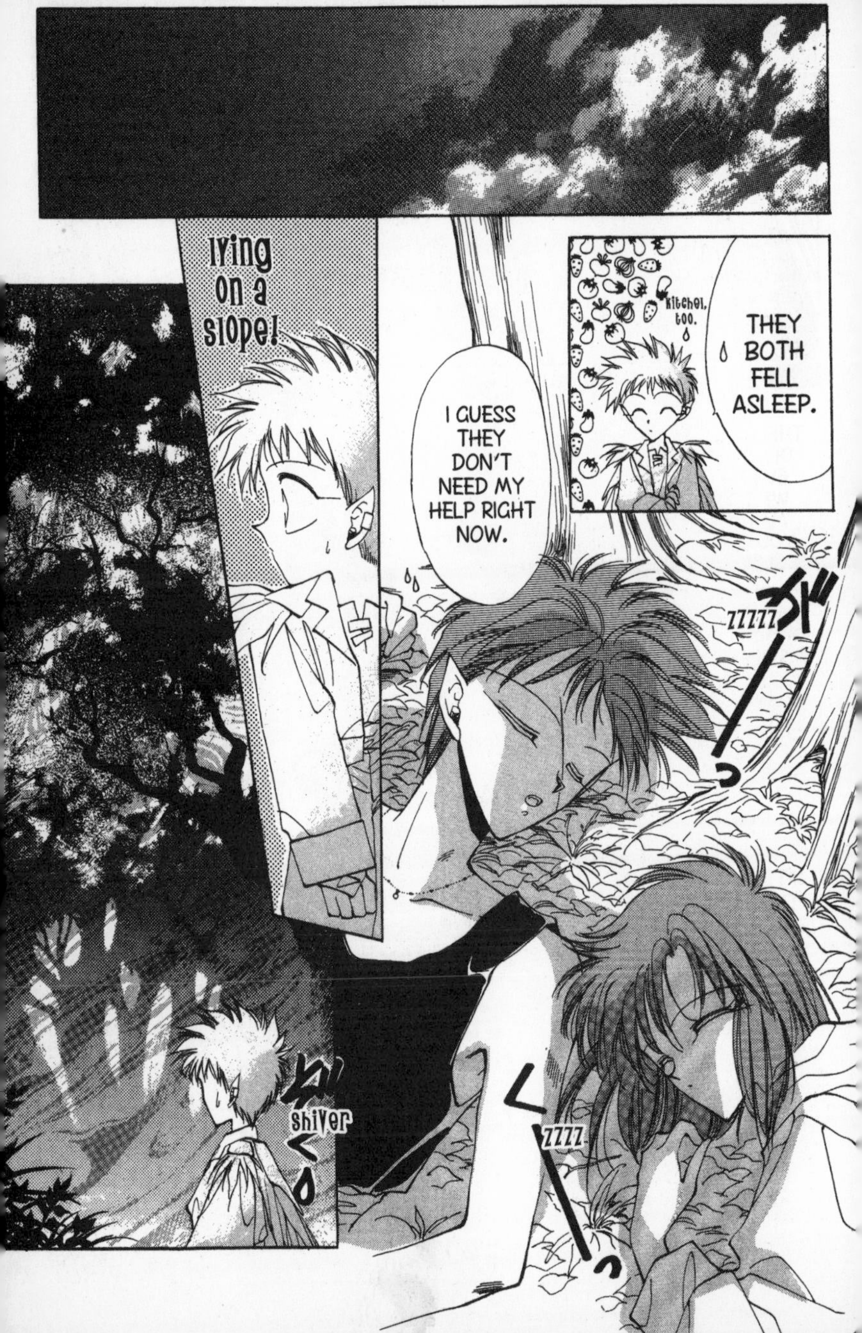
THEY BOTH FELL ASLEEP.
Kitchel, too.
ZZZZZ
I GUESS THEY DON'T NEED MY HELP RIGHT NOW.
lying on a slope!
ZZZZ
shiver

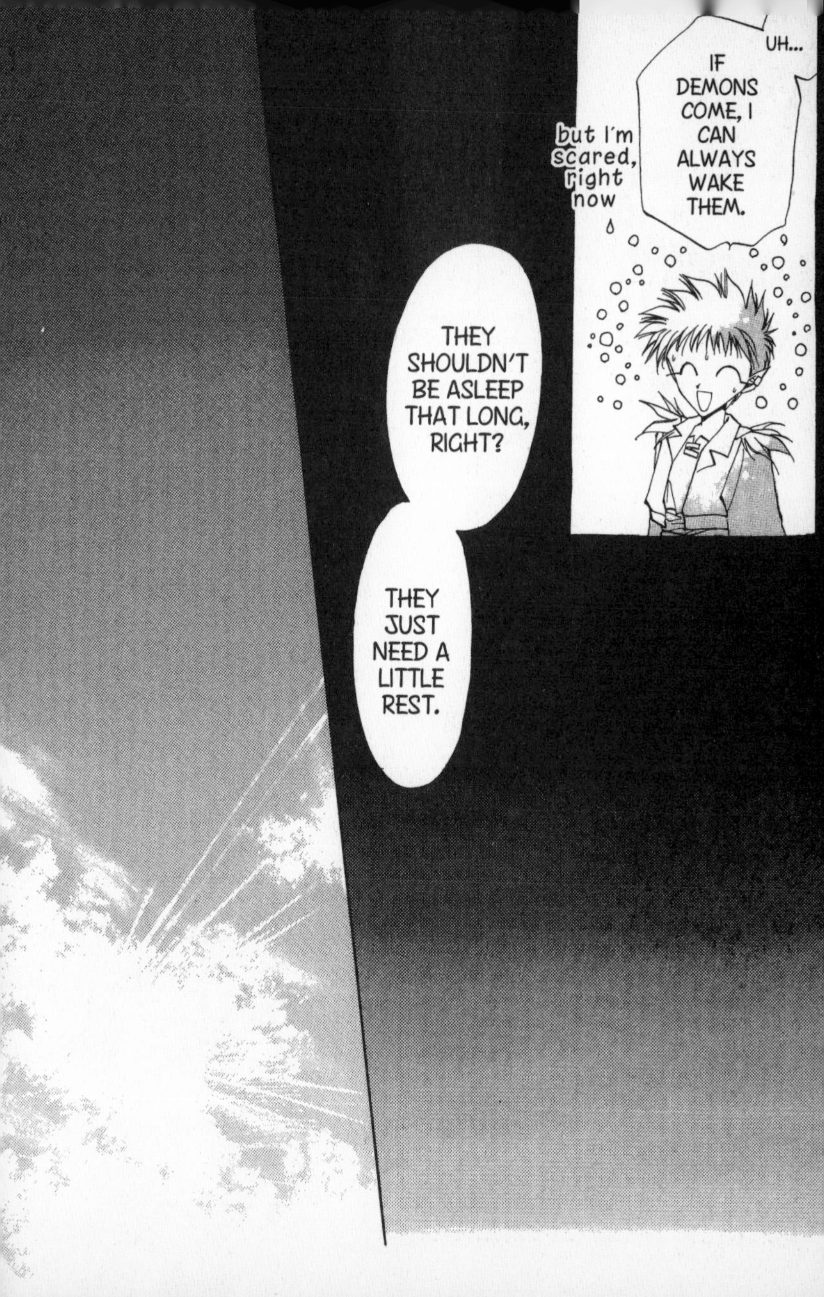
UH...
IF DEMONS COME, I CAN ALWAYS WAKE THEM.
but I'm scared, right now
THEY SHOULDN'T BE ASLEEP THAT LONG, RIGHT?
THEY JUST NEED A LITTLE REST.

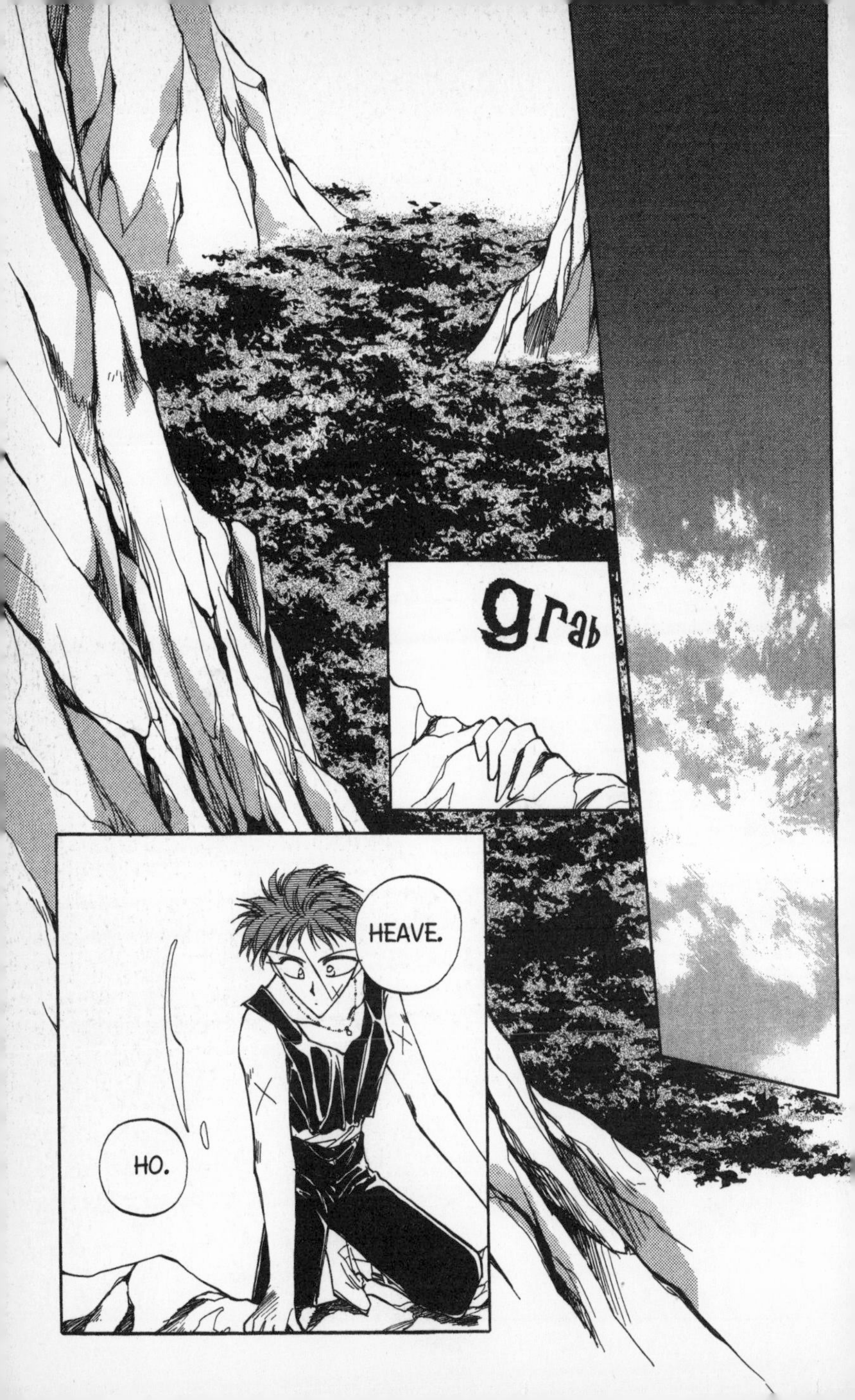
grab
HEAVE.
HO.

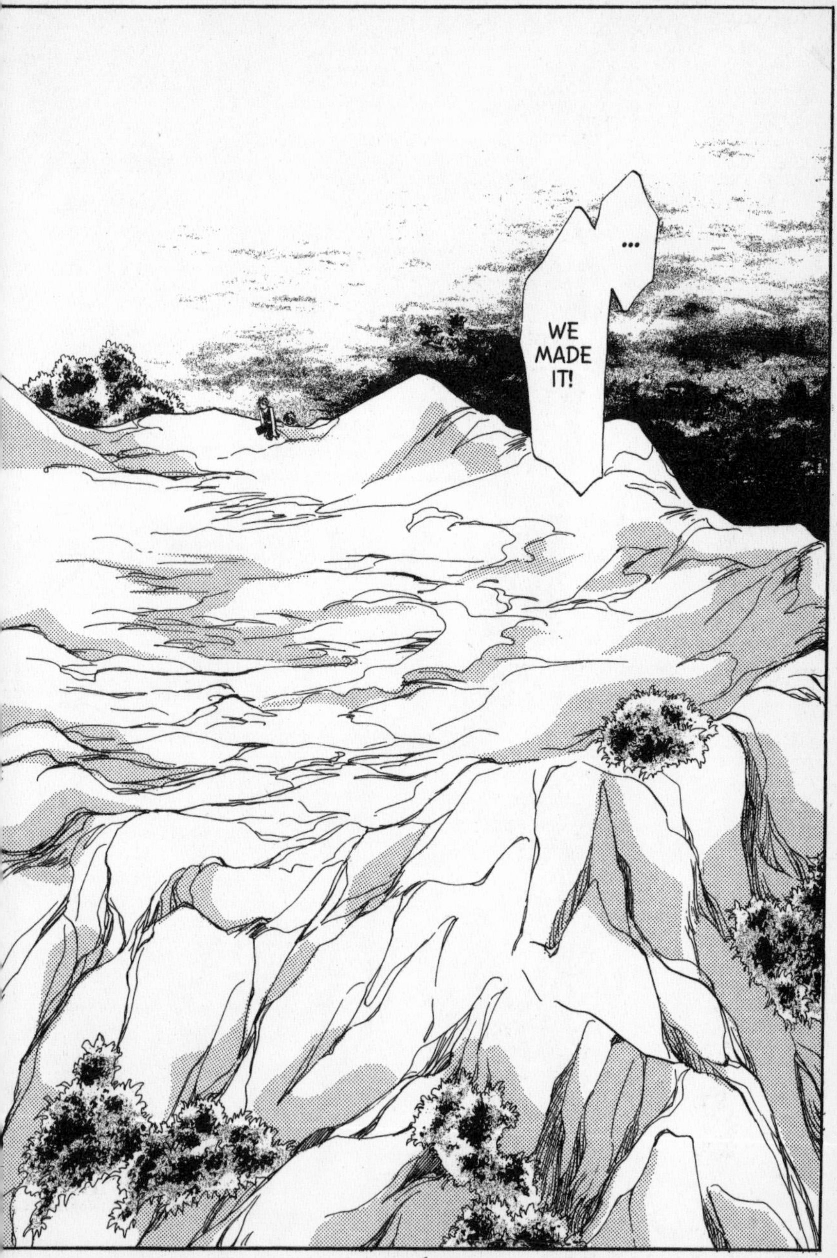
...
WE MADE IT!

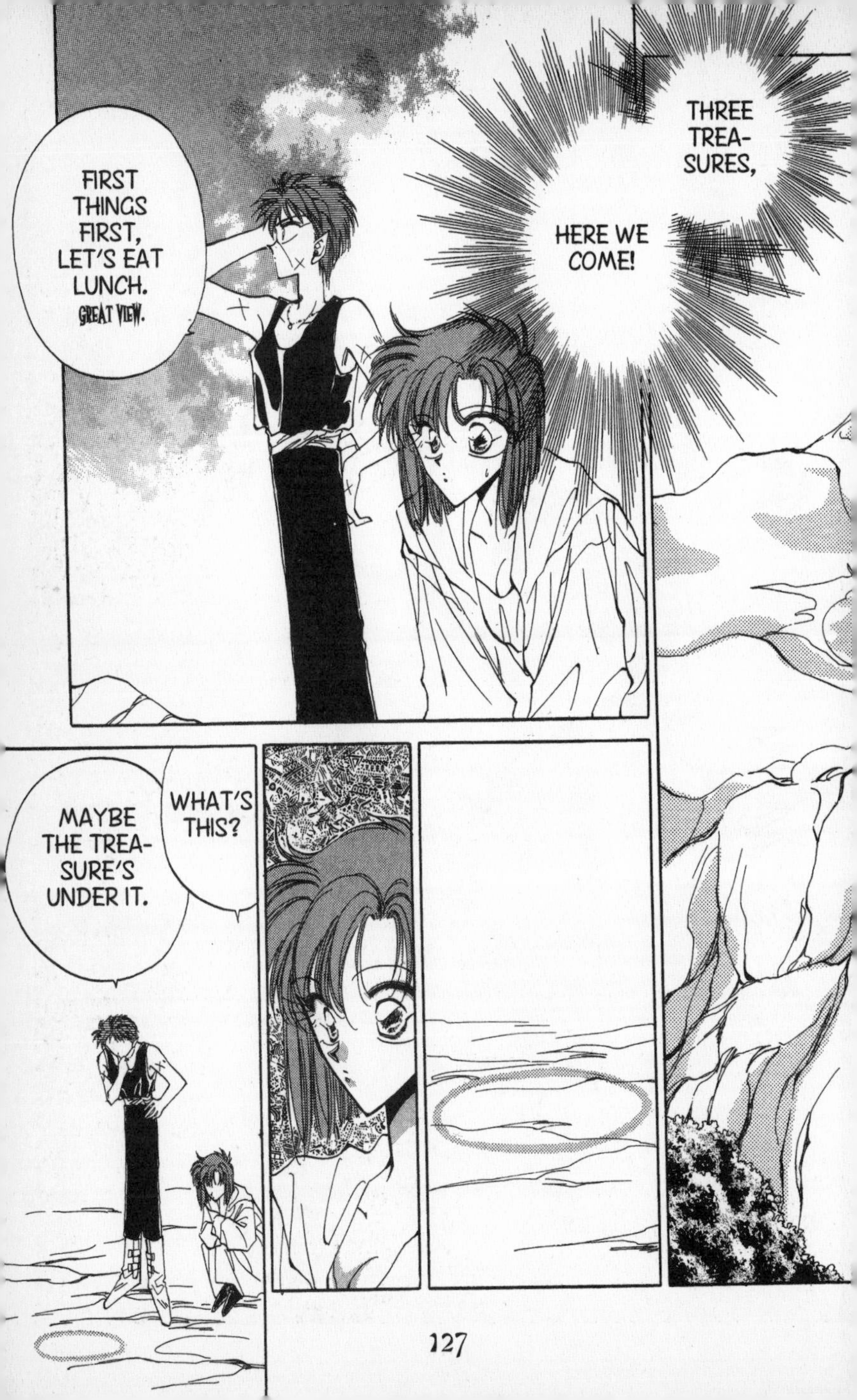
THREE TREA- SURES,
HERE WE COME!
FIRST THINGS FIRST, LET'S EAT LUNCH.
GREAT VIEW.
WHAT'S THIS?
MAYBE THE TREA- SURE'S UNDER IT.

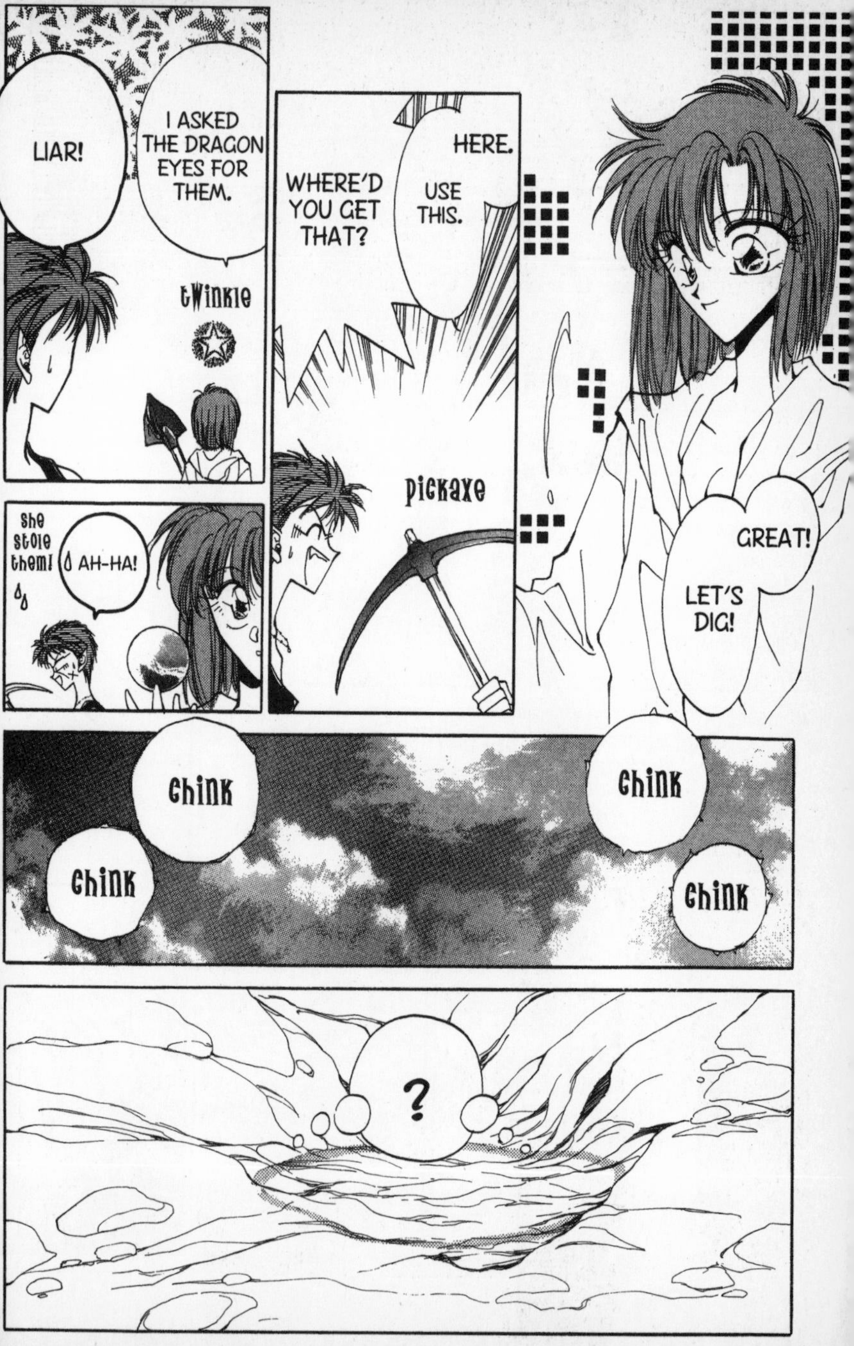
GREAT!
LET'S DIG!
HERE.
USE THIS.
WHERE'D YOU GET THAT?
pickaxe
I ASKED THE DRAGON EYES FOR THEM.
LIAR!
twinkle
AH-HA!
She stole them!
Chink
Chink
Chink
Chink
?

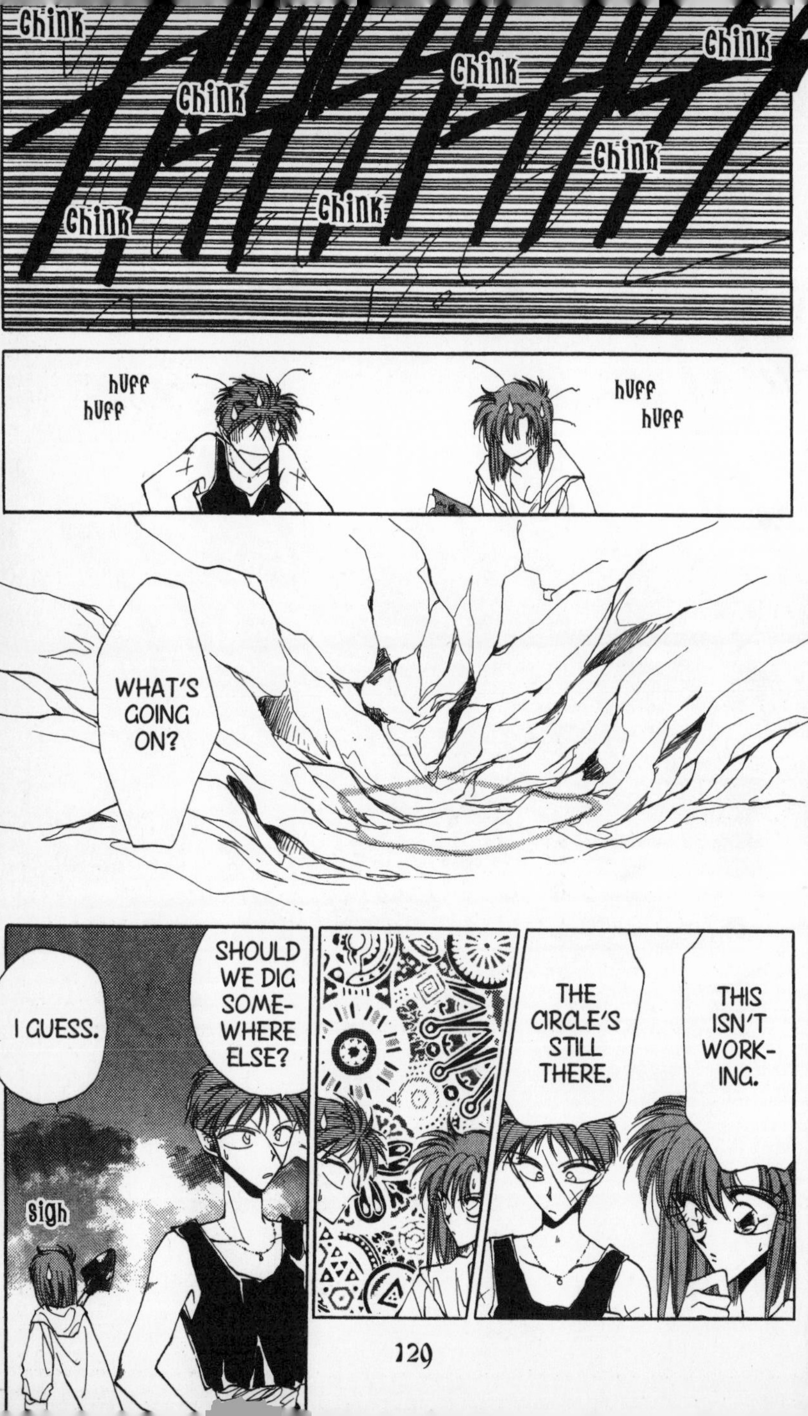
Chink
Chink
Chink
Chink
Chink
Chink
huff huff
huff huff
WHAT'S GOING ON?
THIS ISN'T WORK-ING.
THE CIRCLE'S STILL THERE.
SHOULD WE DIG SOME-WHERE ELSE?
I GUESS.
sigh

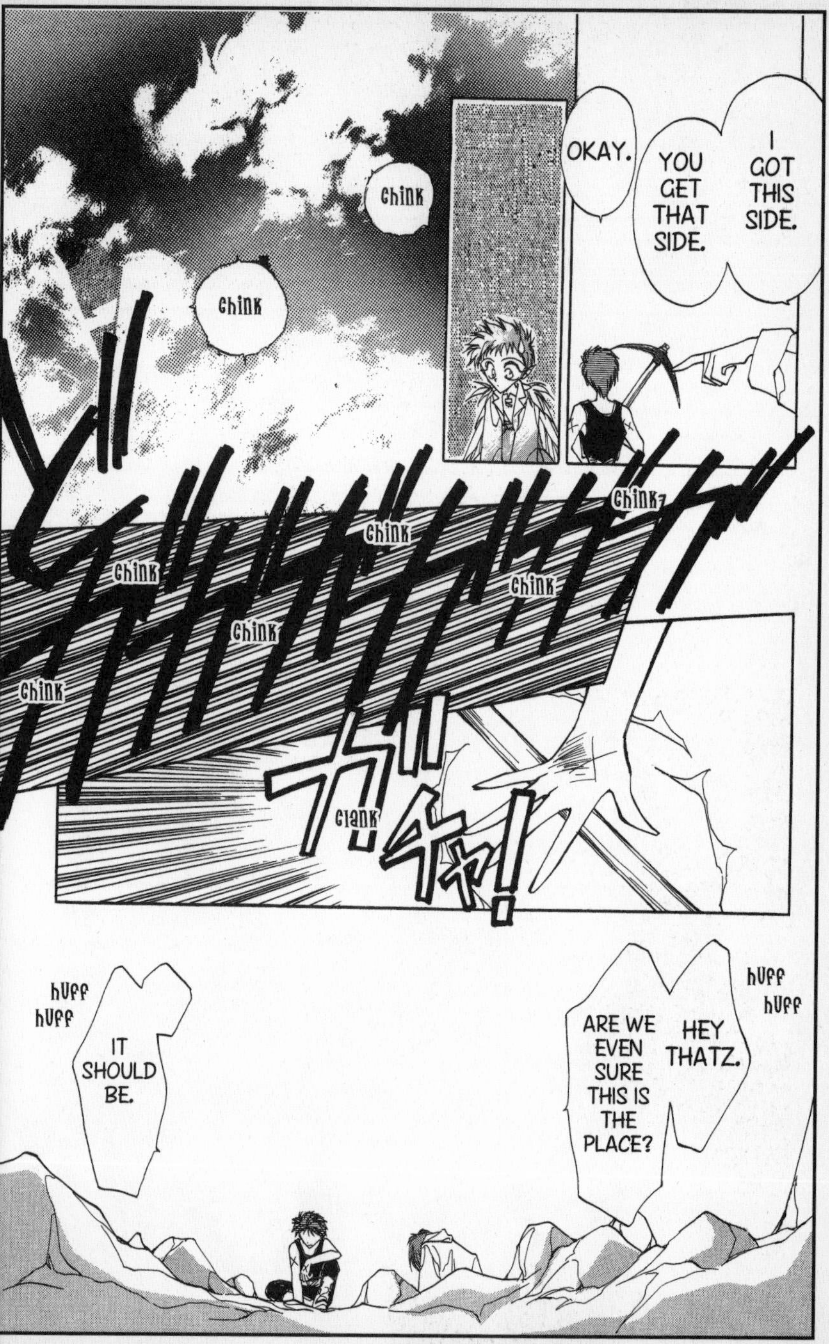
I GOT THIS SIDE.
YOU GET THAT SIDE.
OKAY.
Chink
Chink
Chink
Chink
Chink
Chink
Chink
Chink
CLANK
HEY THATZ.
ARE WE EVEN SURE THIS IS THE PLACE?
huff huff
IT SHOULD BE.
huff huff

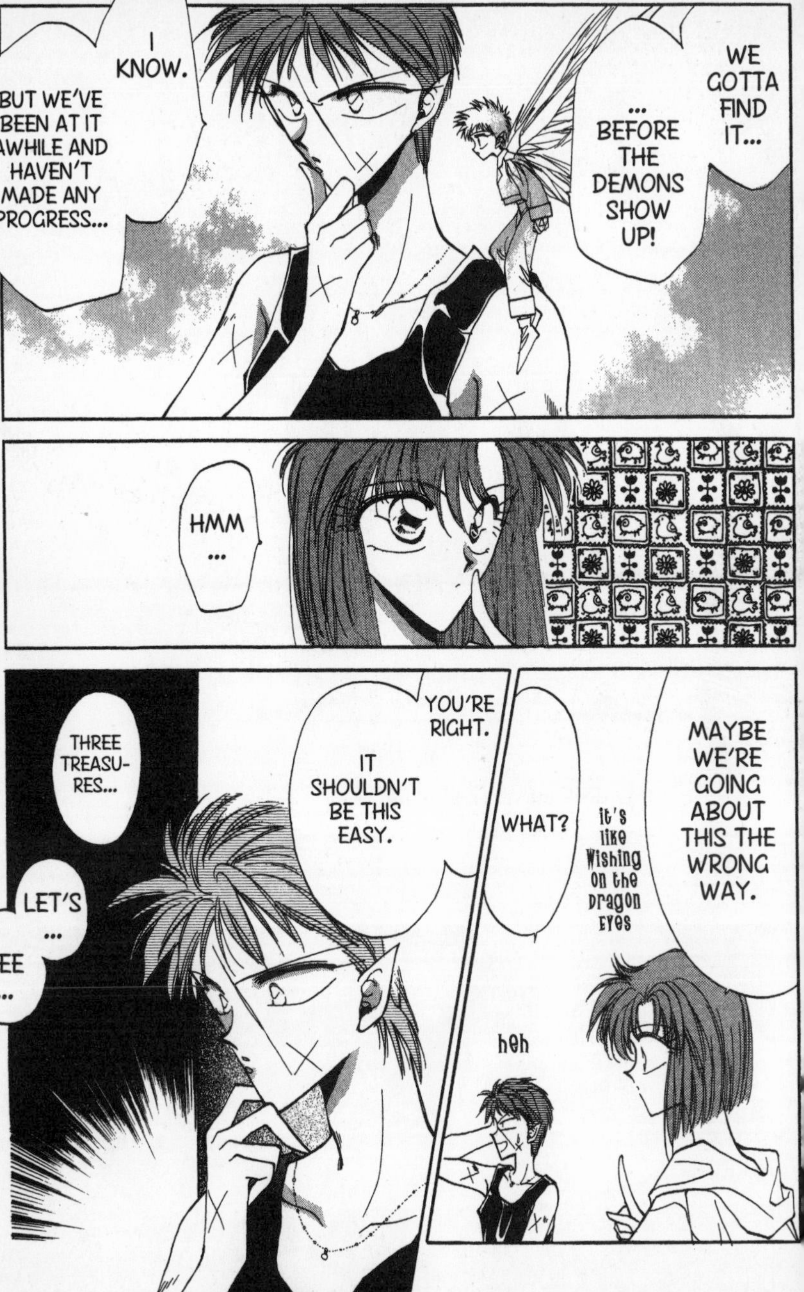
WE GOTTA FIND IT...
... BEFORE THE DEMONS SHOW UP!
I KNOW.
BUT WE'VE BEEN AT IT AWHILE AND HAVEN'T MADE ANY PROGRESS...
HMM ...
MAYBE WE'RE GOING ABOUT THIS THE WRONG WAY.
it's like Wishing on the Dragon Eyes
WHAT?
heh
YOU'RE RIGHT.
IT SHOULDN'T BE THIS EASY.
THREE TREASU-RES...
LET'S ... SEE ...

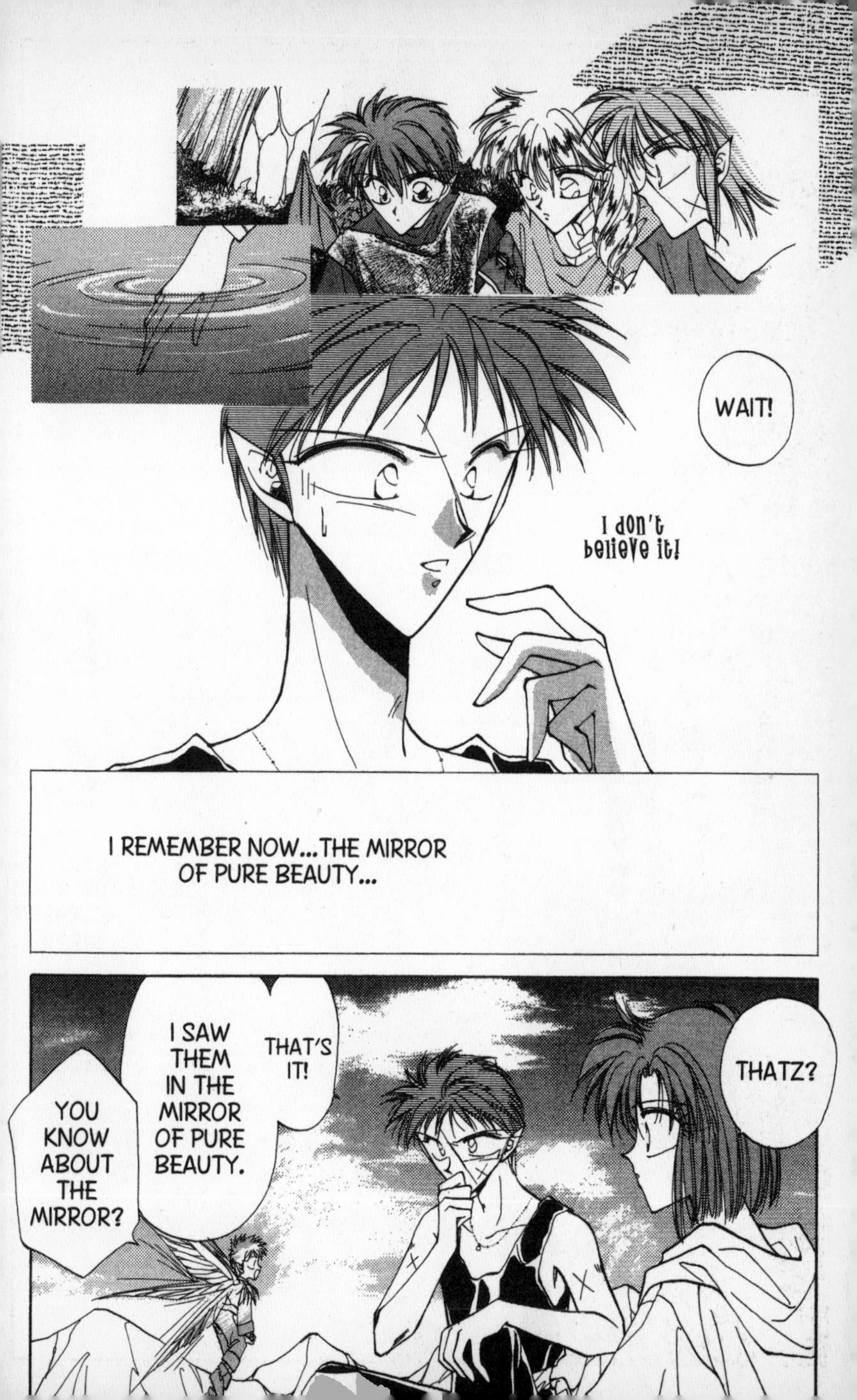
WAIT!
I don't believe it!
I REMEMBER NOW...THE MIRROR OF PURE BEAUTY...
THATZ?
THAT'S IT!
I SAW THEM IN THE MIRROR OF PURE BEAUTY.
YOU KNOW ABOUT THE MIRROR?

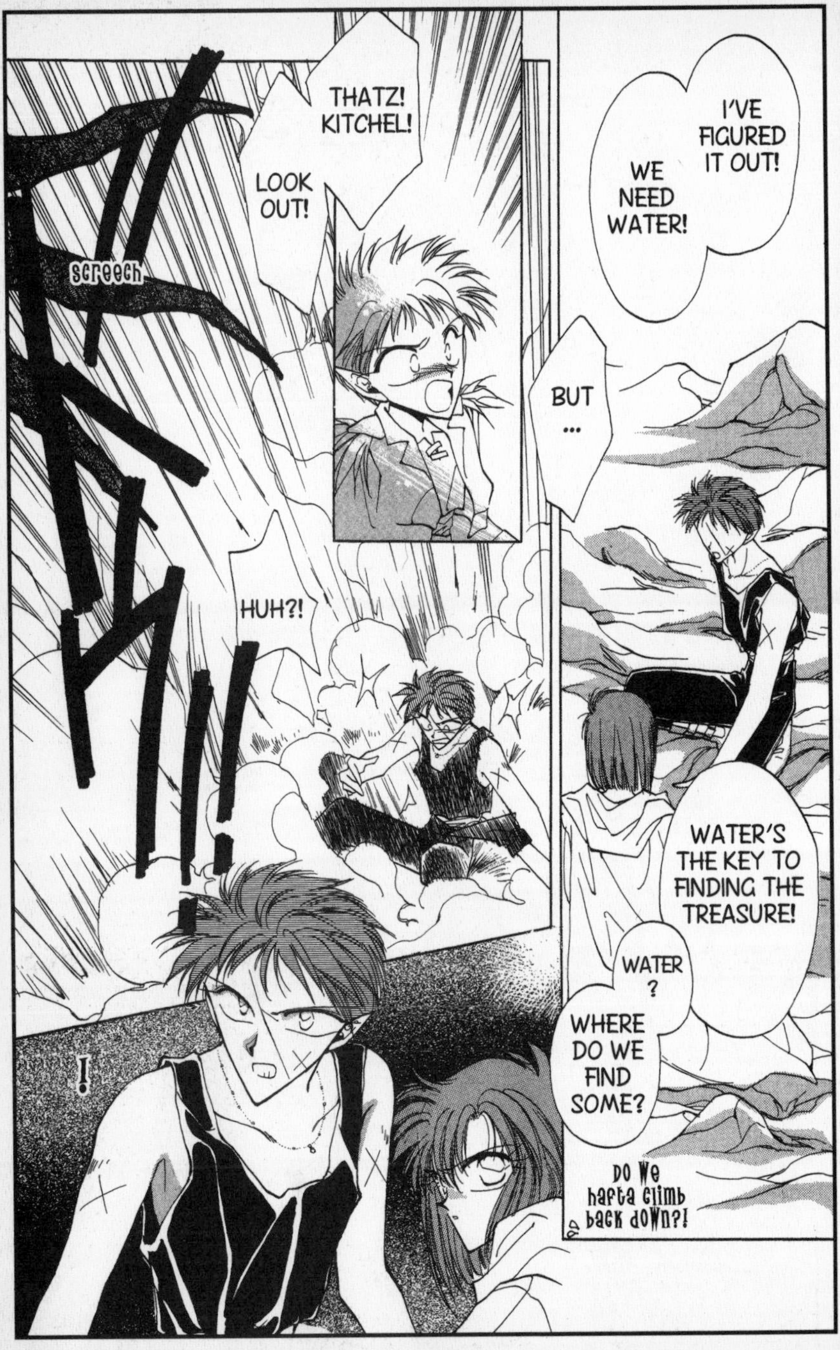
I'VE FIGURED IT OUT!
WE NEED WATER!
BUT ...
WATER'S THE KEY TO FINDING THE TREASURE!
WATER?
WHERE DO WE FIND SOME?
Do we hafta climb back down?!
THATZ! KITCHEL!
LOOK OUT!
HUH?!
screech
!

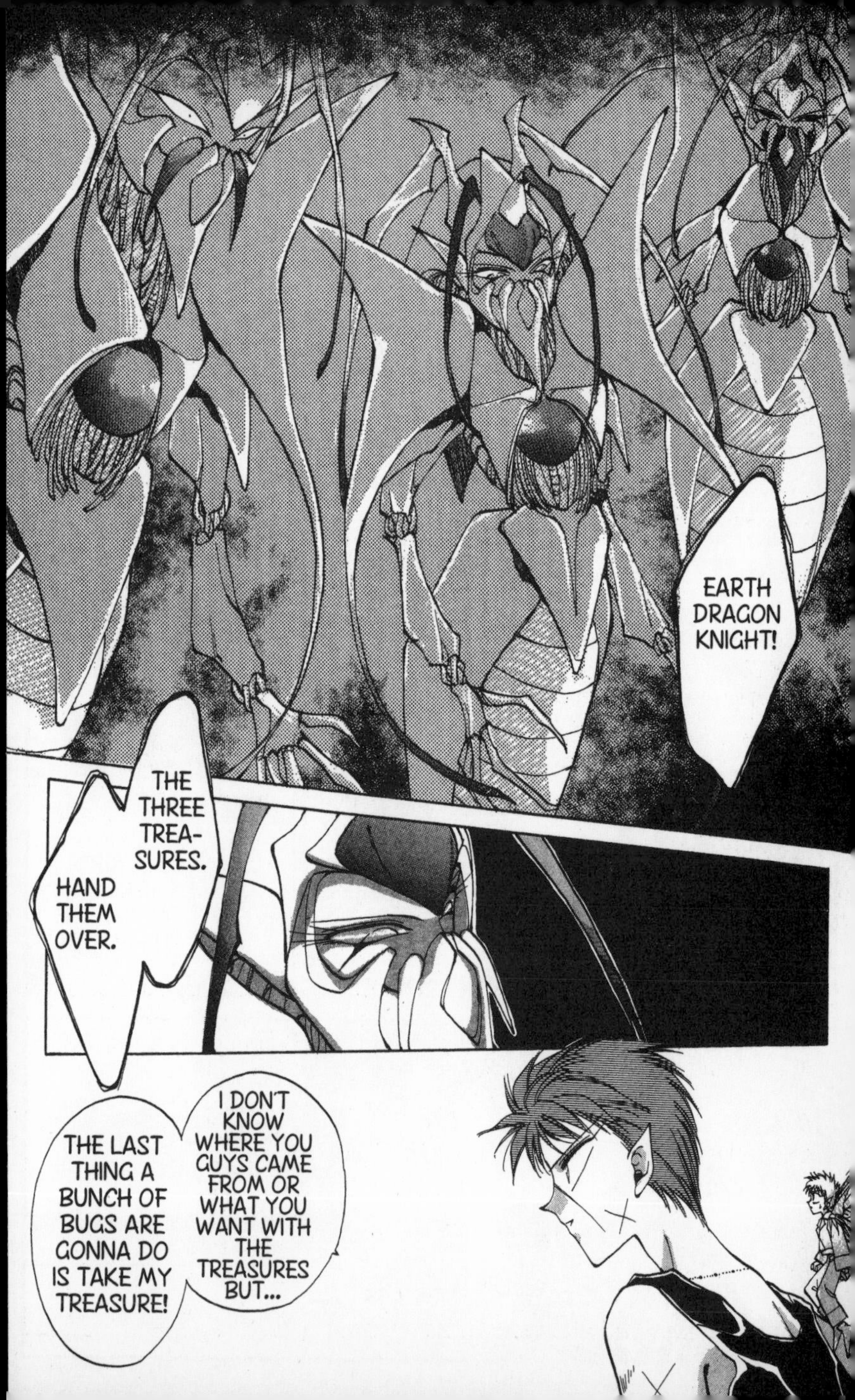
EARTH DRAGON KNIGHT!
THE THREE TREA-SURES.
HAND THEM OVER.
I DON'T KNOW WHERE YOU GUYS CAME FROM OR WHAT YOU WANT WITH THE TREASURES BUT...
THE LAST THING A BUNCH OF BUGS ARE GONNA DO IS TAKE MY TREASURE!

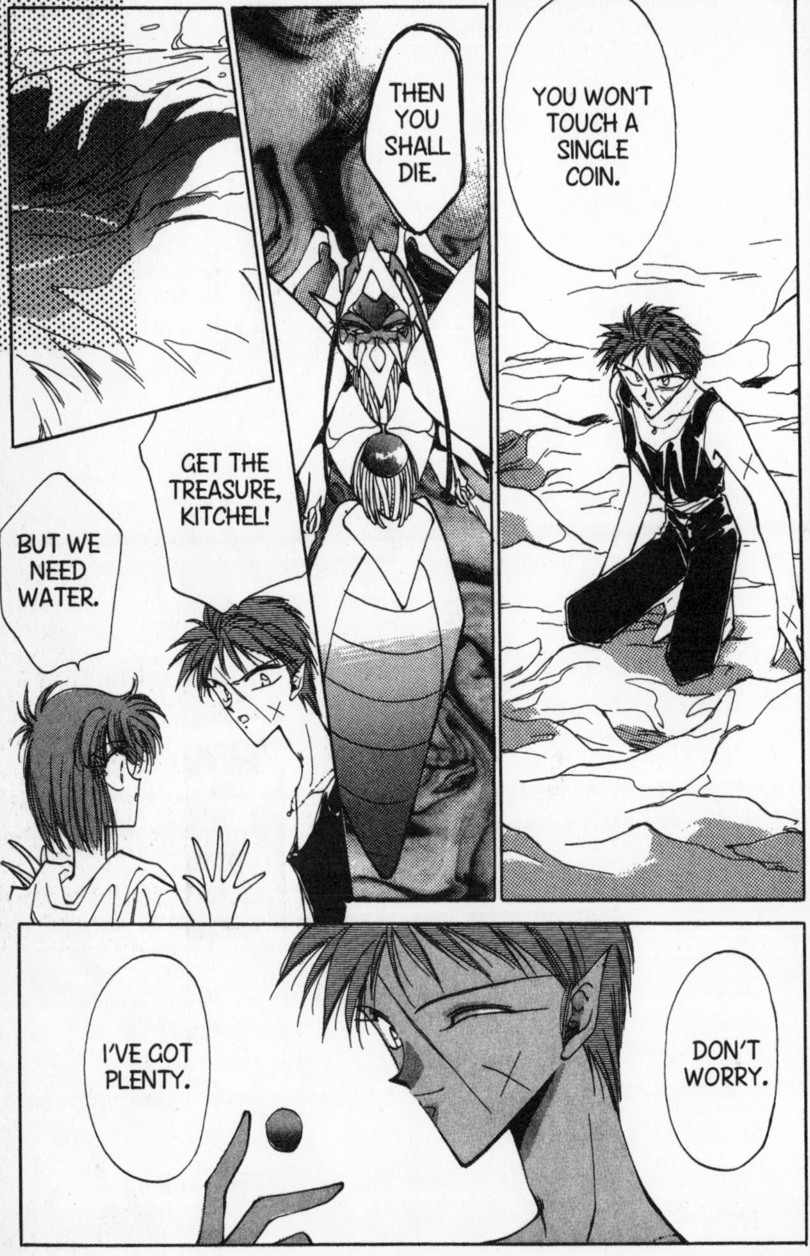
YOU WON'T TOUCH A SINGLE COIN.
THEN YOU SHALL DIE.
GET THE TREASURE, KITCHEL!
BUT WE NEED WATER.
DON'T WORRY.
I'VE GOT PLENTY.

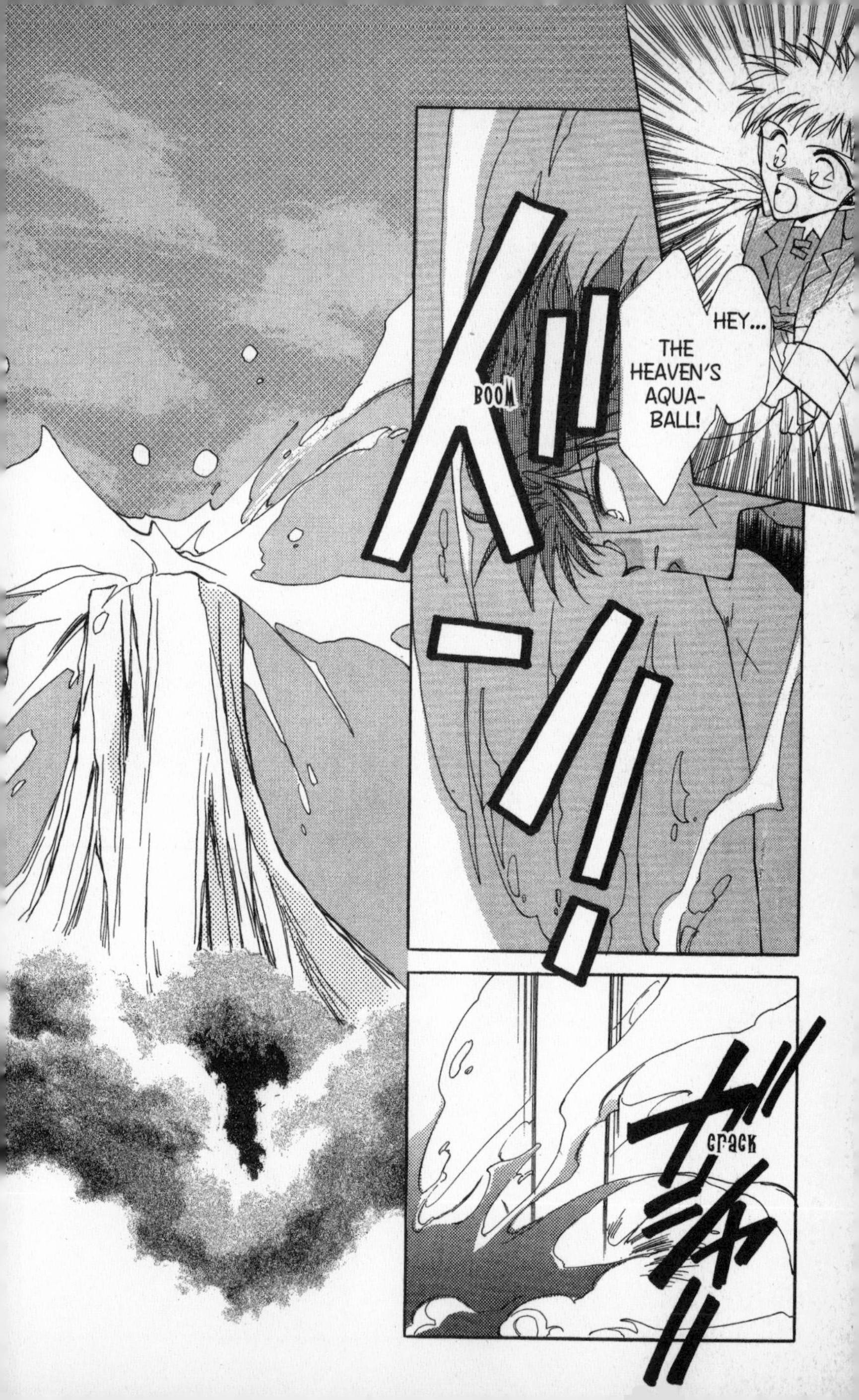
HEY...
THE HEAVEN'S AQUA-BALL!
BOOM
CRACK

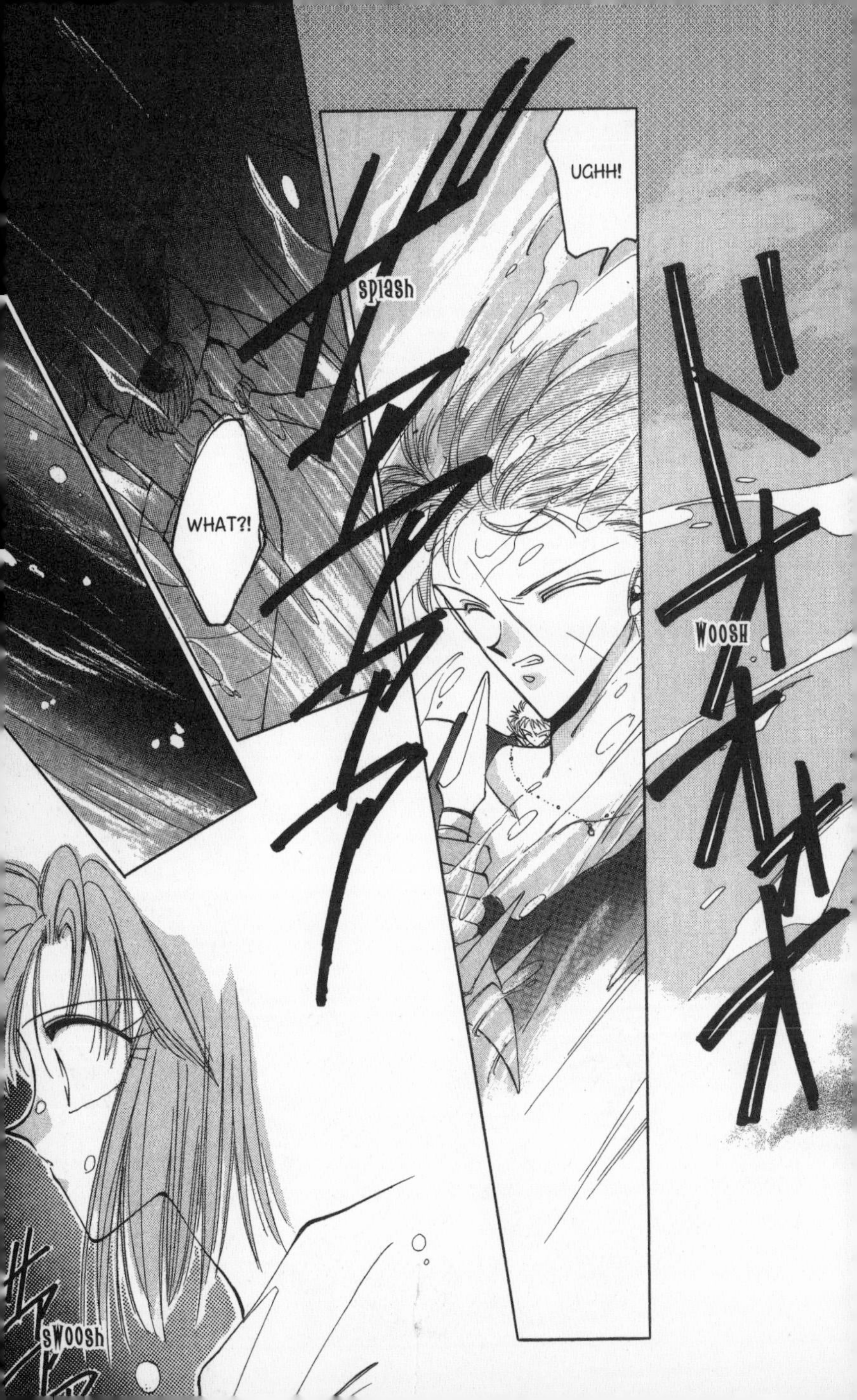
UGHH!
WOOSH
splash
WHAT?!
swoosh

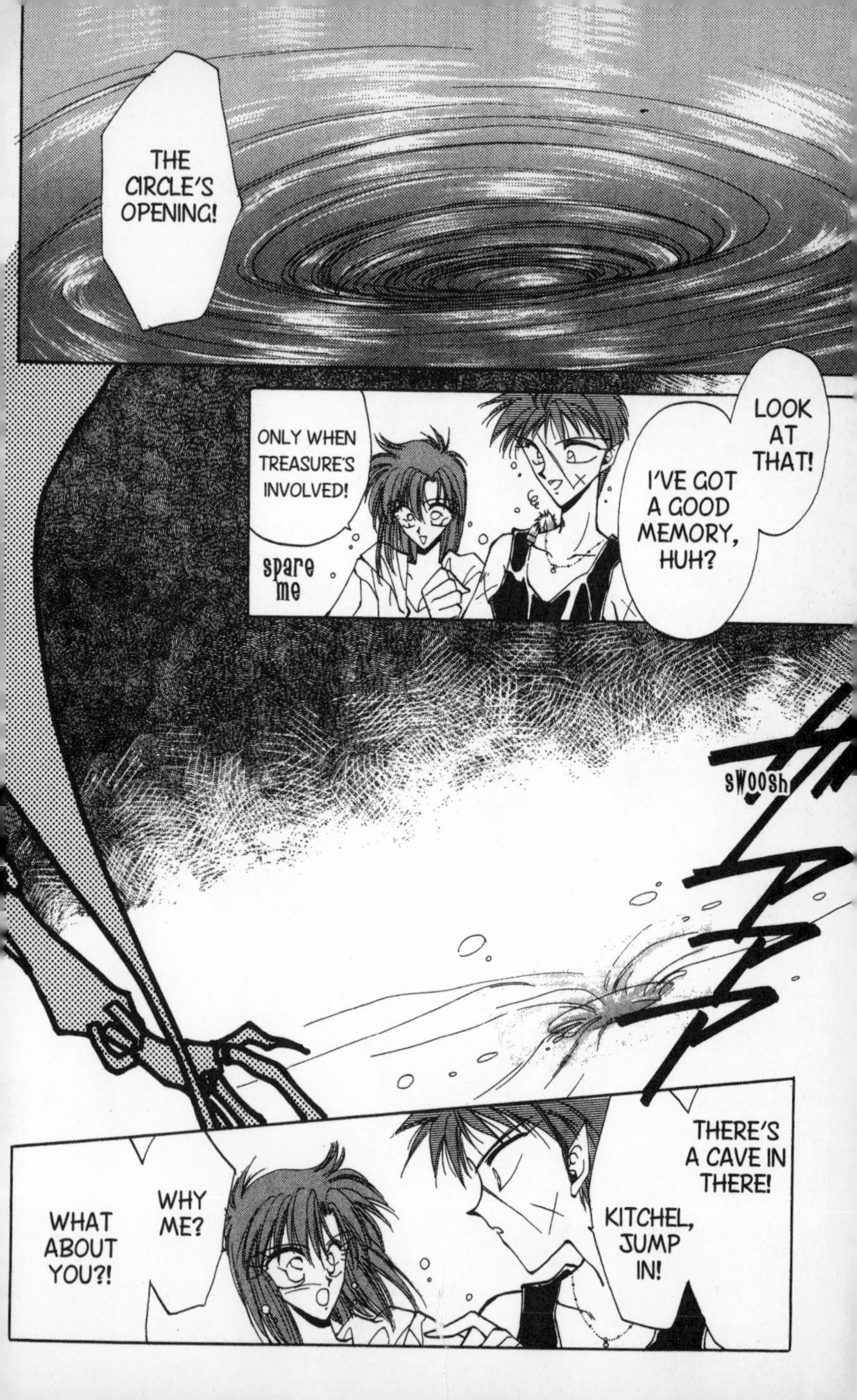
THE CIRCLE'S OPENING!
LOOK AT THAT!
I'VE GOT A GOOD MEMORY, HUH?
ONLY WHEN TREASURE'S INVOLVED!
spare me
sWOOsh
THERE'S A CAVE IN THERE!
KITCHEL, JUMP IN!
WHY ME?
WHAT ABOUT YOU?!

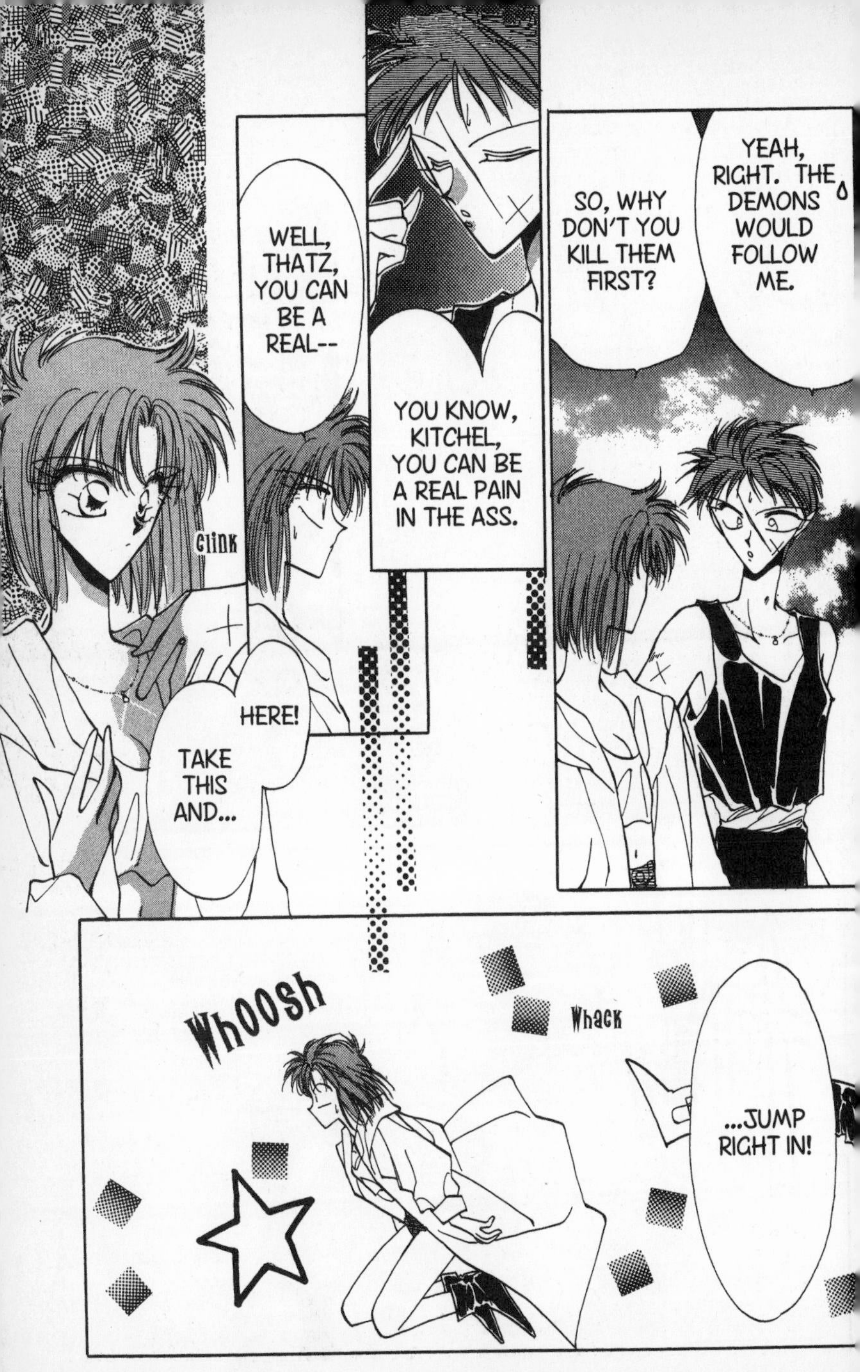
YEAH, RIGHT. THE DEMONS WOULD FOLLOW ME.
SO, WHY DON'T YOU KILL THEM FIRST?
YOU KNOW, KITCHEL, YOU CAN BE A REAL PAIN IN THE ASS.
WELL, THATZ, YOU CAN BE A REAL--
Clink
HERE!
TAKE THIS AND...
...JUMP RIGHT IN!
Whack
Whoosh

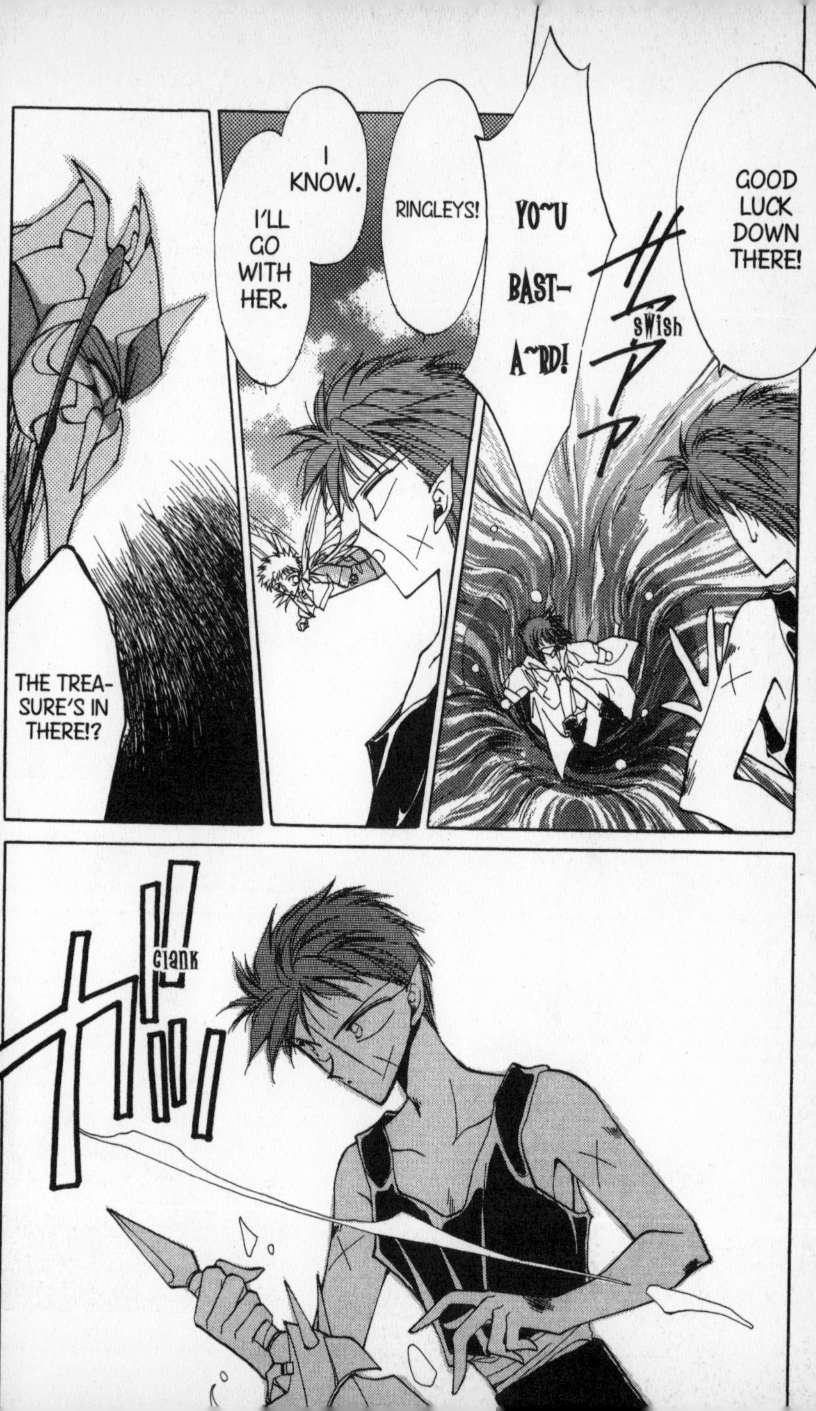
GOOD LUCK DOWN THERE!
SWISH
YO~U BAST-A~RD!
RINGLEYS!
I KNOW. I'LL GO WITH HER.
THE TREA-SURE'S IN THERE!?
CLANK

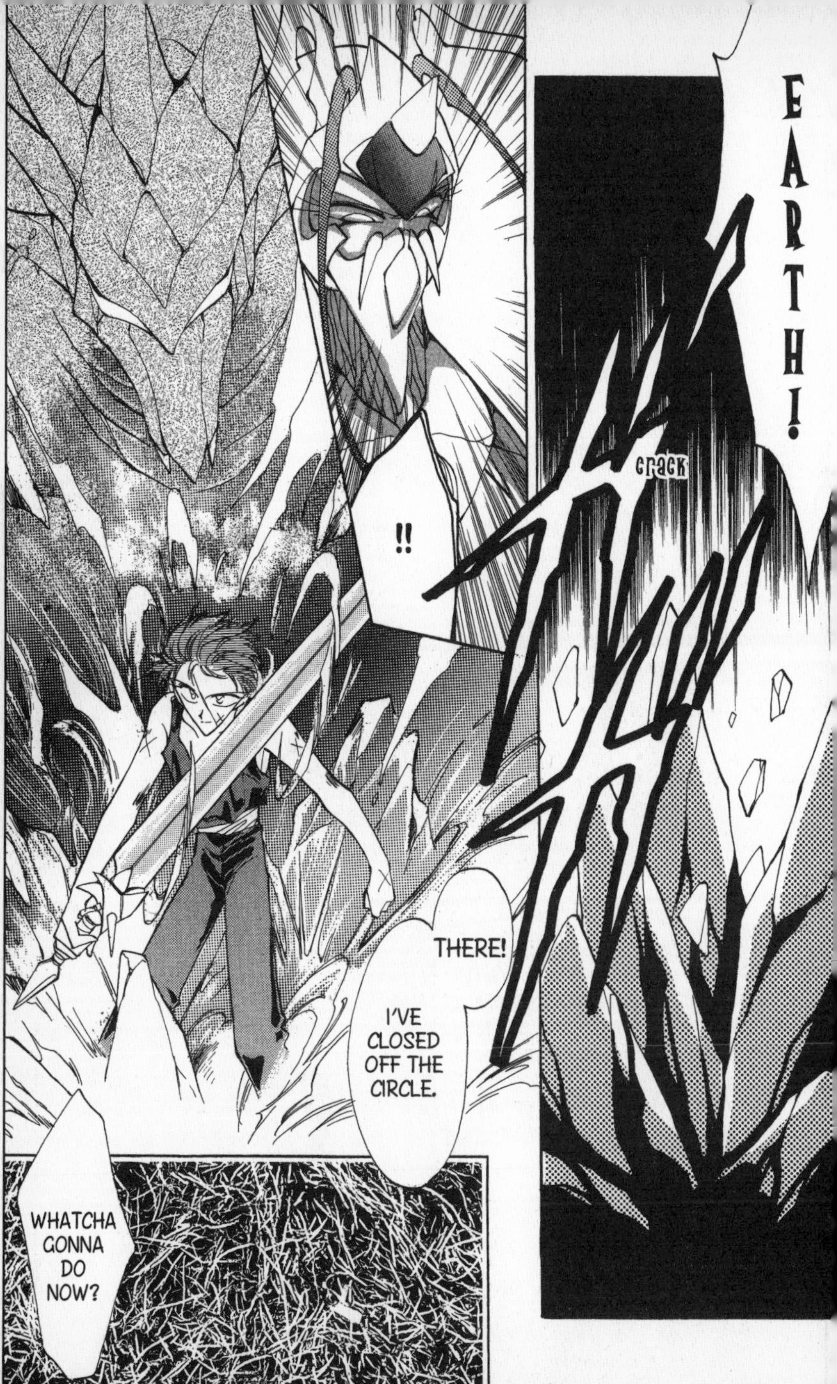
EARTH!
crack
!!
THERE!
I'VE CLOSED OFF THE CIRCLE.
WHATCHA GONNA DO NOW?

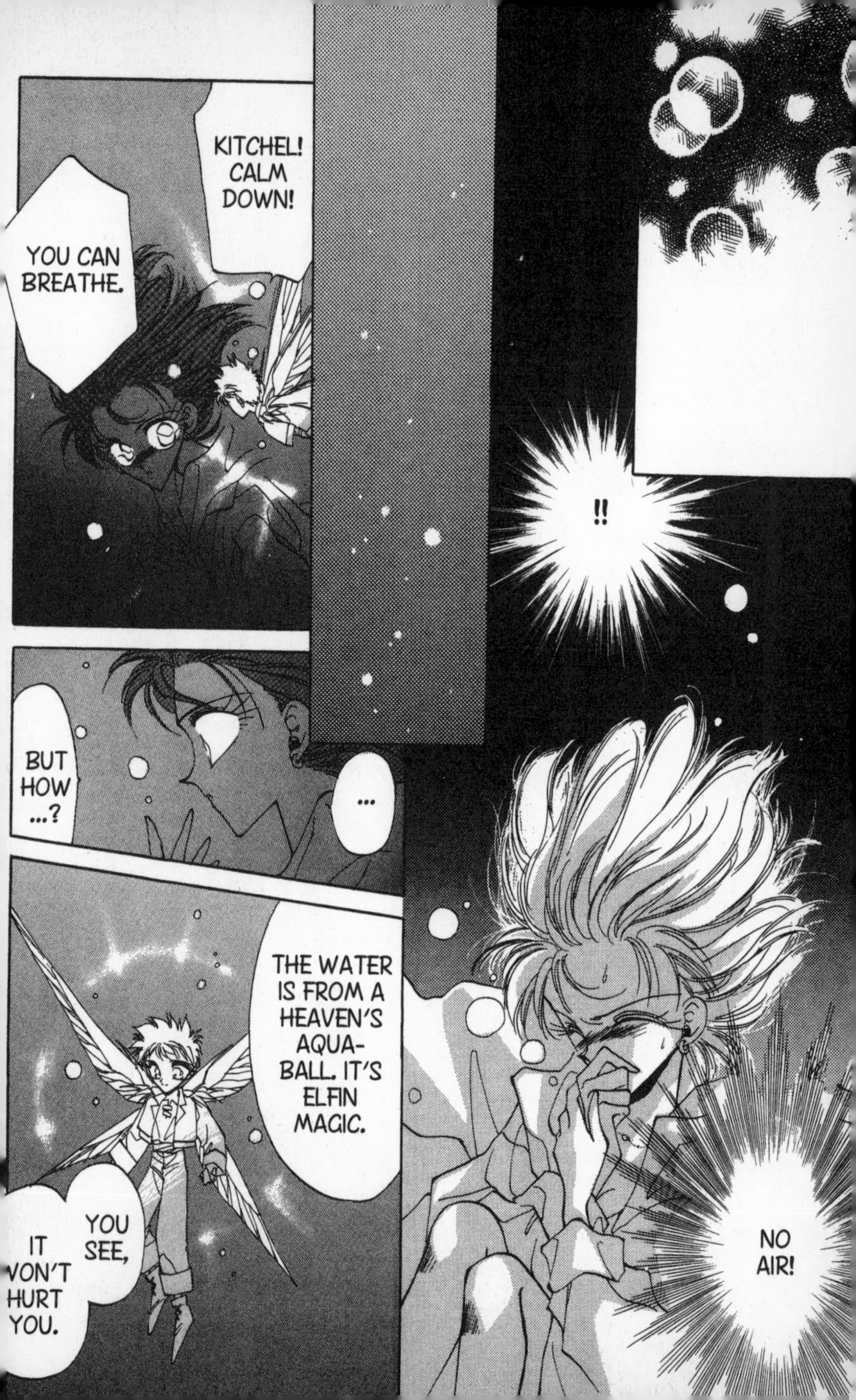
!!
NO AIR!
KITCHEL! CALM DOWN!
YOU CAN BREATHE.
...
BUT HOW ...?
THE WATER IS FROM A HEAVEN'S AQUA-BALL. IT'S ELFIN MAGIC.
YOU SEE,
IT WON'T HURT YOU.

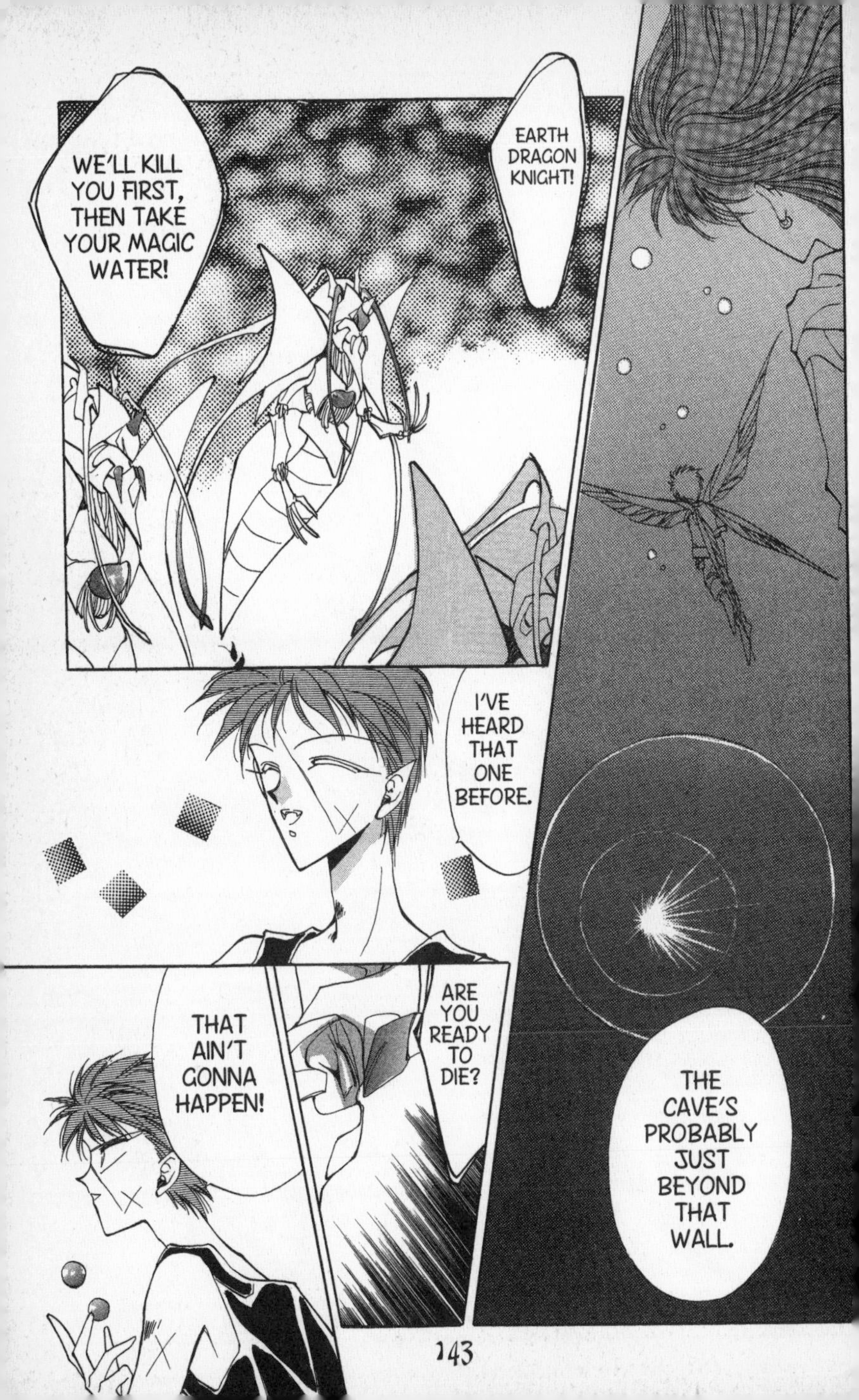
THE CAVE'S PROBABLY JUST BEYOND THAT WALL.
EARTH DRAGON KNIGHT!
WE'LL KILL YOU FIRST, THEN TAKE YOUR MAGIC WATER!
I'VE HEARD THAT ONE BEFORE.
ARE YOU READY TO DIE?
THAT AIN'T GONNA HAPPEN!

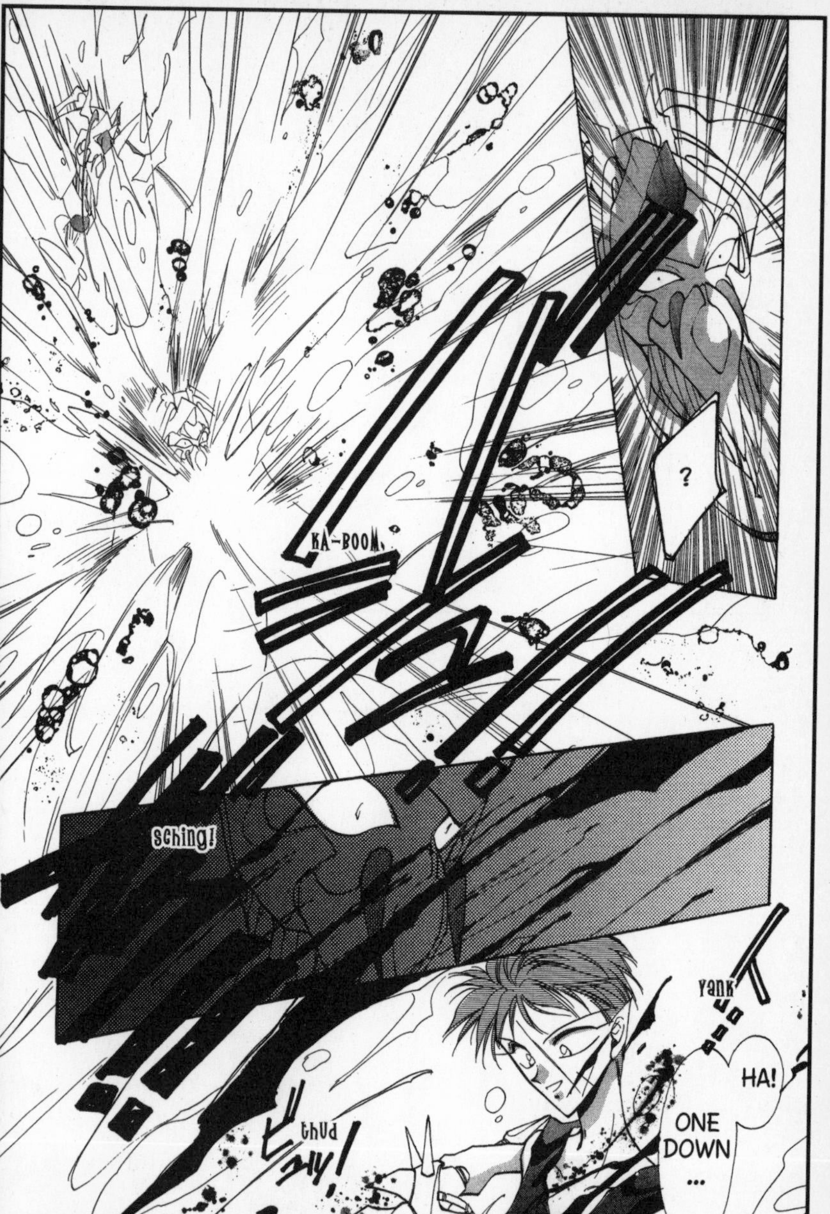
?
KA-BOOM
sching!
yank
HA!
ONE DOWN ...
thud

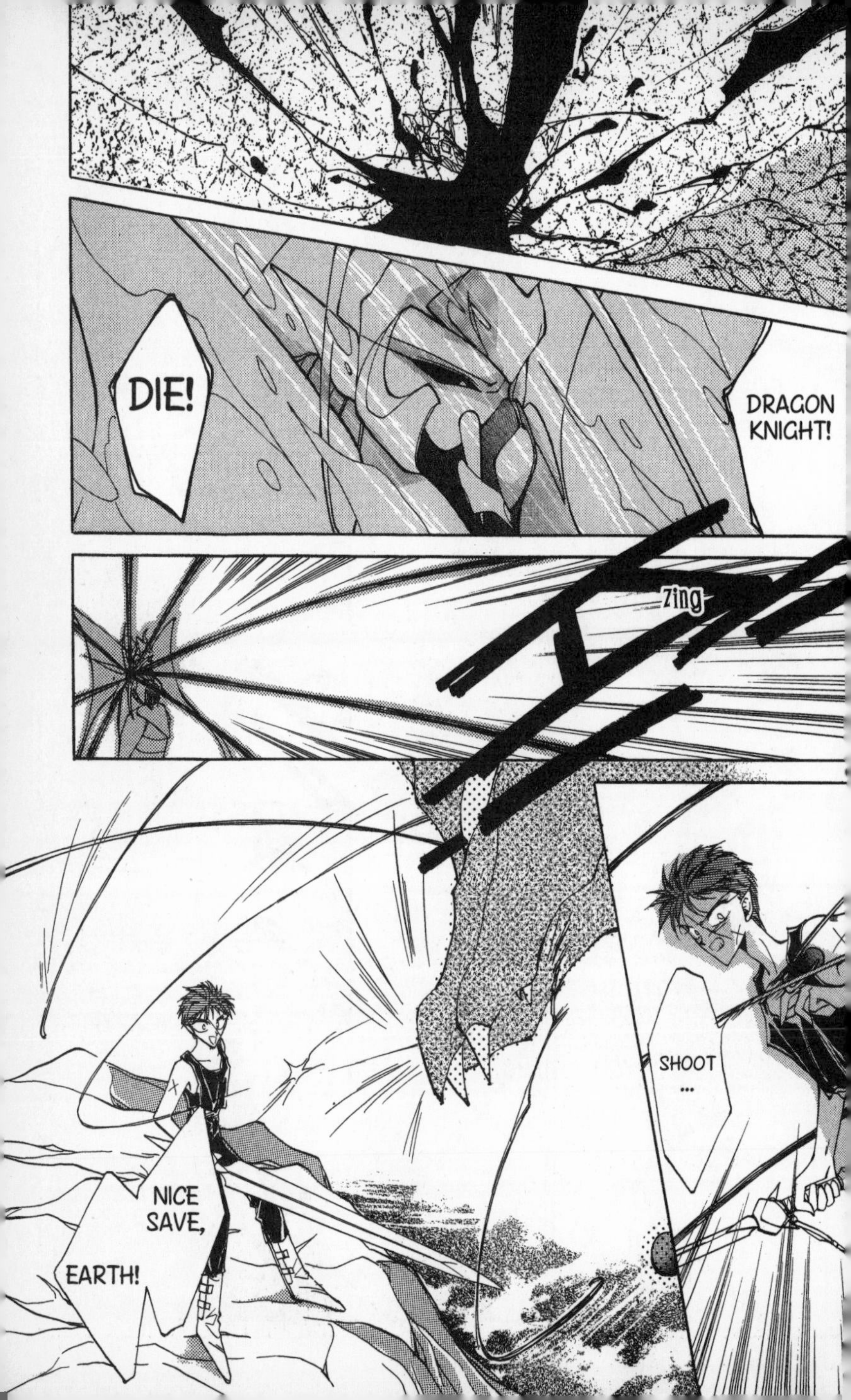
DRAGON KNIGHT!
DIE!
zing
SHOOT ...
NICE SAVE,
EARTH!

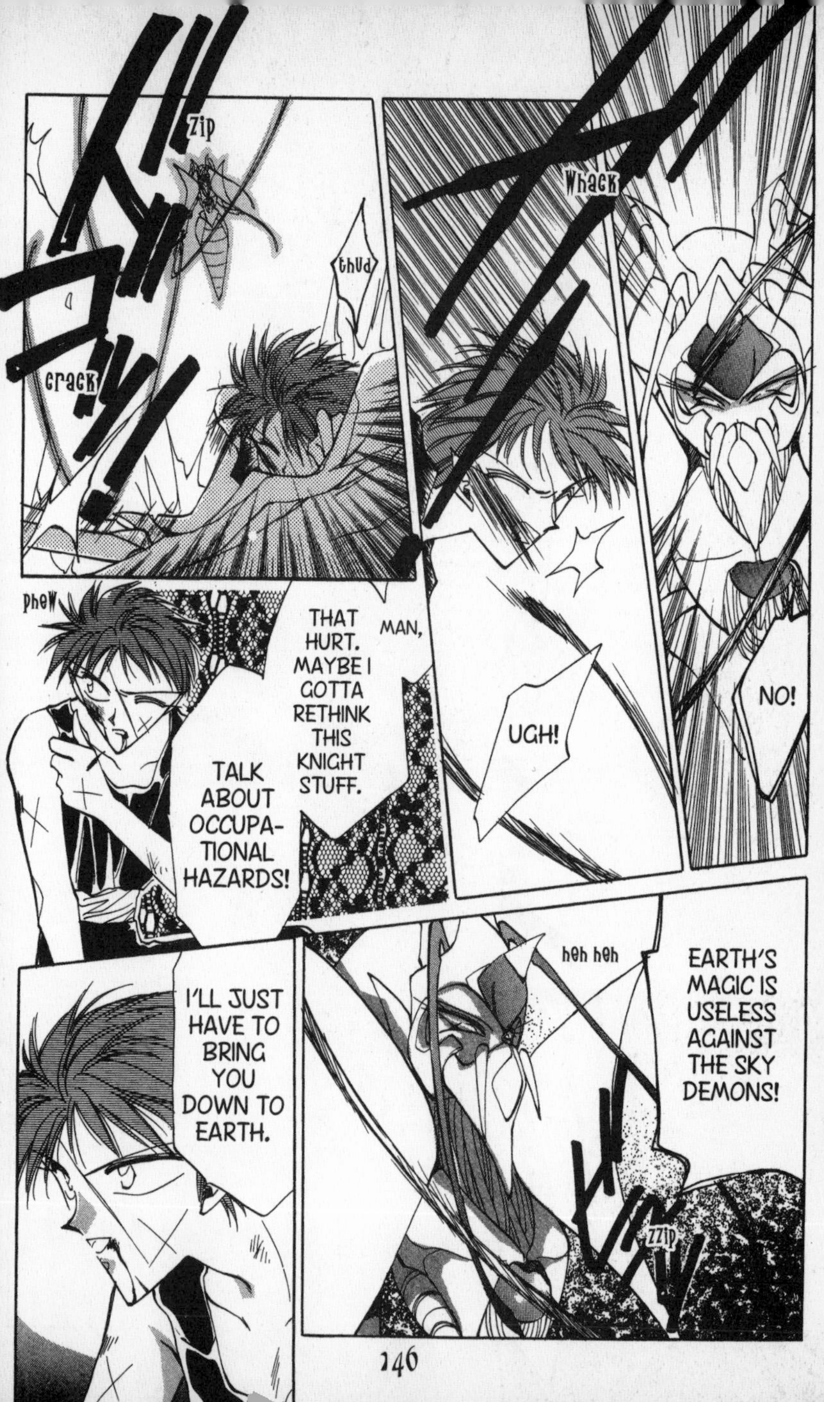
NO!
Whack
UGH!
zip
thud
crack
phew
MAN,
THAT HURT. MAYBE I GOTTA RETHINK THIS KNIGHT STUFF.
TALK ABOUT OCCUPATIONAL HAZARDS!
heh heh
EARTH'S MAGIC IS USELESS AGAINST THE SKY DEMONS!
zzip
I'LL JUST HAVE TO BRING YOU DOWN TO EARTH.

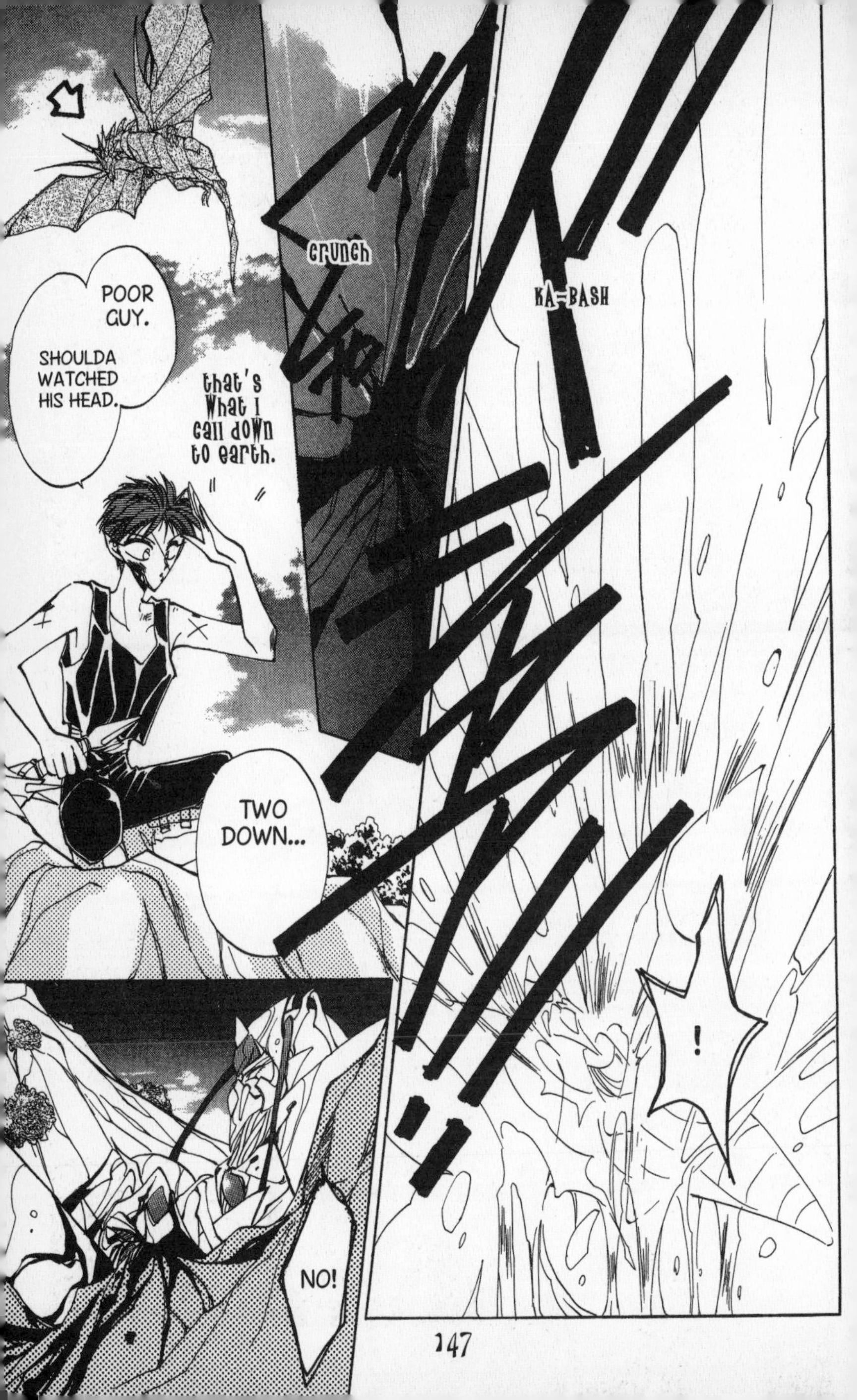
KA-BASH
!
crunch
that's What I call down to earth.
POOR GUY.
SHOULDA WATCHED HIS HEAD.
TWO DOWN...
NO!

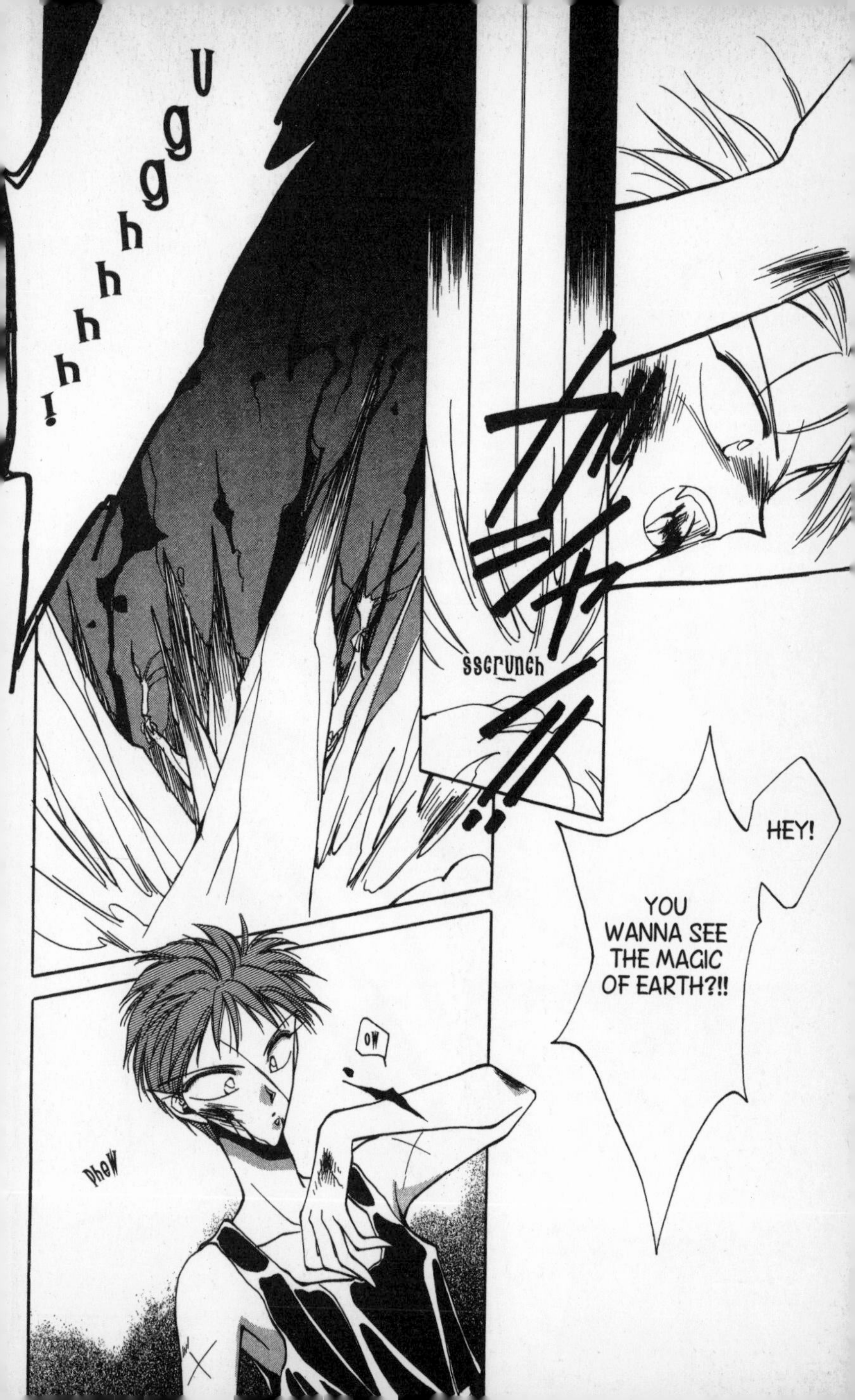
sscrunch
Ugghhhh!
HEY!
YOU WANNA SEE THE MAGIC OF EARTH?!!
ow
phew

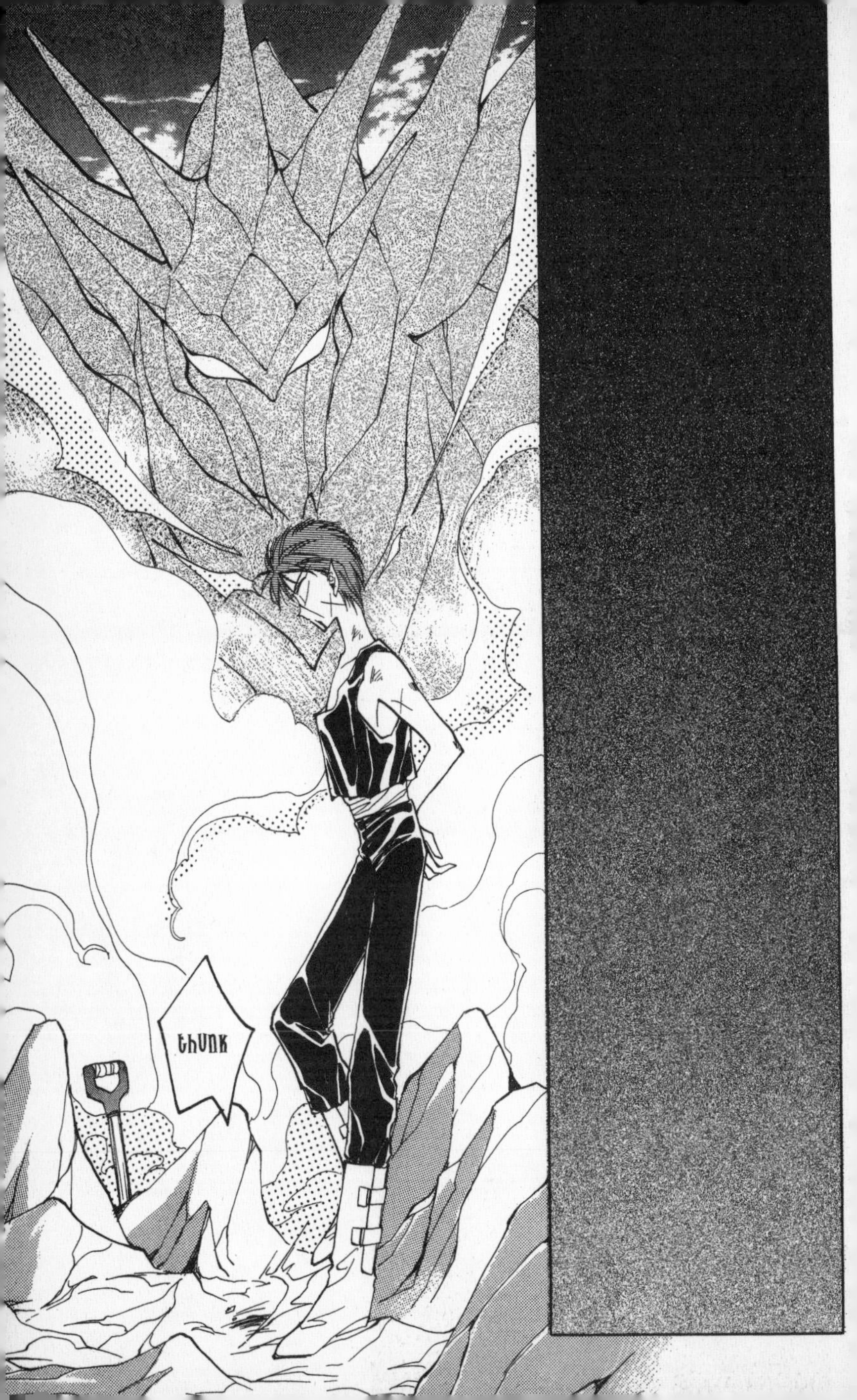
THUNK

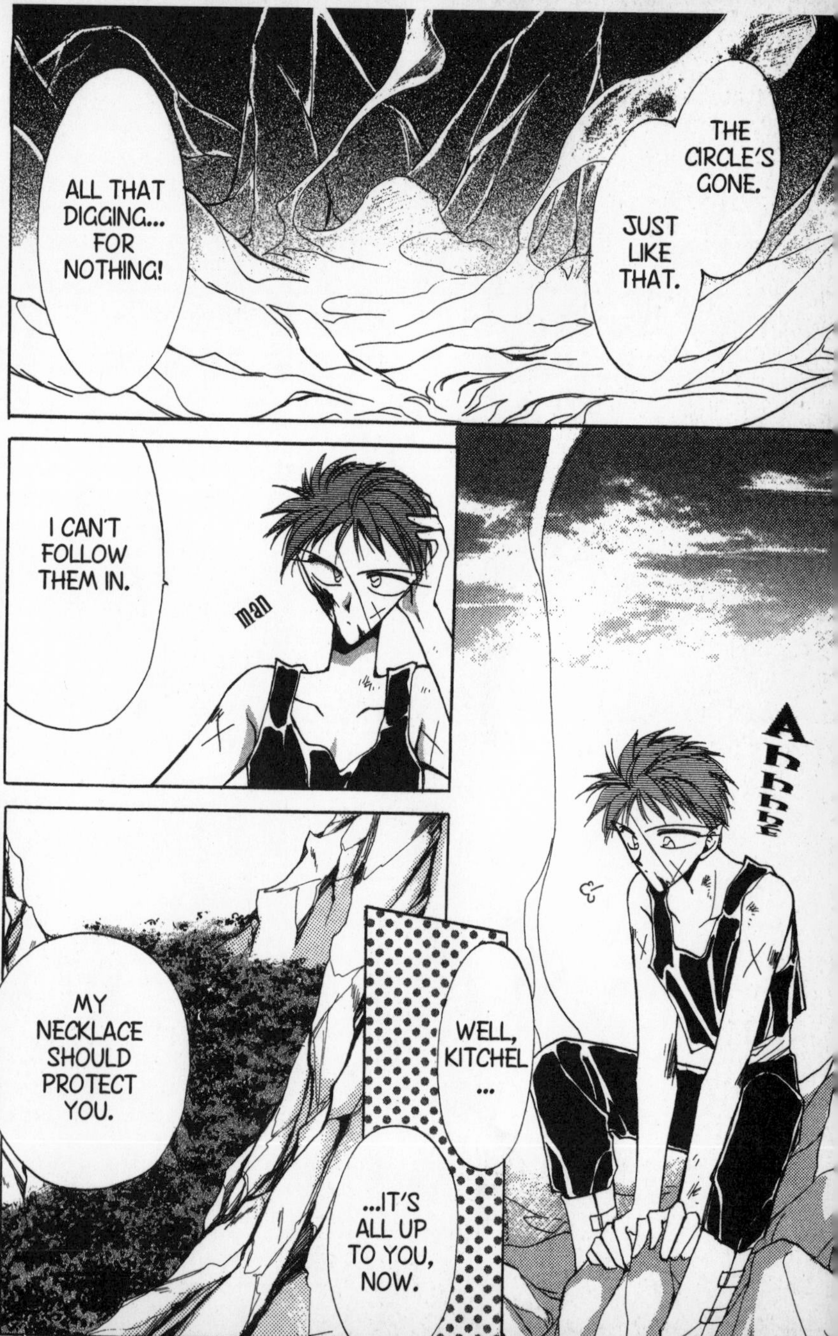
THE CIRCLE'S GONE.
JUST LIKE THAT.
ALL THAT DIGGING... FOR NOTHING!
Ahhhh
WELL, KITCHEL ...
...IT'S ALL UP TO YOU, NOW.
I CAN'T FOLLOW THEM IN.
man
MY NECKLACE SHOULD PROTECT YOU.

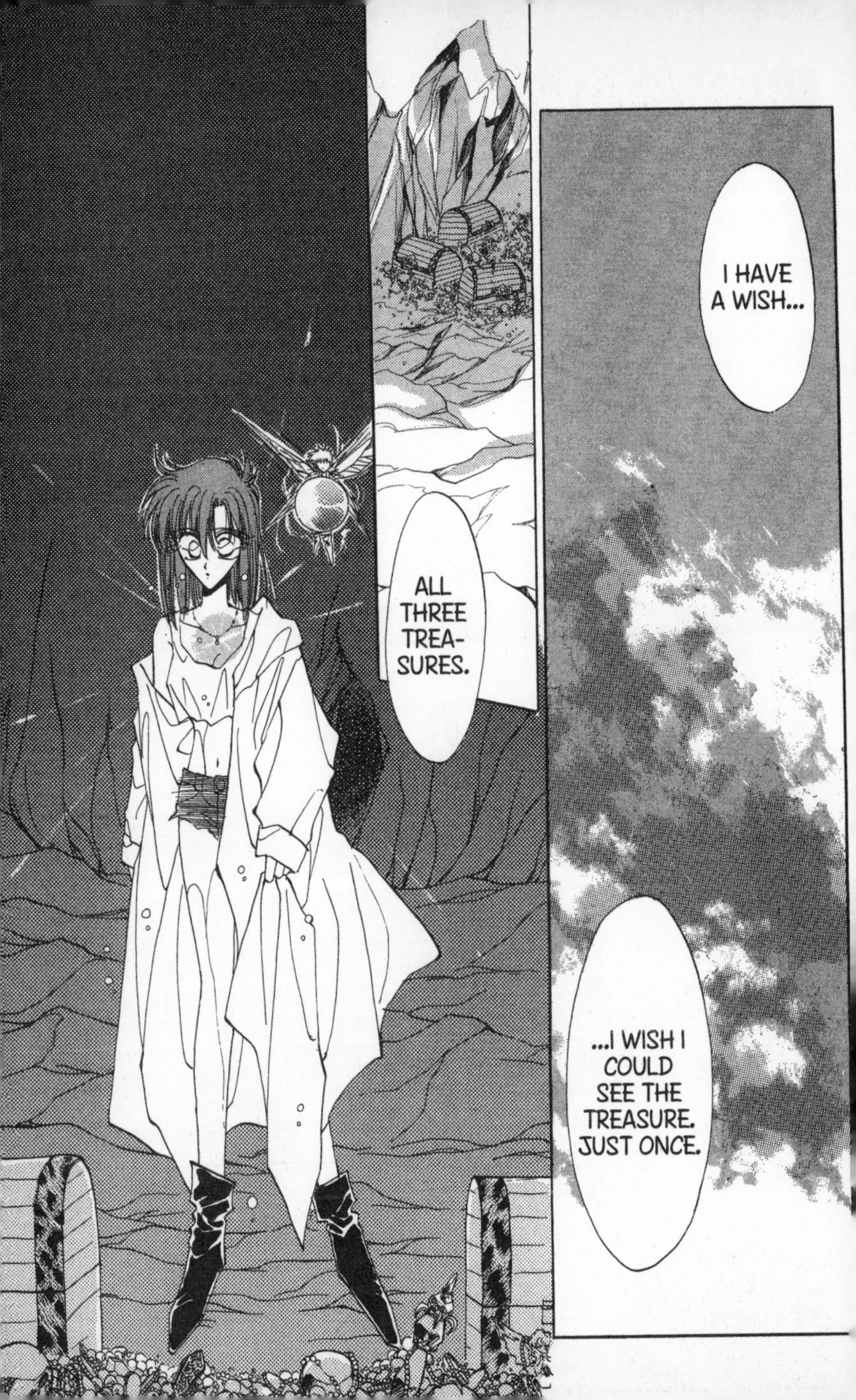
I HAVE A WISH...
...I WISH I COULD SEE THE TREASURE. JUST ONCE.
ALL THREE TREASURES.

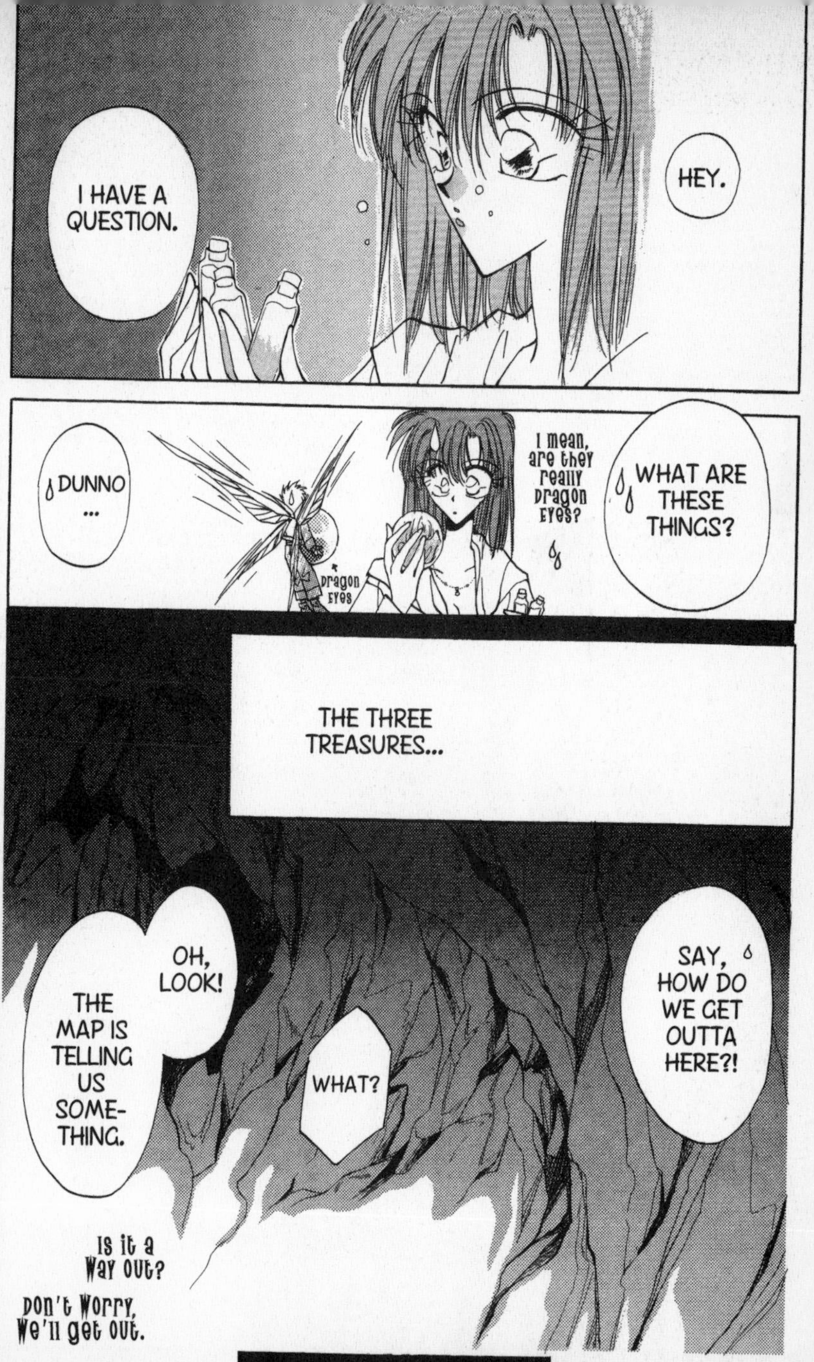
HEY.
I HAVE A QUESTION.
WHAT ARE THESE THINGS?
I mean, are they really Dragon Eyes?
Dragon Eyes
DUNNO ...
THE THREE TREASURES...
SAY, HOW DO WE GET OUTTA HERE?!
WHAT?
OH, LOOK!
THE MAP IS TELLING US SOME-THING.
Is it a way out?
Don't worry, we'll get out.

DRAGON KNIGHTS (TREASURE HUNT) • THE END

BERTHA'S CURSE

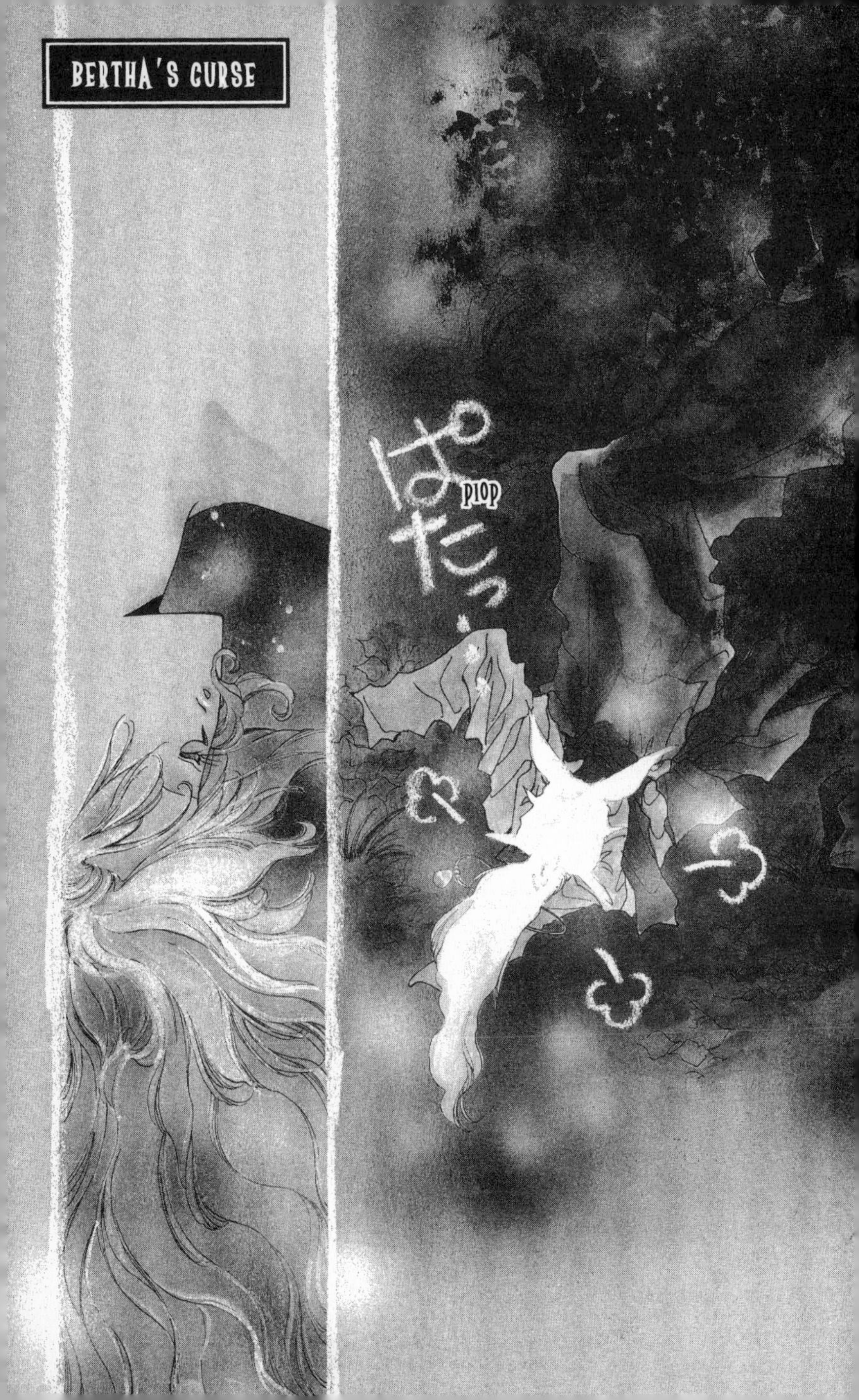
ぱたっ
PLOP

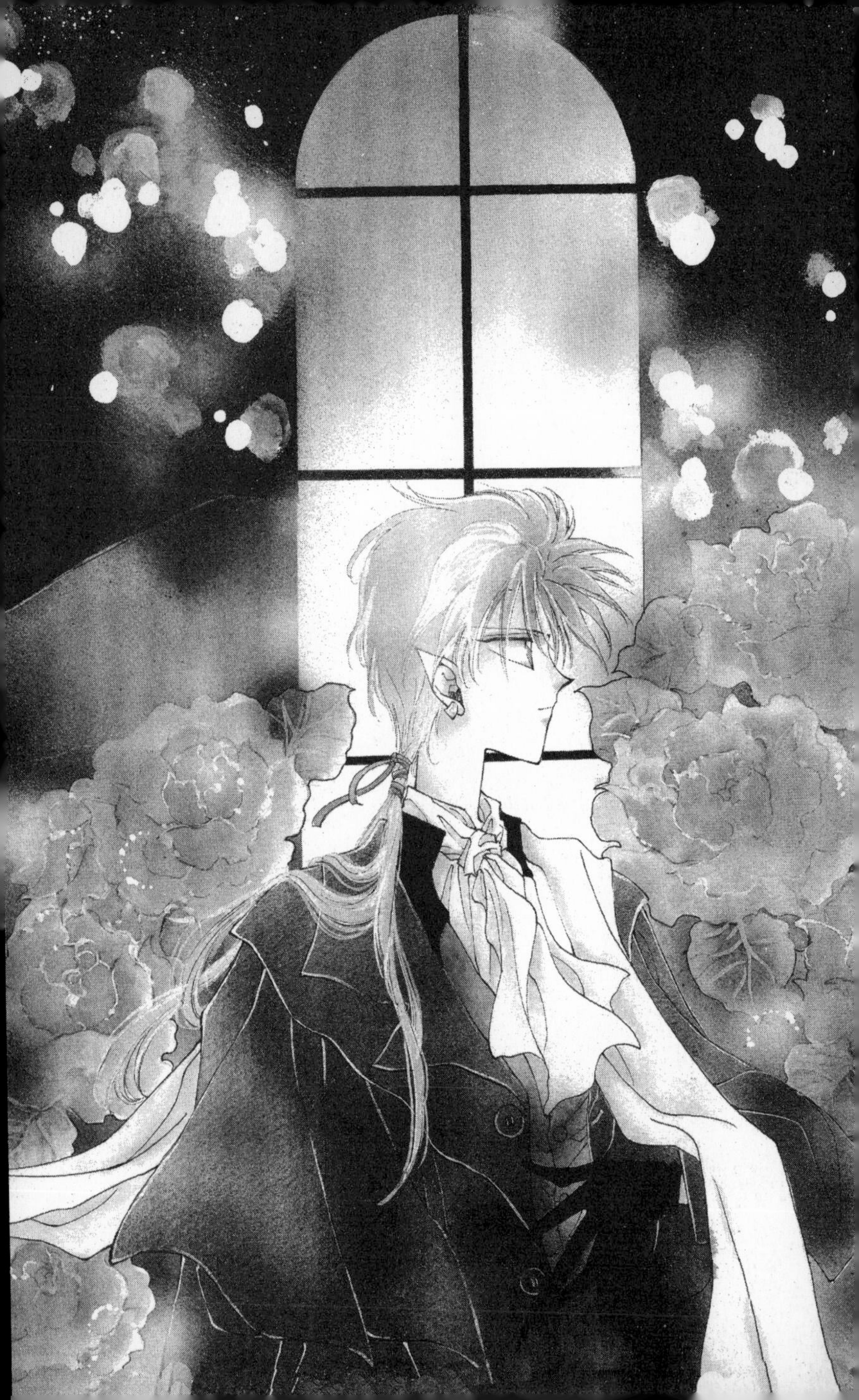

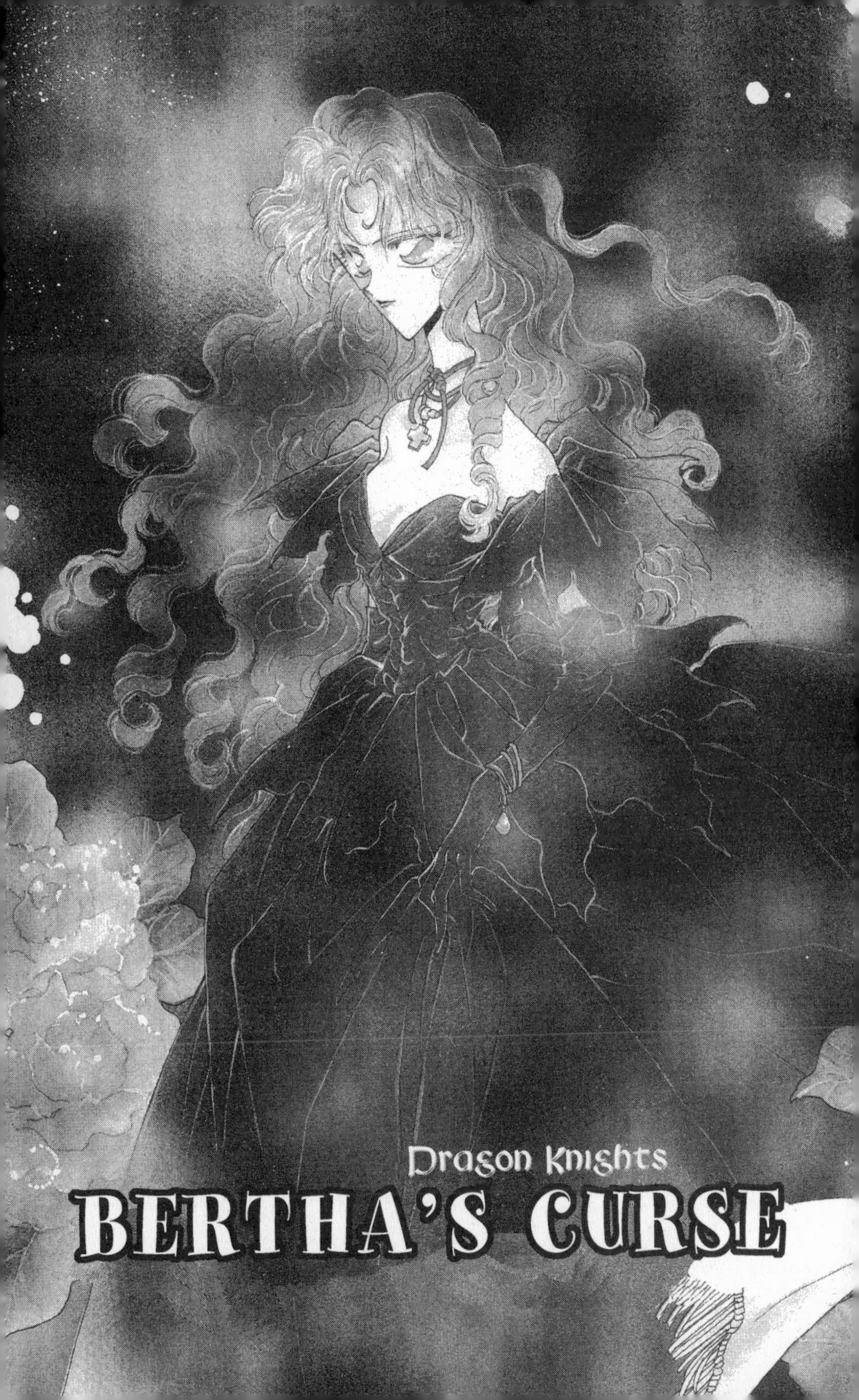
Dragon Knights
BERTHA'S CURSE

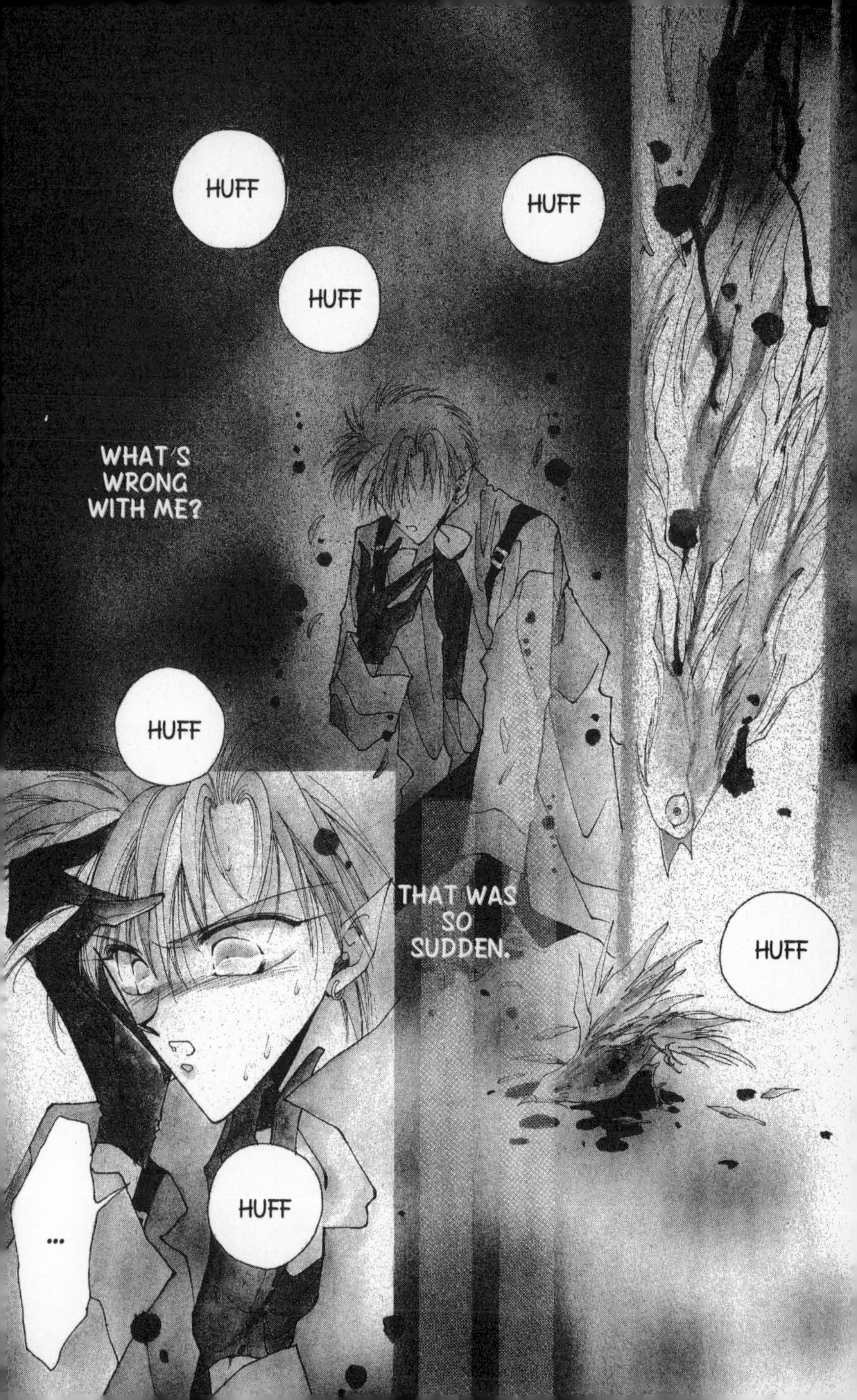
HUFF
HUFF
HUFF
WHAT'S WRONG WITH ME?
HUFF
HUFF
THAT WAS SO SUDDEN.
HUFF
...

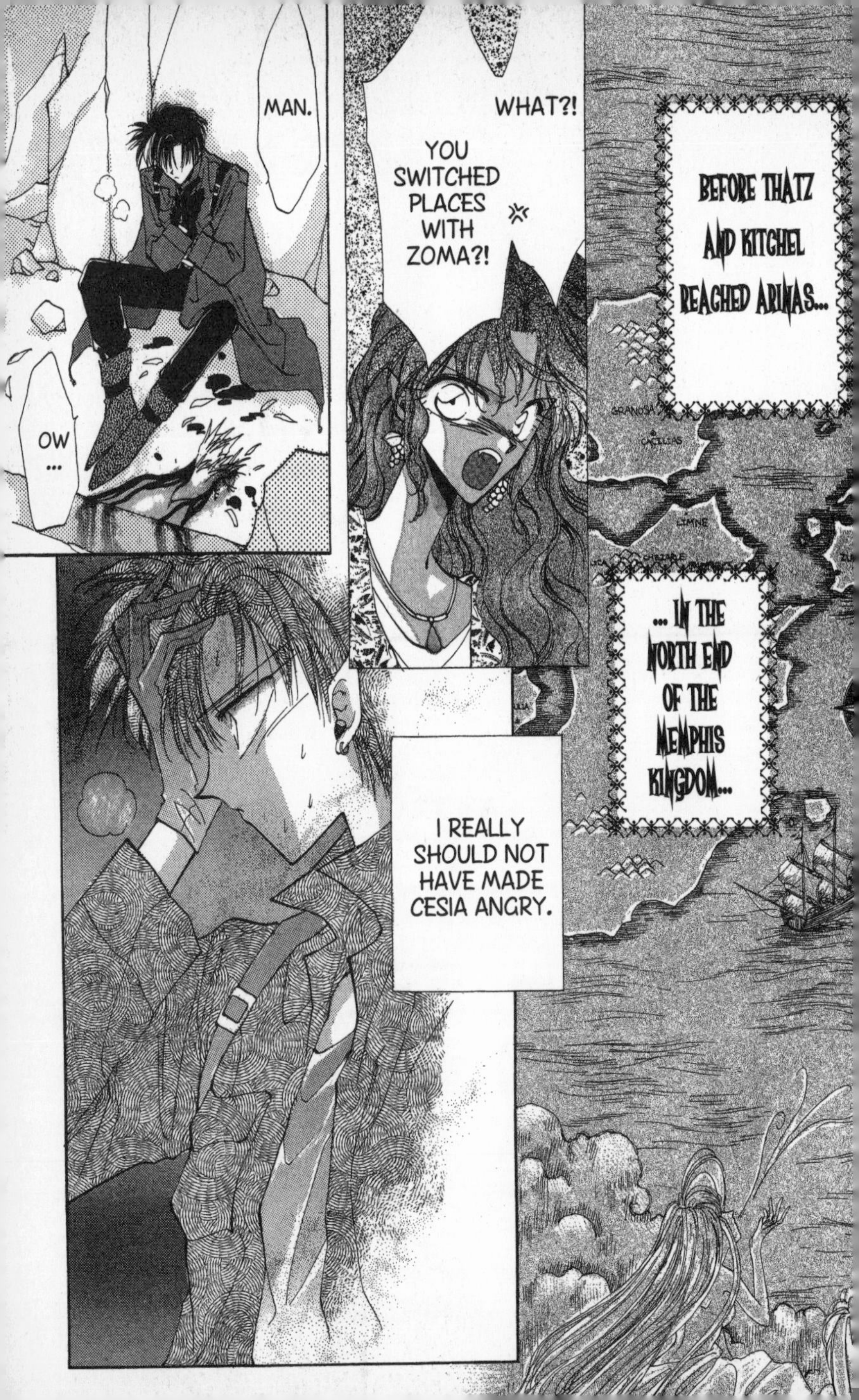
BEFORE THATZ AND KITCHEL REACHED ARINAS...
... IN THE NORTH END OF THE MEMPHIS KINGDOM...
WHAT?!
YOU SWITCHED PLACES WITH ZOMA?!
MAN.
OW ...
I REALLY SHOULD NOT HAVE MADE CESIA ANGRY.

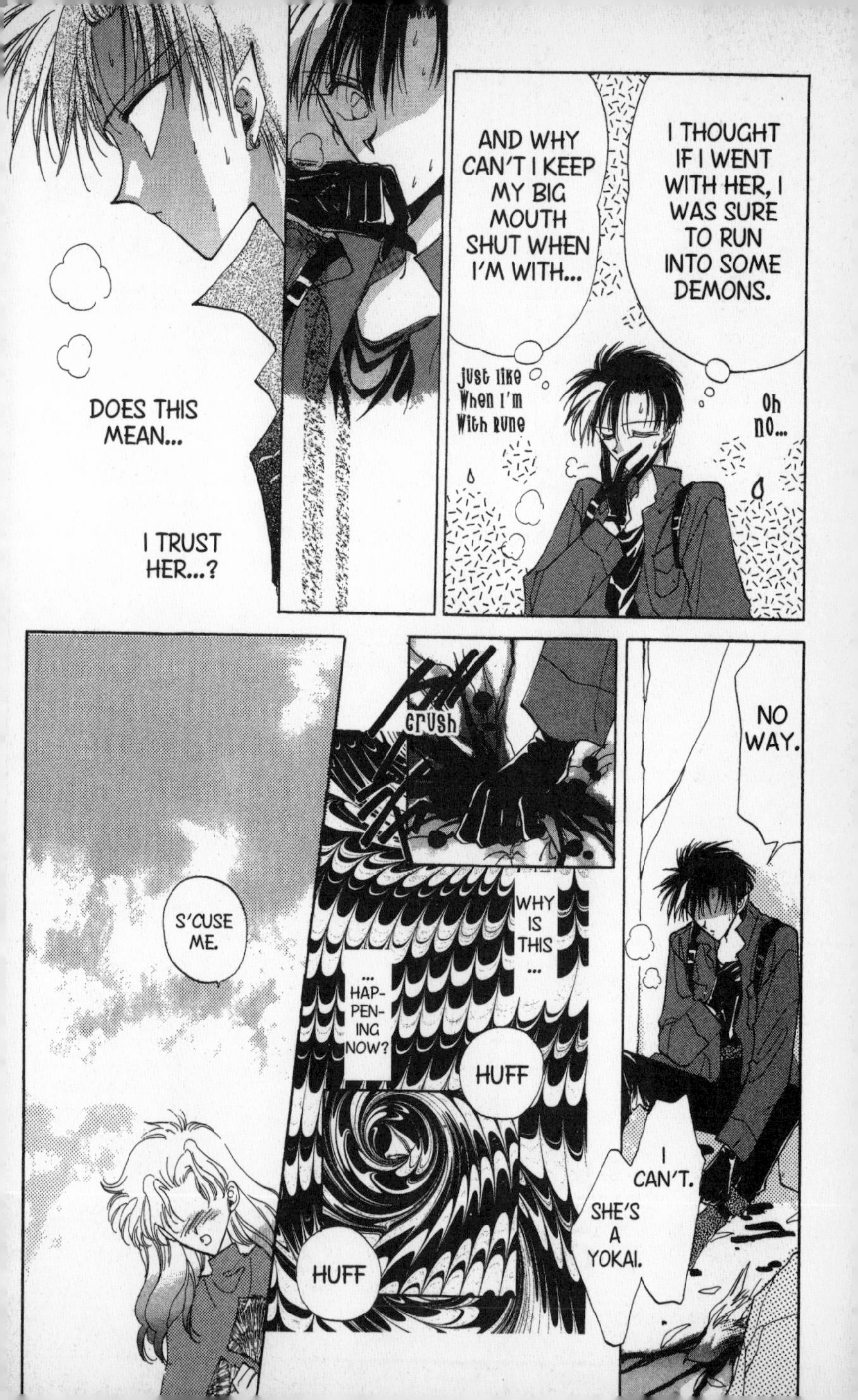
I THOUGHT IF I WENT WITH HER, I WAS SURE TO RUN INTO SOME DEMONS.
AND WHY CAN'T I KEEP MY BIG MOUTH SHUT WHEN I'M WITH...
just like When I'm With Rune
Oh no...
DOES THIS MEAN...
I TRUST HER...?
NO WAY.
I CAN'T.
SHE'S A YOKAI.
crush
WHY IS THIS...
...HAP-PEN-ING NOW?
HUFF
HUFF
S'CUSE ME.

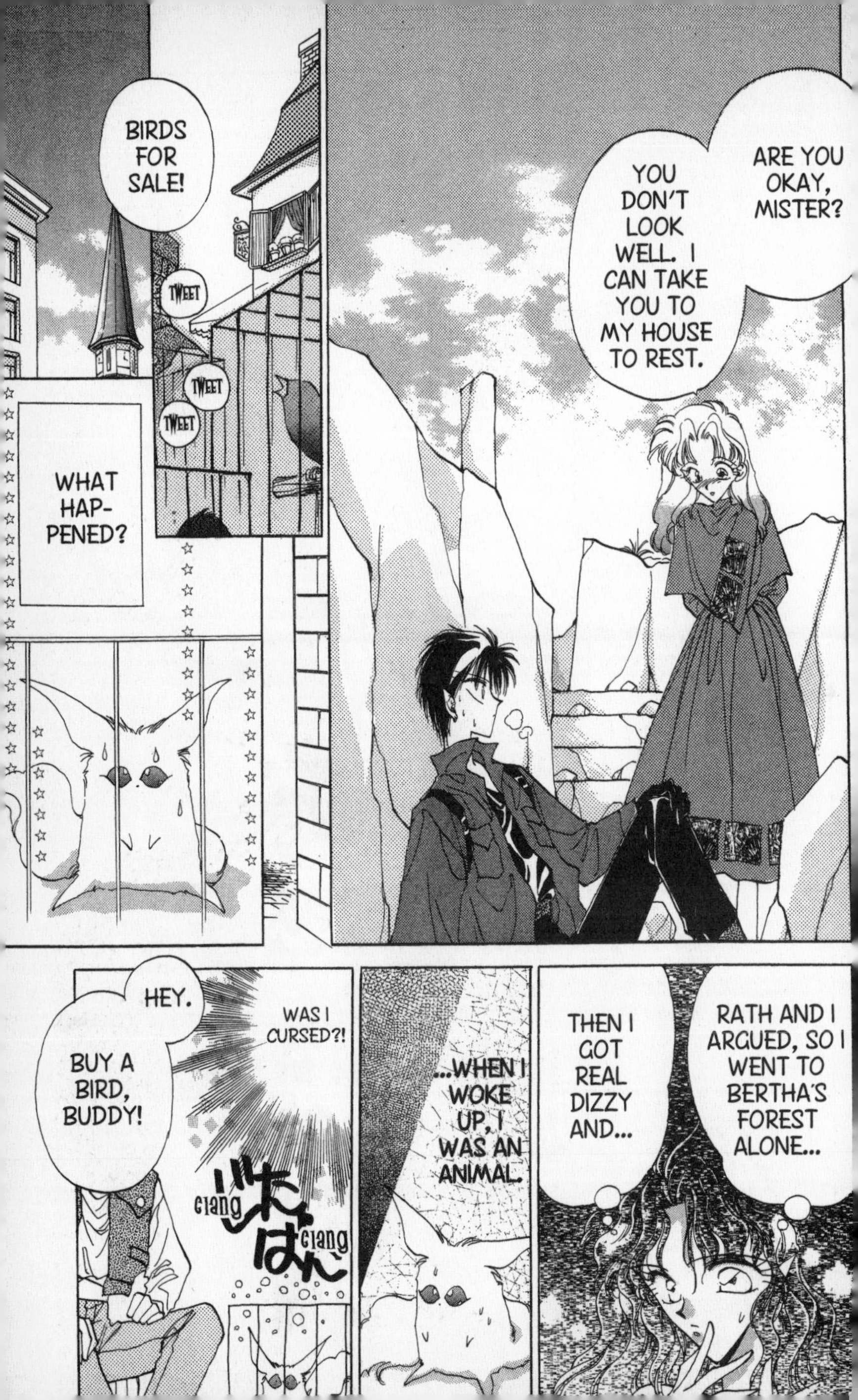
ARE YOU OKAY, MISTER?
YOU DON'T LOOK WELL. I CAN TAKE YOU TO MY HOUSE TO REST.
BIRDS FOR SALE!
TWEET
TWEET
TWEET
WHAT HAP-PENED?
RATH AND I ARGUED, SO I WENT TO BERTHA'S FOREST ALONE...
THEN I GOT REAL DIZZY AND...
...WHEN I WOKE UP, I WAS AN ANIMAL.
WAS I CURSED?!
HEY.
BUY A BIRD, BUDDY!
CLANG
CLANG

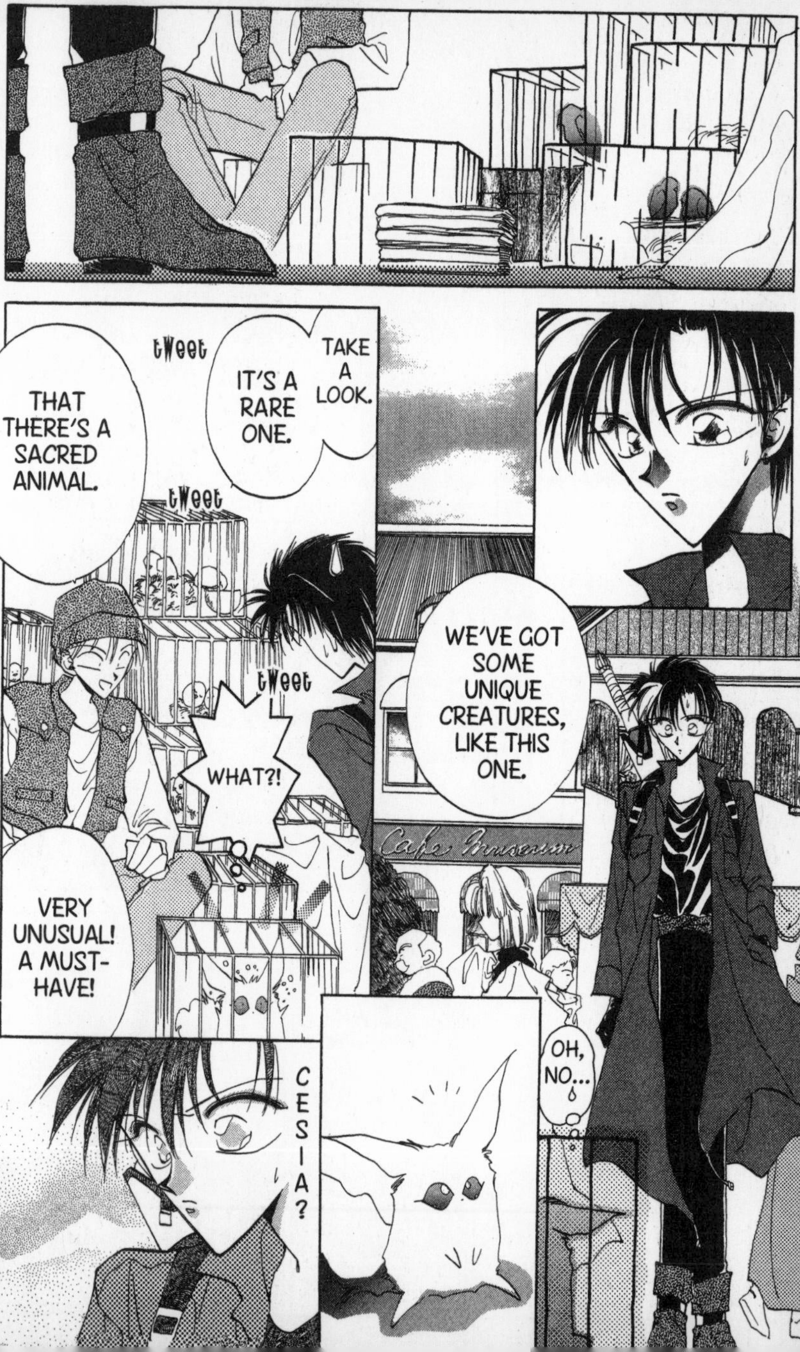
WE'VE GOT SOME UNIQUE CREATURES, LIKE THIS ONE.
OH, NO...
TAKE A LOOK.
IT'S A RARE ONE.
tWeet
THAT THERE'S A SACRED ANIMAL.
tWeet
tWeet
WHAT?!
VERY UNUSUAL! A MUST-HAVE!
Cafe Museum
CESIA?

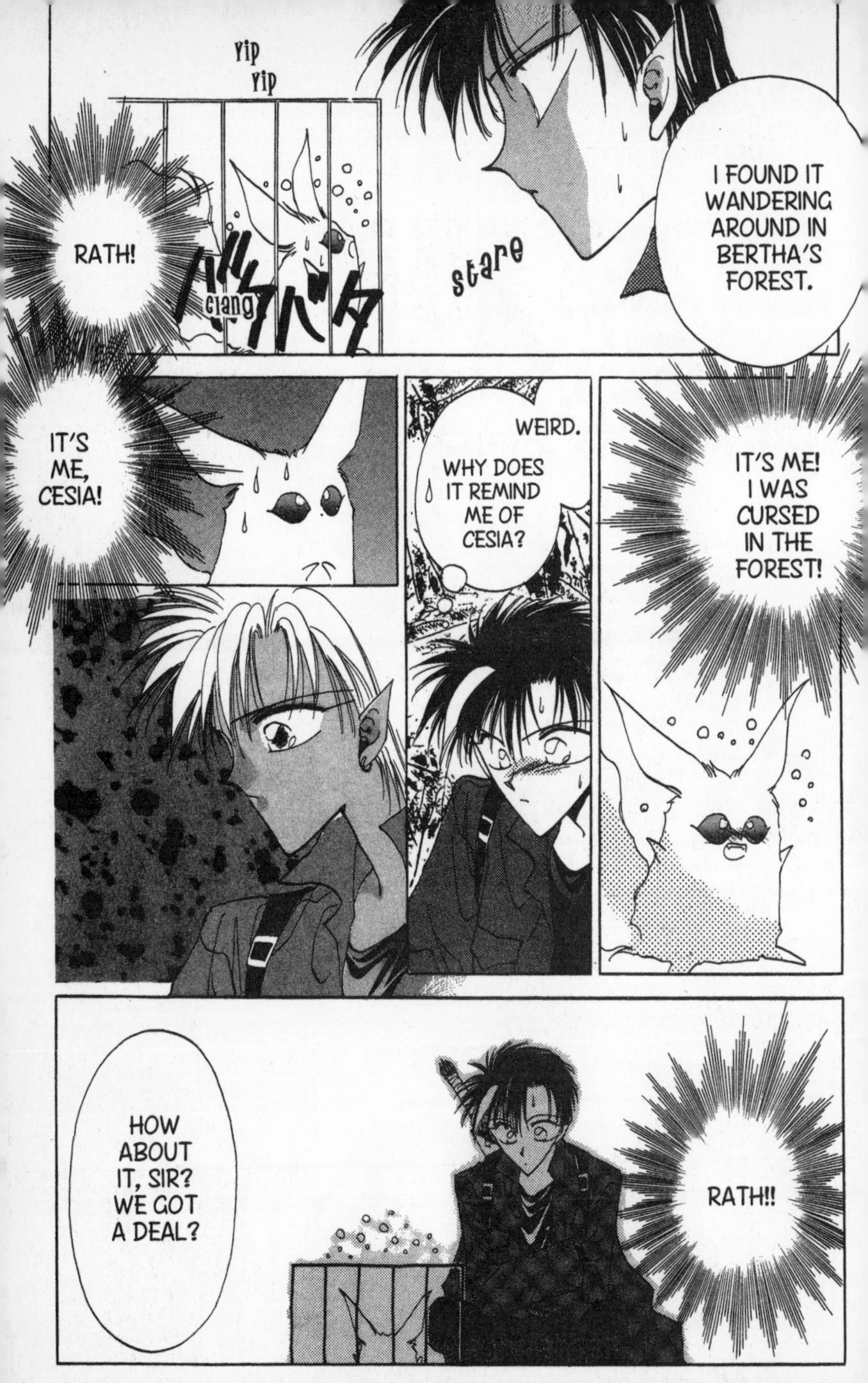
I FOUND IT WANDERING AROUND IN BERTHA'S FOREST.
stare
yip yip
clang
RATH!
IT'S ME! I WAS CURSED IN THE FOREST!
WEIRD. WHY DOES IT REMIND ME OF CESIA?
IT'S ME, CESIA!
RATH!!
HOW ABOUT IT, SIR? WE GOT A DEAL?

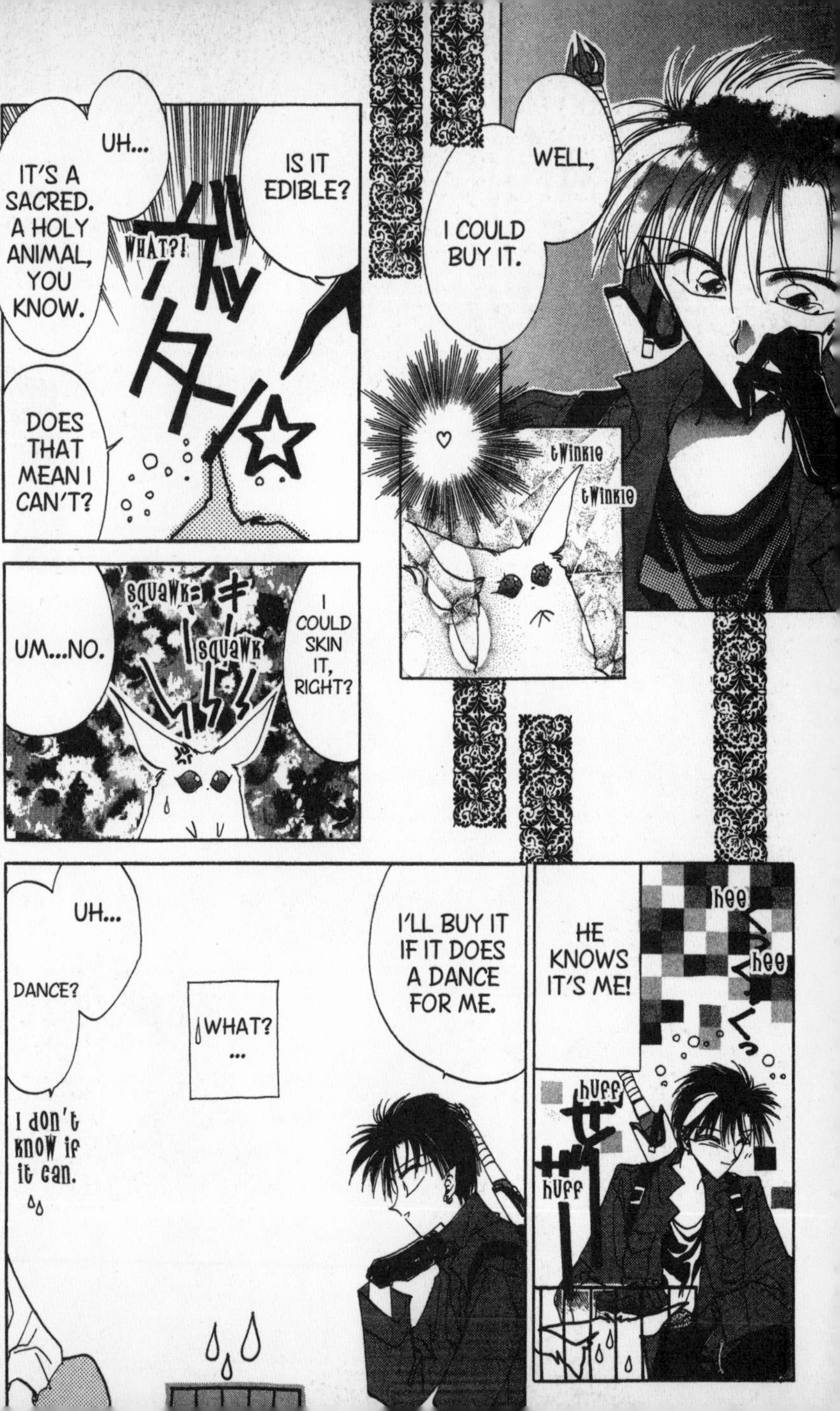
WELL,
I COULD BUY IT.
tWinkle
tWinkle
IS IT EDIBLE?
WHAT?!
UH...
IT'S A SACRED. A HOLY ANIMAL, YOU KNOW.
DOES THAT MEAN I CAN'T?
I COULD SKIN IT, RIGHT?
squaWk
squaWk
UM...NO.
HE KNOWS IT'S ME!
hee
hee
huff
huff
I'LL BUY IT IF IT DOES A DANCE FOR ME.
WHAT? ...
UH...
DANCE?
I don't know if it can.

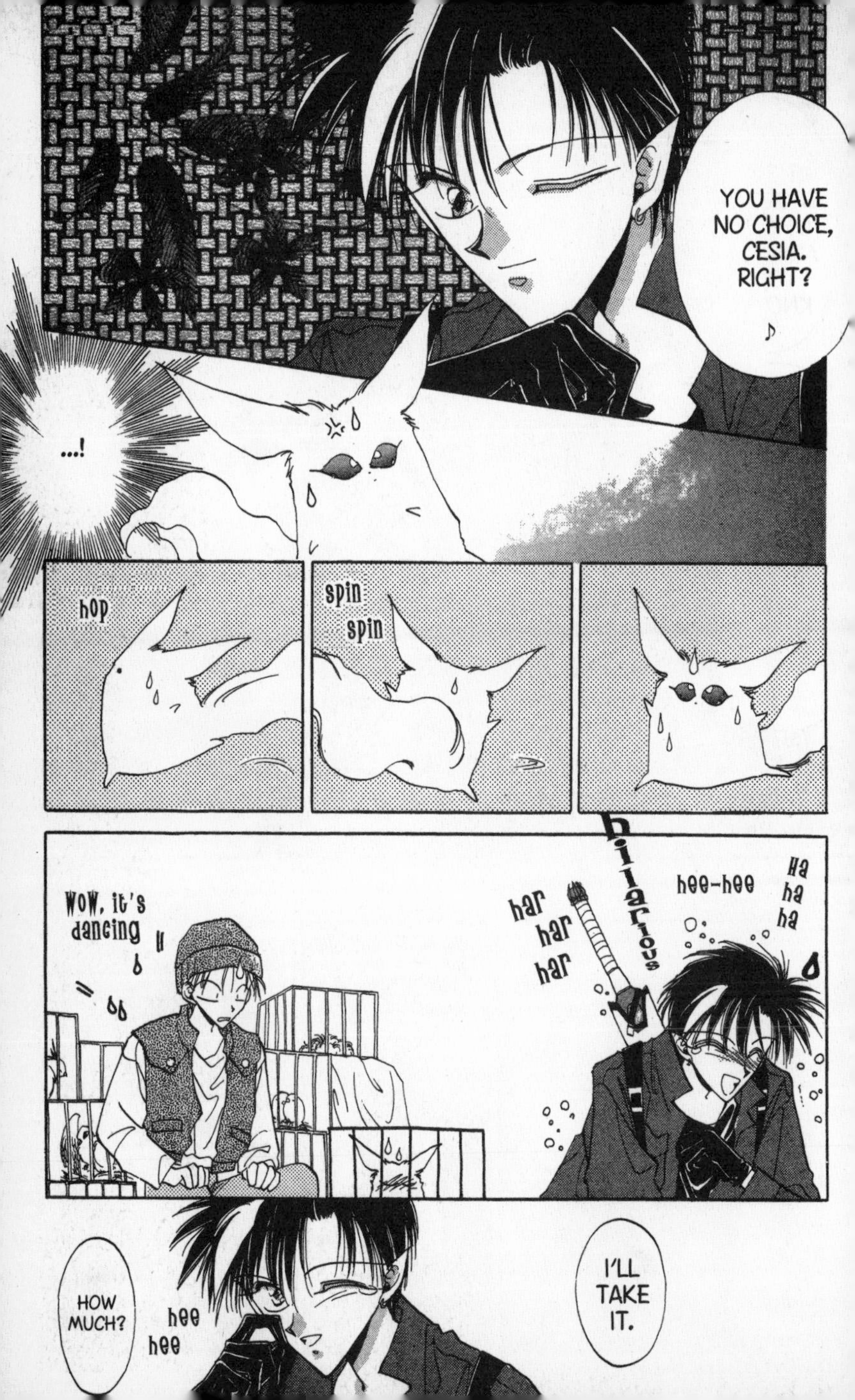
YOU HAVE NO CHOICE, CESIA. RIGHT? ♪
...!
spin spin
hop
Ha ha ha
hee-hee
hilarious
har har har
wow, it's dancing
I'LL TAKE IT.
hee hee
HOW MUCH?

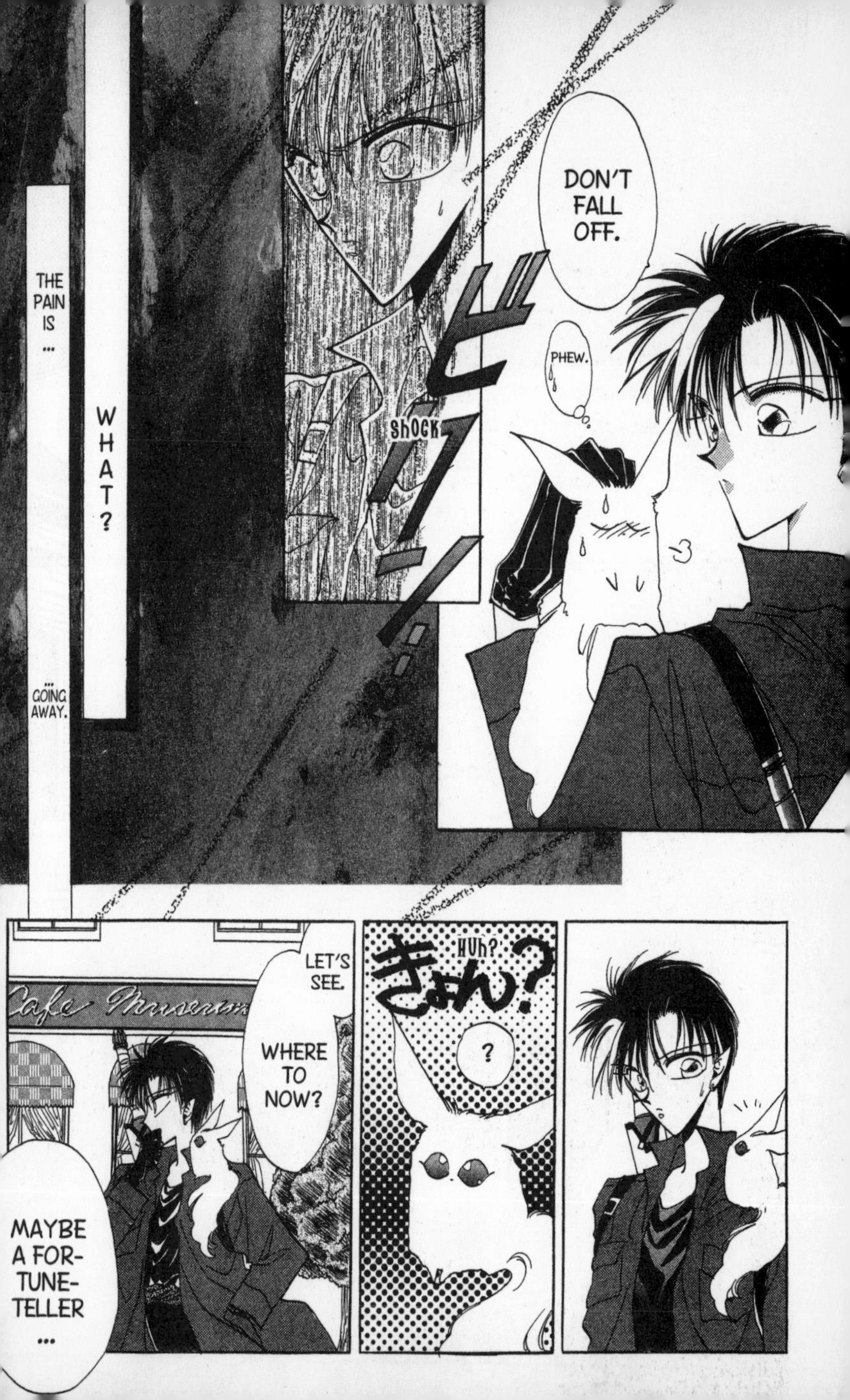

DON'T FALL OFF.
PHEW.
SHOCK
WHAT?
THE PAIN IS ...
... GOING AWAY.
HUH?
きゅん?
?
LET'S SEE.
WHERE TO NOW?
Cafe Museum
MAYBE A FOR-TUNE-TELLER ...

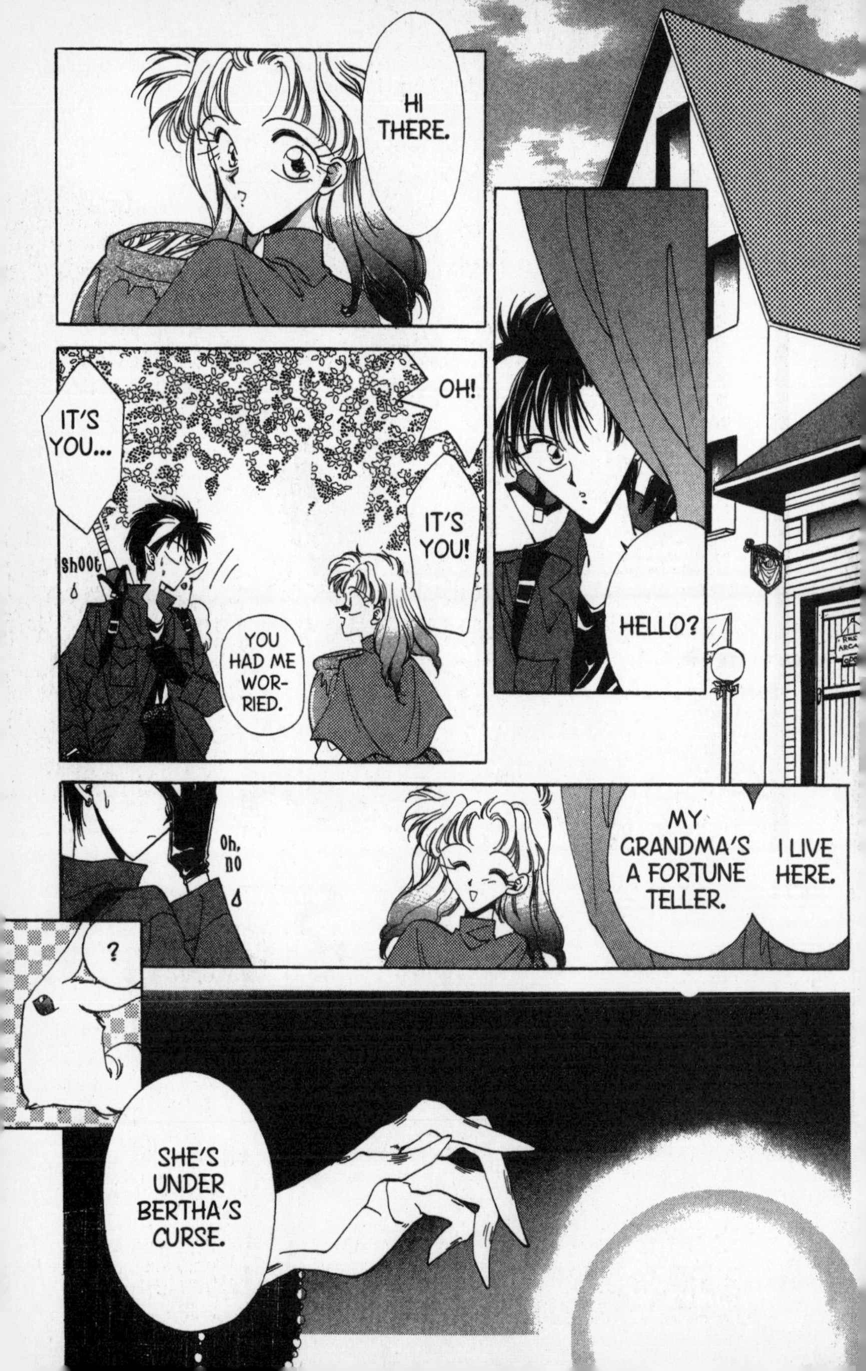
HELLO?
HI THERE.
OH!
IT'S YOU!
IT'S YOU...
YOU HAD ME WOR-RIED.
shoot
I LIVE HERE.
MY GRANDMA'S A FORTUNE TELLER.
Oh, no
?
SHE'S UNDER BERTHA'S CURSE.

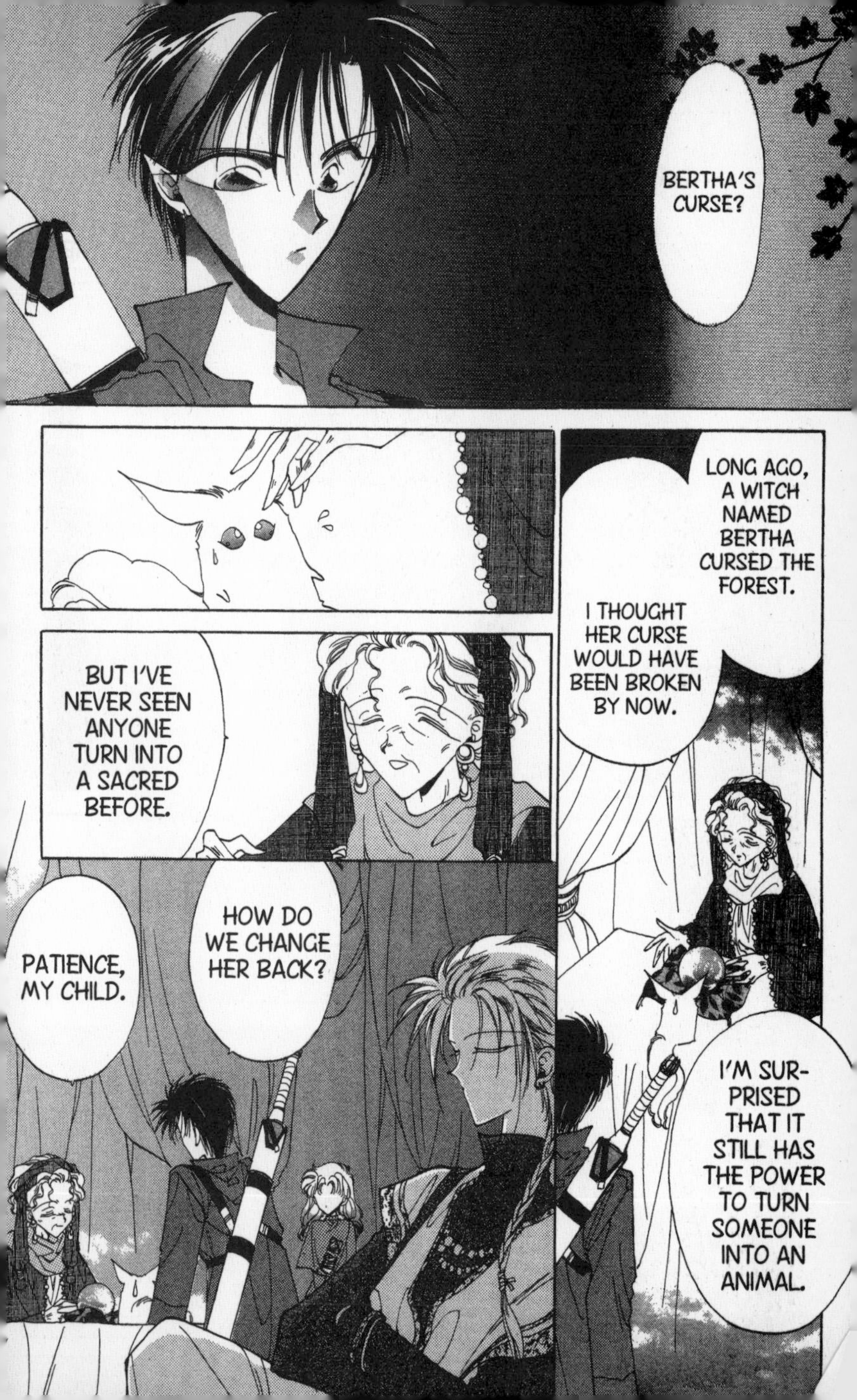
BERTHA'S CURSE?
LONG AGO, A WITCH NAMED BERTHA CURSED THE FOREST.
I THOUGHT HER CURSE WOULD HAVE BEEN BROKEN BY NOW.
I'M SUR-PRISED THAT IT STILL HAS THE POWER TO TURN SOMEONE INTO AN ANIMAL.
BUT I'VE NEVER SEEN ANYONE TURN INTO A SACRED BEFORE.
HOW DO WE CHANGE HER BACK?
PATIENCE, MY CHILD.

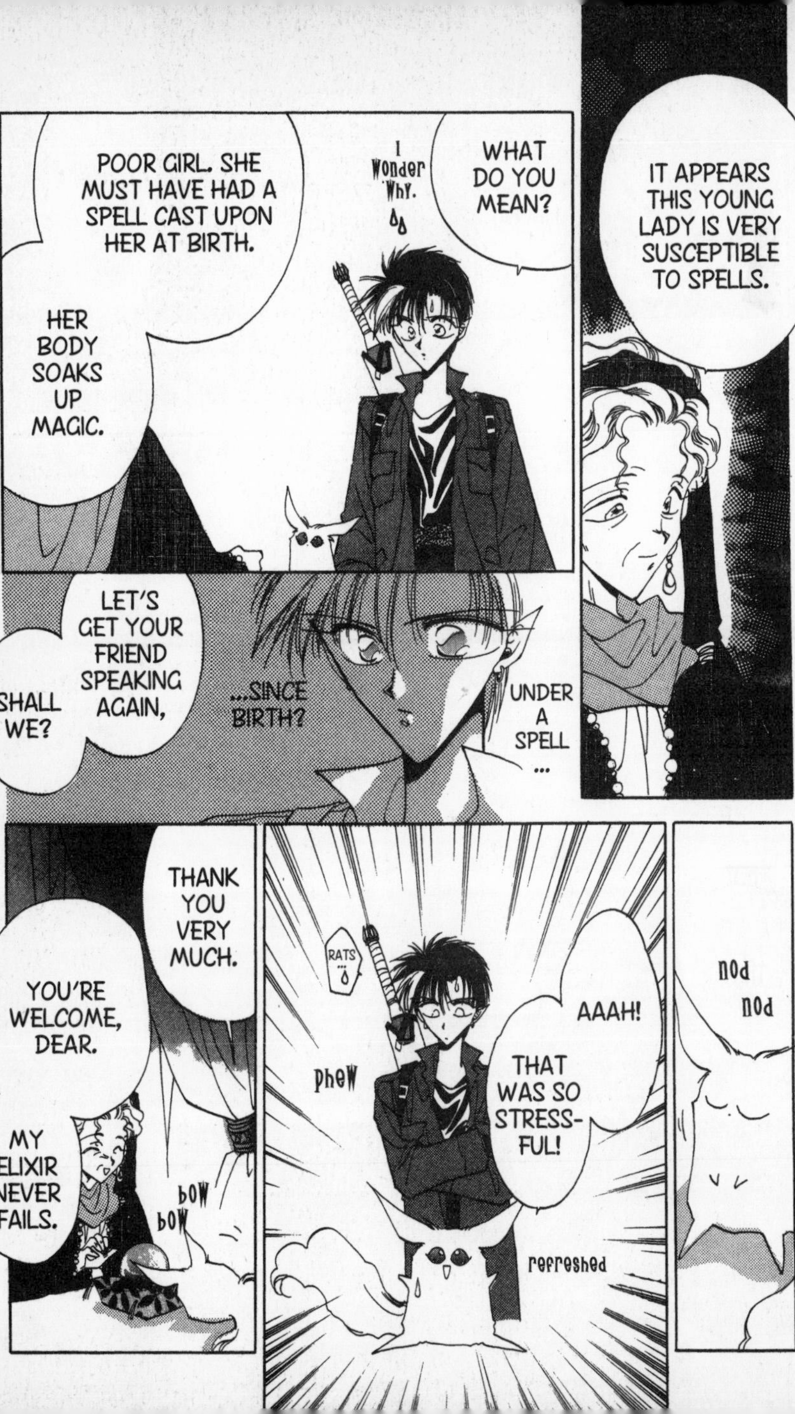
IT APPEARS THIS YOUNG LADY IS VERY SUSCEPTIBLE TO SPELLS.
WHAT DO YOU MEAN?
I wonder why.
POOR GIRL. SHE MUST HAVE HAD A SPELL CAST UPON HER AT BIRTH.
HER BODY SOAKS UP MAGIC.
UNDER A SPELL ...
...SINCE BIRTH?
LET'S GET YOUR FRIEND SPEAKING AGAIN,
SHALL WE?
nod
nod
AAAH!
THAT WAS SO STRESS-FUL!
RATS ...
phew
refreshed
THANK YOU VERY MUCH.
YOU'RE WELCOME, DEAR.
MY ELIXIR NEVER FAILS.
bow
bow

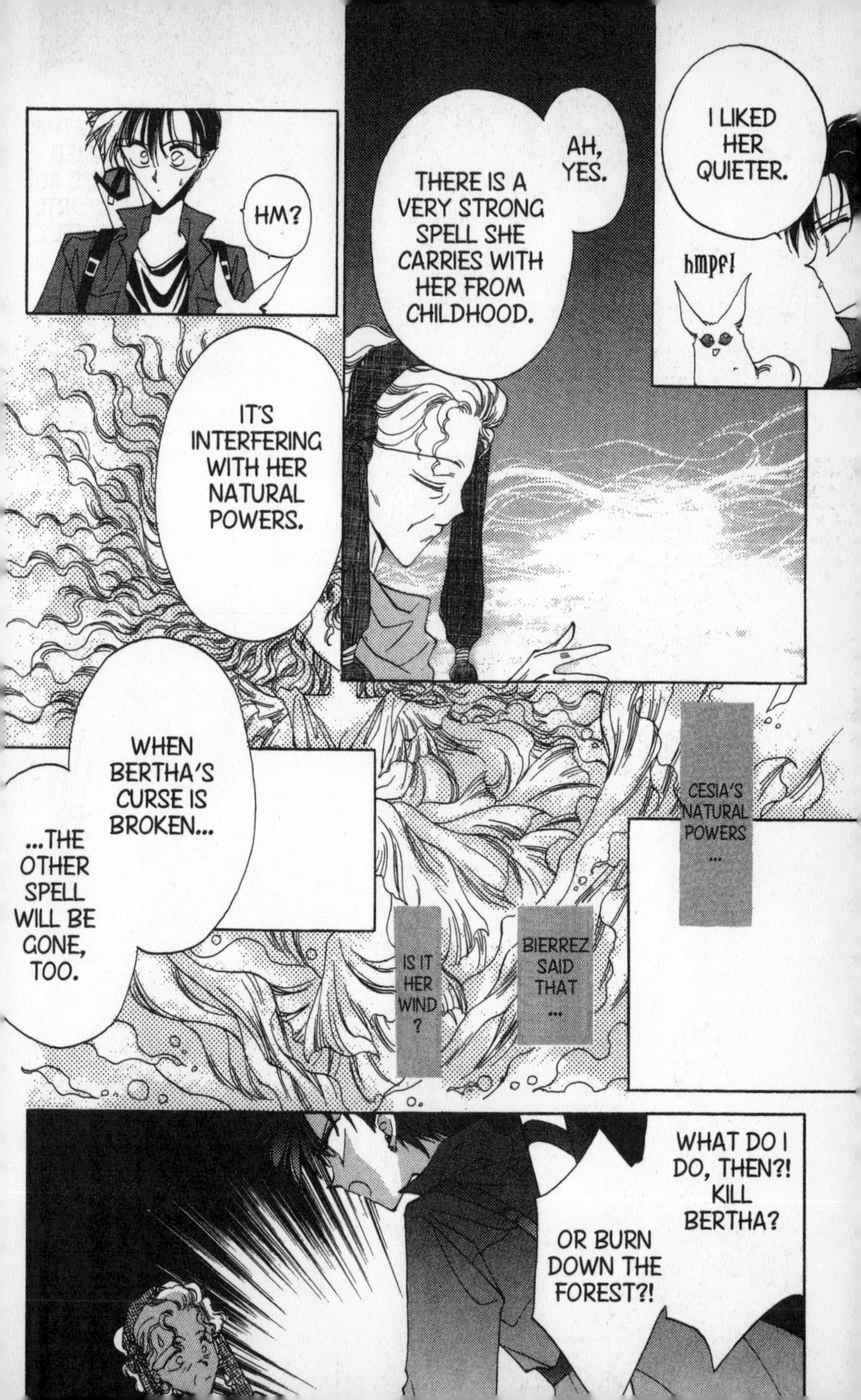
I LIKED HER QUIETER.
hmpf!
HM?
AH, YES.
THERE IS A VERY STRONG SPELL SHE CARRIES WITH HER FROM CHILDHOOD.
IT'S INTERFERING WITH HER NATURAL POWERS.
CESIA'S NATURAL POWERS ...
BIERREZ SAID THAT ...
IS IT HER WIND ?
WHEN BERTHA'S CURSE IS BROKEN...
...THE OTHER SPELL WILL BE GONE, TOO.
WHAT DO I DO, THEN?! KILL BERTHA?
OR BURN DOWN THE FOREST?!

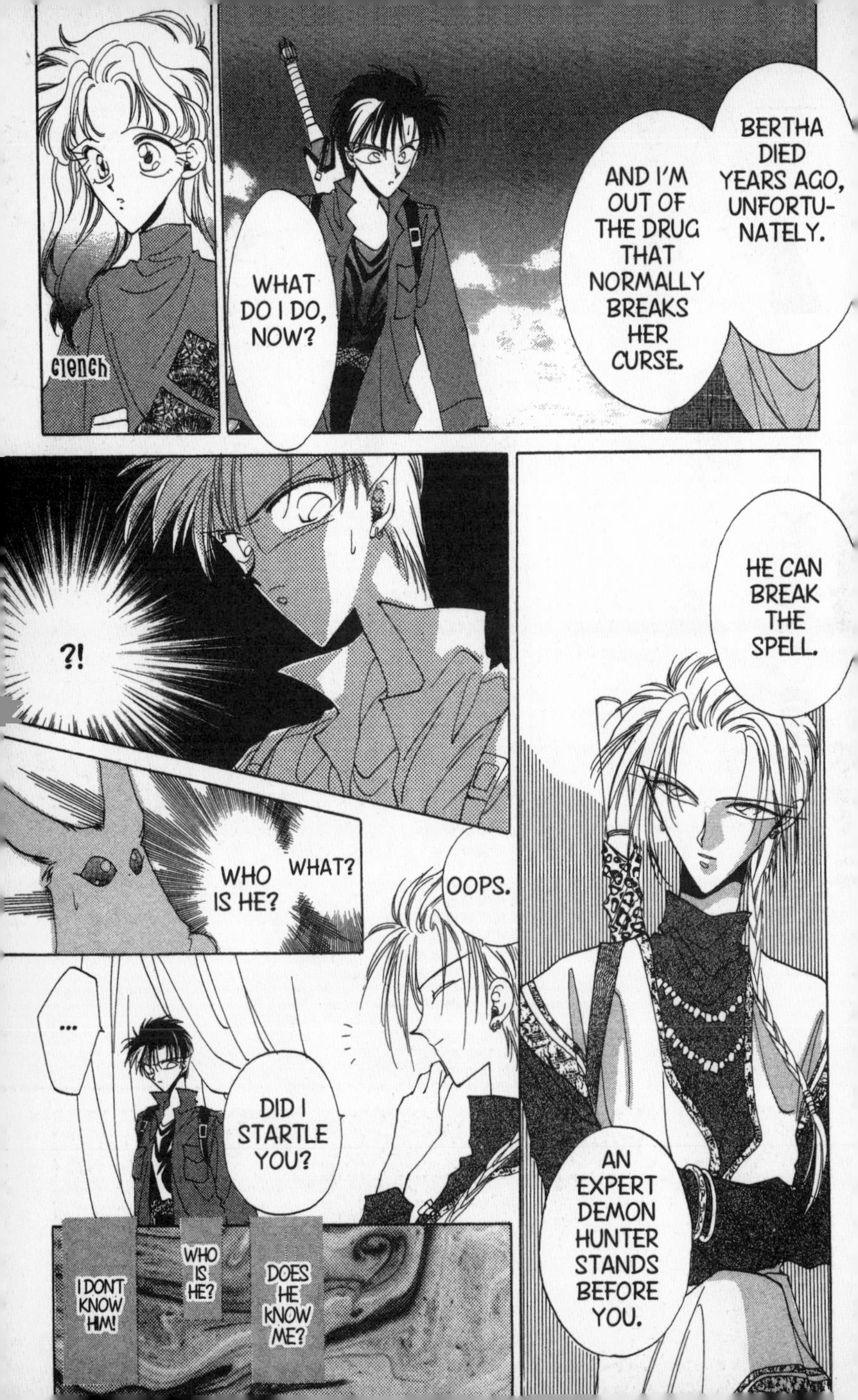
BERTHA DIED YEARS AGO, UNFORTU-NATELY.
AND I'M OUT OF THE DRUG THAT NORMALLY BREAKS HER CURSE.
WHAT DO I DO, NOW?
CLENCH
HE CAN BREAK THE SPELL.
AN EXPERT DEMON HUNTER STANDS BEFORE YOU.
?!
WHAT?
WHO IS HE?
OOPS.
DID I STARTLE YOU?
...
DOES HE KNOW ME?
WHO IS HE?
I DONT KNOW HIM!

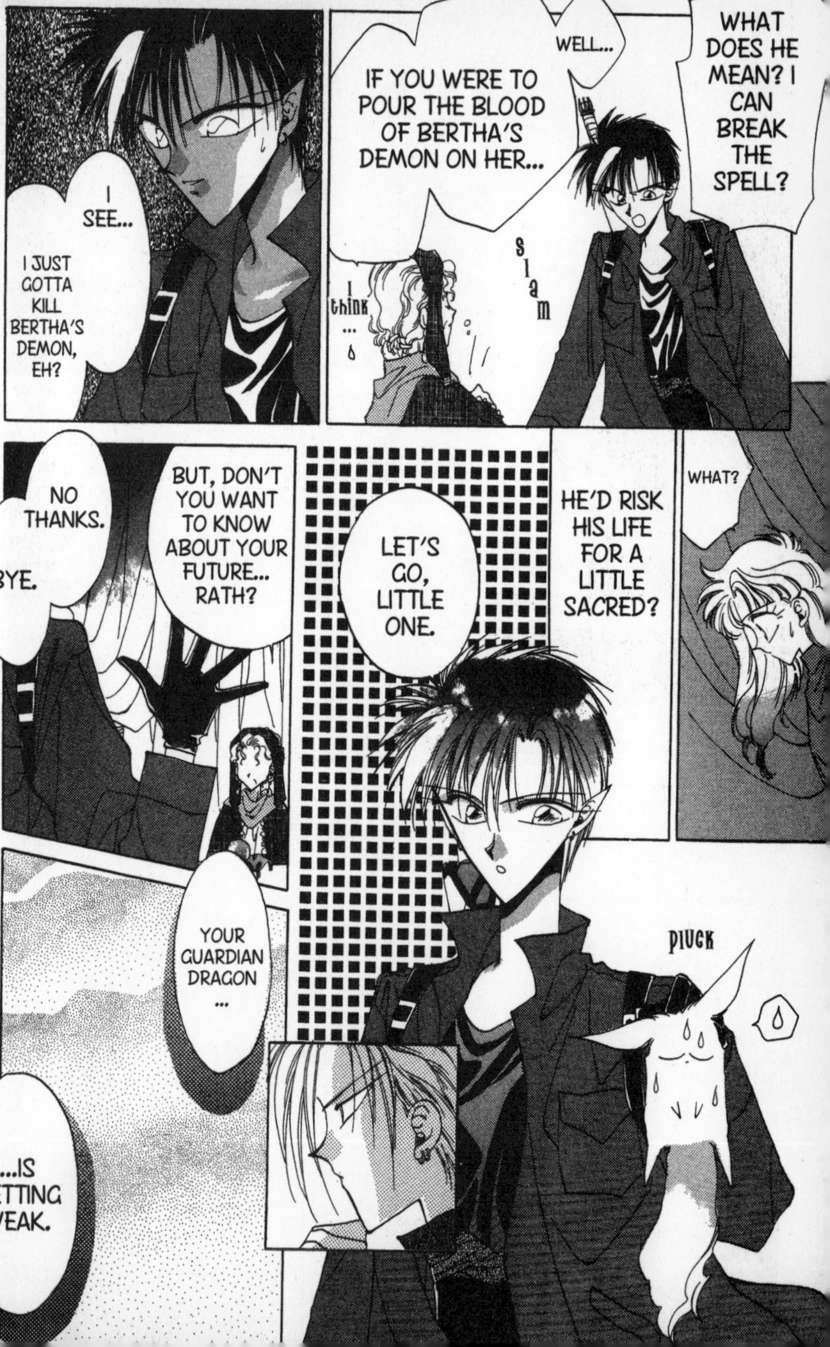
WHAT DOES HE MEAN? I CAN BREAK THE SPELL?
WELL...
IF YOU WERE TO POUR THE BLOOD OF BERTHA'S DEMON ON HER...
slam
I think...
I SEE...
I JUST GOTTA KILL BERTHA'S DEMON, EH?
WHAT?
HE'D RISK HIS LIFE FOR A LITTLE SACRED?
LET'S GO, LITTLE ONE.
pluck
BUT, DON'T YOU WANT TO KNOW ABOUT YOUR FUTURE... RATH?
NO THANKS.
BYE.
YOUR GUARDIAN DRAGON ...
...IS GETTING WEAK.

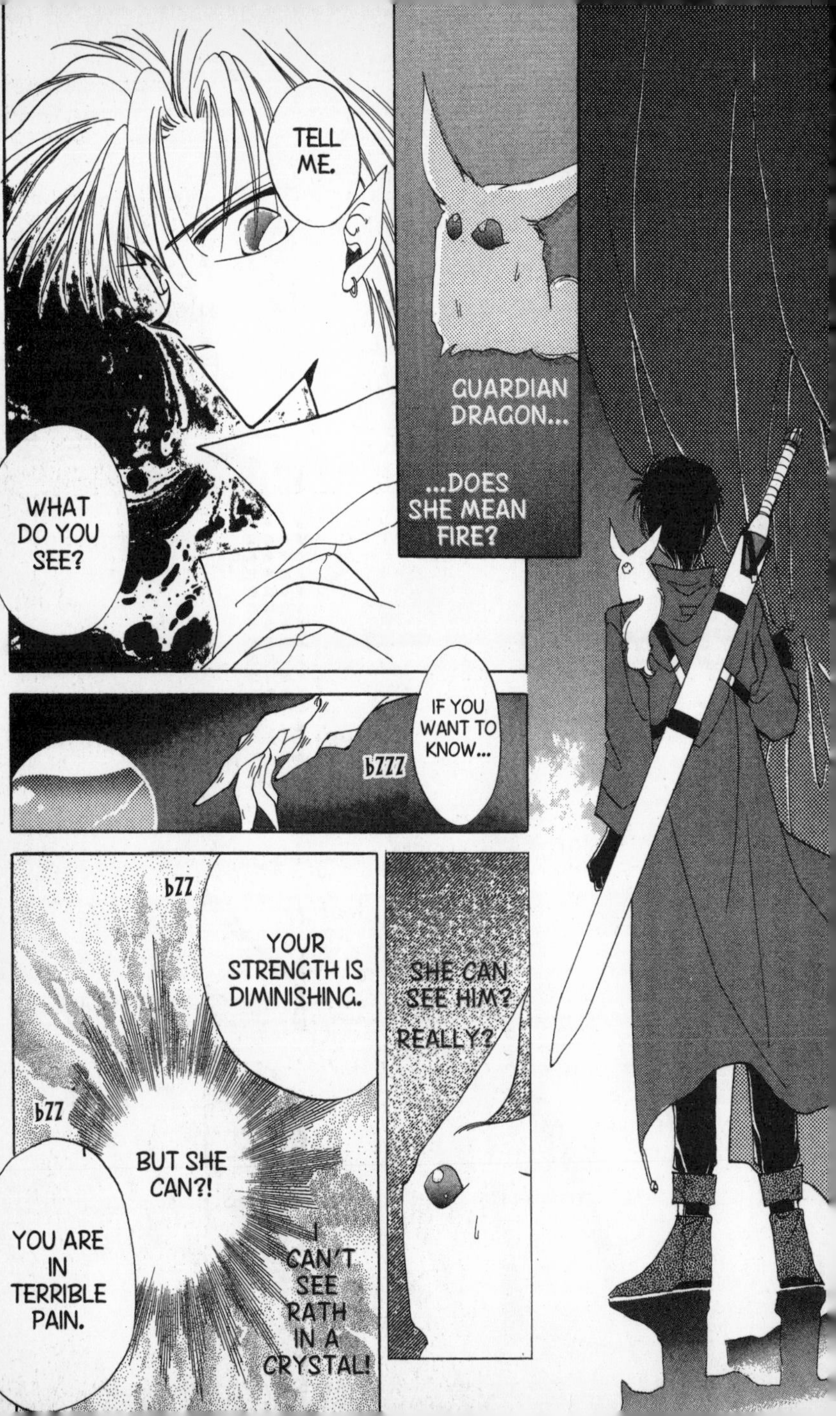
GUARDIAN DRAGON...
...DOES SHE MEAN FIRE?
TELL ME.
WHAT DO YOU SEE?
IF YOU WANT TO KNOW...
bzzz
SHE CAN SEE HIM?
REALLY?
bzz
YOUR STRENGTH IS DIMINISHING.
bzz
YOU ARE IN TERRIBLE PAIN.
I CAN'T SEE RATH IN A CRYSTAL!
BUT SHE CAN?!

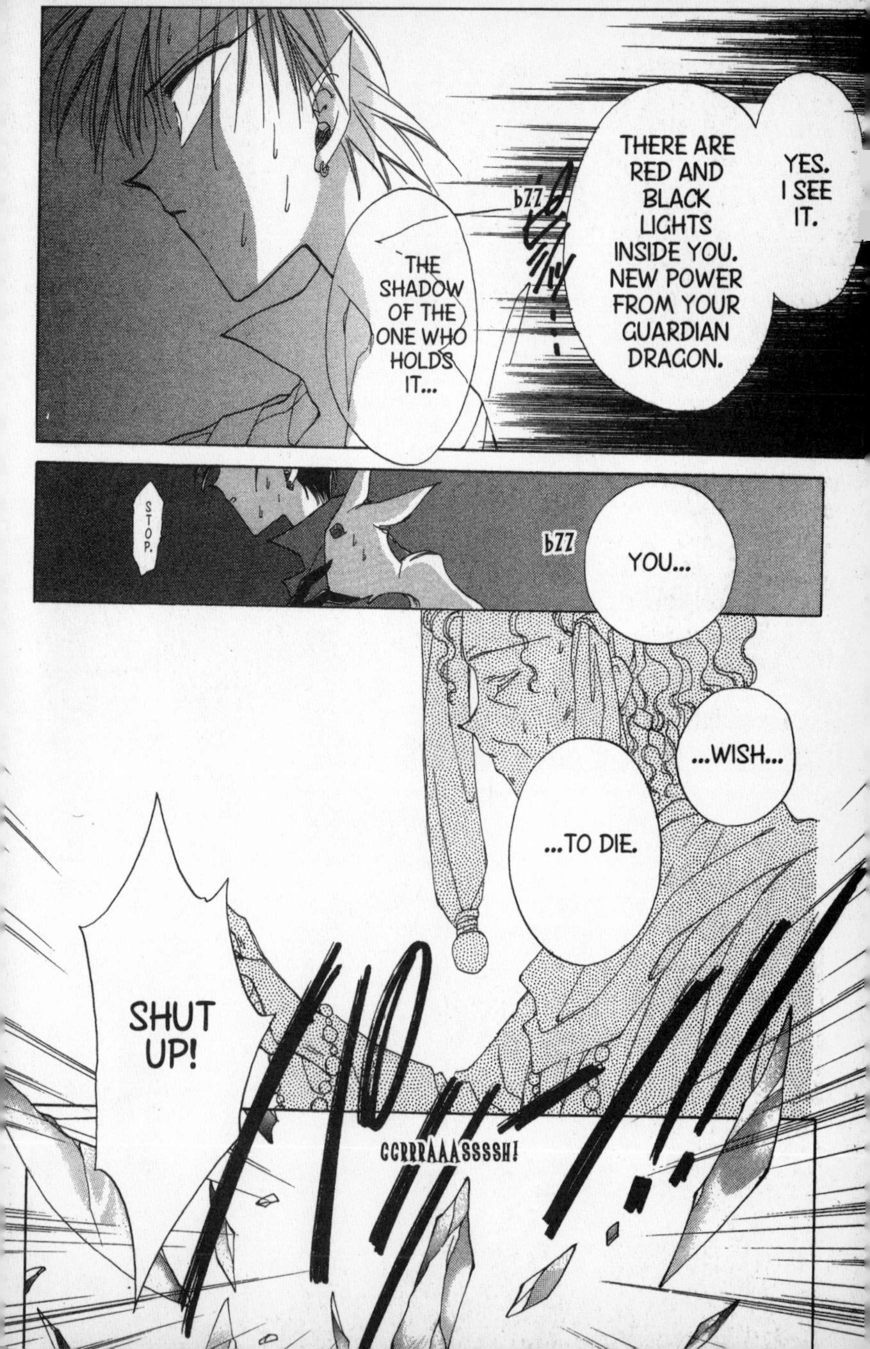
YES. I SEE IT.
THERE ARE RED AND BLACK LIGHTS INSIDE YOU. NEW POWER FROM YOUR GUARDIAN DRAGON.
BZZ
THE SHADOW OF THE ONE WHO HOLDS IT...
YOU...
BZZ
STOP.
...WISH...
...TO DIE.
SHUT UP!
CCRRRAAASSSSH!

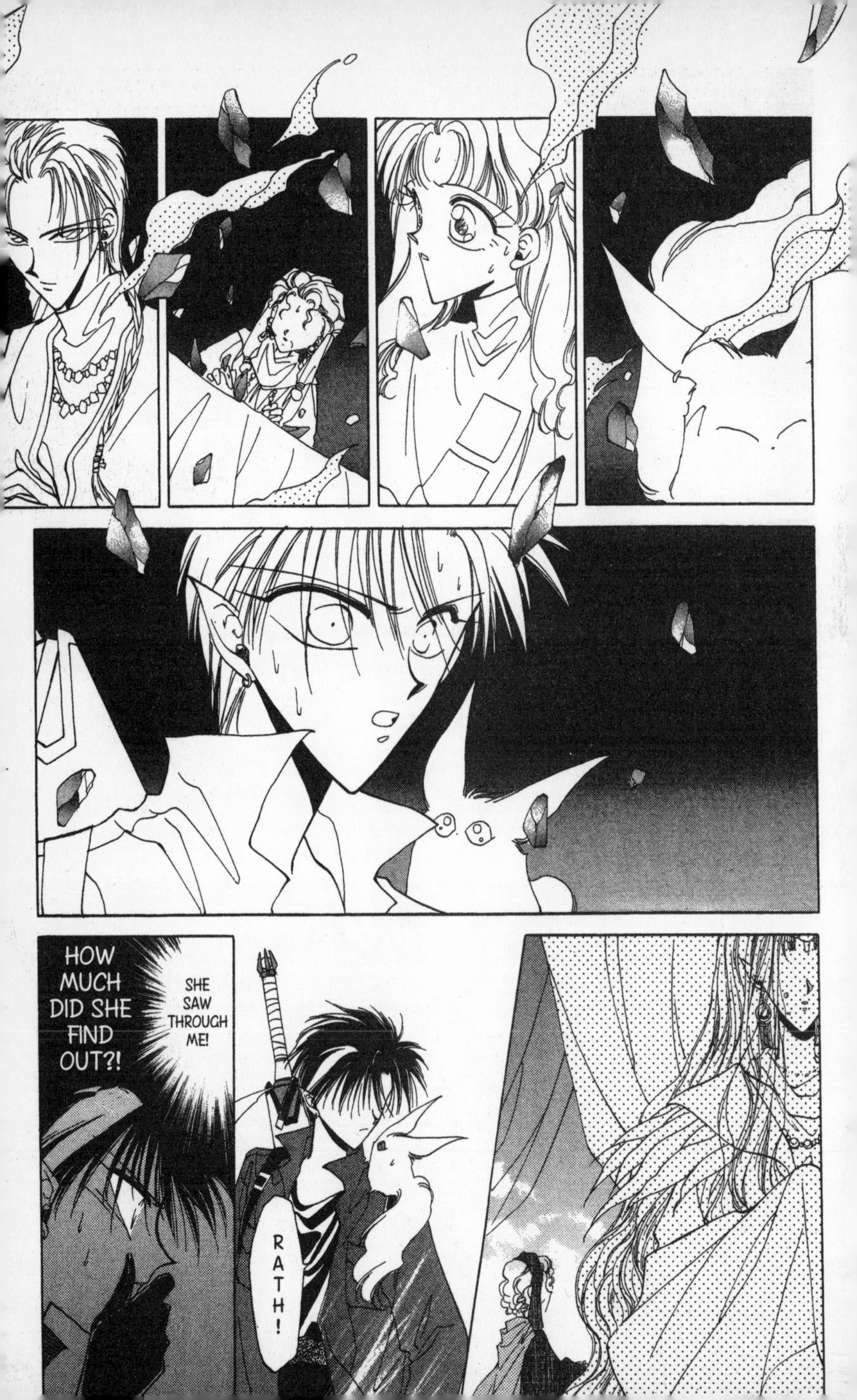
RATH!
SHE SAW THROUGH ME!
HOW MUCH DID SHE FIND OUT?!

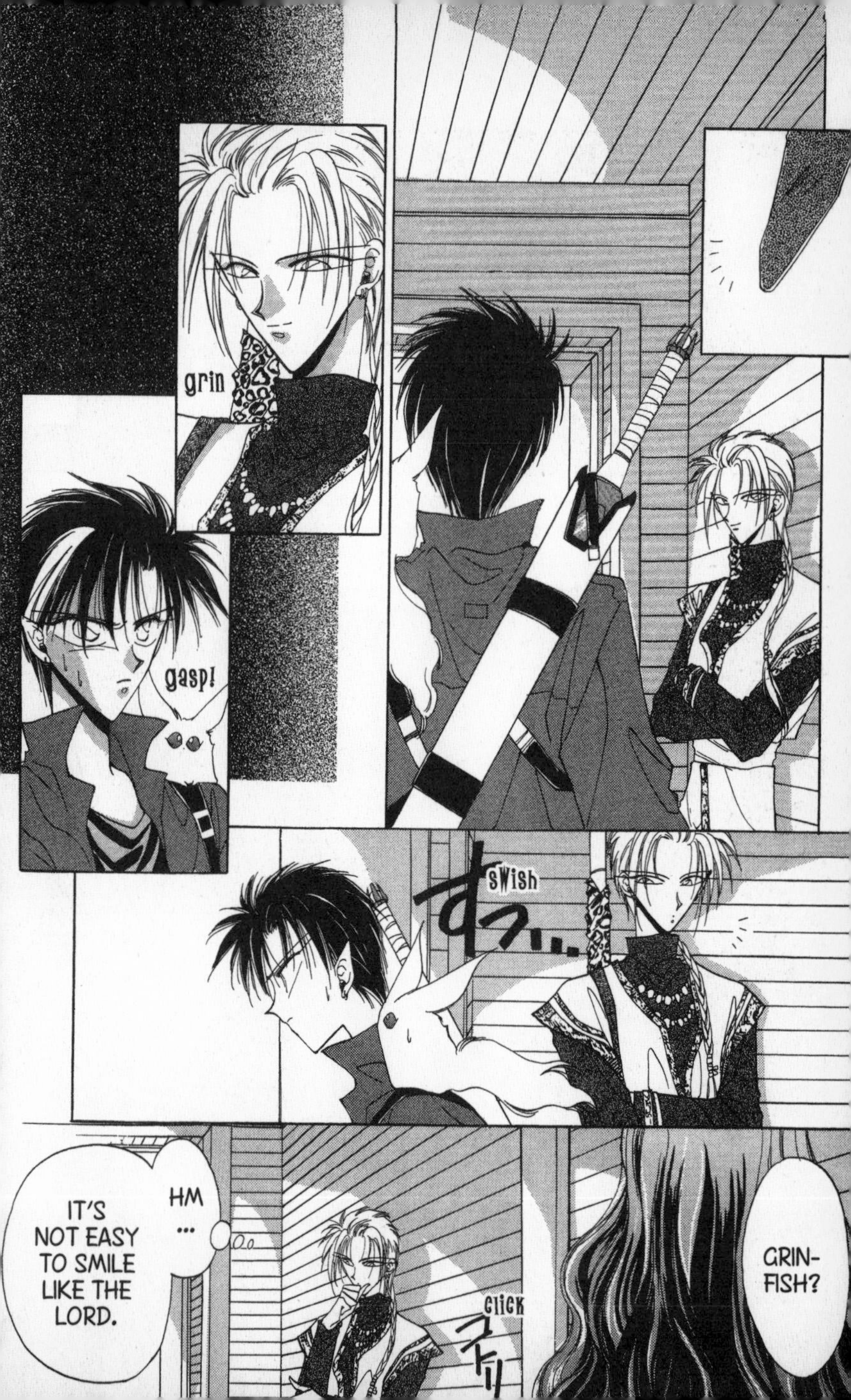
grin
gasp!
SWISH
すっ...
GRIN-FISH?
HM...
IT'S NOT EASY TO SMILE LIKE THE LORD.
CLICK
コトリ

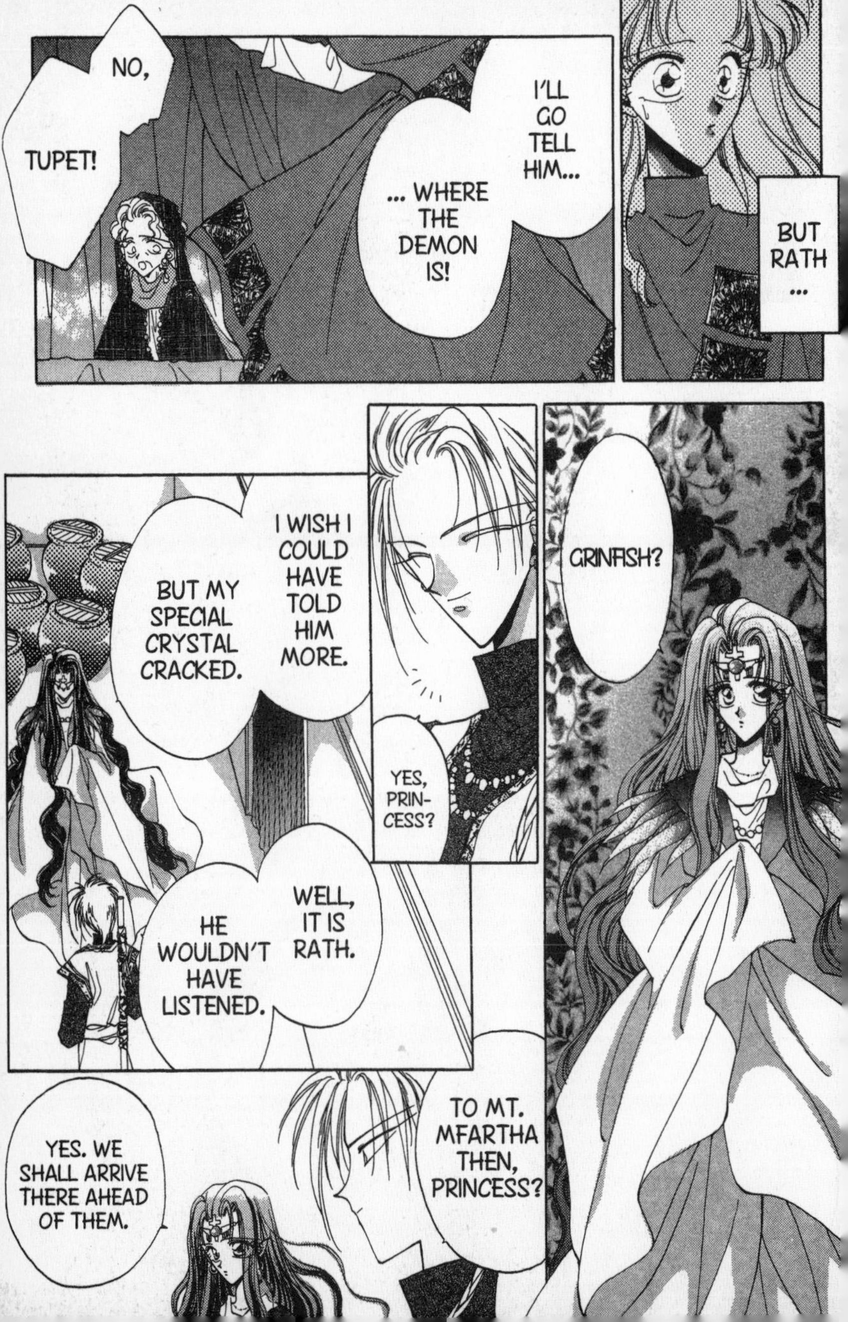
BUT RATH ...
I'LL GO TELL HIM...
... WHERE THE DEMON IS!
NO,
TUPET!
GRINFISH?
YES, PRIN-CESS?
I WISH I COULD HAVE TOLD HIM MORE.
BUT MY SPECIAL CRYSTAL CRACKED.
WELL, IT IS RATH.
HE WOULDN'T HAVE LISTENED.
TO MT. MFARTHA THEN, PRINCESS?
YES. WE SHALL ARRIVE THERE AHEAD OF THEM.

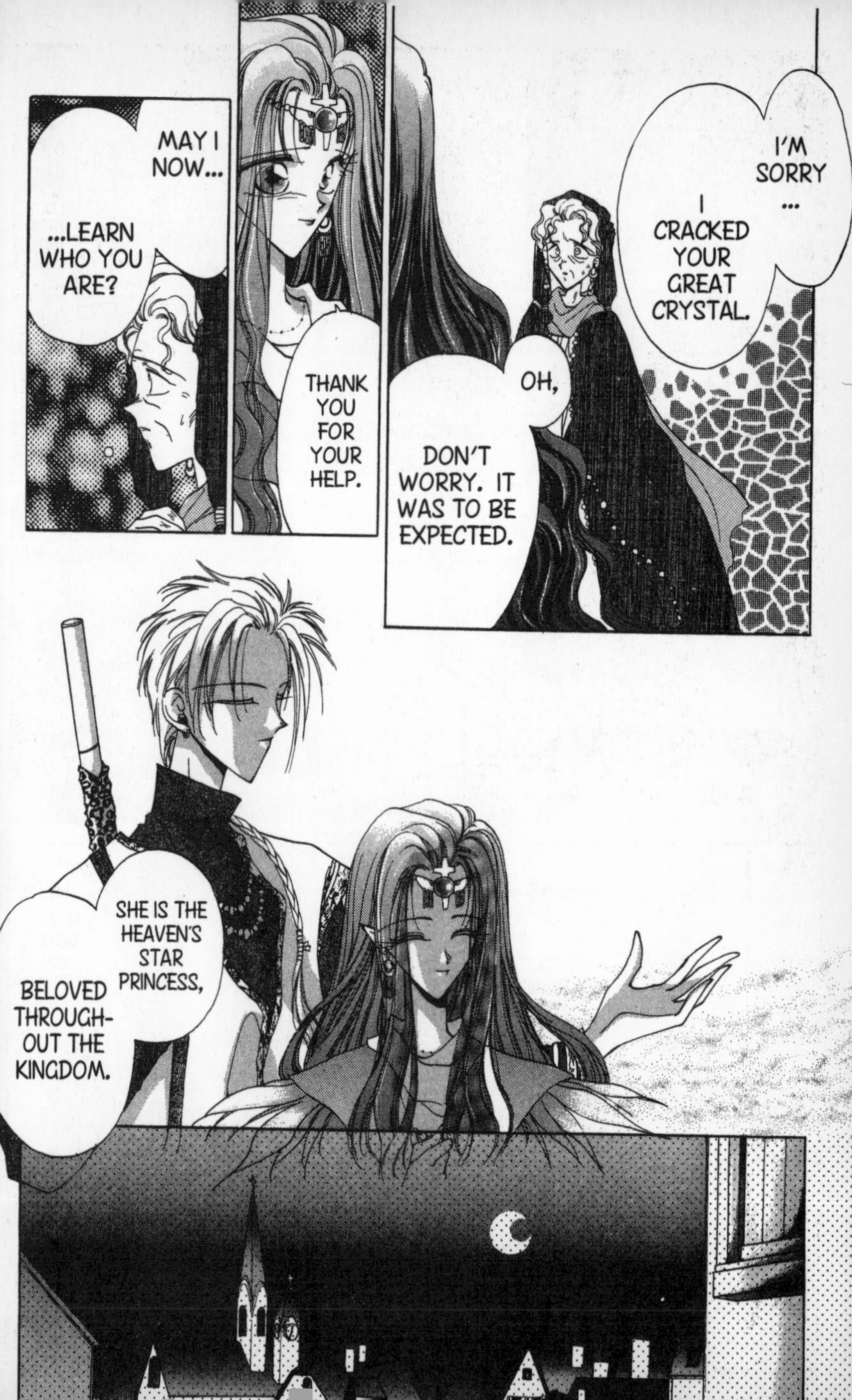
I'M SORRY ... I CRACKED YOUR GREAT CRYSTAL.
OH, DON'T WORRY. IT WAS TO BE EXPECTED.
THANK YOU FOR YOUR HELP.
MAY I NOW...
...LEARN WHO YOU ARE?
SHE IS THE HEAVEN'S STAR PRINCESS,
BELOVED THROUGHOUT THE KINGDOM.

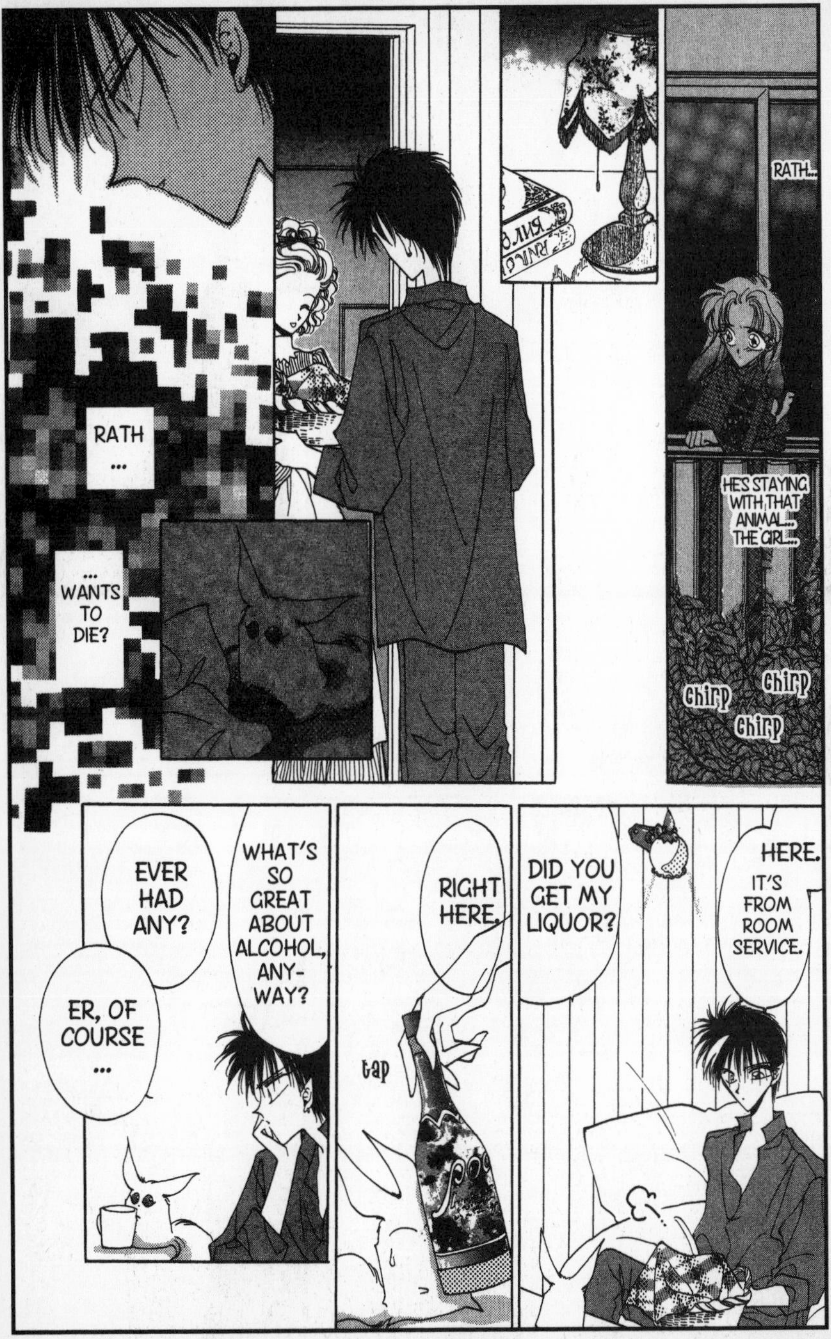
RATH...
HE'S STAYING WITH THAT ANIMAL... THE GIRL...
Chirp
Chirp
Chirp
RATH ...
... WANTS TO DIE?
HERE.
IT'S FROM ROOM SERVICE.
DID YOU GET MY LIQUOR?
RIGHT HERE.
tap
WHAT'S SO GREAT ABOUT ALCOHOL, ANY-WAY?
EVER HAD ANY?
ER, OF COURSE ...

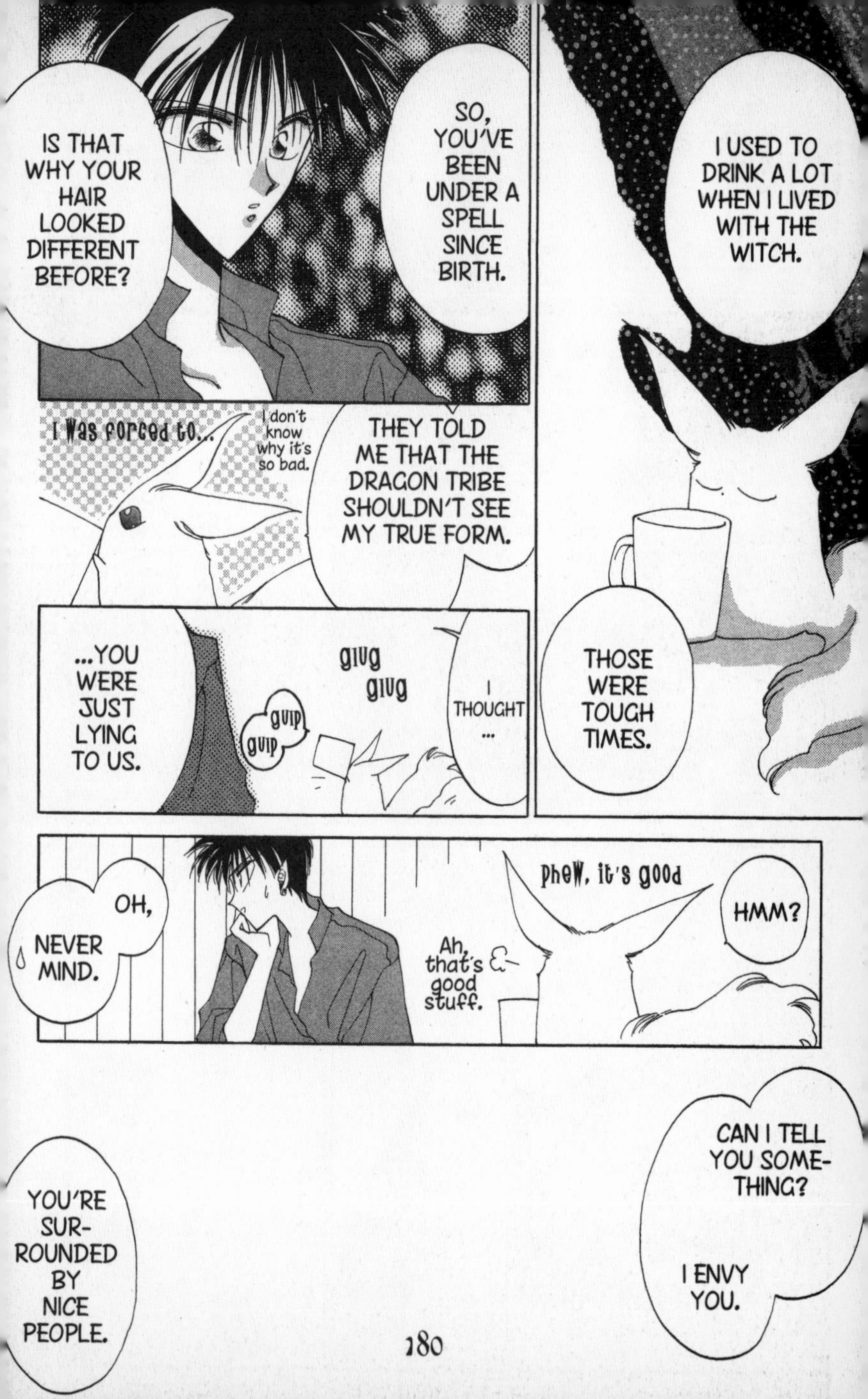
I USED TO DRINK A LOT WHEN I LIVED WITH THE WITCH.
THOSE WERE TOUGH TIMES.
SO, YOU'VE BEEN UNDER A SPELL SINCE BIRTH.
IS THAT WHY YOUR HAIR LOOKED DIFFERENT BEFORE?
THEY TOLD ME THAT THE DRAGON TRIBE SHOULDN'T SEE MY TRUE FORM.
I don't know why it's so bad.
I was forced to...
I THOUGHT...
glug glug
gulp gulp
...YOU WERE JUST LYING TO US.
HMM?
phew, it's good
Ah, that's good stuff.
OH, NEVER MIND.
CAN I TELL YOU SOME-THING?
I ENVY YOU.
YOU'RE SUR-ROUNDED BY NICE PEOPLE.

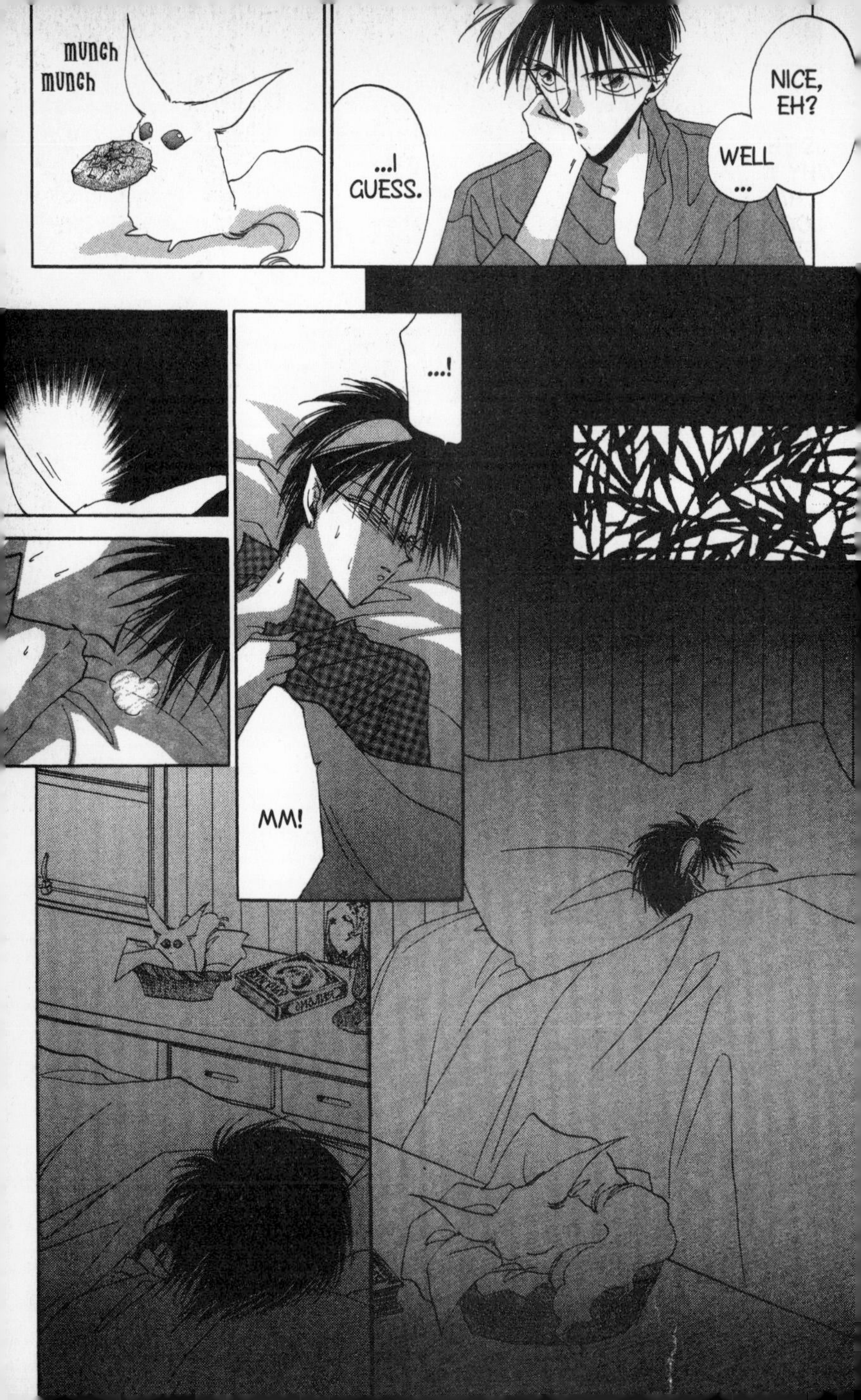
NICE, EH?
WELL ...
...I GUESS.
munch munch
...!
MM!

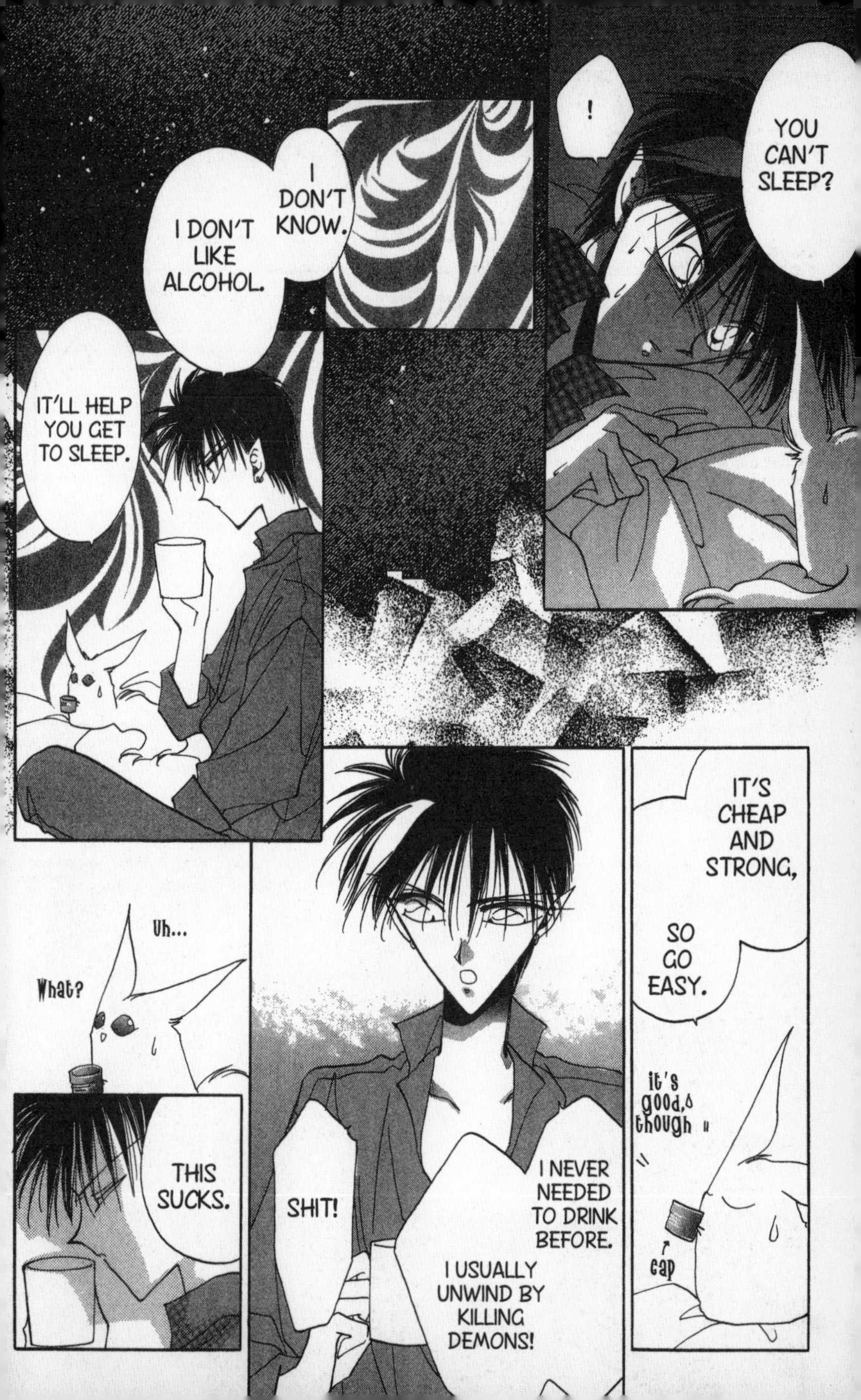
YOU CAN'T SLEEP?
!
I DON'T KNOW.
I DON'T LIKE ALCOHOL.
IT'LL HELP YOU GET TO SLEEP.
IT'S CHEAP AND STRONG,
SO GO EASY.
it's good, though
cap
I NEVER NEEDED TO DRINK BEFORE.
SHIT!
I USUALLY UNWIND BY KILLING DEMONS!
Uh...
What?
THIS SUCKS.

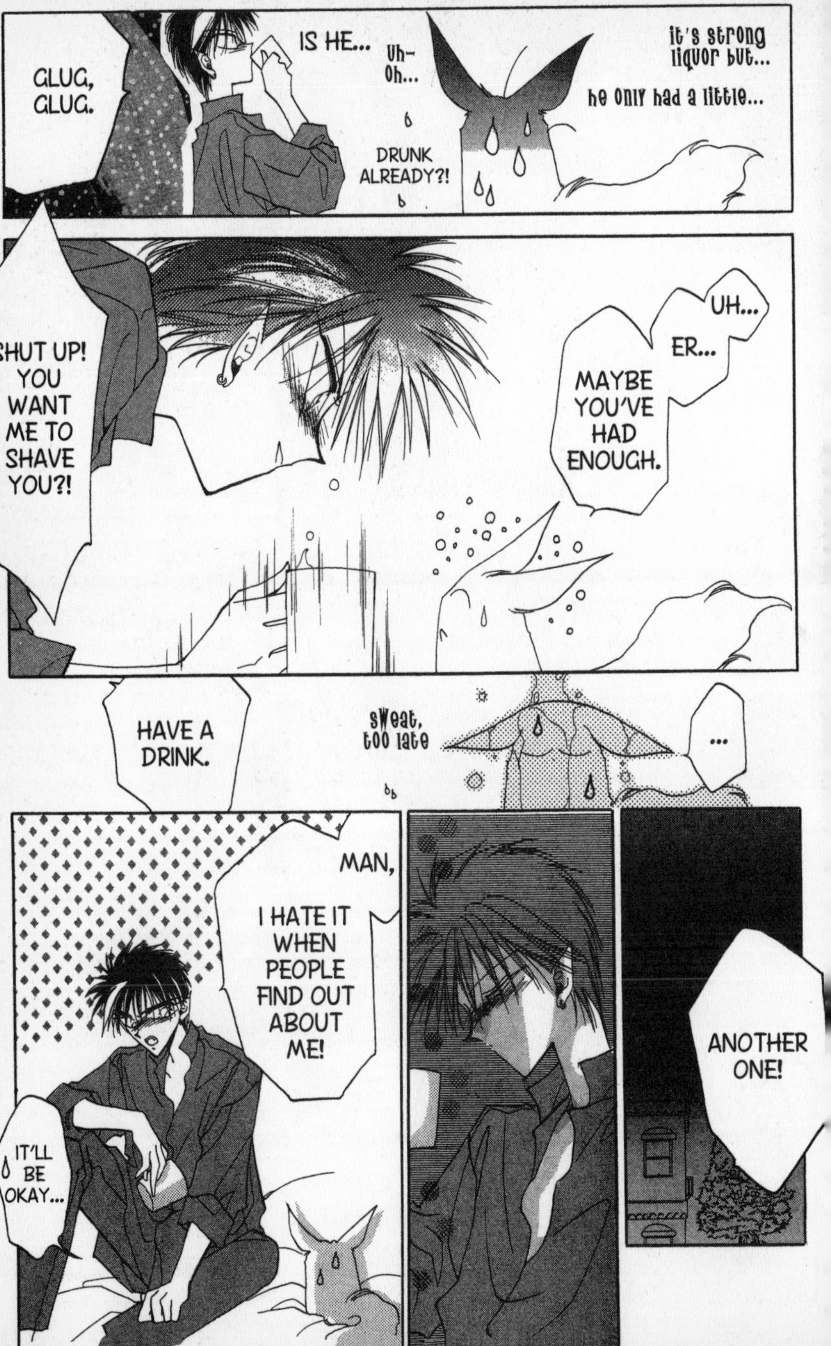
it's strong liquor but...
he only had a little...
Uh- Oh...
IS HE...
DRUNK ALREADY?!
GLUG, GLUG.
UH...
ER...
MAYBE YOU'VE HAD ENOUGH.
SHUT UP! YOU WANT ME TO SHAVE YOU?!
...
sweat, too late
HAVE A DRINK.
ANOTHER ONE!
MAN,
I HATE IT WHEN PEOPLE FIND OUT ABOUT ME!
IT'LL BE OKAY...

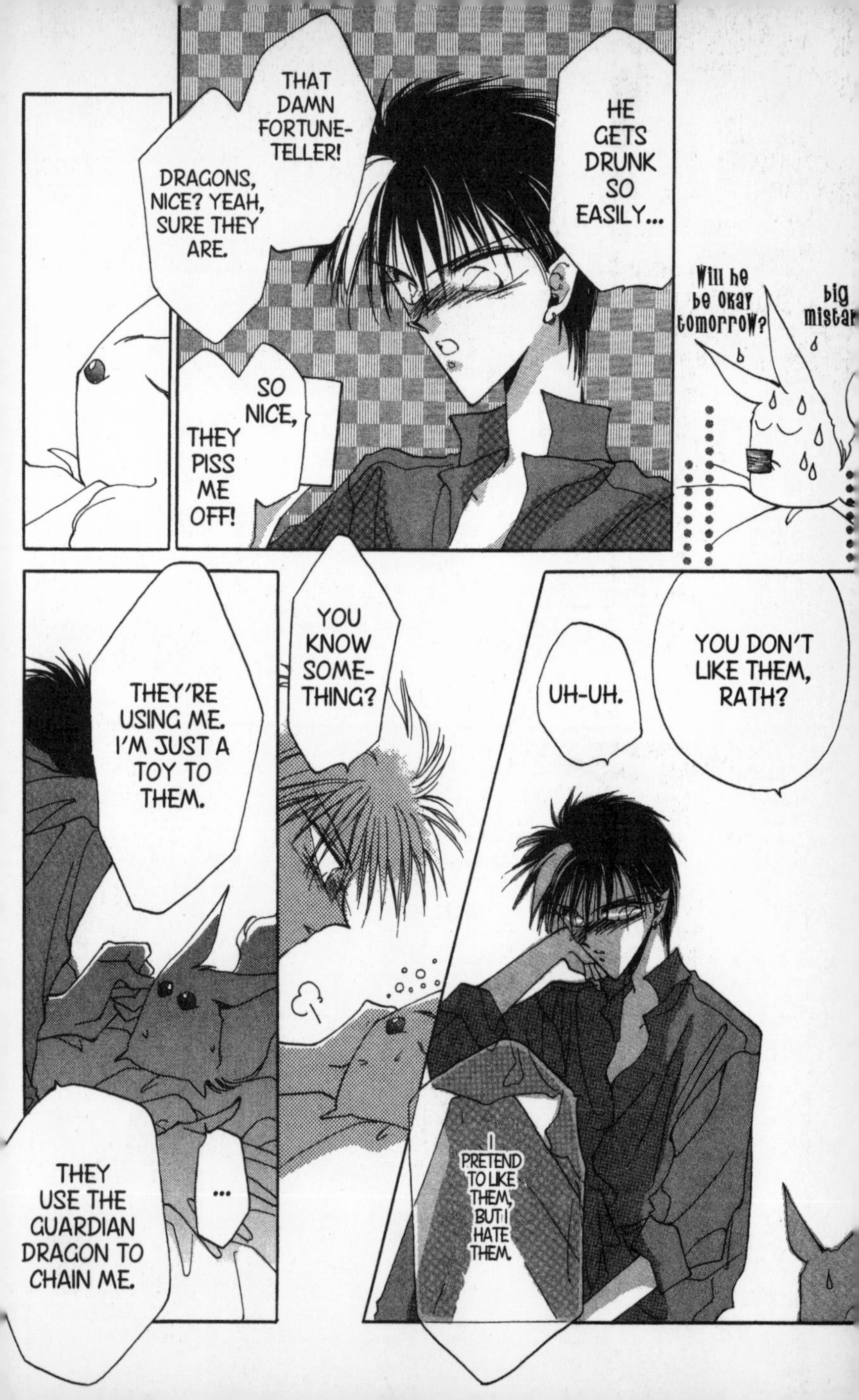
big mista
Will he be okay tomorrow?
HE GETS DRUNK SO EASILY...
THAT DAMN FORTUNE-TELLER!
DRAGONS, NICE? YEAH, SURE THEY ARE.
SO NICE, THEY PISS ME OFF!
YOU DON'T LIKE THEM, RATH?
UH-UH.
I PRETEND TO LIKE THEM, BUT I HATE THEM.
YOU KNOW SOMETHING?
THEY'RE USING ME. I'M JUST A TOY TO THEM.
...
THEY USE THE GUARDIAN DRAGON TO CHAIN ME.

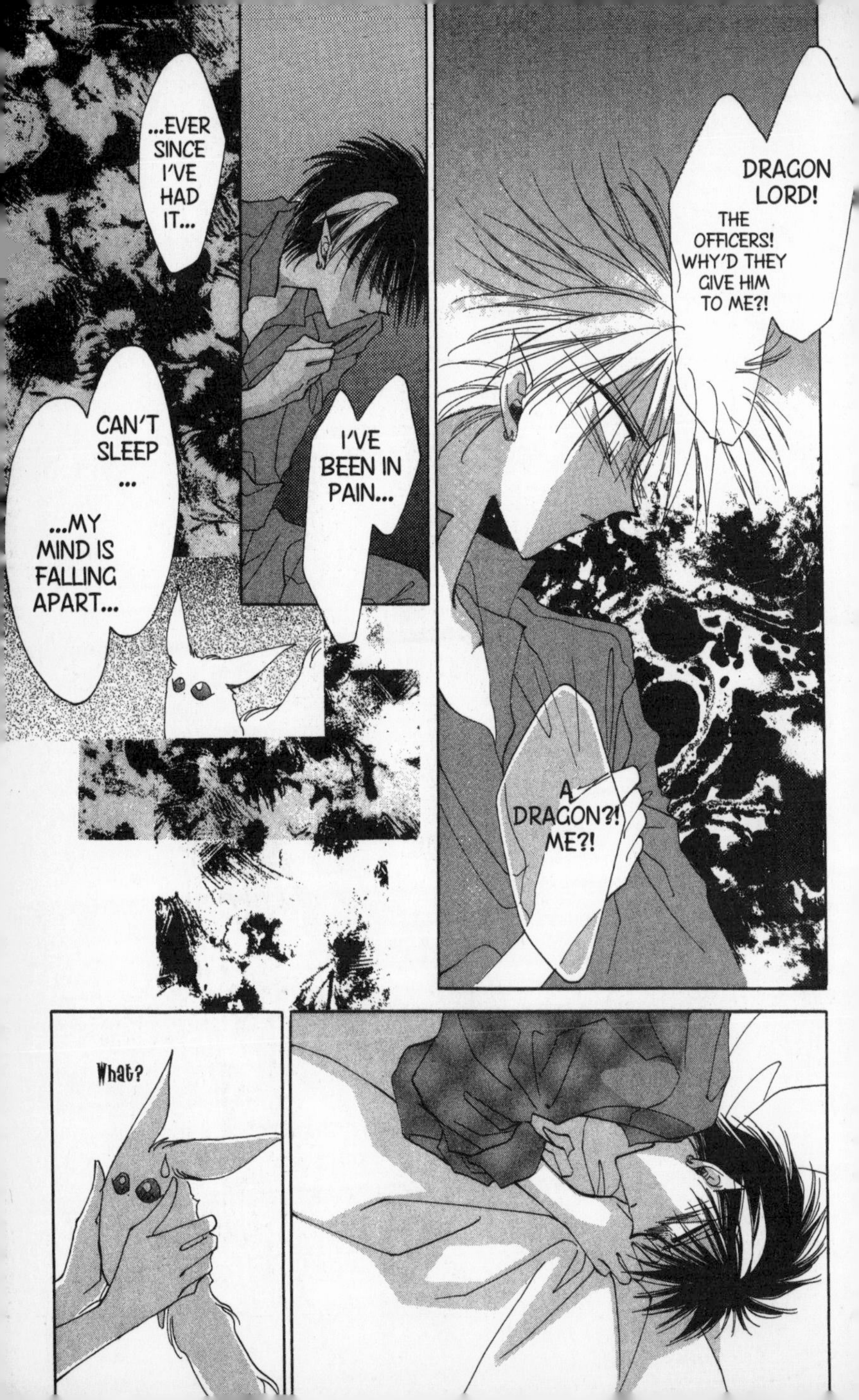
DRAGON LORD!
THE OFFICERS! WHY'D THEY GIVE HIM TO ME?!
A DRAGON?! ME?!
...EVER SINCE I'VE HAD IT...
I'VE BEEN IN PAIN...
CAN'T SLEEP ...
...MY MIND IS FALLING APART...
What?

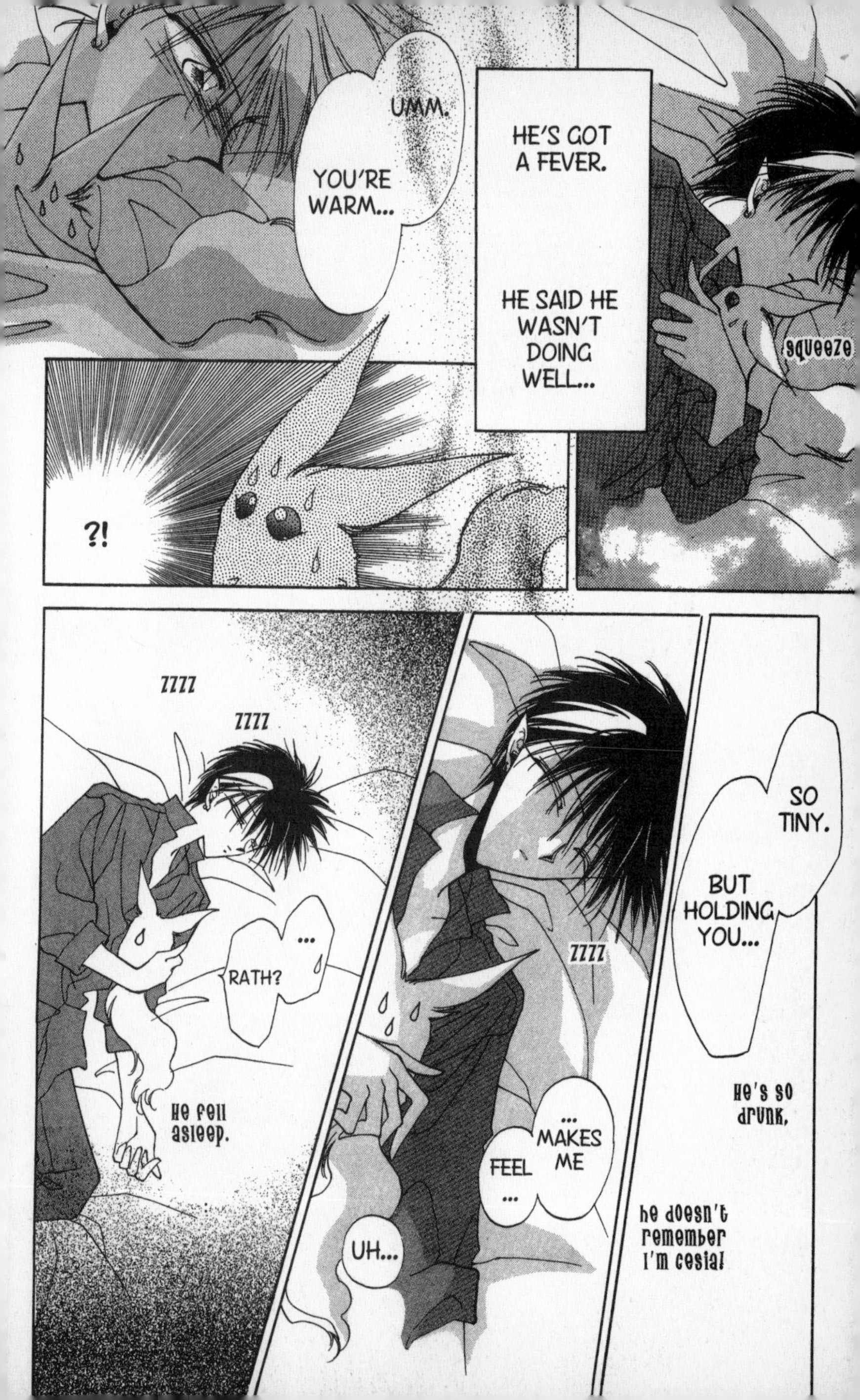
squeeze
HE'S GOT A FEVER.
HE SAID HE WASN'T DOING WELL...
UMM.
YOU'RE WARM...
?!
SO TINY.
BUT HOLDING YOU...
He's so drunk,
he doesn't remember I'm cesia!
ZZZZ
... MAKES ME
FEEL ...
UH...
ZZZZ
ZZZZ
...
RATH?
He fell asleep.

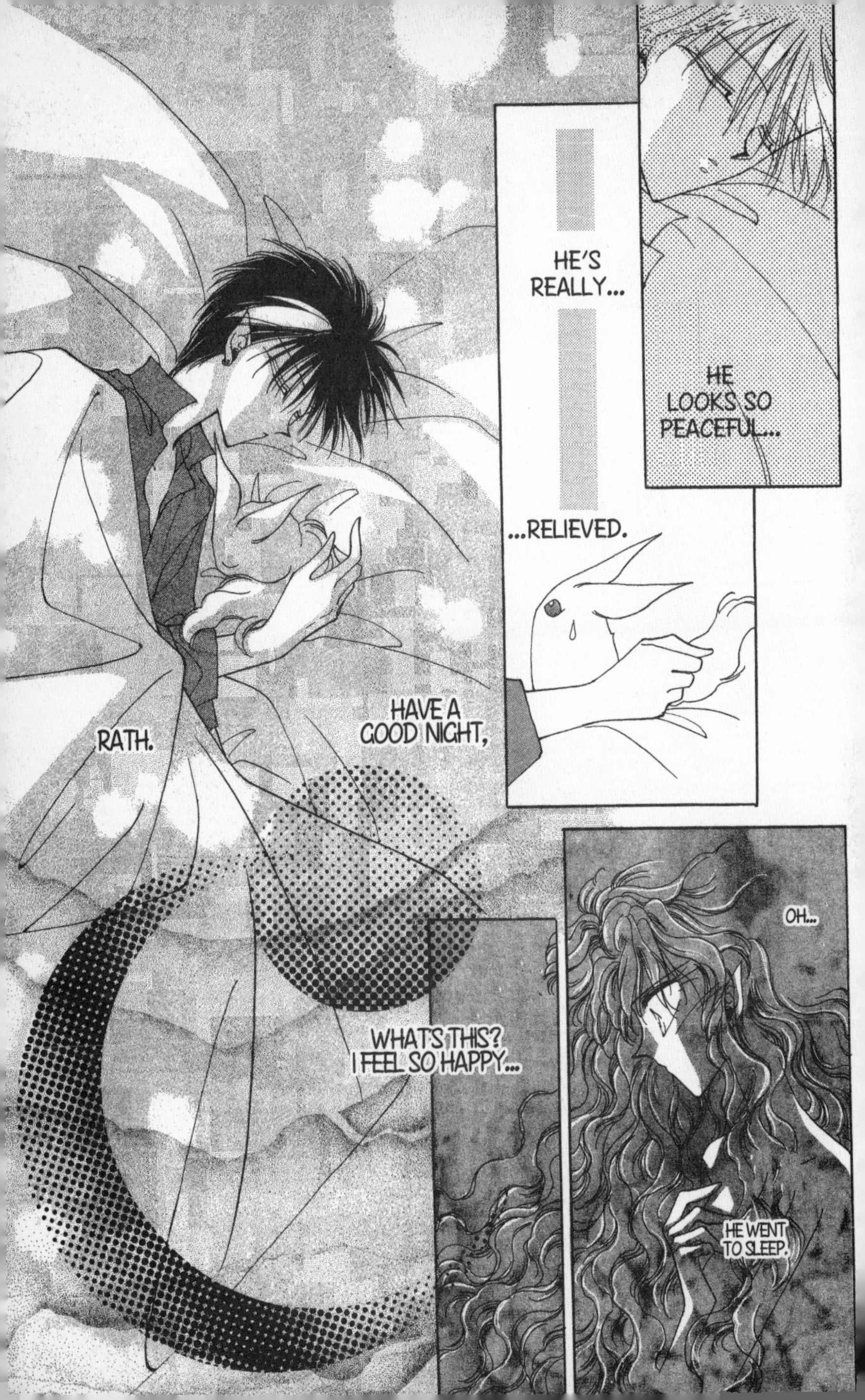
HE LOOKS SO PEACEFUL...
HE'S REALLY...
...RELIEVED.
OH...
HE WENT TO SLEEP.
WHAT'S THIS? I FEEL SO HAPPY...
HAVE A GOOD NIGHT,
RATH.

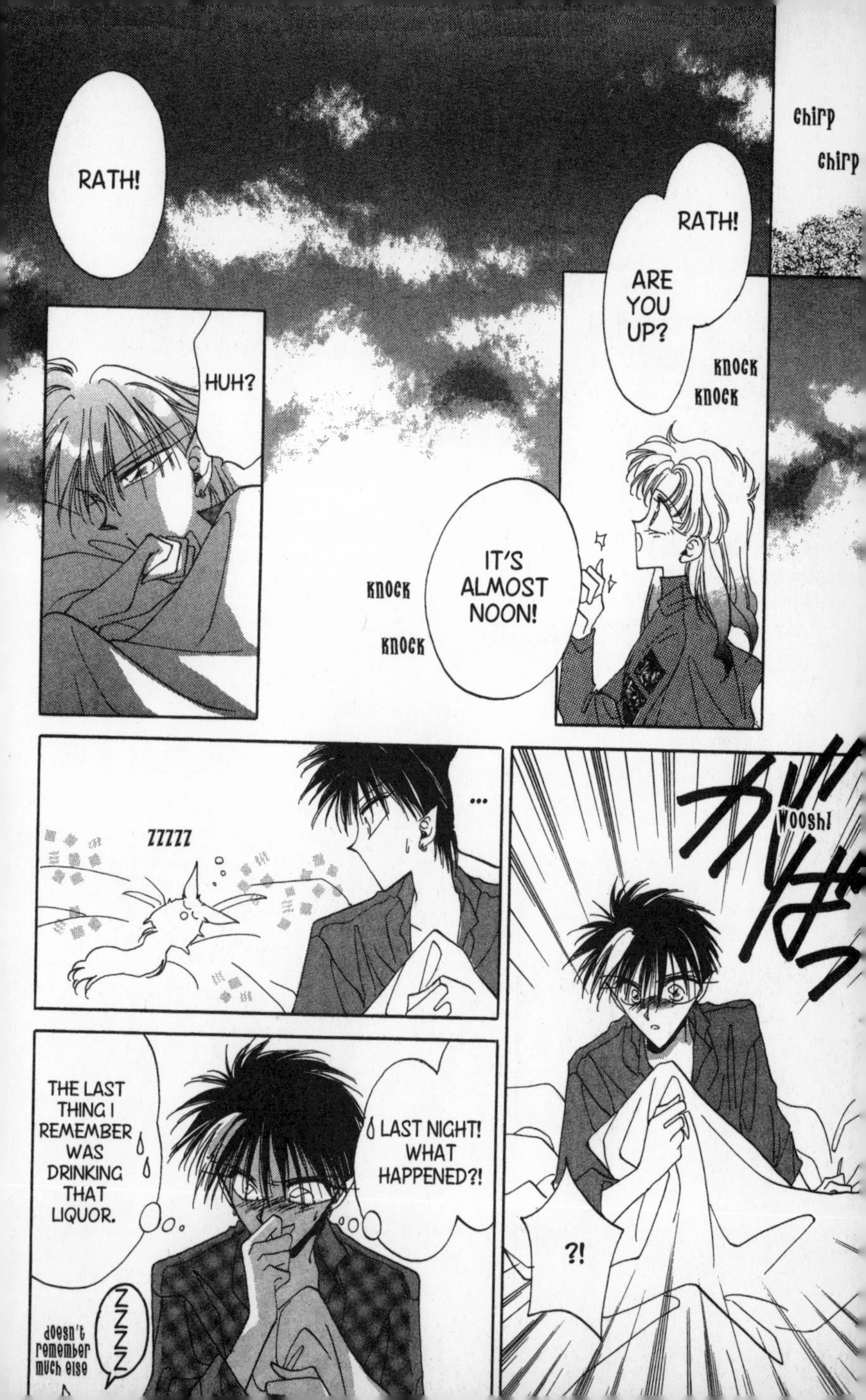
chirp
chirp
RATH!
ARE YOU UP?
knock
knock
IT'S ALMOST NOON!
knock
knock
RATH!
HUH?
がばっ
WOOSH!
?!
...
ZZZZZ
LAST NIGHT! WHAT HAPPENED?!
THE LAST THING I REMEMBER WAS DRINKING THAT LIQUOR.
ZZZZ
doesn't remember much else

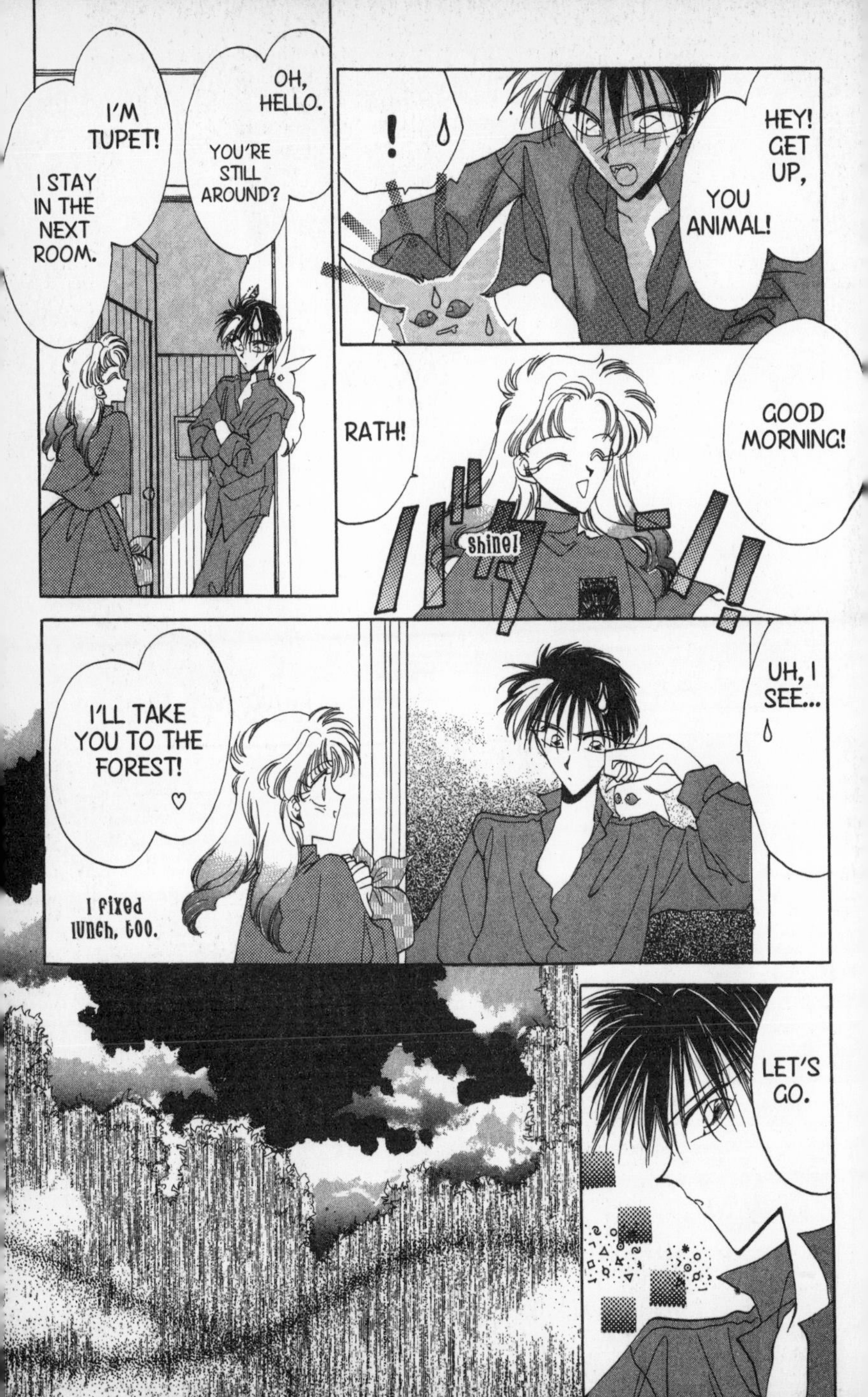
HEY! GET UP, YOU ANIMAL!
GOOD MORNING!
RATH!
Shine!
OH, HELLO.
YOU'RE STILL AROUND?
I'M TUPET!
I STAY IN THE NEXT ROOM.
UH, I SEE...
I'LL TAKE YOU TO THE FOREST! ♡
I fixed lunch, too.
LET'S GO.

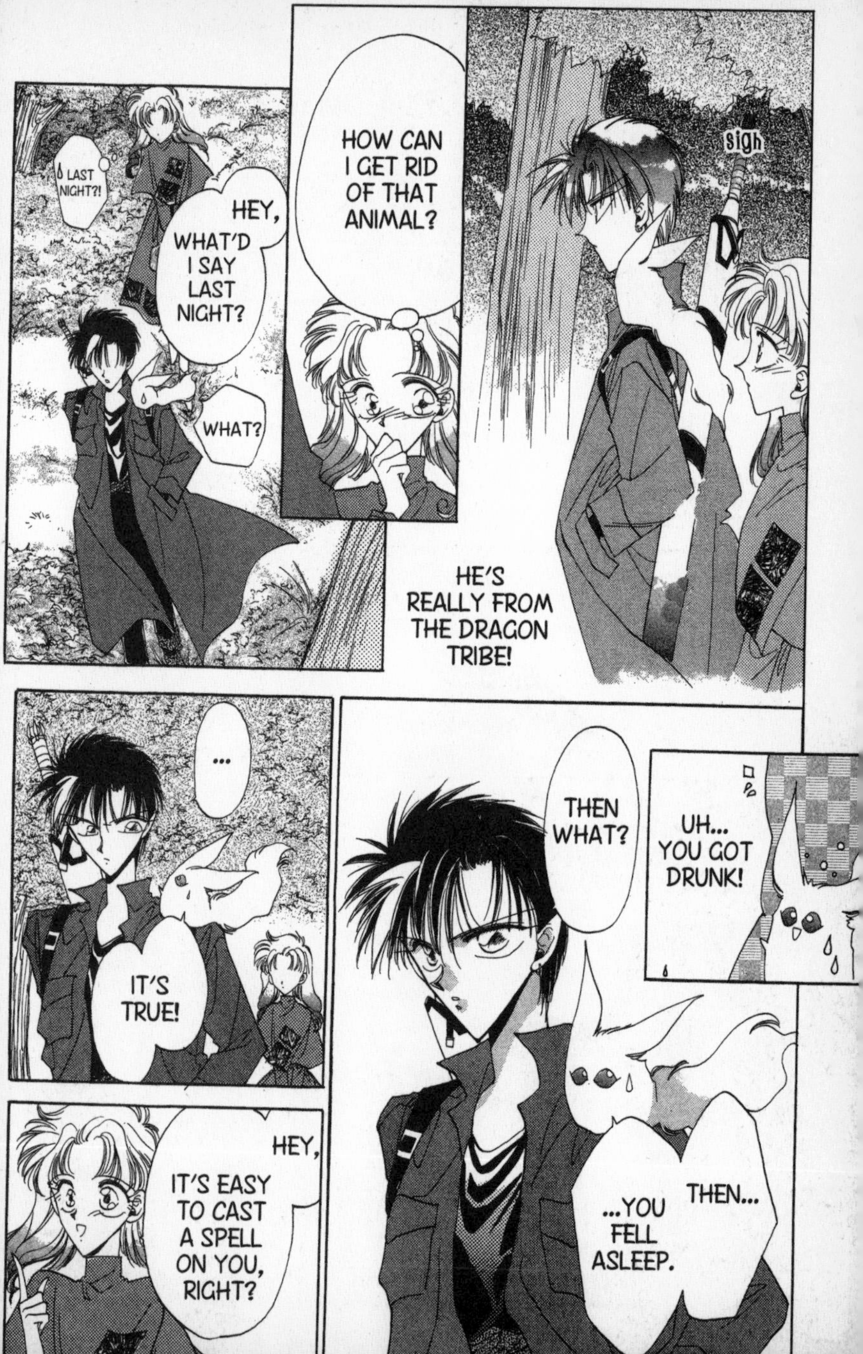
sigh
HE'S REALLY FROM THE DRAGON TRIBE!
HOW CAN I GET RID OF THAT ANIMAL?
HEY, WHAT'D I SAY LAST NIGHT?
LAST NIGHT?!
WHAT?
THEN WHAT?
UH... YOU GOT DRUNK!
THEN...
...YOU FELL ASLEEP.
...
IT'S TRUE!
HEY, IT'S EASY TO CAST A SPELL ON YOU, RIGHT?

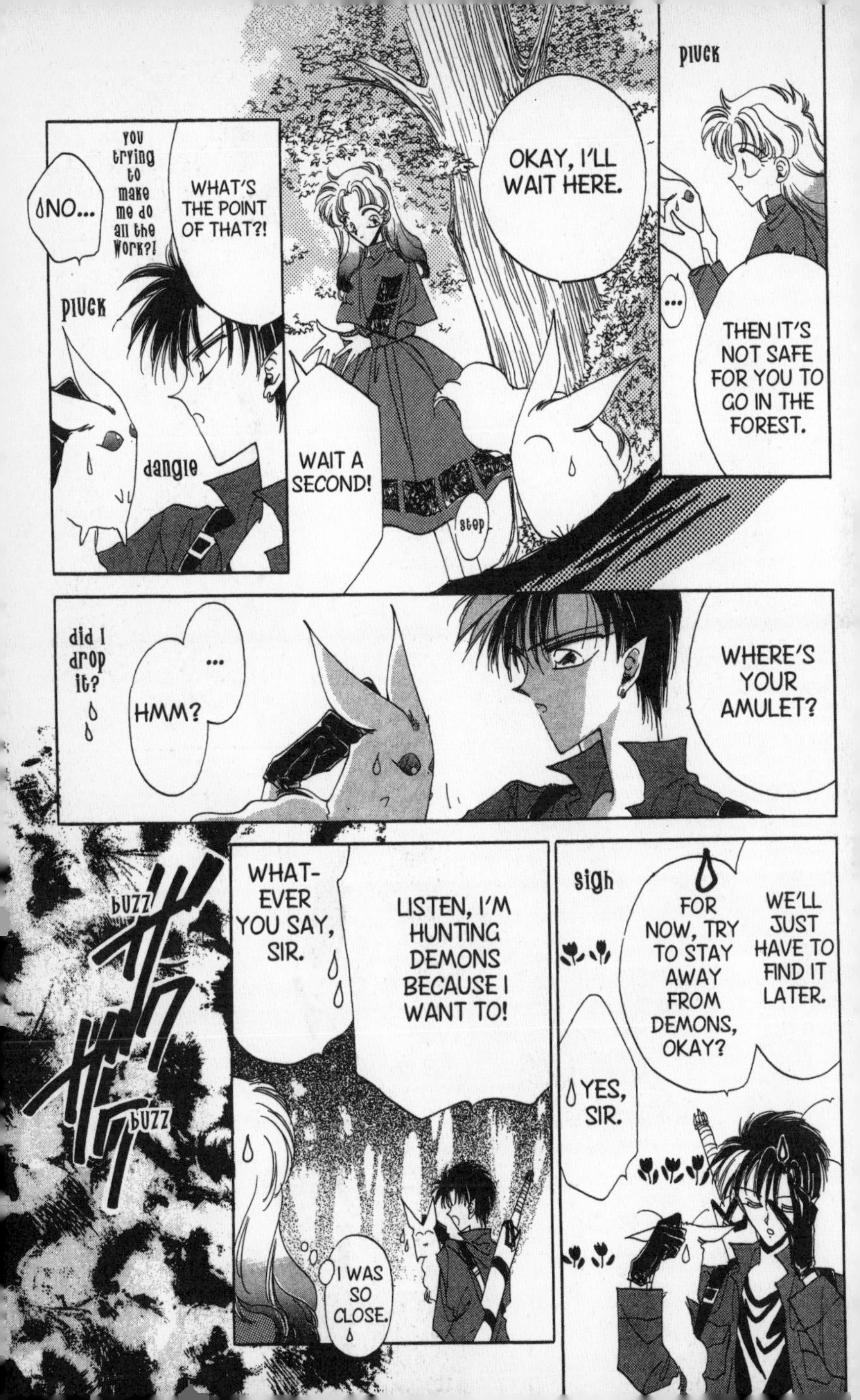
pluck
...
THEN IT'S NOT SAFE FOR YOU TO GO IN THE FOREST.
OKAY, I'LL WAIT HERE.
WAIT A SECOND!
stop
WHAT'S THE POINT OF THAT?!
you trying to make me do all the work?!
NO...
pluck
dangle
WHERE'S YOUR AMULET?
...
HMM?
did I drop it?
WE'LL JUST HAVE TO FIND IT LATER.
FOR NOW, TRY TO STAY AWAY FROM DEMONS, OKAY?
sigh
YES, SIR.
LISTEN, I'M HUNTING DEMONS BECAUSE I WANT TO!
WHAT-EVER YOU SAY, SIR.
I WAS SO CLOSE.
buzz
buzz

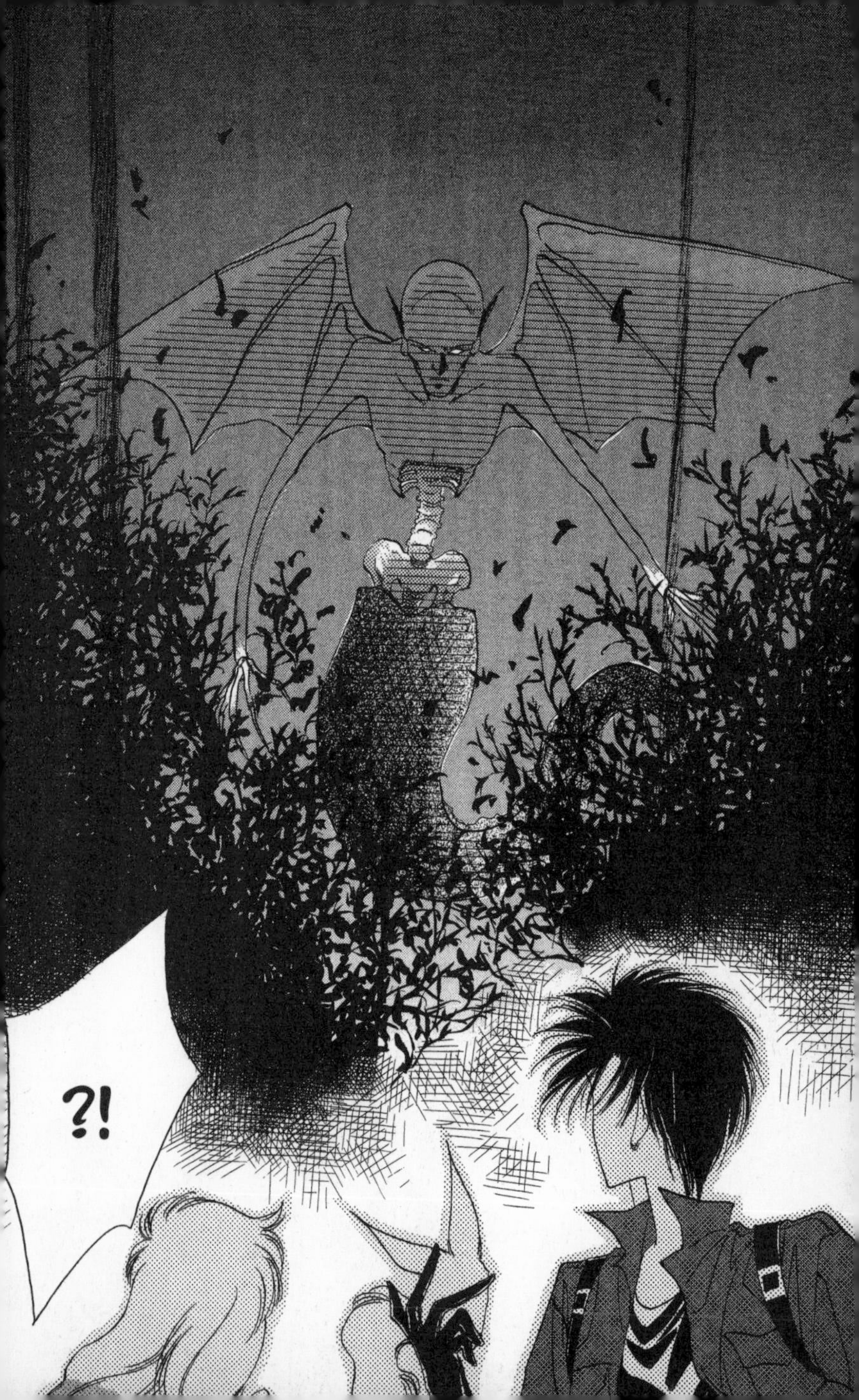
?!

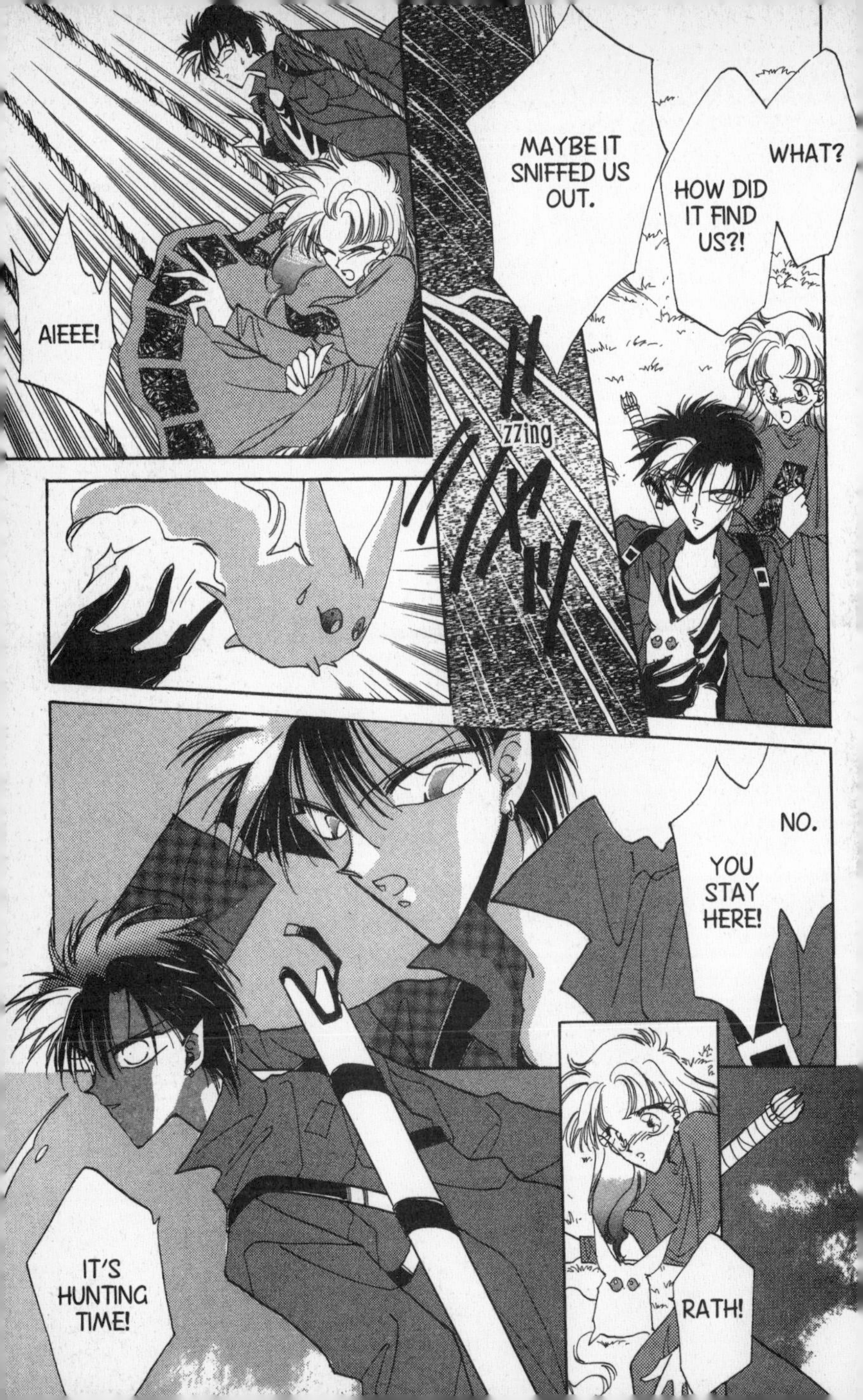
WHAT?
HOW DID IT FIND US?!
MAYBE IT SNIFFED US OUT.
zzing
AIEEE!
NO.
YOU STAY HERE!
RATH!
IT'S HUNTING TIME!

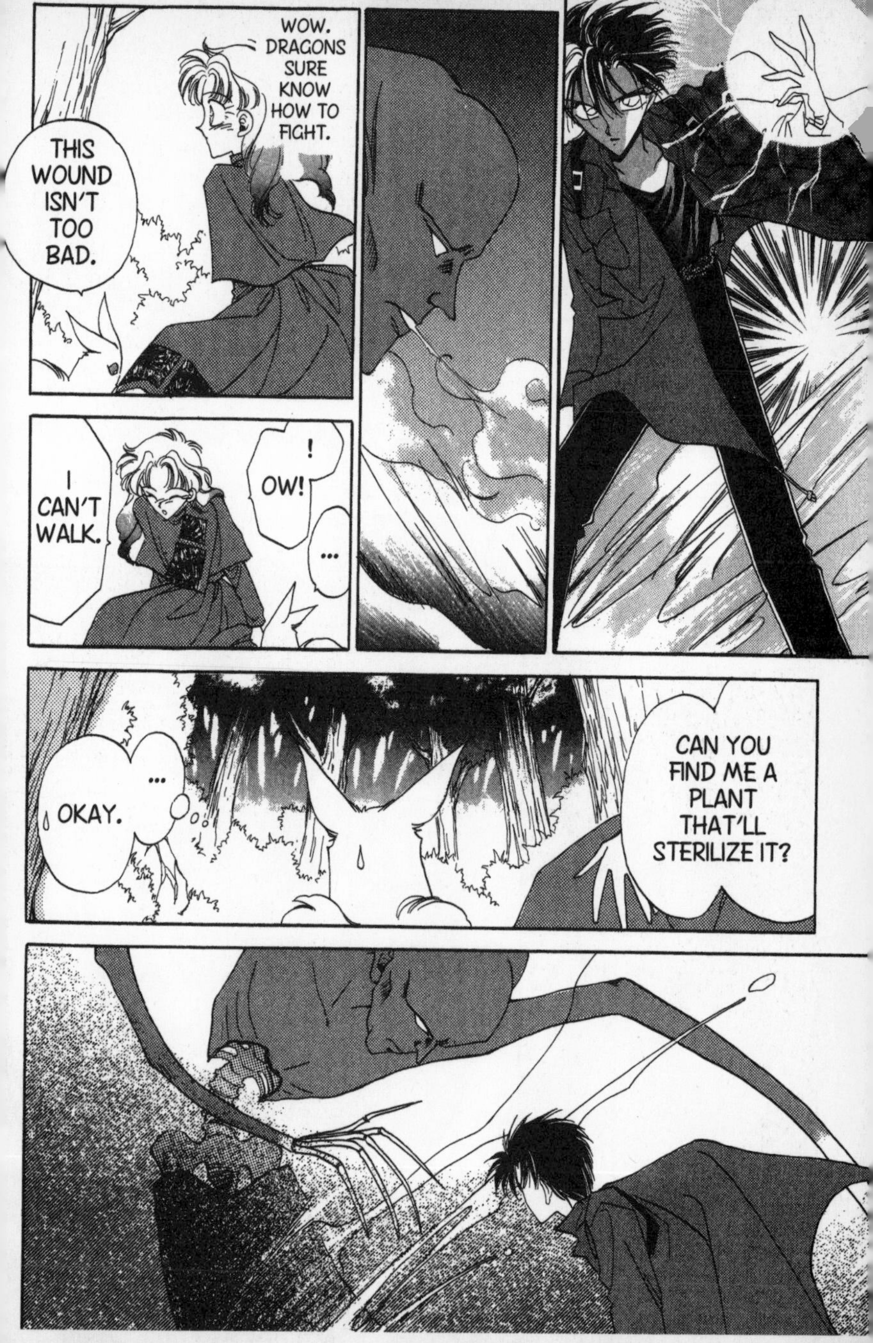
WOW. DRAGONS SURE KNOW HOW TO FIGHT.
THIS WOUND ISN'T TOO BAD.
! OW!
...
I CAN'T WALK.
CAN YOU FIND ME A PLANT THAT'LL STERILIZE IT?
... OKAY.

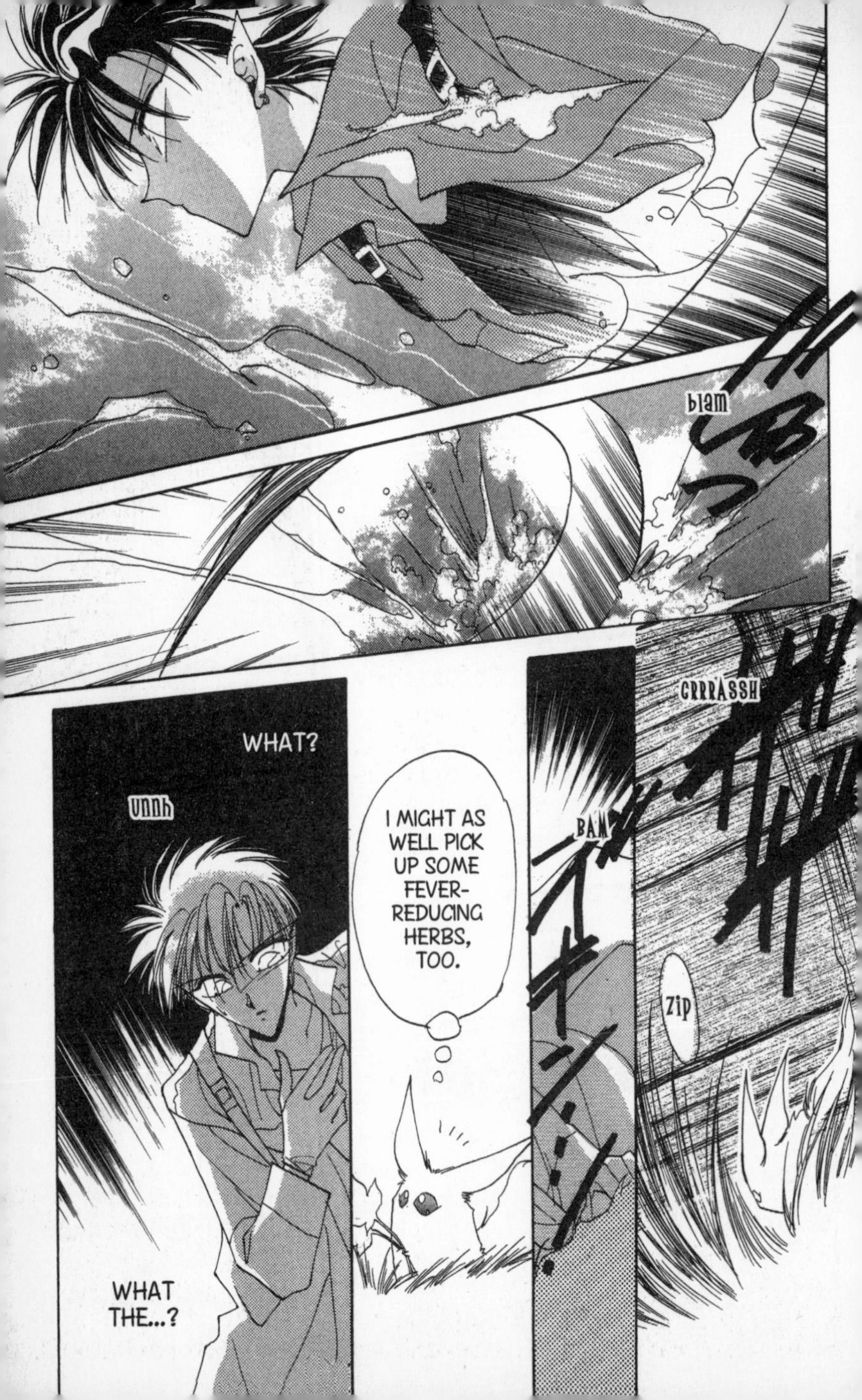
blam
CRRRASSH
zip
BAM
I MIGHT AS WELL PICK UP SOME FEVER-REDUCING HERBS, TOO.
WHAT?
unnh
WHAT THE...?

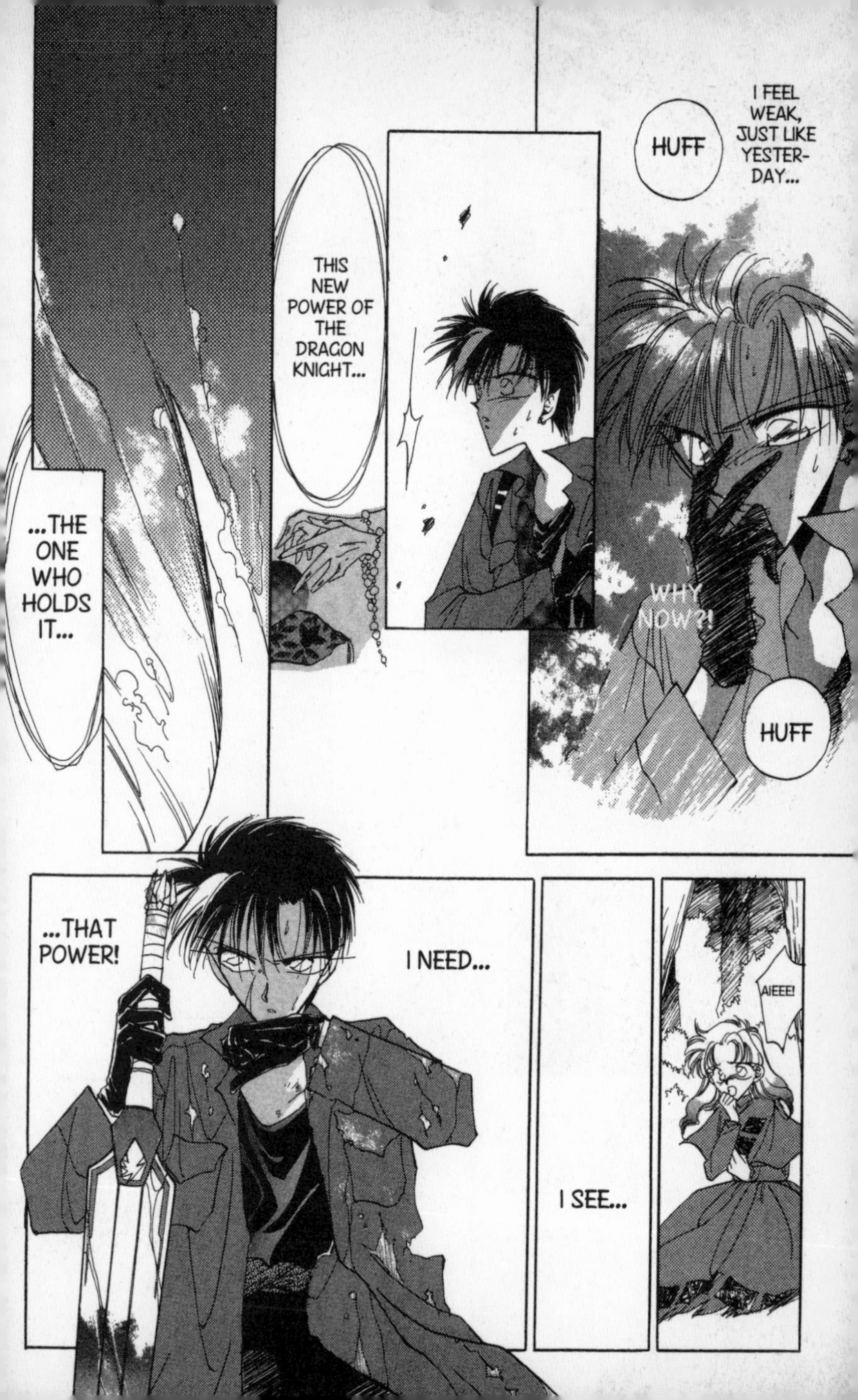
I FEEL WEAK, JUST LIKE YESTER-DAY...
HUFF
WHY NOW?!
HUFF
THIS NEW POWER OF THE DRAGON KNIGHT...
...THE ONE WHO HOLDS IT...
AIEEE!
I SEE...
I NEED...
...THAT POWER!

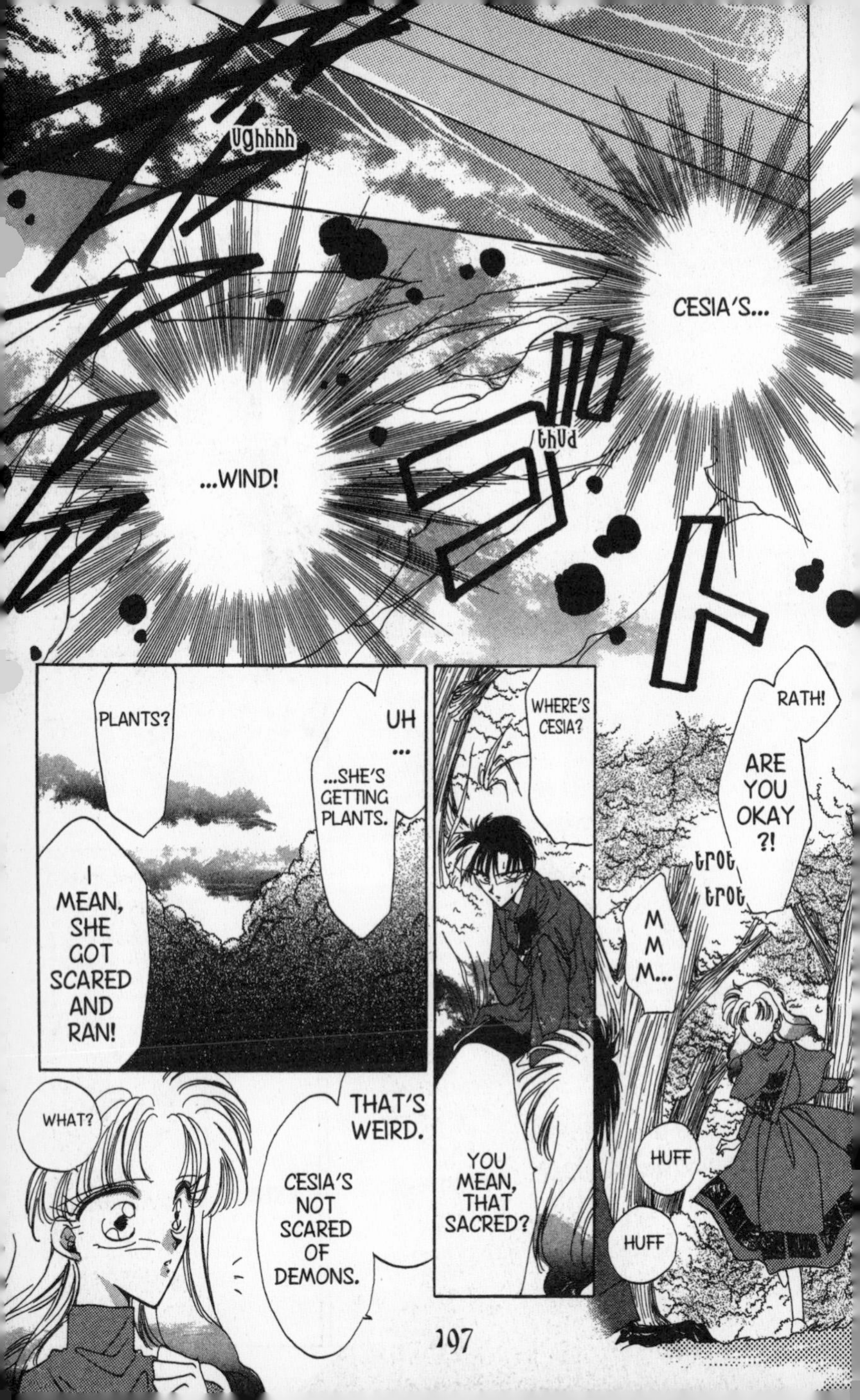
CESIA'S...
...WIND!
thud
ughhhh
RATH!
ARE YOU OKAY?!
trot trot
HUFF
HUFF
MMM...
WHERE'S CESIA?
UH... ...SHE'S GETTING PLANTS.
PLANTS?
I MEAN, SHE GOT SCARED AND RAN!
YOU MEAN, THAT SACRED?
THAT'S WEIRD.
CESIA'S NOT SCARED OF DEMONS.
WHAT?

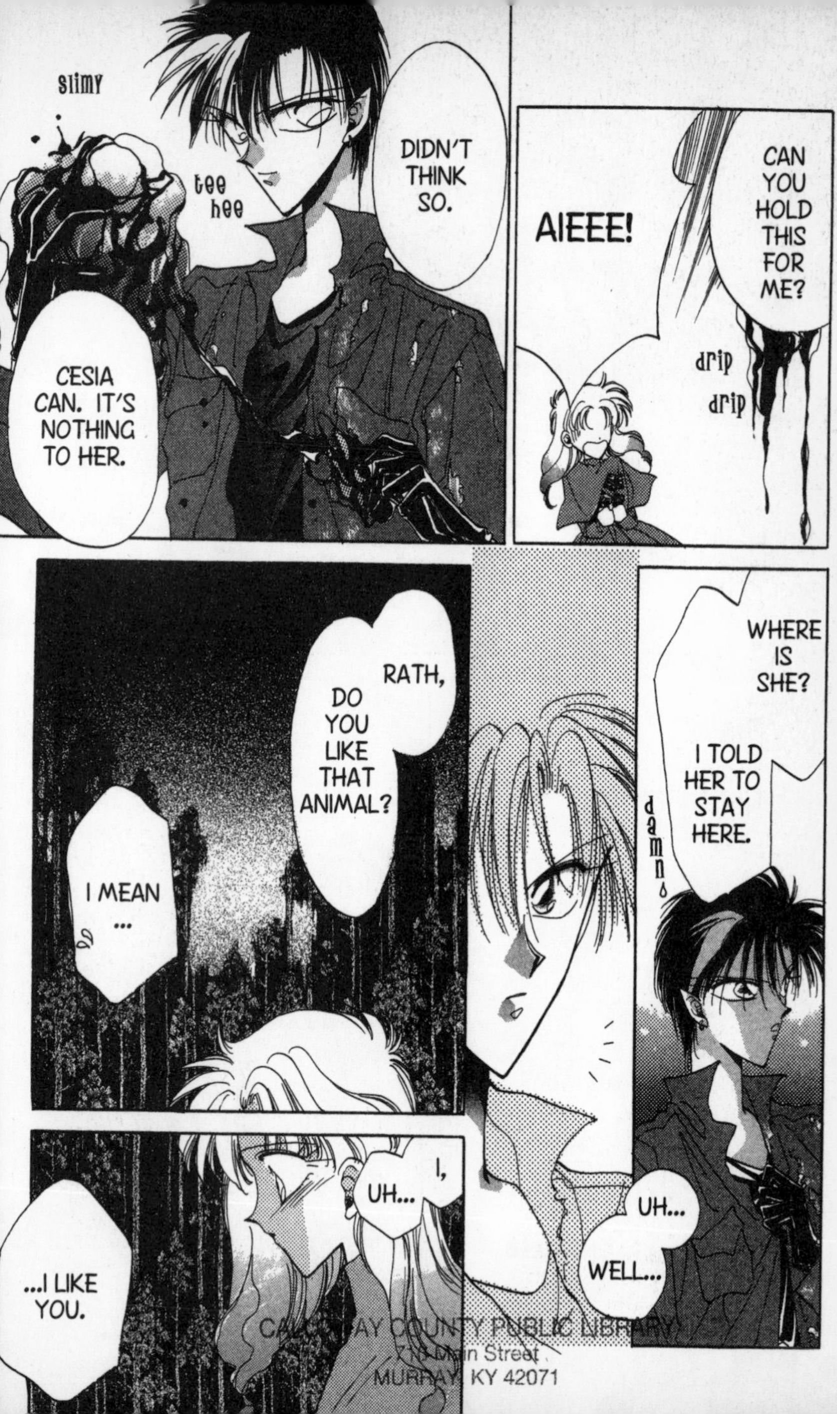
CAN YOU HOLD THIS FOR ME?
drip
drip
AIEEE!
DIDN'T THINK SO.
slimy
tee hee
CESIA CAN. IT'S NOTHING TO HER.
WHERE IS SHE?
I TOLD HER TO STAY HERE.
damn
UH...
WELL...
RATH, DO YOU LIKE THAT ANIMAL?
I MEAN ...
I, UH...
...I LIKE YOU.

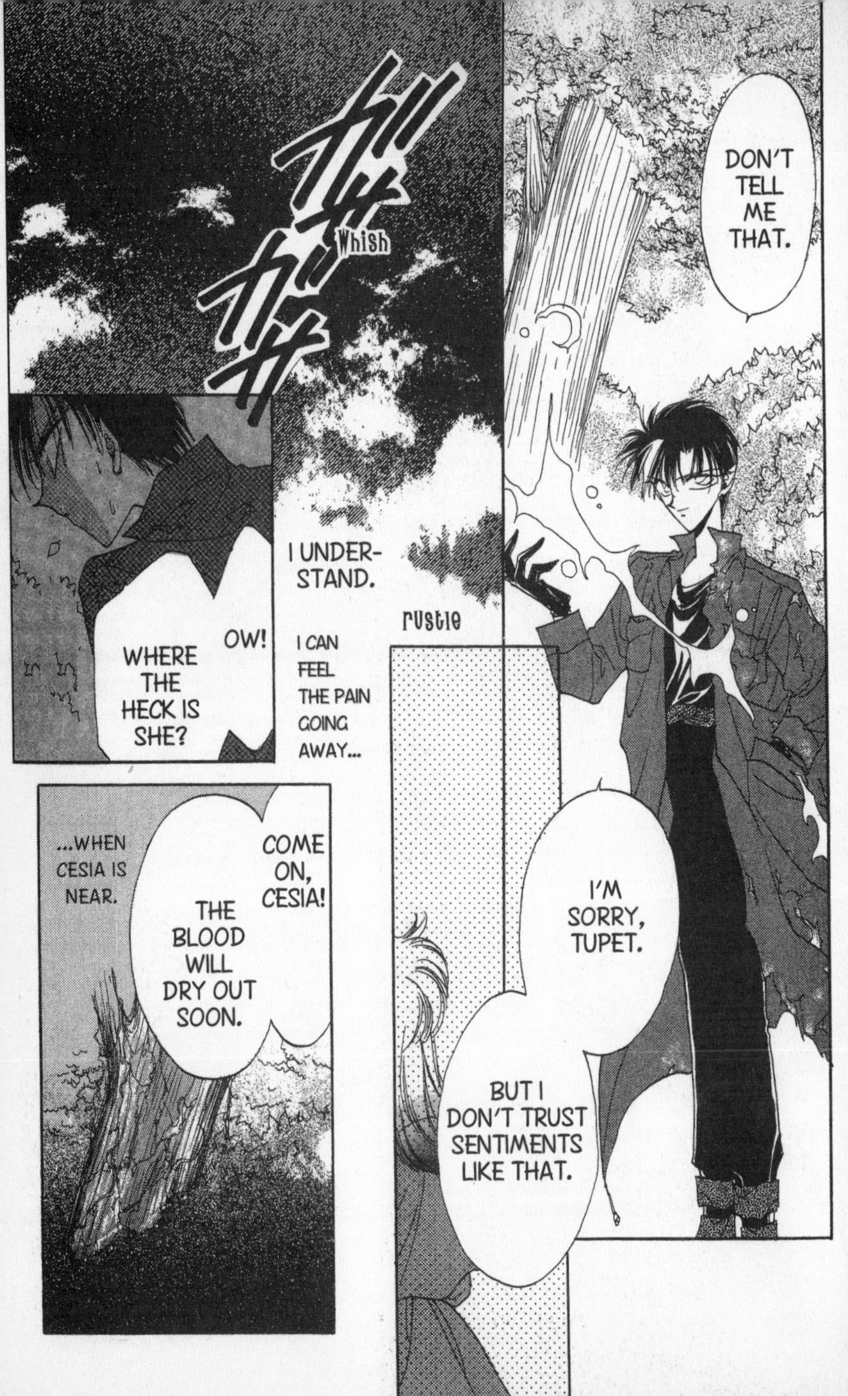
DON'T TELL ME THAT.
rustle
I'M SORRY, TUPET.
BUT I DON'T TRUST SENTIMENTS LIKE THAT.
Whish
OW!
WHERE THE HECK IS SHE?
I UNDER-STAND.
I CAN FEEL THE PAIN GOING AWAY...
COME ON, CESIA!
THE BLOOD WILL DRY OUT SOON.
...WHEN CESIA IS NEAR.

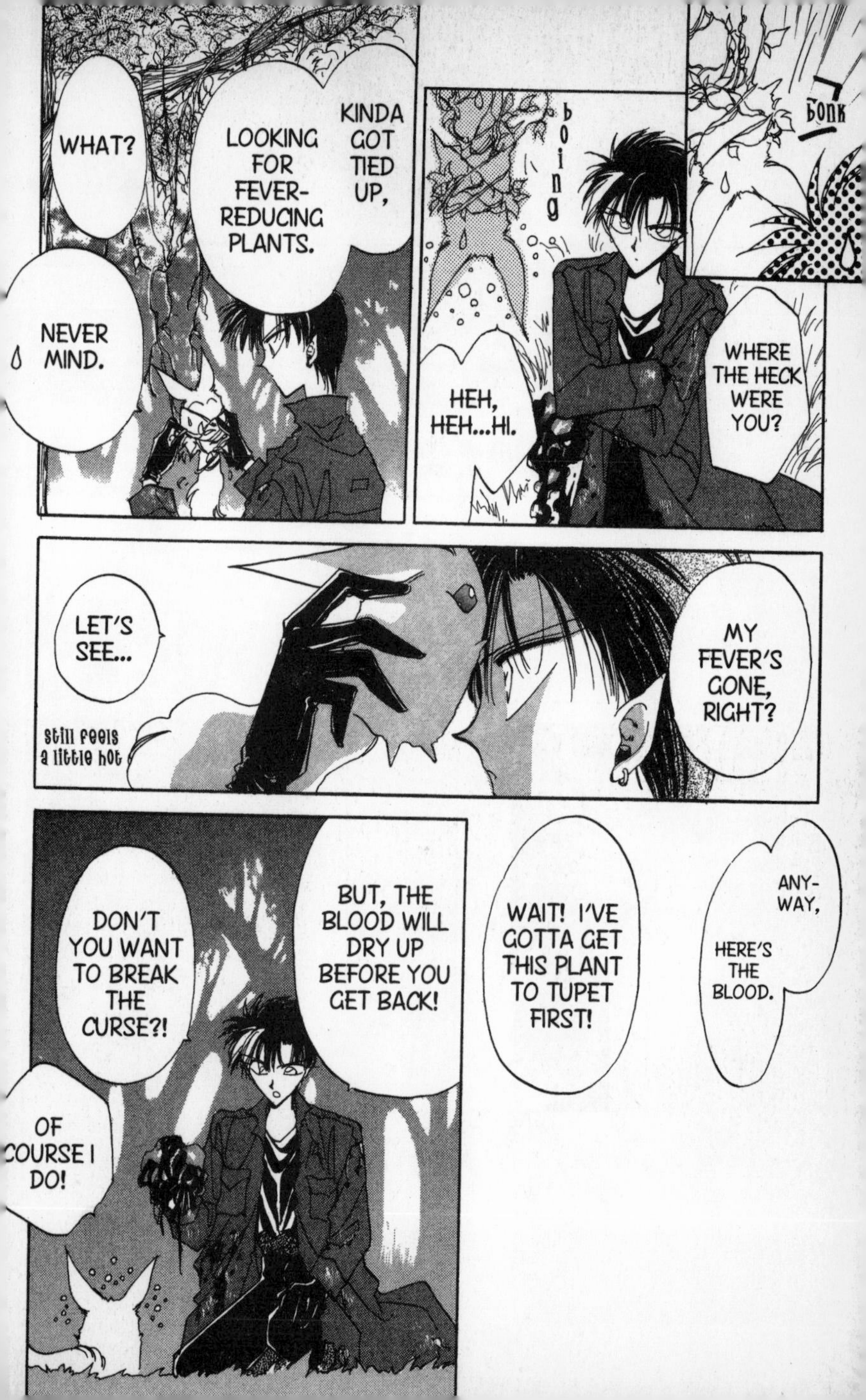
BONK
boing
WHERE THE HECK WERE YOU?
HEH, HEH...HI.
KINDA GOT TIED UP,
LOOKING FOR FEVER-REDUCING PLANTS.
WHAT?
NEVER MIND.
MY FEVER'S GONE, RIGHT?
LET'S SEE...
still feels a little hot
ANYWAY, HERE'S THE BLOOD.
WAIT! I'VE GOTTA GET THIS PLANT TO TUPET FIRST!
BUT, THE BLOOD WILL DRY UP BEFORE YOU GET BACK!
DON'T YOU WANT TO BREAK THE CURSE?!
OF COURSE I DO!

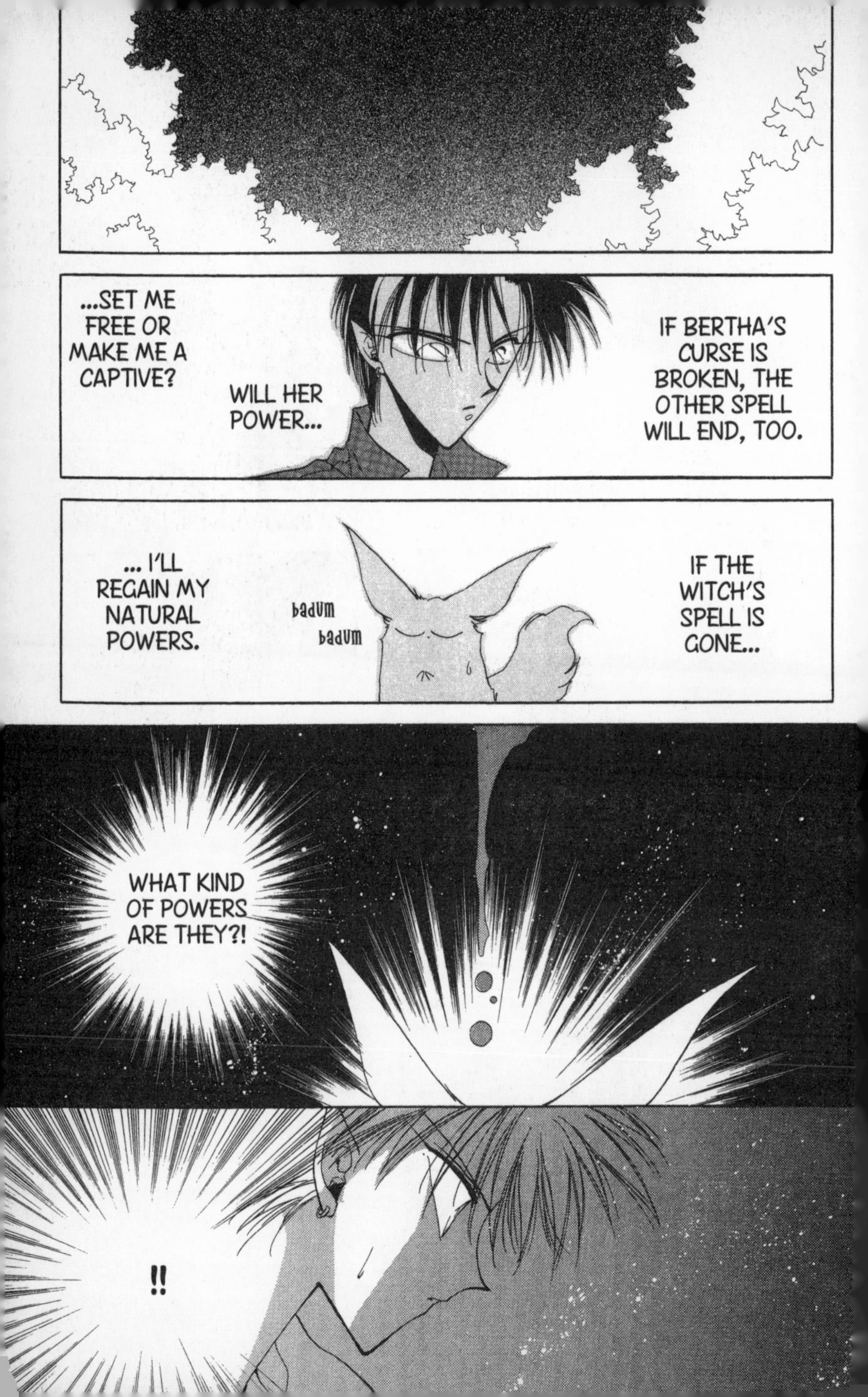
IF BERTHA'S CURSE IS BROKEN, THE OTHER SPELL WILL END, TOO.
WILL HER POWER...
...SET ME FREE OR MAKE ME A CAPTIVE?
IF THE WITCH'S SPELL IS GONE...
badum
badum
... I'LL REGAIN MY NATURAL POWERS.
WHAT KIND OF POWERS ARE THEY?!
!!

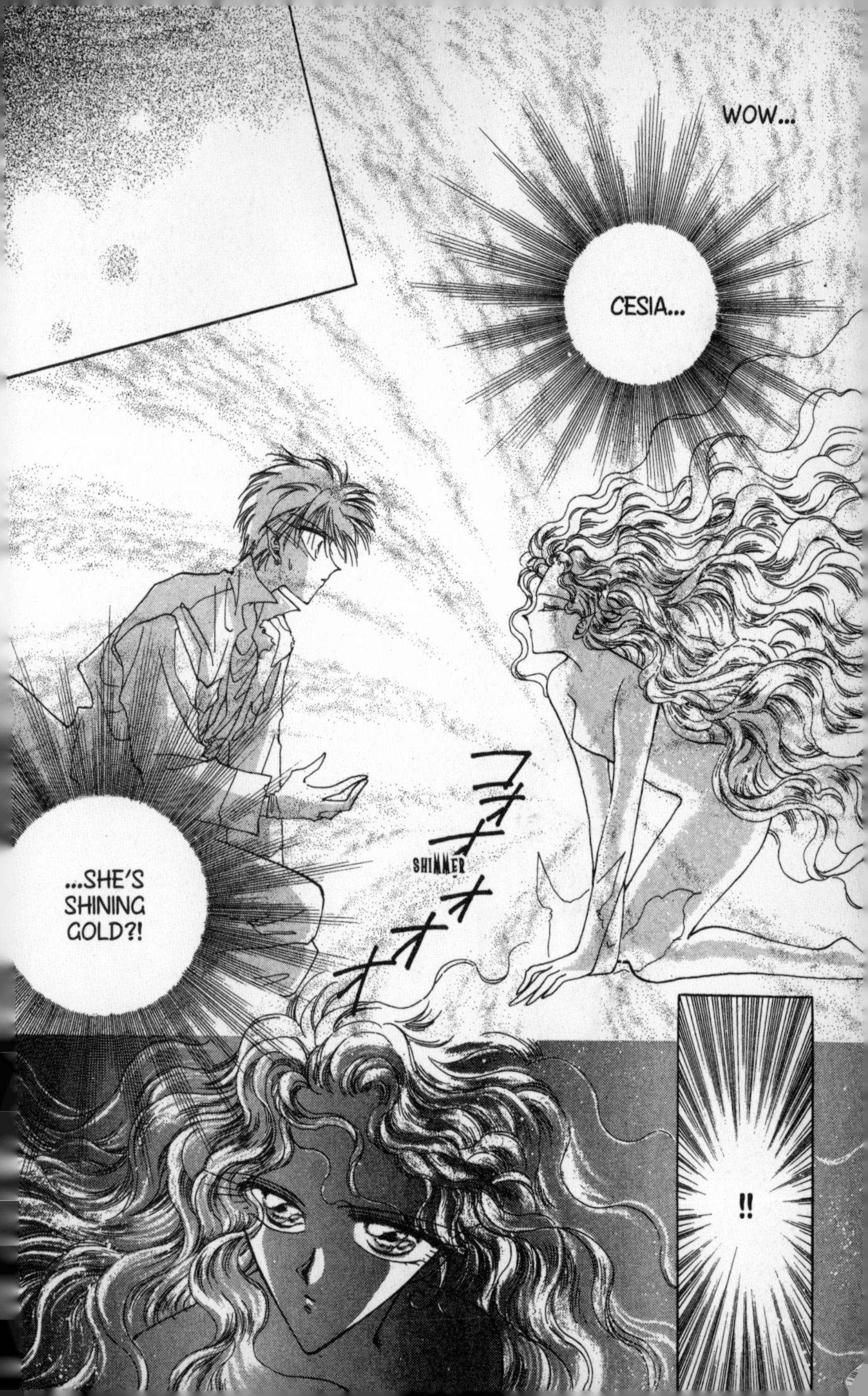
WOW...
CESIA...
SHIMMER
...SHE'S SHINING GOLD?!
!!

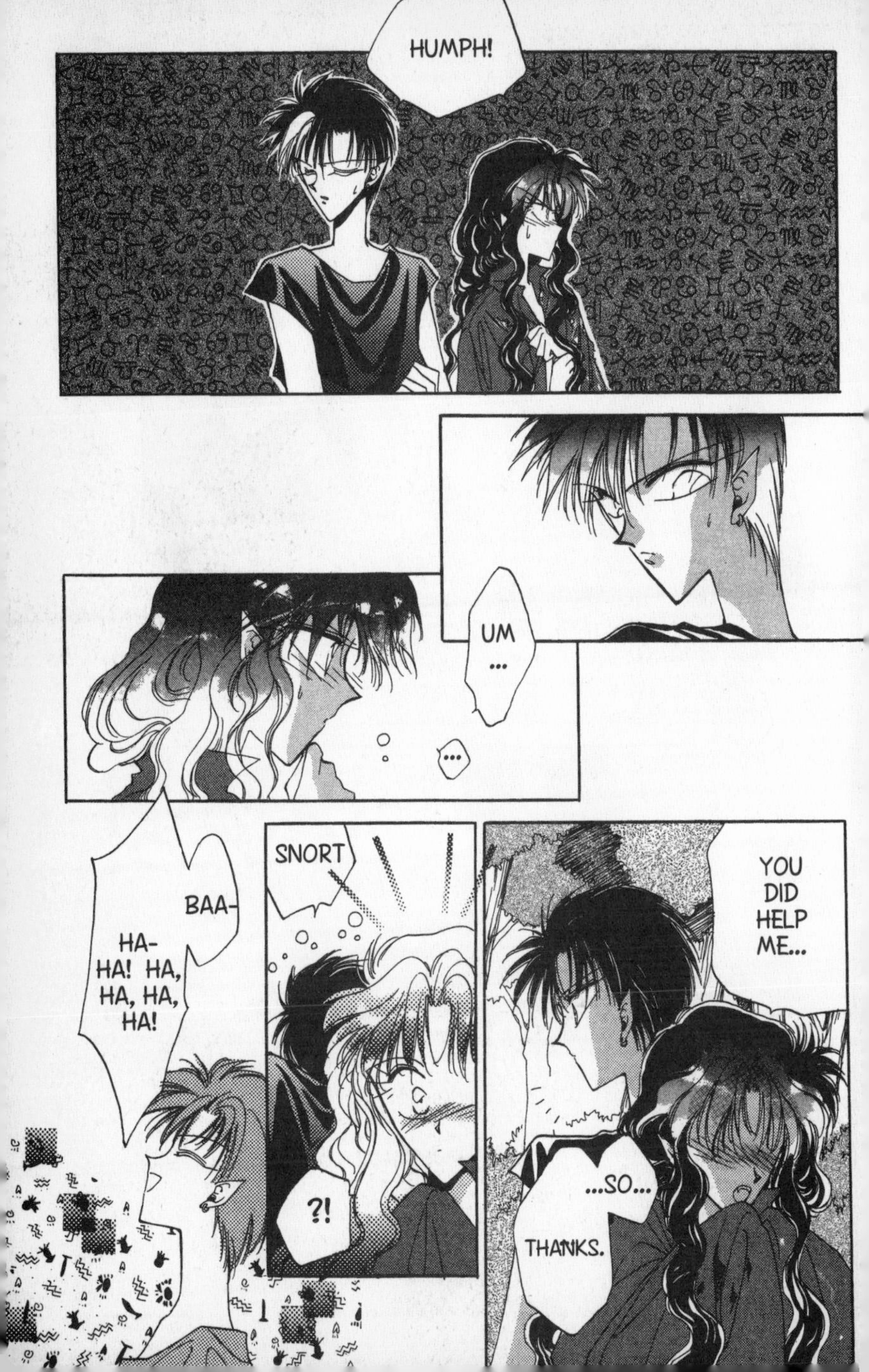
HUMPH!
UM ...
...
YOU DID HELP ME...
...SO...
THANKS.
SNORT
?!
BAA-
HA-HA! HA, HA, HA, HA!

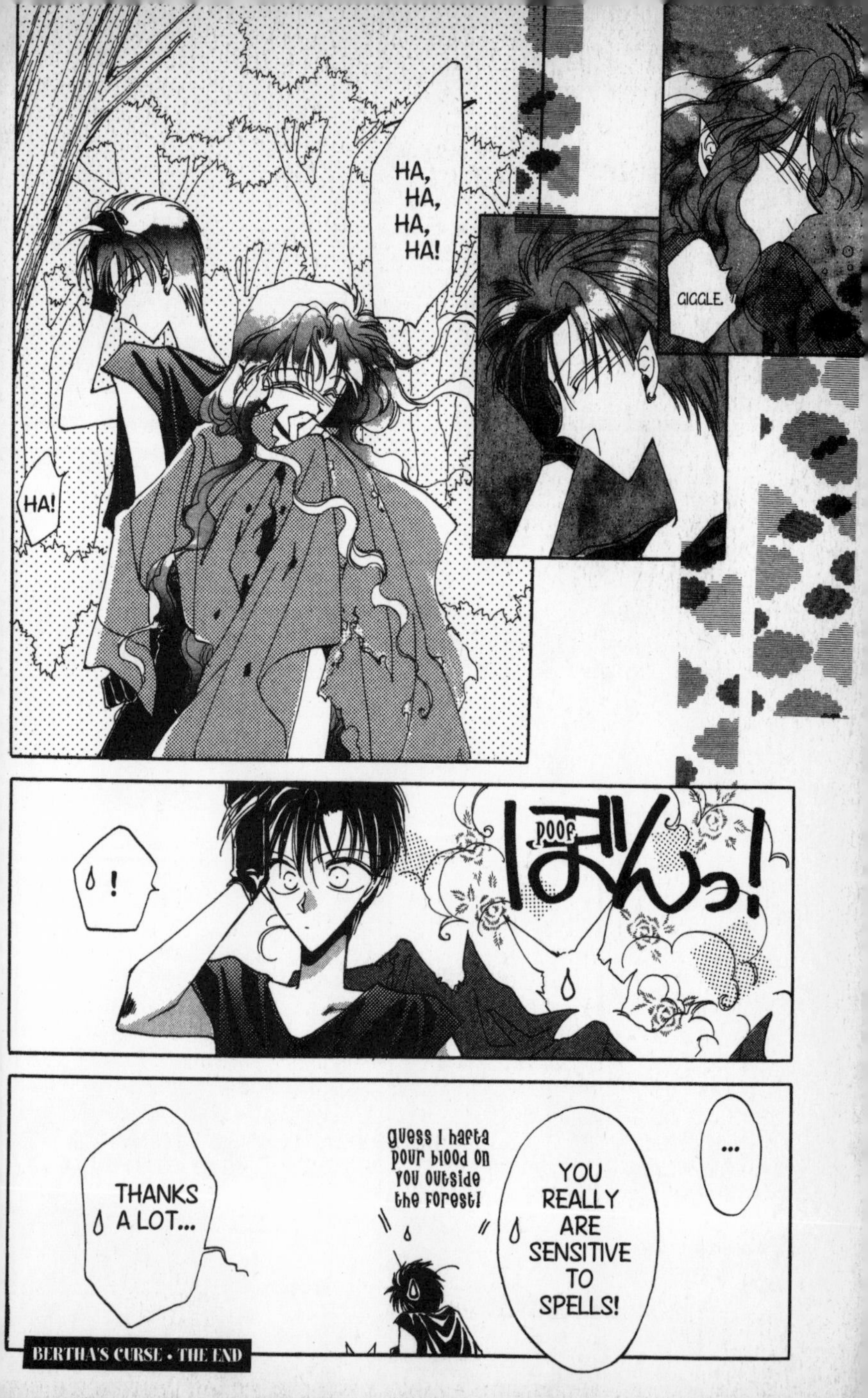
GIGGLE.
HA, HA, HA, HA!
HA!
POOF ぼんっ!
!
...
YOU REALLY ARE SENSITIVE TO SPELLS!
Guess I hafta pour blood on you outside the forest!
THANKS A LOT...
BERTHA'S CURSE • THE END